READINGS IN THE HISTORY OF PHILOSOPHY

SERIES EDITORS:

PAUL EDWARDS
RICHARD H. POPKIN

The Volumes and Their Editors:

GREEK PHILOSOPHY: THALES TO ARISTOTLE
Reginald E. Allen

GREEK AND ROMAN PHILOSOPHY AFTER ARISTOTLE
Jason L. Saunders

MEDIEVAL PHILOSOPHY:
ST. AUGUSTINE TO OCKHAM
Father Allan B. Wolter

THE PHILOSOPHY OF THE SIXTEENTH
AND SEVENTEENTH CENTURIES
Richard H. Popkin

EIGHTEENTH-CENTURY PHILOSOPHY
Lewis White Beck

NINETEENTH-CENTURY PHILOSOPHY:
HEGEL TO NIETZCHE
Patrick Gardiner

TWENTIETH-CENTURY PHILOSOPHY:
THE ANALYTIC TRADITION
Morris Weitz

Greek Philosophy
Thales to Aristotle

THIRD EDITION
REVISED AND EXPANDED

Reginald E. Allen, Editor

THE FREE PRESS

***f*P**

THE FREE PRESS
1230 Avenue of the Americas
New York, NY 10020

Manufactured in the United States of America

20 19 18

Library of Congress Cataloging-in-Publication Data

Greek philosophy : Thales to Aristotle / Reginald E. Allen.—3rd
    ed., rev. and expanded.
        p.   cm.—(Readings in the history of philosophy)
    Includes bibliographical references and index.
    ISBN-13: 978-0-02-900495-1 (Pbk)
    ISBN-10:   0-02-900495-0 (Pbk)
        1. Philosophy.   2. Philosophy, Ancient.   I. Allen, Reginald E.
II. Series.
B171.G74   1991
180—dc20
                                                        91-23279
                                                        CIP

CONTENTS

v

PREFACE TO THE THIRD EDITION

In preparing the third edition of this book, I must again express my thanks for the comments and criticisms of many teachers of Greek philosophy who have used it as a text and suggested improvements. They have strengthened the book and made it more useful.

I have taken occasion, in this edition, to ratchet the English down more tightly to the Greek in the translations of Plato's *Symposium* and Aristotle's *Categories*. I have also added selections on time and infinity from the *Physics*. These last are not only important to an understanding of Aristotle's philosophy, but to an informed contrast between ancient and modern science. They should be read in conjunction with the fragments of Zeno, whose paradoxes altered the course of Greek mathematics in the analysis of infinity and continuity. Aristotle's distinction between potential and actual infinites is explicitly meant as a solution to those paradoxes, especially the paradoxes of motion; leaving out of account issues of vocabulary, the distinction is not idiosyncratic to Aristotle, but represents the best mathematical thinking of his time. See specifically *Physics* VIII 263A 4–B 8, a passage whose import has been neglected in recent discussions of Zeno.

The emphasis of this book has been and remains on metaphysics. It has become evident in recent years how important the study of Greek mathematics and science, and especially the *Physics*, is to an understanding of Greek metaphysics. It is an area in which much hard work remains to be done. The word 'metaphysics,' however accidental its origin, is not accidental in its force.

R. E. A.

INTRODUCTION

The Milesians

Philosophy begins in Miletus, an Ionian city on the Mediterranean shore of what is now Turkey. A great port with a large carrying trade, Miletus served not only Greece but also Egypt and Babylonia, then at the height of their culture. The thought of the Milesian philosophers, Thales, Anaximander, and Anaximenes, shows traces of this influence. If Thales predicted a solar eclipse that occurred in 585 B.C., he must have been born toward the latter part of the seventh century. Anaximander appears to have been his slightly younger contemporary; Anaximenes, a younger contemporary of both.

Thales

Every history of philosophy begins with Thales, and records with proper solemnity his opinion that the source of all things is water. And every beginning student is shocked. Not until he reaches Plato and Aristotle does he find himself in a world recognizably his own, a world whose science, law, and logic are of a type his own experience has made familiar.

The pronouncements of philosophers are usually answers to questions, whether or not the questions are explicitly put. If Thales claimed that the source of all things is water, his question must presumably have been, What is the source of all things?

This seems but little progress: we appear to have passed from a naïve answer to a naïve question. In fact, the question is one of great importance. Questions do not express propositions; they are neither true nor false; but every question assumes that certain propositions are true. Questions arise in a context of beliefs and attitudes, and they turn upon their source, transforming their own assumptions.

Thales' question, understood through its answer, assumes that at

1

least two things are true: that all things have a source, and that the source of all things is one thing. The universe is bound to a single principle, the primordial water, by a single relation, that of derivation. Nature is one whole, with unchanging ways of its own, to be accounted for in terms of a unitary principle of explanation: there is an order in nature, which the mind can comprehend.

The details of Thales' world view are not known with any accuracy. He seems to have supposed that the earth floats on a vast body of water, a clot in a sea of liquid. The liquid itself he must have thought to be "unbounded"—not infinite, since the concept of the infinite had not yet been invented, but rather of indefinite extent. This conception of unbounded, primordial water is not Greek; it is found in the myths of the great river-civilizations of Egypt and Babylonia, and in *Genesis*. The world itself was probably thought by Thales to have grown from this liquid, perhaps, Aristotle suggested, as an animal grows from the moist seed.

Thales thought the primordial water alive, and its life the source of motion: to be alive is to be capable of spontaneous movement. This may have been the reason Thales chose water as his primordial stuff, for water is an ancient symbol of life. Thales, no doubt, thought that it *is* life, thought that, in the living liquid, there was no distinction between its life and its liquidity.

Anaximander

In his account of Anaximander, Aristotle preserves a genuine and important objection to Thales—the first recorded criticism of one philosopher by another. Thales had conceived the primordial element as both unbounded and as water. But, Aristotle remarks:

> There are some (i.e. Anaximander) who make this the Unbounded, and not air or water; in order that the other things may not be destroyed by their unboundness. They are in opposition to one another—air is cold, water is moist, and fire hot—and therefore, if any one of them were unbounded, the rest would have ceased to be by this time. Accordingly, they say that what is unbounded is something other than the elements, and from it the elements arise.
>
> (*Physics* 204b 24). Burnet's translation, slightly altered.

Anaximander's objection evidently was that the hot, the cold, the wet, and the dry, and the things which embody them, stand to each other in a relation of opposition; therefore, if one of them were made primary and unbounded, the others could not continue to exist. So far as we can now tell, Thales could have had no answer to this objection. Anaximander supposed the answer to lie in ridding the primordial principle of its association with any single sensible opposite and making it simply the Unbounded. This is a great leap of the creative imagination, an abstraction of very high order: Anaximander posited as explanatory of the world of sense experience a principle that had no characteristic found in the world of sense experience.

The Unbounded could not merely have been unbounded in extent, for water was unbounded in that sense. It must have been unbounded in that it was internally undifferentiated. This was in fact Aristotle's view, who supposed Anaximander's Boundless to be a mixture of all opposites: the opposites fuse in it as water and wine fuse in watered wine, and it is "boundless" because it is itself of no determinate sort, a thing which is no kind because it is all kinds.

The elements of the world, then, its opposites, separate out or separate off from this primitive mixture, and, once separated, they war upon one another. The one remaining fragment of Anaximander, the oldest remaining fragment of philosophy, bears directly on this point: "The source of coming to be for existent things is that into which destruction, too, happens, 'according to necessity; for they pay penalty and retribution to each other for their injustice according to the assessment of Time.'"

The warring opposites, then, commit injustice upon each other. The concrete case that Anaximander probably had in mind is the perpetual war between winter (the moist and cold) and summer (the hot and dry); the cycle of the seasons, and perhaps the lesser cycle of day and night, prompt this view, as they prompt the predominance in primitive thought of these particular opposites rather than others. Anaximander's view is that one opposite encroaches on the domain of the other, a case of "injustice," and "a reaction takes place through the infliction of punishment by the restoration of equality—of more than equality, since the wrong-doer is deprived of part of his original substance too. This is given to the victim in addition to what was his own, and in turn leads (it might be inferred) to *koros*, surfeit, on the part of the former victim, who now commits injustice on the former aggressor." (Kirk and Raven, p. 119) The cycle of recurring injustice is held in balance by the assessment of Time, which functions as a judge. The world, like a pendulum, maintains equilibrium through the alternation of its extremes.

Anaximenes

Anaximander had presented a question to Thales: How is the qualitative diversity of the world to be reconciled with the primordial unity of its source? Anaximenes undertook to answer that question in a way very different from that of Anaximander, a way of which Thales himself might have approved.

Anaximenes' answer, very simply, was that the primordial unity is to be treated as a stuff, a matter out of which things are made. The diverse elements of the world are to be attributed to changes in this primitive matter, changes that are quantitative. Qualitative differences, that is, are to be accounted for by the thickening and thinning, condensation and rarefaction, of a primordial stuff. This answer has about it an air of distinct modernity. Anaximenes here anticipated Democritus, as well as every modern philosopher who undertakes to derive the colors, sights, and sounds of the world from the arrangement in space of a matter which is qualitatively homogenous.

This primordial stuff Anaximenes believed to be air (or mist, or breath), which when rarefied became fire and when condensed, wind, then cloud, then water, then earth, then stone. Associated with these substances were appropriate qualities, especially the hot and the cold. Condensation is a source of cold, while rarefaction is a source of heat. Anaximenes adduced an empirical argument for this conclusion: breath blown through compressed lips is cold, but with the mouth open, it is warm—a curious observation, but something of a historical landmark.

As in Thales, so in Anaximenes, the primordial stuff is alive or ensouled, and the motion in the world is traced to the living character of its origin. As water is an ancient symbol of life, so is air or breath.

Anaximander and Anaximenes

In the *Physics* (187a 11) Aristotle divides the natural philosophers into two schools: those who hold that there is an underlying body from which other things are generated by thickening and thinning, and those who "separate out" the opposites from a mixture. Anaximander belongs to the latter school, Anaximenes to the former, and the contrast is important.

The principles by which Anaximander interprets the universe are closely linked to that psychology of the tragic passions by which Aeschylus interprets human life. The order of nature is essentially a dramatic order: the agonists are the warring opposites, alternately triumphing in the cycle of days and seasons—a cycle of Hubris and Nemesis, of Excess and Retribution. Separated off from the Unbounded and grown wanton, the opposites pay penalty to each other and lapse once more into their source, "according to the assessment of Time." Seasons return, and in their return we find evidence for a type of causality which is, in a peculiar sense, moral: balance or harmony is a principle of nature, and the equilibrium of the world process is its product. Because harmony is a basic principle of explanation, and because harmony is the harmony of opposites, the opposites themselves are in this scheme irreducible; they are "separated off" from their primitive togetherness, not generated by a combination of prior causes. Implicitly, then, understanding of the universe, for Anaximander, is qualitative and moral: the seeds of the teleological pattern of explanation which was to bulk so large in Plato and Aristotle are already in his thought.

With Anaximenes it is different. The universe is not to be explained by the dramatic tension of qualities and their balance; those qualities are themselves generated by the thickening and thinning of a matter which is qualitatively homogenous. Quantity is prior to quality; causality is implicitly mechanical, not moral. Though Anaximenes' Air is alive, and its life the source of natural motion, there is no hint in this of teleology. The development of speculation in the Ionian tradition will progressively drain the mythical elements from Anaximenes' world view: the primitive life of the world's source will be abandoned, leaving only its physical residue, a spontaneous and uninitiated swirl of atoms, postulated as the origin of motion and change in the world. But Anaximenes' fundamental conception will be kept: the notion that the world consists in matter and its arrangement, that the ultimate explanation of it must be quantitative and mechanical. Anaximenes stands in a direct line with Democritus, where this ultimate reduction is made; and Democritus is perhaps the one Greek who foreshadowed most clearly the scientific world view which has dominated thought from the time of Newton to the present.

In the dawn of philosophy, the outlines of figures are dim. We shall never know as much as we should like to know of Thales, Anaximander, and Anaximenes. But in the distance, their figures seem very much of a size—all men of extraordinary genius, each of whom made a unique contribution to thought. A division in Greek—and modern—philosophy, the division between mechanists and teleologists, is already to be found, in embryo, in their thought. That division arose within a common context of ideas, provided by Thales: the world is a natural whole, with unchanging ways of its own, and it issues from a primitive and unitary source. The result of this claim was revolution, the passage from myth to philosophy. That revolution Thales' pupils carried forward, each in his own way. The magnitude of their achievement may be measured by its fruit.

Pythagoras and Pythagoreanism

Pythagoras was born on the island of Samos, before the middle of the sixth century. As a young man he migrated to Italy, where he founded the society which bore his name.

Contrast to Milesian Speculation

Religion. Pythagoras founded, in effect, a cult society with religious taboos. Philosophy, or inquiry into the nature of things, was understood as a way of life whose aim was salvation—the purification of the soul and its release from the prison of the body. There was nothing of this in the Milesians, who were motivated by simple curiosity, not desire for salvation, and whose work is distinguished by its uncompromising naturalism.

The Soul. The religious impulse in Pythagoreanism led to the doctrine that the soul is immortal, that it undergoes reincarnation in various forms of animal life, and that, therefore, all life is akin—a claim that found practical expression in abstention from meat. Salvation, release from the wheel of rebirth, was to be attained by coming to understand the beauty and order of the cosmos, especially as shown in the circles of the heavens, and by reproducing that order in one's own soul. Philosophy, then, is purification or catharsis, a regimen designed to free the soul from the burden of sense and the corruption of the physical, prominent sources of disorder. Once again, there was nothing of this in the Milesians, for whom soul, or life, though of fundamental importance as an attribute of the primordial stuff, had no ethical or religious implications.

Form and Mathematics. Broadly speaking, the Ionian tradition was materialistic: it sought explanation in such sensible opposites as the hot, the cold, the wet, and the dry—characters proper to perception. The Pythagoreans, on the contrary, sought explanation in terms of structure or form, a form in essence numerical. They assumed that the world is a *harmonia*, an orderly and proportionate adjustment of parts within a complex whole: they assumed that the book of nature—to borrow a metaphor from one of Pythagoras' intellectual heirs, Galileo—is written in the language of mathematics.

Doctrine

Difficulties of Interpretation. Attempts to reconstruct the history of early Pythagoreanism are made difficult by the absence of early documents, a difficulty already encountered by Aristotle and Theophrastus. The Pythagoreans published little, partly because the school was so tightly knit that oral teaching was sufficient, partly because of its character as a cult society, with an emphasis on secrecy. As one ancient testimonium remarks, "their silence was of no ordinary kind." Also, the tradition of the school attributed all discoveries to the founder, which often makes it difficult to decide what is a primitive feature of their thought and what is not. Still, some things may be ascribed to Pythagoras himself with a high degree of probability.

Things Are Numbers. It was universally attested by the ancients that Pythagoras was the author of the doctrine that numbers are the real nature of things. The meaning of this dark saying was obscure even to Aristotle, and scholars have reached no agreement on its interpretation. The doctrine appears to have been suggested by a discovery in music. Pythagoras, experimenting perhaps with a monochord and a movable bridge, found that the perfect consonances which form the basis of musical scales, the fourth, the fifth, and the octave, could be expressed as ratios of the least whole numbers: the octave is 2:1, the fifth 3:2, the fourth 4:3. The welter and chaos of sound, then, is reduced to the beauty and order of music by the introduction of arithmetical proportion. Pythagoras, "recognizing the universal in the clearly known particular," to use Aristotle's description of induction, extended this account to the order of the universe at large. His intuition was very like that of an artist, grasping through significant detail the form of the whole. This is the source of the Pythagorean doctrine, as stated by Aristotle, that "the whole heaven or visible universe is a musical scale or number."

The Tetractys of the Decad. For the Pythagoreans, 10 was (according to Aristotle) "the whole nature of number," presumably because it formed the base of Pythagorean (as well as our own) arithmetic. It is also the sum of 1, 2, 3, and 4—the numbers which occur in the ratios of the perfect consonances: according to Aristotle, ten "contains all the consonances." The tetractys of the decad was a symbol of great significance, and like other such symbols, capable of many interpretations. The symbol is as follows:

$$a$$
$$a \quad a$$
$$a \quad a \quad a$$
$$a \quad a \quad a \quad a$$

Notice that it contains ten units, ranked in four rows, with the rows (from whatever angle approached) containing, progressively, one, two, three, and four units. Also, the symbol is an equilateral triangle, the simplest plane figure; it contains both points and lines; and seen from above, it is a pyramid, the simplest solid figure.

Mathematical Discoveries. The Pythagorean school, in a period of two hundred years, helped to lay the foundations of mathematics as we know it today, inaugurating a tradition that ranks with the poetry of Aeschylus and the philosophy of Plato as among the greatest intellectual contributions of Greece to civilization. Pythagoras found geometry a system of land measurement used in Egypt, not unlike the practical rules of thumb used by carpenters today. He transformed it by making it abstract. He was probably the first man in history to establish theorems by demonstration and to undertake the systematic development of geometry as a science. The ideals of the science he founded—ideals of simplicity, economy, and rigor—were to influence every facet of Greek art and Greek thought. It may be that he himself discovered and demonstrated the so-called "Pythagorean Theorem," at least for the isosceles right triangle: that the square of the hypotenuse of a right triangle is equal to the sum of the squares of its sides, and its corollary, the incommensurability of the diagonal with its sides. To discover that corollary was to discover the existence of incommensurability and irrational ratios, a triumph of mathematical imagination. In addition, Pythagoras probably refined current arithmetical symbolism, and invented the *gnomon* representation of numbers. The *gnomon*, literally, was the carpenter's square. By application of successive *gnomons*, with 1 as base, one could generate all odd numbers; with 2 as base, all even numbers. As follows:

```
a a a a          a a a a a
a a a a          a a a a a
a a a a          a a a a a
a a a a          a a a a a
3 5 7 etc.       4 6 8 etc.
```

The Table of Opposites. The table of opposites described by Aristotle should perhaps be ascribed to Pythagoras himself. It is as follows:

Limit	Unlimited
Odd	Even
One	Many
Right	Left
Male	Female
Rest	Motion
Straight	Curved
Light	Dark
Good	Bad
Square	Oblong

There are ten opposites, whose relations are best understood through the *gnomon* representation of numbers. One generates Odd. Two is Many, and generates Even. The *gnomon* shapes of odd numbers are Square, of even numbers, Oblong. Since the ratio of side to side in odd numbers is always 1:1, the odd is Limited; the ratio of side to side in even numbers is continually different—2:3, 3:4, 4:5, and so on—so that the Even is Unlimited.[1] Since the ratio in odd numbers is always the same, Odd is correlated with Rest; since in even numbers it is always different, Even is correlated with Motion; the same consideration explains Straight and Curved. Good/Bad, Right/Left, Male/Female, and Light/Dark are evaluative terms, respectively associated with Limit and Unlimited. The table of opposites, then, is a unity. It provides the categories in terms of which the Pythagoreans understood the world.

Cosmology. Aristotle's testimony tends to indicate that Pythagoreanism was dualistic, containing as primitive principles both Limit and Unlimited. If true, this is in sharp contrast to the Milesians, who were monists.

Heraclitus

Heraclitus was born in Ephesus after the middle of the sixth century, a younger contemporary of Pythagoras and an elder contemporary of Parmenides. The riddling, gnomic character of his writings won him the name of "the dark one" in later antiquity.

His view of the universe turns on his concept of *logos*—an untranslatable word which in fact means "word," but which has connotations of proportion, measure, and perhaps even here pattern. The *logos* is the first principle of knowledge: understanding of the world involves understanding of the structure or pattern of the world, a pattern concealed from the eyes of ordinary men. The *logos* is also the first principle of existence, that unity of the world process which sustains it as a process. This unity lies beneath the surface, for it is a unity of diverse and conflicting opposites, in whose strife the *logos* maintains a continuing balance: the world, in being drawn asunder, is drawn together—a backstretched connection, as in the bow and the lyre. The *logos* itself is an ever-living fire, kindling and dying out in measures. As it dies, it produces sea and earth, which in turn kindle into fire, measure answering to measure. The world process is a circle, in which the way up and the way down are continually balanced, and thus, in some sense, the same.

Heraclitus' thought differs from the Milesians in its concern for ethics and the soul; on these topics, and in the prominence he gives to the *logos*, a structural principle, he in some ways resembles the Pythagoreans. Yet the *logos* is identified with a perceptible element, fire, and its function in Heraclitus' world view is very like that of Time in Anaximander. Like Time, the *logos* is a principle of isonomy, maintaining

---

[1] This conjecture is confirmed by Aristotle, *Physics* 203a 10.

proportion in the world process. But whereas Anaximander's Time produces equilibrium in a cyclical alteration of excess, the *logos* maintains equilibrium in the universe at every moment. The reason for this is that, though the opposites continually war on one another, as they did in Anaximander, they are maintained constantly in equal measures, and are even, perhaps, fundamentally one and the same.

Both Plato and Aristotle ascribed to Heraclitus the doctrine of perpetual flux: "all things change, and nothing remains at rest." It is to be remembered, however, that the *logos* is itself stable, the measured pattern of flow.

Heraclitus' vision of the universe—a universe in which enemies sustain each others in and through their enmity, in which war and contention are inseparable elements of unity and peace, in which identity is identity in difference, and difference, difference in identity—has never ceased to grip the imaginations of his successors.

The Eleatics

The Eleatics, with their claim for priority of reason over the senses and their radical skepticism of common sense, sharply altered the course of future philosophy. The great pluralistic systems of the fifth century, and even the work of Plato and Aristotle in the fourth, are largely concerned to answer questions they first raised. The most prominent members of the school were Parmenides, its founder, and Zeno, his pupil.

Parmenides

Parmenides was born about 515 B.C. in Elea, a Greek city on the coast of Italy. He was associated in his youth with the Pythagoreans, against whom he later reacted. Most of the first section of his poem in hexameter verse, the *Way of Truth*, has been preserved.

The *Way of Truth* is the first philosophical demonstration in history. It is modeled upon, and meant to exhibit the cogency of, geometry. The demonstration rests upon a disjunction which, reduced to its lowests terms, is simply "It is, or It is not." No antecedent for "It" is supplied and none is intended. The first disjunct is the true way of inquiry. The second disjunct is to be wholly rejected: it is unthinkable, unknowable, not to be uttered, for the same thing exists for thinking and for being. The second way of inquiry, in brief, is not really a way at all.

In the proem of the *Way of Truth* (Fr. 1), the goddess who grants Parmenides his deductive revelation promises to reveal to him, not only "the unshaken heart of well-rounded Truth," that is, reality itself, but also "the opinions of mortals in which is no true belief at all," and to teach him "how, passing right through all things, one should judge the things that seem to be." After the disjunction of the two ways is laid down, this promise is fulfilled. To "It is" and "It is not" we are to add what appears to be another way, "It is and is not." (Fr. 6) This is the way of mortal opinion, which supposes real the world of nature, whose contents come to be and cease to be. This way has often been supposed distinct, a third way derived from the combination of the first two. The text, however, forbids that view: it is explicitly stated that there are two, and *only* two, ways, (Fr. 2), and later, after their combination has been discussed, the original disjunction is again recalled and treated as exhaustive. (Fr. 8) There are not, then, three ways; the third way is merely an aspect of the second. "It is and is not" reduces to "It is not."

The primary object of Parmenides' poem is to demonstrate that the common-sense belief in the reality of the physical world, a world of plurality and change, is mistaken, and to set in its place a One Being, unchanging, ungenerated, indestructible, shaped as a sphere. The characteristics with which Parmenides qualifies the One resemble the Limited side of the Pythagorean table of opposites. It is perhaps worth noting that the One is not qualified by both of any pair of opposites.

Parmenides' distinction between appearance and reality and between opinion and knowledge laid the foundation for Platonism; his objections to change and plurality helped to inspire, in Aristotle's thought, the identification of matter and potentiality, and in Plato, the doctrine that the sensible world is lower in degree of reality than the world apprehended by intelligence. But despite the stimulus he lent his successors, it has become the fashion to locate the springs of his argument in a simple logical fallacy, the confusion between existential and predicative statements. Kirk and Raven[2] put the view as follows:

Parmenides is attacking those who believe, as all men always had believed, that it is possible to make a significant negative predication; but he is enabled to attack them only because of his own confusion between a negative predication and a negative existential judgement. The gist of this difficult and important fragment (Fr. 2) is therefore this: Either it is right only to think or say of a thing, "it is . . . " (i.e., "it is so-and-so, e.g. white"), or else it is right to think and say only "it is not . . ." (i.e., "it is not something else, e.g., black"). This latter is to be firmly rejected on the ground (a mistaken one, owing to the confusion between existential and predicative) that it is impossible to conceive of Not-being, the non-existent. Any propositions about Not-being are necessarily meaningless; the only significant thoughts or statements concern Being.

---

[2] P.269.

This interpretation ascribes two assumptions to Parmenides. The first is that negative predicative statements, of the form "*a* is not *F*," imply negative existential statements, of the form "*a* does not exist." The second is that negative existential statements are meaningless, or otherwise logically absurd.

The first claim is false. It may be dismissed on the textual ground that Parmenides qualifies his One with negative predicates—it is *un*-generated, *in*destructible, *un*changing—and further, that he would surely have agreed that it therefore is *not* changing, *not* generated, *not* destructible. Beyond this, the claim falls on the common-sense ground that a man who habitually inferred from "Jones is not bald" to "Jones does not exist" would not be a philosopher, but either a lunatic or a sophist. Parmenides was presumably neither.

The second claim is true, logically independent of the first, and the key to the problem. Parmenides' position appears to be this: To think (but when do we really think, if ever?) is to think of what is, and what is is intelligible. Suppose, then, that we think of some individual, *a*, which has come to be and will pass away; it follows that we can think of *a* that it is not. But we cannot think this, since to think is to think of what is; therefore *a* is not an object of thought, for the thought of it is self-contradictory; and since what exists can be thought of, *a* does not exist. This argument assumes (i) that existence is attributable to individuals, (ii) that thought or discourse has for its object what exists.

Zeno

Zeno was born in approximately 490 B.C. and became a pupil of Parmenides while still a young man. His philosophical activity was primarily negative, devoted to refutation rather than construction; his pattern of argument, the *reductio ad absurdum,* he borrowed from the geometers.

Aristotle, and the doxographical tradition that followed him, supposed that Zeno's arguments were directed, in the interests of Eleatic Monism, against the existence of any sort of plurality and motion, however conceived—directed, not only against other philosophers, but against common-sense belief in the reality of the empirical world.

The Pluralists

Parmenides posed a simple problem to his successors, that of reconciling the sensible world with criteria of reality it cannot satisfy. To be real is to be intelligible and therefore free from generation or destruction; since the sensible world does not fulfill these conditions, it cannot be real. But an unreal world is a philosophical embarrassment, especially when it happens to be a world in which we live; such a world must in *some* sense exist, even to be illusion.

The Pluralists—Empedocles, Anaxagoras, and the Atomists, Leucippus and Democritus—all undertook to solve this difficulty, undertook to justify the reality of motion and the existence of the sensible world. In broad outline, their solution was in each case the same, resting on a distinction between elements, which satisfy the Parmenidean requirements, and compounds of those elements, which do not. Anaxagoras (Fr. 17) summed up the point admirably: "No object comes-to-be or passes away, but is mixed or separated from existing objects." Parmenides' denial of generation and destruction is accepted; his denial of plurality is itself denied.

Empedocles

Empedocles was born in Acragas, a Greek city in Sicily, in the early years of the fifth century. His philosophy may be read as an attempt to restate the world view of Anaximander and Heraclitus, while yet taking account of the criticism of Parmenides. From Parmenides he takes his insistence that coming to be and passing away are alike impossible; from Parmenides too he takes the Sphere of Being, everywhere full. But the Sphere is now full of four sensible opposites, the hot, the cold, the wet, and the dry, which change places in the sphere, combine and separate in varying proportions, under the impulse of the cosmic forces of Love and Strife. The various complex substances of the world—its men and tables, horses and trees—come to be and pass away; but that is because they are mere arrangements of elements that do not.

By distinguishing between simple elements and their compounds, Empedocles justified the world of coming to be and passing away which Parmenides' strictures had threatened to destroy. Like Anaximander and Heraclitus, his world view makes qualities primitive in the explanation of nature, and in the balanced alternation of his cosmic forces we have an echo of Heraclitus' *logos* and Anaximander's Time. The peculiar way in which this alternation is exhibited—the rearrangement of qualities in space—perhaps owes something to Anaximenes.

Anaxagoras

Anaxagoras was born in Clazomenae, in Asia Minor, at the beginning of the fifth century. As a young man he came to Athens, where he taught for many years. A friend of Pericles, he played an important role in the intellectual life of the city in its golden age. He was exiled from Athens in middle life, and retired to Lampsacus, a colony of Miletus, where he founded a school.

Like Empedocles, Anaxagoras denied that things come to be and pass away. He held that generation and destruction are really mixture and separation of ingenerable and indestructible elements. His account of mixture and separation, however, is difficult to interpret. It involves two principles. The first is homoeomereity: a natural substance, such as gold or bone, consists solely of parts which are like the whole. Divide gold however finely, and the remnants are still gold. The second principle, that there is a portion of everything in everything, appears to mean that a piece of gold, or of any other natural substance, contains portions of everything else.

These two principles, as stated, are inconsistent with each other, and it is unclear how their inconsistency is to be resolved. One suggestion is that Anaxagoras, however little he would have put it in these terms, means for us to distinguish between physical division and analysis. If one *divides* a natural substance, one is left with parts which are identical in kind to the whole: a piece of gold is still gold. But if one *analyzes* a natural substance, one will find in it portions, or shares, which are also to be found in every other natural substance.

What are these portions, portions of? Not of other natural substances, presumably, for that leads to a vicious circle. The answer must be, portions of opposites, portions of hot, cold, wet, dry, light, dark, and so on. These are not physically separable from things, but are discriminable elements in things.

If this interpretation is correct, Anaxagoras anticipated Plato. He certainly anticipated him, and Aristotle too, in the crucial place he gives to Mind as cause of motion.

The Atomists: Leucippus and Democritus

Very little is known of Leucippus. His writings have mainly been lost, and his very birthplace is uncertain, though there is a tradition connecting him with Elea and Parmenides. He has survived in and through the work of his follower, Democritus, whose elder contemporary he was. Democritus was born about 460 B.C., and founded a school at Abdera in Thrace.

Parmenides had denied the existence of empty space, or void, on the ground that since Being is, void could only be where Being is not, and therefore cannot be. Leucippus and Democritus accepted the argument but denied the conclusion, maintaining that "Not-being exists as much as being." The remark may seem self-contradictory, but in fact is not. Parmenides' concept of Being contained the latent confusion of existence with material existence—a confusion Plato was the first to detect. The Atomists' claim, stated as a paradox, amounts to this: material bodies are not the only things that exist, since space exists as well.

The universe of Leucippus and Democritus consists of atoms, physically indivisible material particles that differ in size and shape and move about at random in empty space. The characteristics of these particles are geometrical, not perceptual; the colors and sounds and tastes of the world are secondary qualities, which arise in virtue of the interaction of certain kinds of physical objects (such as eyes and ears) with others (such as tables and chairs).

The atoms move, but no cause of motion, nothing analogous to the Love and Strife of Empedocles or the Mind of Anaxagoras, impels them. This theory called forth severe criticism from Aristotle, who supposed, with most Greeks, that rest is the natural state of things and that motion must always be explained by prior causes. In fact, the atomists' treatment of motion closely anticipated the modern account of inertia.

In their atomism, their theory of motion, their distinction between primary and secondary qualities, and most of all, in their insistence that explanation of natural processes shall be mechanical, the atomists anticipated much in the world view of modern science, and many historians have hailed them as far in advance of their time. It is well to remember, however, that their doctrines were not the result of empirical inquiry: they were posited a priori, to meet the difficulty Parmenides had first put, that out of nothing nothing comes and that generation or destruction is impossible. That same difficulty, it may be added, was to prompt in Aristotle a very different solution, that matter is potentiality.

The Sophists

The sophists were the wandering teachers of Greece in the latter part of the fifth century, traveling from city to city to lecture for a fee. They taught a variety of subjects—literary criticism, for example, especially of the poets, and grammar—but their chief aim was to provide training in rhetoric, the techniques and devices of winning over opinion in courts of law and public assemblies. There was need for their services. The decay of aristocratic institutions in Greece toward the end of the sixth century and the subsequent rise of democracy—direct, not representative, democracy—made skill in rhetoric important not only to those ambitious for political advancement, but to ordinary citizens concerned to safeguard before the law their property, their citizenship, and their lives. Sophism was not a doctrine, hardly even an attitude of mind, but a social movement, which could contain men of genuine intellectual eminence such as Protagoras and Gorgias and contain also Euthydemus and his brother Dionysodorus, a pair of elderly ex-athletes who took to lecturing when they found it hard to stay in shape. But the movement was tinged from the beginning with a certain skepticism which increasingly brought it into disrepute. Much prejudice arose from the very task which sophistry performed. Rhetoric aims at persuasion, not truth, and the popular charge that the sophists undertook to make the weak argument stronger and the strong argument weak was quite correct.

An important trait of sophism was its skepticism of the intellect, in large measure prompted, paradoxically enough, by Parmenides. Parmenides had divorced the world of thought from the world of fact, had put the claims of logic in sharp opposition to the claims of experience. Faced with a choice, Parmenides rejected experience. The sophists, facing the same choice, rejected logic. Protagoras offered a subjective theory of truth and claimed that man is the measure of all things; he meant, or so Plato thought, that what seems true to each man is true, that nothing is true or false but thinking makes it so. Mathematics, which provides truths independent of anyone's opinions, Protagoras dealt with by denying its relevance to the world of fact; there are, after all, no examples in nature of the geometer's lengthless points and breadthless lines. Gorgias, again, reacting to Parmenides' claim that what exists must be one and unchanging, concluded that nothing exists; that if anything did exist, it would be unknowable; and that if it were knowable, it would be incommunicable.

Skepticism of the intellect was coupled with moral skepticism: many sophists challenged the objective validity of the attitudes and beliefs of Greek moral and political life. This challenge took the form of a contrast between *phusis* and *nomos*, "nature," and "convention" or "law." By nature, men are selfish and self-seeking: their appetites are directed toward pleasure, power, and self-aggrandisement and are exercised without regard to, or at the expense of, their neighbors. If men do not behave in society solely as their appetites direct, the reason is that they are checked and inhibited by convention and law. The sole sanction for law is compulsion; where no compulsion is present, men are bound by no obligation.

This thesis to some degree was prompted by anthropology. It is perhaps no accident that most of the sophists came from the periphery of the Greek world—Protagoras from Abdera in Thrace, Prodicus from Ceos in the Aegean, Gorgias from Leontini in Sicily—from cities in constant contact with foreign culture. As Aristotle once remarked, fire burns both here and in Persia; but if fire is constant, morals are not, and the sophists inferred, as many modern anthropologists have done, that the basis of morality lies solely in custom and law. This is the thesis of cultural relativity, a thesis which has two parts. The first is that what is regarded as right or morally good in one culture may be regarded as wrong or morally bad in another. The second is that there are no "absolute" standards by which to judge whether anything is right or wrong in itself, apart from the attitude a given society takes to it. The first claim is empirical, a matter of fact; the second is a claim in moral philosophy, and indeed metaphysics, a claim in no way implied by the fact.

Cultural relativity, if taken not simply as a theory, but as a working basis for political and private conduct, is a heady doctrine. For if moral standards are subjective in that they are relative to culture, it is an easy inference that they are subjective in that they are further relative to the individual—that nothing is either right or wrong but thinking makes it so. Many sophists and their pupils drew this conclusion, which Socrates was to make it the main purpose of his life to challenge.

Socrates and Plato

Socrates was born in 469 B.C. in Athens, within whose walls, except for brief periods of military service, he spent his entire life. He wrote nothing; it is upon Plato's portrait of him that we chiefly rely for information.

The inner life of the man is mysterious, and will always remain so. Socrates was an ugly man, walleyed, snub-nosed, bald in later life, with a peculiar rolling walk that reminded observers of a duck. But Alcibiades, in the *Symposium,* compared him to the statues of Silenus the satyr, that were sold in the Agora. Cleverly hinged, they opened to reveal within them the golden image of a god. Alcibiades had perhaps put his finger on the source of the mystery.

Inscribed on the portals of the temple at Delphi were the words of Apollo: "Know Thyself." And it was at Delphi, as the *Apology* tells us, that Socrates' mission began. Before Socrates, the significance of the Delphic injunction had been primarily understood as social: "Know Thyself" meant, "Know thy station and its duties, and do not usurp a position not thine by right." Peasants were not to act like kings, nor kings like gods.

Socrates transformed the meaning of the injunction by turning it inward. The true aim of life, as he puts it in the *Apology,* is to "make one's soul as good as possible"; human happiness consists in spiritual perfection, and spiritual perfection implies and is implied by self-knowledge. The claim of morality on a man is ultimately the claim of his own human nature on itself; only when a man has come clearly to understand himself, has come to know who he is and what he is, can he truly know good from evil. It is for this reason that "the unexamined life is not worth living," and it is this knowledge, rather than knowledge of natural causes, which deserves the name of Wisdom.

As a moral teacher, Socrates was peculiar in that he did not preach, but questioned, wearing all the while a mask of ironic ignorance. All of us, in moral matters, think we know what we do not know. The first aim of Socrates' questioning was to disperse this false conceit of knowledge. Socratic dialectic begins with refutation. Ask a man to tell you the meaning of some simple term, a term like courage, or justice; then question him about his definition and test it to see if it holds water. If it does not, bring him to see for himself the weakness of his vision. When the ground has thus been cleared, you can both enlist together in the common cause of finding out what is really the case, in a cooperative effort to discover the truth. What has been gained in this process by the respondent cannot be taken from him; he will come to see for himself, with the full clarity of immediate insight, the nature of the virtue which before he had only dimly understood. It is because each man must see the truth for himself that virtue cannot be taught. You can teach a man what has usually been thought about virtue, for that is a fact and facts may be learned by rote. But in order to understand virtue, one must apprehend it as directly and immediately as a theorem in geometry; and that apprehension cannot fail to reorder life. It was for this reason that Socrates identified knowledge with goodness in his paradoxical statement, "virtue is knowledge." It would be more accurate to say, perhaps, that virtue is self-knowledge, knowledge of the nature of one's own soul, of the true end of life and the means to attain it.

Socrates' relentless examinations often called in question the rules and customs of conventional Greek morality. The very basis of his ethics challenged the morality of social habit in the name of a higher morality of spiritual aspiration. Each man must see his own good, must come to understand for himself. The goal is the autonomous moral life of the wise man, which cannot be governed by any set of rules imposed from without. But the latter part of the fifth century, particularly in Athens, was a time of social disorder, a time when men were in doubt who did not know how to doubt. For many Athenians, the old order, which they knew to be passing away, became a symbol of all that was fair in the life of Greece; criticism became heresy and change, unthinkable. And because Socrates criticized, and refused to give over, he was regarded as a sophist and put to death. The charge against him could hardly have been more ironic: he had corrupted the youth and introduced strange gods.

Plato was born in 428 B.C., of distinguished Athenian parentage, shortly after the death of Pericles. He came under the influence of Socrates as a very young man, perhaps through his older brothers, Glaucon and Adeimantus. When Socrates was put to death in 399, at the age of seventy, Plato undertook to justify his memory and carry on his work by writing a series of dialogues which were to be consciously faithful to the memory of the master. The *Apology* and the *Euthyphro* belong to this group of dialogues, works of Plato's early period.

In 387, at the age of forty, Plato traveled in Italy and Sicily, where he met Archytas of Tarentum, the Pythagorean mathematician and philosopher, and visited the court of Dionysius I, the tyrant of Syracuse. He returned the next year to Athens to found the first university in Europe, the Academy, and to write the great dialogues of his middle period, the *Meno, Phaedo, Symposium, Republic, Phaedrus,* and *Parmenides*. These dialogues resemble the early dialogues in style but differ from them in content. The early dialogues are concerned almost exclusively with ethics; there is little or no emphasis on mathematics, politics, or metaphysics. They are brief, and given less to positive teaching than to questioning and refutation. They are critical and exploratory rather than dogmatic and they make no use of myth. In all these respects, the middle dialogues differ. In them, the ethical concern of the early dialogues is grounded in a new metaphysics whose chief doctrines are the immortality and divinity of the rational soul and the reality and unchangeability of the objects of its knowledge. These doctrines constitute, to borrow the metaphor of F. M. Cornford, the twin pillars of Platonism: the architrave of those pillars is Anamnesis, the doctrine that learning is recollection and that the truth of all things is always in the soul. The seed planted by Socrates in the waters of the human spirit had grown, under Plato's hands, into a tree whose branches embraced the heavens.

Plato's view of reality is that there are two worlds, a world of Knowledge and a world of Opinion. The world of Knowledge is fully real; its contents are Forms, divine, immaterial, and fully intelligible exemplars of such characteristics as Justice, Goodness, and Equality, which may be apprehended only by reason. The world of Opinion is not fully real but it is not wholly unreal either; its contents are the changing particulars of the material world, which are apprehended by sensation and cannot be known. The relation between these worlds is one of participation, or imitation: particulars stand to Forms as shadows and reflections of material objects stand to the material objects which cast them; the less real stands to the more real as the dependent (image) stands to the independent (original). Plato thus solved, or undertook to solve, the Parmenidean problem of Not-Being by giving a genuine, though dependent, status to the way of Seeming. In a strict and literal sense, the material world was made the seal and symbol of the intelligible. The moral ideal for men was to attain to knowledge, thereby introducing the beauty and order of the divine into their own souls, and, hopefully, into society as well.

In 367, and again in 361, Plato returned to Syracuse to take in hand the education of Dionysius II, who had ascended to the throne on the death of his father. Plato's object, almost certainly, was to rear a philosopher-king, or an approximation, in the unlikely soil of Sicily. It is not surprising—nor was it, in all likelihood, surprising to Plato—that the attempt failed, but the circumstances of failure saddened, and perhaps to some degree embittered, Plato's remaining years. In any case, Plato returned in 360 to Athens and the Academy, not to leave again. In the years following 367, Plato wrote his last, his most technical, and in the opinion of many philosophers, his greatest dialogues, the *Theaetetus, Sophist, Statesman, Timaeus, Philebus,* and *Laws.* He died in 348 at the age of eighty, writing to the last.

Aristotle

Aristotle was born in 384 B.C. at Stagira, in Thrace, the son of a physician to the court of Macedon. In 368, at the age of seventeen, he came to Athens, to the Academy, where he remained as a student until Plato's death in 348. At that time he left Athens and founded a branch of the Academy at Assos, in the Troad in Asia Minor. In 343 he was invited to the court of Macedon at Pella to undertake the education of the heir apparent, Alexander, who was to become, in a few short years, the conqueror of the world. When Alexander succeeded to the throne in 336, Aristotle left Pella, and returned the following year to Athens. There he founded his own school, the Lyceum, a school dedicated both to teaching and research, in the precincts of Apollo Lyceus. Aristotle continued in the Lyceum until 323, when political difficulties arose in Athens due to his association with Macedon; he then withdrew to Chalcis in Euboea, where he died in 322.

Aristotle's writings were of two main kinds. First, there were the "exoteric" works, written for publication, of which only scattered fragments remain. They appear to have been written in early life as dialogues, in the manner of Plato, and they reveal Aristotle as himself deeply under the spell of Platonism, explaining the doctrine of recollection, the theory of forms, and the separability and immortality of the soul. His prose style in these works was praised by no less an authority than Cicero as "golden." Second, there were the "esoteric" works, works meant not for publication, but for the use of students. Most of these—and they include all of the selections which follow—were first delivered in the form of lectures, and date from a later period of Aristotle's life than the dialogues. In them, the doctrines that have come to be regarded as characteristically Aristotelian were developed.

Aristotle's thought is in some ways a mirror-image of Plato's. Plato had been a rationalist: he believed that reality can only be grasped by intuitive reason, and that the role of perception in knowledge is merely to remind us of what we already in some sense know. Aristotle, on the contrary, was an empiricist: he did not suppose, as many empiricists have, that all knowledge is limited to perceptible objects, but he did suppose that perception is our only direct avenue to reality, and that our concepts, one and all, are derived from, if not therefore exhausted in, sense experience. Again, Plato had been an idealist: reality consisted, for him, not in things one could touch, taste, and handle, but in transcendent Forms or exemplars, which served as ideal standards to which the changing material world approximates, and on which it depends for its existence. Aristotle, however, was a realist: he located reality in the individual substances that compose our perceptible world, in its plants and animals, its elements of earth and air, fire and water. He agreed with Plato that such things as these were intelligible only through their form, but held that form exists, not apart from things enformed, but *in* them: except in the case of God, form exists only in relation to matter, which is itself to be construed as potentiality for receiving form. Thus the material world, which for Plato had been only an object of opinion, for Aristotle became an object of knowledge. But though Platonism in any explicit sense had been abandoned, its traces remain, particularly in the doctrine that God, or the Unmoved Mover, is pure form, existing independently of matter.

PRESOCRATIC PHILOSOPHY

THE SOURCES

No work of the Presocratics has come down in its entirety. We possess fragments preserved by later authors, and testimony. The major sources are as follows:

A. Philosophers

(i) Plato gives useful information about his predecessors. Since he himself was not a historian of philosophy, his remarks must be treated with caution.

(ii) Aristotle surveyed his predecessors' testimony on the philosophical problems with which he himself was concerned. The Presocratics are thus made parties to his argument, not left to speak for themselves, and this often introduces a cast into his interpretation. Nevertheless, he was not without a sense of history, and his work is, and will remain a major source of knowledge.

(iii) The Stoics' method of interpretation was syncretistic: they undertook to show that their predecessors agreed with Stoic doctrine, and with each other.

(iv) Sceptics, such as Sextus Empiricus, were concerned to exhibit the contradictions of earlier philosophy, but preserved valuable fragments.

(v) The Neo-Platonists, especially Proclus, Alexander, and Simplicius, commented on Plato and Aristotle; with the library of the Academy at their disposal, they too preserved many fragments.

B. The Doxographical Tradition

Theophrastus, Aristotle's successor in the Lyceum, continued the Peripatetic interest in history. As part of the encyclopedia of knowledge

Texts in this part reprinted by permission of the publisher from G. S. Kirk and J. E. Raven, *The Presocratic Philosophers* (Cambridge University Press, 1957).

projected by the school, Theophrastus wrote *On the Opinions of the Physical Philosophers*, parts of which have come down to us. He consulted the original texts of the Presocratics, but his historical judgment was much influenced by Aristotle.

Theophrastus' work became the standard authority in the ancient world. The doxographers are those who derive their material, directly or indirectly, from the *Opinions (doxai)*. The main sources in the doxographical tradition are Diogenes Laertius (probably third century A.D.), Plutarch (first-second century A.D.), and John Stobeaus (fifth century A.D.).

Readings

Burnet, *Early Greek Philosophy*, pp. 31–38.
Guthrie, *A History of Greek Philosophy*, Vol. I, p. xiii ff.
Kirk and Raven, *The Presocratic Philosophers*, pp. 1–7.

THE MILESIANS

Thales

Testimony

The Typical Philosopher

A witty and attractive Thracian servant-girl is said to have mocked Thales for falling into a well while he was observing the stars and gazing upwards, declaring that he was eager to know the things in the sky, but that what was behind him and just by his feet escaped his notice. (Plato, *Theaetetus* 174a)

When they reproached him because of his poverty, as though philosophy were no use, it is said that, having observed through his study of the heavenly bodies that there would be a large olive crop, he raised a little capital while it was still winter and paid deposits on all the olive presses in Miletus and Chios, hiring them cheaply because no one bid against him. When the appropriate time came there was a sudden rush of requests for the presses. He then hired them out on his own terms and so made a large profit, thus demonstrating that it is easy for philosophers to be rich, if they wish, but that it is not in this that they are interested. (Aristotle, *Politics* 1259a 9)

Astronomy and Practical Activities

In the sixth year of the war, which [the Medes and Lydians] had carried on with equal fortunes, an engagement took place in which it turned out that when the battle was in progress the day suddenly became night. This alteration of the day Thales the Milesian foretold to the Ionians, setting as its limit this year in which the change actually occurred. (Herodotus I, 74)

Some say he was the first to study the heavenly bodies and to foretell eclipses of the sun and solstices, as Eudemus says in his history of astronomy; for which reason both Xenophanes and Herodotus express admiration; and both Heraclitus and Democritus bear witness for him. (Diogenes Laertius I, 23)

For the victory belonged to Thales, who was clever in judgment, not least because he was said to have measured out the little stars of the Wain, by which the Phoenicians sail. (Callimachus, *Iambus* I, 52, fr. 191, Pfeiffer)

Useful also was the opinion, before the destruction of Ionia, of Thales, a man of Miletus, being a Phoenician by ultimate descent, who advised the Ionians to have a single deliberative chamber, saying that it should be in Teos, for this was in the middle of Ionia; the other cities should continue to be inhabited but should be regarded as if they were demes. (Herodotus I, 170)

When he came to the Halys river, Croesus then, as I say, put his army across by the existing bridges; but, according to the common account of the Greeks, Thales the Milesian transferred the army for him. For it is said that Croesus was at a loss how his army should cross the river, since these bridges did not yet exist at this period; and that Thales, who was present in the army, made the river, which flowed on the left of the army, flow on the right hand also. He did so in this way; beginning upstream of the army he dug a deep channel, giving it a crescent shape, so that it should flow around the back of where the army was encamped, being diverted in this way from its old course by the channel, and passing the camp should flow into its old course once more. The result was that as soon as the river was divided it became fordable in both parts. (Herodotus I, 75)

Cosmology

Others say that the earth rests on water. For this is the most ancient account we have received, which they say was given by Thales the Milesian, that it stays in place through floating like a log or some other such thing (for none of these rests by nature on air, but on water)—as though the same argument did not apply to the water supporting the earth as to the earth itself. (Aristotle, *de caelo* 294a 28)

For [Thales] said that the world is held up by water and rides like a ship, and when it is said to "quake" it is actually rocking because of the water's movement. (Seneca, *Qu. Nat.* III, 14)

Most of the first philosophers thought that principles in the form of matter were the only principles of all things: for the original source of all existing things, that from which a thing first comes-into-being and into which it is finally destroyed, the substance persisting but changing its qualities, this they declare is the element and first principle of existing things, and for this reason they consider that there is no absolute coming-to-be or passing away, on the ground that such a nature is always preserved . . . for there must be some natural substance, either one or more than one, from which the other things come-into-being, while it is preserved. Over the number, however, and the form of this kind of principle they do not all agree; but Thales, the founder of this type of philosophy, says it is water (and therefore declared that the earth is on water), perhaps taking this supposition from seeing the nurture of all things to be moist, and the warm itself coming-to-be from this and living by this (that from which they come-to-be being the principle of all things—taking the supposition both from this and from the seeds of all things having a moist nature, water being the natural principle of moist things. (Aristotle, *Metaphysics* 983b 6)

Thales, too, seems, from what they relate, to have supposed that the soul was something kinetic, if he said that the [Magnesian] stone possesses soul because it moves iron. (Aristotle, *de anima* 405a 19)

Aristotle and Hippieas say that he gave a share of soul even to inanimate objects, using Magnesian stone and amber as indications. (Diogenes Laertius I, 24)

And some say that [soul] is intermingled in the universe, for which reason, perhaps, Thales also thought that all things are full of gods. (Aristotle, *de anima* 411a 7)

Thales said that the mind of the world is god, and that the sum of things is besouled, and full of daimons [spirits]; right through the elemental moisture there penetrates a divine power that moves it. (Aetius I, 7, 11)

Anaximander

Testimony

Scientific Activities

Anaximander the Milesian, a disciple of Thales, first dared to draw the inhabited world on a tablet; after him Hecataeus the Milesian, a much travelled man, made the map more accurate, so that it became a source of wonder. (Agathemerus I, 1)

I smile when I see that many have drawn circuits of the earth, up to now, and none of them has explained the matter sensibly; they draw Ocean running around the earth, which is drawn as though with a compass, and make Asia equal to Europe. (Herodotus IV, 36)

Anaximander son of Praxiades, of Miletus, philosopher, was a kinsman, pupil and successor of Thales. He first discovered the equinox and solstices and hour-indicators, and that the earth lies in the center. He introduced the *gnomon* and in general made known an outline of geometry. (Suda, s.v.)

Cosmology

Of those who say that it is one, moving, and infinite, Anaximander, son of Praxiades, a Milesian, the successor and pupil of Thales, said that the principle and element of existing things was the Indefinite, being the first to introduce this name of the material principle. He says that it is neither water nor any other of the so-called elements, but some other indefinite nature, from which came into being all the heavens and the worlds in them. And the source of coming-to-be for existing things is that into which destruction, too, happens "according to necessity; for they pay penalty and retribution to each other for their injustice according to the assessment of Time," as he describes it in these rather poetical terms. (Simplicius, *Phys.* 24, 13)

Two types of explanation are given by the physicists. Those who have made the subsisting body one, either one of the three [elements— air, fire, water] or something else which is thicker than fire and finer than air, generate the rest by condensation and rarefaction, making it into many. . . . But the others say that the opposites are separated out from the One, being present in it, as Anaximander says and all who say that there are one and many, like Empedocles and Anaxagoras; for these, too, separate out the rest from the mixture. (Aristotle, *Physics* 187a 12)

Nor can the infinite body be one and simple, whether it be, as some say, that which is beside the elements, from which they generate the elements, or whether it be expressed simply. For there are some people who make what is beside the elements the infinite, and not air or water, so that the rest be not destroyed by their infinite substance; for the elements are opposed to each other (for example, air is cold, water moist, and fire hot), and if one of those were infinite the rest would already have been destroyed. But as it is, they say that the infinite is different from these, and that they came into being from it. (Aristotle, *Physics* 204b 22)

Of the infinite there is no beginning . . . but this seems to be the beginning of the other things, and to surround all things and steer all, as all those say who do not postulate other causes, such as mind or love, above and beyond the infinite. And this is the divine; for it is immortal and indestructible, as Anaximander says and most of the physical speculators. (Aristotle, *Physics* 203b 7)

Others say that the opposites are separated out from the One, being present in it, as Anaximander says and all who say that there are one and many, like Empedocles and Anaxagoras; for these, too, separate out the rest from the mixture. (Aristotle, *Physics* 187a 20)

The World Order

[Anaximander] says that that which is productive from the eternal of hot and cold was separated off at the coming-to-be of this world, and that a kind of sphere of flame from this was formed round the air surrounding the earth, like bark around a tree. When this was broken off and shut off in certain circles, the sun and the moon and the stars were formed. (Ps.-Plutarch, *Strom.* 2)

He says that the earth is cylindrical in shape, and that its depth is a third of its width. (Ps.-Plutarch, *Strom.* 2)

Its shape is curved, round, similar to the drum of a column; of its flat surfaces we walk on one, and the other is on the opposite side. (Hippolytus, *Ref.* I, 6, 3)

There are some who say, like Anaximander among the ancients, that (the earth) stays still because of its equilibrium. For it behooves that which is established at the center, and is equally related to the extremes, not to be borne one whit more either up or down or to the sides; and it is impossible for it to move simultaneously in opposite directions, so that it stays fixed by necessity. (Aristotle, *de caelo* 295b 10)

The heavenly bodies come into being as a circle of fire separated off from the fire in the world, and enclosed by air. There are breathing-holes, certain pipe-like passages, at which the heavenly bodies show themselves; accordingly eclipses occur when the breathing-holes are blocked up. The moon is seen now waxing, now waning, according to the blocking or opening of the channels. The circle of the sun is 27 times the size of the earth, that of the moon 18 times; the sun is highest, and the circles of the fixed stars are lowest. (Hippolytus, *Ref.* I, 6, 4-5)

(On thunder, lightning, thunderbolts, whirlwinds, and typhoons). Anaximander says that all these things occur as a result of wind: for whenever it is shut up in a thick cloud and then bursts out forcibly, through its fineness and lightness, then the bursting makes the noise, while the rift against the blackness of the cloud makes the flash. (Aetius III, 3, 1-2)

For first of all the whole area round the earth is moist, but being dried by the sun the part that is exhaled makes winds and turnings of the sun and moon, they say, while that which is left is sea; therefore they think that the sea is actually becoming less through being dried up, and that some time it will end up by ending all dry. (Aristotle, *Meteor.* 353b 6)

Anaximander said that the first living creatures were born in moisture, enclosed in thorny barks; and that as their age increased they came forth on to the drier part and, when the bark had broken off, they lived a different kind of life for a short time. (Aetius V, 19, 4)

Further he says that in the beginning man was born from creatures of a different kind; because other creatures are soon self-supporting, but man alone needs prolonged nursing. For this reason he would not have survived if this had been his original form. (Ps.-Plutarch, *Strom.* 2)

Anaximenes

Testimony

Cosmology

Anaximenes, son of Eurystratus of Miletus, was a pupil of Anaximander . . . He said that the material principle was air and the infinite; and that the stars move, not under the earth, but round it. He used simple and unsuperfluous Ionic speech. (Diogenes Laertius II, 3)

Anaximenes . . . also says that the underlying nature is one and infinite like [Anaximander], but not undefined as Anaximander said but definite, for he identifies it as air; and it differs in its substantial nature by rarity and density. Being made finer it becomes fire, being made thicker it becomes wind, then cloud, then (when thickened still more) water, then earth, then stones; and the rest come into being from these. He, too, makes motion eternal, and says that change, also, comes about through it. (Theophrastus *ap.* Simplicium, *Phys.* 24, 26)

Anaximenes said that infinite air was the principle, from which the things that are becoming, and that are, and that shall be, and gods and things divine, all come into being, and the rest from its products. The form of air is of this kind: whenever it is most equable it is invisible to sight, but is revealed by the cold and the hot and the damp and by movement. It is always in motion: for things that change do not change unless there be movement. Through becoming denser or finer it has different appearances; for when it is dissolved into what is finer it becomes fire, while winds again, are air that is becoming condensed, and cloud is produced from air by felting. When it is condensed still more, water is produced; with a further degree of condensation earth is produced, and when condensed as far as possible, stone. The result is that the most influential components of generation are opposites, hot and cold. (Hippolytus, *Ref.* I, 7, 1)

As Anaximenes thought of old, let us leave neither the cold nor the hot as belonging to substance, but as common dispositions of matter that supervene on changes; for he says that matter which is compressed and condensed is cold, while that which is fine and 'relaxed' (using this very word) is hot. Therefore, he said, the dictum is not an unreasonable one, that man releases both warmth and cold from his mouth: for the breath is chilled by being compressed and condensed with the lips, but when the mouth is loosened the breath escapes and becomes warm through its rarity. (Plutarch, *de prim. frig.* 7, 947f)

Anaximenes says that the air is god. (Aetius I, 7, 13)

The World Order

All things are produced by a kind of condensation, and again rarefaction, of (air). Motion, indeed, exists from everlasting; he says that when the air felts, there first of all comes into being the earth, quite flat—therefore it accordingly rides on the air; and sun and moon and the remaining heavenly bodies have their source of generation from earth. At least, he declares the sun to be earth, but that through the rapid motion it obtains heat in great sufficiency. (Ps.-Plutarch *Strom.* 3)

The heavenly bodies have come into being from earth and through the exhalation arising from it; when the exhalation is rarefied fire comes into being, and from fire raised on high the stars are composed. (Hippolytus, *Ref.* I 7, 5)

The earth is flat, being borne upon air, and similarly sun, moon, and the other heavenly bodies, which are all fiery, ride upon the air through their flatness. (Hippolytus, *Ref.* I, 7, 4)

He says that the heavenly bodies do not move under the earth, as others have supposed, but round it, just as if a felt cap turns round our head; and that the sun is hidden not by being under earth, but through being covered by the higher parts of the earth and through its increased distance from us. (Hippolytus, *Ref.* I, 7, 6)

Anaximenes said the same as (Anaximander), adding what happens in the case of sea, which flashes when cleft by oars—Anaximenes said that clouds occur when the air is further thickened; when it is compressed further rain is squeezed out, and hail occurs when the descending water coalesces, snow when some windy portion is included together with the moisture. (Aetius III, 3, 2)

Anaximenes says that the earth, through being drenched and dried off, breaks asunder, and is shaken by the peaks that are thus broken off and fall in. Therefore earthquakes happen in periods both of drought and again of excessive rains; for in droughts, as has been said, it dries up and cracks, and being made over-moist by the waters it crumbles apart. (Aristotle, *Meteor.* 365b 6)

Anaximenes . . . of Miletus, declared that air is the principle of existing things; for from it all things come-to-be and into it they are again dissolved. As our soul, he says, being air holds us together and controls us, so does wind and air enclose the whole world. (Aetius I, 3, 4)

Readings

Burnet, *Early Greek Philosophy*, Ch. I.
Collingwood, *Idea of Nature*, Pt. I, Ch. I.
Cornford, *The Unwritten Philosophy*, Ch. I, III.
Guthrie, *A History of Greek Philosophy*, Vol. I, Ch. II, III.
Kirk and Raven, *The Presocratic Philosophers*, Ch. I-IV.
Whitehead, *Science and the Modern World*, Ch. I.

PYTHAGORAS AND PYTHAGOREANISM

Testimony

Religion

The following became universally known: first, that he maintains that the soul is immortal; next, that it changes into other kinds of living things; also that events recur in certain cycles, and that nothing is ever absolutely new; and finally, that all living things should be regarded as akin. Pythagoras seems to have been the first to bring these beliefs into Greece. (Porphyry, *Vita Pythagorae* 19)

The Egyptians are the first to have maintained the doctrine that the soul of man is immortal, and that, when the body perishes, it enters into another animal that is being born at the time, and when it has been the complete round of the creatures of the dry land and of the sea and of the air it enters again into the body of a man at birth; and its cycle is completed in 3000 years. There are some Greeks who have adopted this doctrine, some in former times and some in later, as if it were their own invention; their names I know but refrain from writing down. (Herodotus II, 123)

On the subject of reincarnation Xenophanes bears witness in an elegy which begins: "Now I will turn to another tale and show the way." What he says about Pythagoras runs thus: "Once they say that he was passing by when a puppy was being whipped, and he took pity and said: 'Stop, do not beat it; for it is the soul of a friend that I recognised when I heard it giving tongue.'" (Diogenes Laertius VIII, 36)

Above all else he forbade the eating of red mullet and black-tail; and he enjoined abstinence from the heart and from beans. (Diogenes Laertius VIII, 19)

Let the rules to be pondered be these: (1) When you are going out to a temple, worship first, and on your way neither say nor do anything else connected with your daily life. (2) On a journey neither enter a temple nor worship at all, not even if you are passing the very doors.

(3) Sacrifice and worship without shoes on. (6) Follow the gods and restrain your tongue above all else. (8) Stir not the fire with iron. (12) Speak not of Pythagorean matters without light. (21) Let not a swallow nest under your roof. (22) Do not wear a ring. (26) Be not possessed by irrepressible mirth. (29) When you rise from bed roll the bed-clothes together and smooth out the place where you lay. (39) Abstain from living things. (Iamblichus, *Protr.* 21)

Religion and Inquiry

Life, he said, is like a festival; just as some come to the festival to compete, some to ply their trade, but the best people come as spectators, so in life the slavish men go hunting for fame or gain, the philosophers for the truth. (Diogenes Laertius VIII, 8)

Pythagoras turned geometrical philosophy into a form of liberal education by seeking its first principles in a higher realm of reality. (Proclus, *in Eucl.* 65 Friedl.)

The Pythagoreans, according to Aristoxenus, practised the purification of the body by medicine, that of the soul by music. (Cramer, *An. Par.* I 172)

Do we hear of Homer in his own lifetime presiding, like Pythagoras, over a band of intimate disciples who loved him for the inspiration of his society and handed down a Homeric way of life, like the way of life which the Pythagoreans called after their founder and which to this day distinguishes them from the rest of the world? (Plato, *Republic* 600B, trans. Cornford)

The form of this instruction was twofold: one group of his followers were called the Mathematicians, the other the Acousmatics. The Mathematicians were those who had learnt the more detailed and exactly elaborated version of his knowledge, the Acousmatics those who had heard only the summary headings of his writings, without the more exact exposition. (Porphyry, *Vita Pythagorae* 37)

Cosmology

Ten is the very nature of number. All Greeks and all barbarians alike count up to ten, and having reached ten revert again to the unit. And again, Pythagoras maintains, the power of the number ten lies in the number four, the tetrad. This is the reason: if one starts at the unit and adds the successive numbers up to four, one will make the number ten; and if one exceeds the tetrad, one will exceed ten too. If, that is, one takes the unit, adds two, then three and then four, one will make up the number ten. So that number by the unit resides in the number ten, but potentially in the number four. And so the Pythagoreans used to invoke the tetrad as their most binding oath: "Nay, by him that gave to our generation the tetractys, which contains the fount and root of eternal nature." (Aetius I, 3, 8)

"The square on the hypotenuse of a right-angle triangle is equal to the sum of the squares on the sides enclosing the right angle." If we pay any attention to those who like to recount ancient history, we may find some of them referring this theorem to Pythagoras, and saying that he sacrificed an ox in honour of his discovery. (Proclus *in Eucl.* 426 Friedl.)

The Pythagoreans, as they are called, devoted themselves to mathematics; they were the first to advance this study, and having been brought up in it they thought its principles were the principles of all things. Since of these principles numbers are by nature the first, and in numbers they seemed to see many resemblances to the things that exist and come into being—more than in fire and earth and water (such and such a modification of numbers being justice, another being soul and reason, another being opportunity—and similarly almost all other things being numerically expressible); since, again, they say that the attributes and ratios of the musical scales were expressible in numbers; since, then, all other things seemed in their whole nature to be modelled after numbers, and numbers seemed to be the first things in the whole of nature, they supposed the elements of numbers to be the elements of all things, and the whole heaven to be a musical scale and a number. And all the properties of numbers and scales which they could show to agree with the attributes and parts and the whole arrangement of the heavens, they collected and fitted into their scheme; and if there was a gap anywhere, they readily made additions so as to make their whole theory coherent. E.g. as the number 10 is thought to be perfect and to comprise the whole nature of numbers, they say that the bodies which move through the heavens are ten, but as the visible bodies are only nine, to meet this they invent a tenth—the 'counter-earth'. . . . Evidently, then, these thinkers also consider that number is the principle both as matter for things and as forming their modifications and their permanent states, and hold that the elements of number are the even and the odd, and of these the former is unlimited, and the latter limited; and the 1 proceeds from both of these (for it is both even and odd), and number from the 1; and the whole heaven, as has been said, is numbers. Other members of this same school say there are ten principles, which they arrange in two columns of cognates—limit and unlimited, odd and even, one and plurality, right and left, male and female, resting and moving, straight and crooked, light and darkness, good and bad, square and oblong. (Aristotle, *Metaphysics* 985b 23)

The Pythagoreans identify the infinite with the even. For this, they say, when it is taken in and limited by the odd, provides things with the element of infinity. An indication of this is what happens with numbers. If the gnomons are placed round the one, and without the one, in the one construction the figure that results is always different, in the other it is always the same. (Aristotle, *Physics* 203a 10)

The Pythagoreans, because they saw many attributes of numbers belonging to sensible bodies, supposed real things to be numbers—not separable numbers, however, but numbers of which real things consist. (Aristotle, *Metaphysics* 1090a 20)

Pythagoras first attempted to discuss goodness, but not in the right way; for by referring the virtues to numbers he made his study of them inappropriate; for justice is not a square number. (Aristotle, *Magna Moralia* 1182a 11)

For 1 is the point, 2 is the line, 3 the triangle, and 4 the pyramid. All these are primary, the first principle of individual things of the same class . . . and the same hold in generation too; for the first principle in magnitude is the point, the second the line, the third surface and the fourth the solid. (Speusippus *ap. Theologumena Arithmeticae* 84, 10 de Falco)

There are some who, because the point is the limit and extreme of the line, the line of the plane, and the plane of the solid, think there must be real things of this sort. (Aristotle, *Metaphysics* 1090b 5)

The World Order

The Pythagoreans, too, held that void exists and that breath and void enter from the Unlimited into the heaven itself which, as it were, inhales; the void distinguishes the natures of things, being a kind of separating and distinguishing factor between terms in series. This happens primarily in the case of numbers; for the void distinguishes their nature. (Aristotle, *Physics* 213b 22)

Most people think that the earth lies at the center of the universe, . . . but the Italian philosophers known as Pythagoreans take the contrary view. At the center, they say, is fire, and the earth is one of the stars, creating night and day by its circular motion about the center. (Aristotle, *de caelo* 293a 18)

From all this it is clear that the theory that the movement of the stars produces a harmony, i.e., that the sounds they make are concordant, in spite of the grace and originality with which it has been stated, is nevertheless untrue. Some thinkers suppose that the motion of bodies of that size must produce a noise, since on our earth the motion of bodies far inferior in size and speed of movement has that effect. Also, when the sun and the moon, they say, and all the stars, so great in number and in size, are moving with so rapid a motion, how should they not produce a sound immensely great? Starting from this argument and the observation that their speeds, as measured by their distances, are in the same ratios as musical concordances, they assert that the sound given forth by the circular movement of the stars is a harmony. Since, however, it appears unaccountable that we should not hear this music, they explain this by saying that the sound is in our ears from the very moment of birth and is thus indistinguishable from its contrary silence, since sound and silence are discriminated by mutual contrast. What happens to men, then, is just what happens to coppersmiths, who are so accustomed to the noise of the smithy that it makes no difference to them. (Aristotle, *de caelo* 290b 12)

The sixth tetractys is of things that grow. The seed is analogous to the unit and point, growth in length to the dyad and the line, growth in breadth to the triad and the plane, growth in depth to the tetrad and the solid. (Theo Smyrnaeus 97, 17 Hiller)

The theory held by the Pythagoreans seems to have the same purport; for some of them said that the soul is the motes in the air, others that it is what moves them. They spoke of motes because they are evidently in continual motion, even when there is a complete calm. (Aristotle, *de anima* 404a 16)

Readings

Burnet, *Early Greek Philosophy*, Ch. II.
Cornford, *Plato and Parmenides*, Ch. I; *Unwritten Philosophy*, Ch. II.
Guthrie, *A History of Greek Philosophy*, Vol. I, Ch. IV.
Kirk and Raven, *Presocratic Philosophers*, Ch. IX.

HERACLITUS

Fragments

The Logos

Of the Logos which is as I describe it men always prove to be un-comprehending, both before they have heard it and when once they have heard it. For although all things happen according to this Logos men are like people of no experience, even when they experience such words and deeds as I explain, when I distinguish each thing according to its constitution and declare how it is; but the rest of men fail to notice what they do after they wake up just as they forget what they do when asleep. (Fr. 1)[1]

Therefore it is necessary to follow the common; but although the Logos is common the many live as though they had a private under-standing. (Fr. 2)

Listening not to me but to the Logos it is wise to agree that all things are one. (Fr. 50)

The real constitution of things is accustomed to hide itself. (Fr. 123)

Human disposition does not have true judgement, but divine dis-position does. (Fr. 78)

The things of which there is seeing and hearing and perception, these do I prefer. (Fr. 55)

Evil witnesses are eyes and ears for men, if they have souls that do not understand their language. (Fr. 107)

The Unity of Opposites

The path up and down is one and the same. (Fr. 60)

Disease makes health pleasant and good, hunger satiety, weariness rest. (Fr. 111)

---

[1] Here and throughout, fragments are numbered according to Diels-Kranz, *Die Fragmente der Vorsokratiker*.

Sea is the most pure and most polluted water; for fishes it is drinkable and salutary, for men it is undrinkable and deleterious. (Fr. 61)

And as the same thing there exists in us living and dead and the waking and the sleeping and young and old: for these things having changed round are those, and those having changed round are these. (Fr. 88)

Things taken together are whole and not whole, something which is being brought together and brought apart, which is in tune and out of tune; out of all things there comes a unity, and out of a unity all things. (Fr. 10)

God is day night, winter summer, war peace, satiety hunger; he undergoes alteration in the way that fire, when it is mixed with spices, is named according to the scent of each of them. (Fr. 67)

They do not apprehend how being at variance it agrees with itself; there is a back-stretched connection, as in the bow and the lyre. (Fr. 51)

War is father of all and king of all, and some he shows as gods, others as men; some he makes slaves, others free. (Fr. 53)

Heraclitus rebukes the author of the line "would that strife might be destroyed from among gods and men"; for there would be no musical scale unless high and low existed, nor living creatures without female and male, which are opposites. (Aristotle, *Eudemian Ethics* 123a 25)

Fire and the World Order

This world-order did none of gods or men make, but it always was and is and shall be: an everlasting fire, kindling in measures and going out in measures. (Fr. 30)

Fire's turnings: first sea, and of sea the half is earth, . . . (earth) is dispersed as sea, and is measured so as to form the same proportion as existed before it became earth. (Fr. 31)

All things are an equal exchange for fire and fire for all things, as goods are for gold and gold for goods. (Fr. 90)

Thunderbolt steers all things. (Fr. 64)

Heraclitus somewhere says that all things are in process and nothing stays still, and likening existing things to the stream of a river he says that you would not step twice into the same river. (Plato, *Cratylus* 402a)

And some say not that some existing things are moving, and not others, but that all things are in motion all the time, but that this escapes our perception. (Aristotle, *Physics* 253b 9)

Upon those that step into the same rivers different and different waters flow. . . . It scatters and . . . gathers . . . it comes together and flows away . . . approaches and departs. (Fr. 12)

Wisdom and Morals

The wise is one thing, to be acquainted with true judgement, how all things are steered through all. (Fr. 41)

One thing, the only truly wise, does not and does consent to be called by the name of Zeus. (Fr. 32)

For souls it is death to become water, for water it is death to become earth; from earth water comes-to-be, and from water, soul. (Fr. 36)

A dry soul is wisest and best. (Fr. 118)

A man when he is drunk is led by an unfledged boy, stumbling and not knowing where he goes, having his soul moist. (Fr. 117)

For you would not find out the boundaries of soul, even by travelling along every path: so deep a measure does it have. (Fr. 45)

It is hard to fight with anger; for what it wants it buys at the price of soul. (Fr. 85)

I sought for myself. (Fr. 101)

Insolence is more to be extinguished than a conflagration. (Fr. 43)

Man's character is his daimon [fate]. (Fr. 119)

The people must fight on behalf of the law as though for the city wall. (Fr. 44)

Those who speak with sense must rely on what is common to all, as a city must rely on its law, and with much greater reliance. For all the laws of men are nourished by one law, the divine law; for it has as much power as it wishes and is sufficient for all and is still left over. (Fr. 114)

The secret rites practised among men are celebrated in an unholy manner. (Fr. 14)

They vainly purify themselves with blood when they are defiled with blood, as though one who had stepped into mud were to wash with mud; he would seem to be mad, if any of men noticed him doing this. Further, they pray to statues, as if one were to carry on a conversation with houses, not recognising the true nature of gods or demi-gods. (Fr. 5)

Readings

Burnet, *Early Greek Philosophy*, Ch. III.
Guthrie, *A History of Greek Philosophy*, Vol. I, Ch. VII.
Kirk and Raven, *Presocratic Philosophers*, Ch. VI.

THE ELEATICS

Parmenides

Fragments

The Way of Truth

The steeds that carry me took me as far as my heart could desire, when once they had brought me and set me on the renowned way of the goddess, which leads the man who knows through every town. On that way I was conveyed; for on it did the wise steeds convey me, drawing my chariot, and maidens led the way. And the axle glowing in the socket—for it was urged round by well-turned wheels at each end—was making the holes of the naves sing, while the daughters of the Sun, hastening to convey me into the light, threw back the veils from off their faces and left the abode of night. There are the gates of Night and Day, fitted above with a lintel and below with a threshold of stone. They themselves, high in the air, are closed by mighty doors, and avenging Justice controls the double bolts. Her did the maidens entreat with gentle words and cunningly persuade to unfasten without demur the bolted bar from the gates. Then, when the doors were thrown back, they disclosed a wide opening, when their brazen posts fitted with rivets and nails swung in turn on their hinges. Straight through them, on the broad way, did the maidens guide the horses and the car. And the goddess greeted me kindly, and took my right hand in hers, and spake to me these words: "Welcome, O youth, that comest to my abode on the car that bears thee, tended by immortal charioteers. It is no ill chance, but right and justice, that has sent thee forth to travel on this way. Far indeed does it lie from the beaten track of men. Meet it is that thou shouldst learn all things, as well the unshaken heart of well-rounded truth, as the opinions of mortals in which is no true belief at all. Yet none the less shalt thou learn these things also—how, passing right through all things, one should judge the things that seem to be. (Fr. 1)

Come now, and I will tell thee—and do thou hearken and carry my word away—the only ways of enquiry that exist for thinking: the one way, that it is and cannot not-be, is the path of Persuasion, for it attends upon Truth; the other, that it is-not and needs must not-be, that I tell thee is a path altogether unthinkable. For thou couldst not know that which is-not (that is impossible) nor utter it; for the same thing exists for thinking and for being. (Fr. 2)

That which can be spoken and thought needs must be; for it is possible for it, but not for nothing, to be; that is what I bid thee ponder. This is the first way of enquiry from which I hold thee back, and then from that way also on which mortals wander knowing nothing, two-headed; for helplessness guides the wandering thought in their breasts; they are carried along, deaf and blind at once, altogether dazed—hordes devoid of judgement, who are persuaded that to be and to be-not are the same, yet not the same, and that of all things the path is backward-turning. (Fr. 6)

For never shall this be proved, that things that are not are; but do thou hold back thy thought from this way of enquiry, nor let custom, born of much experience, force thee to let wander along this road thy aimless eye, thy echoing ear or thy tongue; but do thou judge by reason the strife-encompassed proof that I have spoken. (Fr. 7)

One way only is left to be spoken of, that it is; and on this way are full many signs that what is is uncreated and imperishable, for it is entire, immovable and without end. It was not in the past, nor shall it be, since it is now, all at once, one, continuous; for what creation wilt thou seek for it? How and whence did it grow? Nor shall I allow thee to say or to think, "from that which is not"; for it is not to be said or thought that it is not. And what need would have driven it on to grow, starting from nothing, at a later time rather than an earlier? Thus it must either completely be or be not. Nor will the force of true belief allow that, beside what is, there could also arise anything from what is not; wherefore Justice looseth not her fetters to allow it to come into being or perish, but holdeth it fast; and the decision on these matters rests here; it is or it is not. But it has surely been decided, as it must be, to leave alone the one way as unthinkable and nameless (for it is no true way), and that the other is real and true. How could what is thereafter perish? And how could it come into being? For if it came into being, it is not, nor if it is going to be in the future. So coming into being is extinguished and perishing unimaginable. Nor is it divisible, since it is all alike; nor is there more here and less there, which would prevent it from cleaving together, but it is all full of what is. So it is all continuous; for what is clings close to what is. But motionless within the limits of mighty bonds, it is without beginning or end, since coming into being and perishing have been driven far away, cast out by true belief. Abiding the same in the same place it rests by itself, and so abides firm where it is; for strong Necessity holds it firm within the bonds of the limit that keeps it back on every side, because it is not lawful that what is should be unlimited; for it is not in need—if it were, it would need all. But since there is a furthest limit, it is bounded on every side, like the bulk of a well-rounded sphere, from the center equally balanced in every direction; for it needs must not be somewhat more here or somewhat less there. For neither is there that which is not, which might stop it from meeting its like, nor can what is be more here and less there than what is, since it is all inviolate; for being equal to itself on every side, it rests uniformly within its limits. What can be thought is only the thought that it is. For you will not find thought without what is, in relation to which it is uttered; for there is not, nor shall be, anything else besides what is, since Fate fettered it to be entire and immovable. Wherefore all these are mere names which mortals laid down believing them to be true—coming into being and perishing, being and not being, change of place and variation of bright color. (Fr. 8. Lines 42–49 and 34–41 transposed.)

The Way of Seeming

Parmenides effects the transition from the objects of reason to the objects of sense, or, as he himself puts it, from truth to seeming, when he writes: "Here I end my trustworthy discourse and thought concerning truth; henceforth learn the beliefs of mortal men, listening to the deceitful ordering of my words"; and he then himself makes the elemental principles of created things the primary opposition of light and darkness, as he calls them, or fire and earth, or dense and rare, or sameness and difference; for he says immediately after the lines quoted above: "For they made up their minds to name two forms, of which it is not right to name so much as one[1]—that is where they have gone astray—and distinguished them as opposite in appearance and assigned to them manifestations different one from the other—to one the aitherial flame of fire, gentle and very light, in every direction identical with itself, but not with the other; and that other too is in itself just the opposite, dark night, dense in appearance and heavy. The whole ordering of these I tell thee as it seems likely, that so no thought of mortal men shall ever outstrip thee." (Simplicius, *Phys.* 30, 14)

To give an account, in accordance with popular opinion, of the com-

---

[1]Cornford's translation. Kirk and Raven render, "of which they must not name one only."

ing into being of sensible things, he makes the first principles two. (Theophrastus, *Phys. Op.* fr. 6)

And when all things have been named light and night, and things corresponding to their powers have been assigned to each, everything is full of light and of obscure night at once, both equal, since neither has any share of nothingness. (Fr. 9)

According to the mixture that each man has in his wandering limbs, so thought is forthcoming to mankind; for that which thinks is the same thing, namely, the substance of their limbs, in each and all men; for that of which there is more is thought. (Fr. 16)

Parmenides said that there were rings wound one around the other, one formed of the rare, the other of the dense; and that there were others between these compounded of light and darkness. That which surrounds them like a wall is, he says, by nature solid; beneath it is a fiery ring; and likewise what lies in the middle of them all is solid; and around it is again a fiery ring. The middlemost of the mixed rings is the primary cause of movement and of coming into being from them all, and he calls it the goddess that steers all, the holder of the keys, Justice and Necessity. The air, he says, is separated off from the earth, vaporized owing to earth's stronger compression; the sun is an exhalation of fire, and so is the circle of the Milky Way. The moon is compounded of both air and fire. Aither is outermost, surrounding all; next comes the fiery thing we call the sky; and last comes the region of the earth. (Aetius II, 7, 1)

Readings

Burnet, *Early Greek Philosophy*, Ch. IV.
Cornford, *Plato and Parmenides*, Ch. II.
Kirk and Raven, *The Presocratic Philosophers*, Ch. X.

Zeno

Testimony

Arguments Against Motion

Zeno's arguments about motion, which cause such trouble to those who try to solve the problems that they present, are four in number. (Aristotle, *Physics* 239b 9)

(1) *The Stadium.* The first asserts the non-existence of motion on the ground that that which is in locomotion must arrive at the half-way stage before it arrives at the goal. (Aristotle, *Physics* 239b 11)

Hence Zeno's argument makes a false assumption in asserting that it is impossible for a thing to pass over or severally come in contact with infinite things in a finite time. For there are two senses in which length and time and generally anything continuous are called "infinite": they are called so either in respect of divisibility or in respect of their extremities. So while a thing in a finite time cannot come in contact with things quantitatively infinite, it can come in contact with things infinite in respect of divisibility: for in this sense the time itself is also infinite: and so we find that the time occupied by the passage over the infinite is not a finite but an infinite time, and the contact with the infinites is made by means of moments not finite but infinite in number. (Aristotle, *Physics* 233a 21)

(2) *Achilles and the Tortoise.* The second is the so-called Achilles, and it amounts to this, that in a race the quickest runner can never overtake the slowest, since the pursuer must first reach the point whence the pursuit started, so that the slower must always hold a lead. This argument is the same in principle as that which depends on bisection, though it differs from it in that the spaces with which we successively have to deal are not divided by halves. (Aristotle, *Physics* 239b 14)

(3) *The Flying Arrow.* The third is . . . to the effect that the flying arrow is at rest, which result follows from the assumption that time is composed of moments: if this assumption is not granted, the conclusion will not follow. (Aristotle, *Physics* 239b 30)

(4) *The Moving Rows.* The fourth argument is that concerning the two rows of bodies, each row being composed of an equal number of bodies of equal size, passing each other on a race-course as they proceed with equal velocity in opposite directions, the one row originally occupying the space between the goal and the middle point of the course and the other that between the middle point and the starting-post. This, he thinks, involves the conclusion that half a given time is equal to double that time. The fallacy of the reasoning lies in the assumption that a body occupies an equal time in passing with equal velocity a body that is in motion and a body of equal size that is at rest; which is false. (Aristotle, *Physics* 239b 33)

Arguments Against Plurality

If there is plurality, things will be both great and small; so great as to be infinite in size, so small as to have no size at all. If what is had no size, it would not even be. For if it were added to something else that is, it would make it no larger; for being no size at all, it could not, on being added, cause any increase in size. And so what was added would clearly be nothing. Again if, when it is taken away, the other thing is no smaller, just as when it is added it is not increased, obviously what was added or taken away was nothing. But if it is, each thing must have a certain size and bulk, and one part of it must be a certain distance from another; and the same argument holds about the part in front of it—it too will have some size and there will be something in front of it. And it is the same thing to say this once and to go on saying it indefinitely; for no such part of it will be the last, nor will one part ever be unrelated to another. So, if there is a plurality, things must be both small and great; so small as to have no size at all, so great as to be infinite. (Fr. 1 and 2)

If there is a plurality, things must be just as many as they are, no more and no less. And if they are just as many as they are, they must be limited. If there is a plurality, the things that are are infinite; for there will always be other things between the things that are, and yet others between those others. And so the things that are are infinite. (Fr. 3)

Readings

Black, *Problems of Analysis*, Part II: "Zeno's Paradoxes."
Burnet, *Early Greek Philosophy*, Ch. VIII.
Cornford, *Plato and Parmenides*, Ch. III.
Kirk and Raven, *The Presocratic Philosophers*, Ch. XI.
Owen, *Proceedings of the Aristotelian Society* (1958), 199 ff.
Tannery, *Pour l'histoire de la science hellène*, Ch. 10.

THE PLURALISTS

Empedocles

Fragments

Fools—for they have no far-reaching thoughts—who fancy that that which formerly was not can come into being or that anything can perish and be utterly destroyed. For coming into being from that which in no way is is inconceivable, and it is impossible and unheard-of that that which is should be destroyed. For it will ever be there wherever one may keep pushing it. (Fr. 11)

Nor is any part of the whole either empty or over-full. (Fr. 13)

Hear first the four roots of all things: shining Zeus, life-bringing Hera, Aidoneus and Nestis who with her tears fills the springs of mortal man with water. (Fr. 6)

And these things never cease from continual shifting, at one time coming together, through Love, into one, at another each borne apart from the others through Strife. (Fr. 17)

But come, consider with all thy powers how each thing is manifest, neither holding sight in greater trust as compared with hearing, nor loud-sounding hearing above the clear evidence of thy tongue, nor withhold thy trust from any of the other limbs, wheresoever there is a path for understanding, but think on each thing in the way by which it is manifest. (Fr. 3, 1. 9)

Equal [to itself] from every side and quite without end, [it] stays fast in the close covering of Harmony, a rounded sphere rejoicing in [its] circular solitude. (Fr. 28)

A double tale will I tell: at one time it grew to be one only from many, at another it divided again to be many from one. There is a double coming into being of mortal things and a double passing away. One is brought about, and again destroyed, by the coming together of all things, the other grows up and is scattered as things are again di-

49

vided. And these things never cease from continual shifting, at one time all coming together, through Love, into one, at another each borne apart from the others through Strife. So, in so far as they have learnt to grow into one from many, and again, when the one is sundered, are once more many, thus far they come into being and they have no lasting life; but in so far as they never cease from continual interchange of places, thus far are they ever changeless in the cycle. But come, hearken to my words; for learning increaseth wisdom. As I said before when I declared the limits of my words, a double tale will I tell: at one time it grew to be one only from many, at another it divided again to be many from one, fire and water and earth and the vast height of air, dread Strife too, apart from these, everywhere equally balanced, and Love in their midst, equal in length and breadth. On her do thou gaze with they mind, and sit not with dazed eyes; for she is recognised as inborn in mortal limbs; by her they think kind thoughts and do the works of concord, calling her Joy by name and Aphrodite. . . . For all these are equal, and of like age, but each has a different prerogative and its own character, and in turn they prevail as time comes round. And besides these nothing else comes into being nor ceases to be; for if they were continually being destroyed, they would no longer be; and what could increase this whole, and whence could it come? And how could these things perish too, since nothing is empty of them? Nay, there are these things alone, and running through one another they become now this and now that and yet remain ever as they are. (Fr. 17)

He makes the material elements four in number, fire, air, water, and earth, all eternal, but changing in bulk and scarcity through mixture and separation; but his real first principles, which impart motion to these, are Love and Strife. The elements are continually subject to an alternate change, at one time mixed together by Love, at another separated by Strife; so that the first principles are, by his account, six in number. (Simplicius, *Phys.* 25, 21)

Readings

Burnet, *Early Greek Philosophy*, Ch. V.
Kirk and Raven, *The Presocratic Philosophers*, Ch. XIV.

Anaxagoras

Fragments

The Greeks are wrong to recognise coming into being and perishing; for nothing comes into being nor perishes, but is rather compounded or dissolved from things that are. So they would be right to call coming into being composition and perishing dissolution. (Fr. 17)

All things were together, infinite in respect of both number and smallness; for the small too was infinite. And while all things were together, none of them were plain because of their smallness; for air and aither covered all things, both of them being infinite; for these are the greatest ingredients in the mixture of all things, both in number and in size. (Fr. 1)

And since these things are so, we must suppose that there are many things of all sorts in everything that is being aggregated, seeds of all things with all sorts of shapes and colours and tastes. . . . But before these things were separated off, while all things were together, there was not even any colour plain; for the mixture of all things prevented it, of the moist and the dry, the hot and the cold, the bright and the dark, and of much earth in the mixture and of seeds countless in number and in no respect like one another. For none of the other things either are like one to the other. And since this is so, we must suppose that all things are in the whole. (Fr. 4)

And when these things have been thus separated, we must know that all things are neither more nor less (for it is not possible that there should be more than all), but all things are always equal. (Fr. 5)

Neither is there a smallest part of what is small, but there is always a smaller (for it is impossible that what is should cease to be). Likewise there is always something larger than what is large. And it is equal in number to what is small, each thing, in relation to itself, being both large and small. (Fr. 3)

All other things have a portion of everything, but Mind is infinite and self-ruled, and is mixed with nothing but is all alone by itself. For if it was not by itself, but was mixed with anything else, it would have a share of all things if it were mixed with any; for in everything there is a portion of everything . . . ; and the things that were mingled with it would hinder it so that it could control nothing in the same way as it does now being alone by itself. For it is the finest of all things and the purest, it has all knowledge about everything and the greatest power; and mind controls all things, both the greater and the smaller, that have life. Mind controlled also the whole rotation, so that it began to rotate in the beginning. . . . And the things that are mingled and separated and divided off, all are known by Mind. And all things that were to be, all things that were but are not now, all things that are now or that shall be, Mind arranged them all, including this rotation in which are now rotating the stars, the sun and moon, the air and the aither that are being separated off. And this rotation caused the separating off. And the dense is separated from the rare, the hot from the cold, the bright from the dark and the dry from the moist. But there are many portions of many things, and nothing is altogether separated off nor divided one from the other except Mind. Mind is all alike, both the greater and the smaller quantities of it, while nothing else is like anything else, but each single body is and was most plainly those things of which it contains most. (Fr. 12)

And when Mind initiated motion, from all that was moved separation began, and as much as Mind moved was all divided off; and as things moved and were divided off, the rotation greatly increased the process of dividing. (Fr. 13)

But Mind, which is, is assuredly even now where everything else is too, in the surrounding mass and in the things that have been either aggregated or separated. (Fr. 14)

And since the portions of the great and of the small are equal in number, so too all things would be in everything. Nor is it possible that they should exist apart, but all things have a portion of everything. Since it is not possible that there should be a smallest part, nothing can be put apart nor come to be all by itself, but as things were originally, so they must be now too, all together. In all things there are many ingredients, equal in number in the greater and in the smaller of the things that are being separated off. (Fr. 6)

In everything there is a portion of everything except Mind; and there are some things in which there is Mind as well. (Fr. 11)

The things in the one world-order are not separated one from the other nor cut off with an axe, neither the hot from the cold nor the cold from the hot. (Fr. 8)

The theory of Anaxagoras that the principles are infinite in number was probably due to his acceptance of the common opinion of the physicists that nothing comes into being from not-being. For this is the reason why they use the phrase "all things were together," and the coming into being of such and such a thing is reduced to change of quality, while others speak of combination and separation. Moreover, the fact that the opposites proceeded from each other led them to the same conclusion. The one, they reasoned, must have already existed in the other; for since everything that comes into being must arise either from what is or from what is not, and it is impossible for it to arise from what is not (on this point all the physicists agree), they thought that the truth of the alternative necessarily followed, namely that things come into being out of existent things, i.e., out of things already present, but imperceptible to our senses because of the smallness of their bulk. So they assert that everything is mixed in everything, because they saw everything arising out of everything. But things, as they say, appear different from one another and receive different names according to the nature of the thing that is numerically predominant among the innumerable constituents of the mixture. For nothing, they say, is purely and entirely white or black or sweet or flesh or bone, but the nature of a thing is held to be that of which it contains the most. (Aristotle, *Physics* 187a 25)

Readings

Bailey, *The Greek Atomists and Epicurus,* Appendix 1.
Burnet, *Early Greek Philosophy,* Ch. VI.
Cornford, *Classical Quarterly* 24 (1930), 14 ff. and 83 ff.
Kirk and Raven, *The Presocratic Philosophers,* Ch. XV.

The Atomists: Leucippus and Democritus

Fragments and Testimony

Leucippus and Democritus

Leucippus and his associate Democritus hold that the elements are the full and the void; they call them being and not-being respectively. Being is full and solid, not-being is void and rare. Since the void exists no less than body, it follows that not-being exists no less than being. The two together are the material causes of existing things. And just as those who make the underlying substance one generate other things by its modifications, and postulate rarefaction and condensation as the origin of such modifications, in the same way these men too say the differences in atoms are the causes of other things. They hold that these differences are three—shape, arrangement, and position; being, they say, differs only in "rhythm, touching, and turning," of which "rhythm" is shape, "touching" is arrangement, and "turning" is position: for A differs from N in shape, AN from NA in arrangement, and I from H in position. (Aristotle, *Metaphysics* 985b 4)

Democritus . . . calls space by these names—"the void," "nothing," and "the infinite," while each individual atom he calls . . . the "compact," and "being." He thinks they are so small as to elude our senses, but they have all sorts of forms and shapes and differences in size. So he is already enabled from them, as from elements, to create by aggregation bulks that are perceptible to sight and the other senses. (Aristotle, *On Democritus,* apud Simplicius, *de caelo* 295, 1)

They (Leucippus, Democritus, Epicurus) said that the first principles were infinite in number, and thought they were indivisible atoms and impassible owing to their compactness, and without any void in them; divisibility comes about because of the void in compound bodies. . . . (Simplicius, *de caelo* 242, 18)

Leucippus holds that the whole is infinite . . . part of it is full and part void. . . . Hence arise innumerable worlds, and are resolved again into these elements. The worlds come into being as follows: many bodies of all sorts move "by abscission from the infinite" into a great void; they come together there and produce a single whirl, in which, colliding with one another and revolving in all manner of ways, they begin to separate apart, like to like. But when their multitude prevents them from rotating any longer in equilibrium, those that are fine go out towards the surrounding void as if shifted, while the rest "abide together" and, becoming entangled, unite their motions and make a first spherical structure. This structure stands apart like a "membrane" which contains in itself all kinds of bodies; and as they whirl around owing to the resistance of the middle, the surrounding membrane becomes thin, while contiguous atoms keep flowing together owing to contact with the whirl. So the earth came into being, the atoms that had been borne to the middle abiding together there. . . . Some of the bodies that get entangled form a structure that is at first moist and muddy, but as they revolve with the whirl of the whole they dry out and then ignite to form the substance of the heavenly bodies. (Diogenes Laertius ix, 31)

Democritus holds the same view as Leucippus about the elements, full and void. . . . He spoke as if the things that are were in constant motion in the void; there are innumerable worlds, which differ in size. (Hippolytus, *Ref.* I, 13, 2)

Everything happens according to necessity; for the cause of the coming-into-being of all things in the whirl, which [Democritus] calls necessity. (Diogenes Laertius ix, 45)

Nothing occurs at random, but everything for a reason and by necessity. (Leucippus, fr. 2)

When Democritus says that "a whirl was separated off from the whole, of all sorts of shapes" (and he does not say how or through what cause), he seems to generate it by accident or chance. (Simplicius, *Phys.* 327, 24)

Democritus distinguishes heavy and light by size. . . . Nevertheless in compound bodies the lighter is that which contains more void, the heavier that which contains less. Sometimes he expressed it thus, but elsewhere he says simply that the fine is the light. (Theophrastus, *de sensu* 61)

So Leucippus and Democritus, who say that their primary bodies are always in motion in the infinite void, ought to specify what kind of motion—that is, what is the motion natural to them. (Aristotle, *de caelo* 300b 8)

Readings

Bailey, *The Greek Atomists and Epicurus.*
Burnet, *Early Greek Philosophy*, Ch. IX.
Kirk and Raven, *The Presocratic Philosophers*, Ch. XVII.

PLATO

EUTHYPHRO

Characters and Setting (2a–5c)

EUTHYPHRO. What has happened, Socrates, to make you leave your 2a
accustomed pastimes in the Lyceum and spend your time here today at
the King's Porch? You can hardly have a suit pending before the King,
as I do.

SOCRATES. In Athens, Euthyphro, it is not called a suit, but an indictment.

EUTHYPHRO. Really? Someone must have indicted you. For I will b
not suspect you of indicting someone else.

SOCRATES. Certainly not.

EUTHYPHRO. But someone you?

SOCRATES. Yes.

EUTHYPHRO. Who is he?

SOCRATES. I do not know the man well, Euthyphro; it appears he
is young and not prominent. His name, I think, is Meletus. He belongs
to the deme of Pitthus, if you recall a Pithean Meletus with lanky hair
and not much beard, but a hooked nose.

EUTHYPHRO. I have not noticed him, Socrates. But what is the c
charge?

SOCRATES. Charge? One that does him credit, I think. It is no small
thing, young as he is, to be knowledgeable in so great a matter, for he
says he knows how the youth are being corrupted and who is corrupting
them. No doubt he is wise, and realizing that, in my ignorance, I corrupt his comrades, he comes to the city as to a mother to accuse me.
He alone seems to me to have begun his political career correctly, for d
the right way to begin is to look after the young men of the City first
so that they will be as good as possible, just as a good farmer naturally
looks after his young plants first and the rest later. So too with Meletus.
He will perhaps first weed out those of us who blight the young shoots, 3a
as he claims, and afterwards he will obviously look after their elders and

57

become responsible for many great blessings to the City, the natural result of so fine a beginning.

EUTHYPHRO. I would hope so, Socrates, but I fear lest the opposite may happen. He seems to me to have started by injuring the City at its very hearth in undertaking to wrong you. But tell me, what does he say you do to corrupt the youth?

b   SOCRATES. It sounds a bit strange at first hearing, my friend. He says I am a maker of gods, and because I make new ones and do not worship the old ones, he indicted me on their account, he says.

EUTHYPHRO. I see, Socrates. It is because you say the divine sign comes to you from time to time. So he indicts you for making innovations in religious matters and hales you into court to slander you,
c   knowing full well how easily such things are misrepresented to the multitude. Why I, even me, when I speak about religious matters in the Assembly and foretell the future, why, they laugh at me as though I were mad. And yet nothing I ever predicted has failed to come true. Still, they are jealous of people like us. We must not worry about them, but face them boldly.

SOCRATES. My dear Euthyphro, being laughed at is perhaps a thing of little moment. The Athenians, it seems to me, do not much mind if they think a man is clever as long as they do not suspect him of teaching his cleverness to others; but if they think he makes others like himself they become angry, whether out of jealousy as you suggest, or for some
d   other reason.

EUTHYPHRO. On that point I am not very anxious to test their attitude toward me.

SOCRATES. Perhaps they think you give yourself sparingly, that you are unwilling to teach your wisdom. But I fear my own generosity is such that they think I am willing to pour myself out in speech to any man—not only without pay, but glad to pay myself if only someone will listen. So as I just said, if they laugh at me as you say they do you, it
e   would not be unpleasant to pass the time in court laughing and joking. But if they are in earnest, how it will then turn out is unclear—except to you prophets.

EUTHYPHRO. Perhaps it will not amount to much, Socrates. Perhaps you will settle your case satisfactorily, as I think I will mine.

SOCRATES. What about that, Euthyphro? Are you plaintiff or defendant?

EUTHYPHRO. Plaintiff.

SOCRATES. Against whom?

4a   EUTHYPHRO. Someone I am again thought mad to prosecute.

SOCRATES. Really? Has he taken flight?

EUTHYPHRO. He is far from flying. As a matter of fact, he is well along in years.

SOCRATES. Who is he?

EUTHYPHRO. My father.

SOCRATES. Your *father*, dear friend?

EUTHYPHRO. Yes, indeed.

SOCRATES. But what is the charge? What is the reason for the suit?

EUTHYPHRO. Murder, Socrates.

SOCRATES. Heracles! Surely, Euthyphro, the majority of people must be ignorant of what is right. Not just anyone would undertake a thing like that. It must require someone quite far gone in wisdom.

EUTHYPHRO. Very far indeed Socrates.

SOCRATES. Was the man your father killed a relative? But, of course, he must have been—you would not be prosecuting him for murder in behalf of a stranger.

EUTHYPHRO. It is laughable, Socrates, your thinking it makes a difference whether or not the man was a relative, and not this, or this alone; whether his slayer was justified. If so, let him off. If not, prosecute him, even if he shares your hearth and table. For if you knowingly associate with a man like that and do not cleanse both yourself and him by bringing action at law, the pollution is equal for you both. Now as a matter of fact, the dead man was a day-labourer of mine, and when we were farming in Naxos he worked for us for hire. Well, he got drunk and flew into a rage with one of our slaves and cut his throat. So my father bound him hand and foot, threw him in a ditch, and sent a man here to Athens to consult the religious adviser as to what should be done. In the meantime, my father paid no attention to the man he had bound; he neglected him because he was a murderer and it made no difference if he died. Which is just what he did. Before the messenger got back he died of hunger and cold and his bonds. But even so, my father and the rest of my relatives are angry at me for prosecuting him for murder in behalf of a murderer. He did not kill him, they claim, and even if he did, still, the fellow was a murderer, and it is wrong to be concerned in behalf of a man like that—and anyway, it is unholy for a son to prosecute his father for murder. They little know, Socrates, how things stand in religious matters regarding the holy and the unholy.

SOCRATES. But in the name of Zeus, Euthyphro, do you think you yourself know so accurately how matters stand respecting divine law, and things holy and unholy, that with the facts as you declare you can prosecute your own father without fear that it is you, on the contrary, who are doing an unholy thing?

EUTHYPHRO. I would not be much use, Socrates, nor would Eu-

5a thyphro differ in any way from the majority of men, if I did not know all such things as this with strict accuracy.

SOCRATES. Well then, my gifted friend, I had best become your pupil. Before the action with Melètus begins I will challenge him on these very grounds. I will say that even in former times I was much concerned to learn about religious matters, but that now, in view of his claiming that I am guilty of loose speech and innovation in these things, I have become your pupil. "And if, Meletus," I shall say, "if you agree

b that Euthyphro is wise in such things, then assume that I worship correctly and drop the case. But if you do not agree, then obtain permission to indict my teacher here in my place for corrupting the old—me and his own father—by teaching me, and by chastising and punishing him." And if I can not persuade him to drop charges or to indict you in place of me, may I not then say the same thing in court I said in my challenge?

EUTHYPHRO. By Zeus, if he tried to indict me, I would find his

c weak spot, I think, and the discussion in court would concern him long before it concerned me.

The Request for a Definition (5c-6e)

SOCRATES. I realize that, my friend. That is why I want to become your pupil. I know that this fellow Meletus and no doubt other people too pretend not even to notice you; but he saw through me so keenly and easily that he indicted me for impiety. So now in Zeus' name, tell me what you confidently claimed just now that you knew: what sort of thing do you say the pious and impious are, with respect to murder and

d other things as well? Or is not the holy, just by itself, the same in every action? And the unholy, in turn, the opposite of all the holy—is it not like itself, and does not everything which is to be unholy have a certain single character with respect to unholiness?

EUTHYPHRO. No doubt, Socrates.

SOCRATES. Then tell me, what do you say the holy is? And what is the unholy?

EUTHYPHRO. Well, I say that the holy is what I am doing now, prosecuting murder and temple theft and everything of the sort, whether

e father or mother or anyone else is guilty of it. And not prosecuting is unholy. Now, Socrates, examine the proof I give you that this is a dictate of divine law. I have offered it before to other people to show that it is established right not to let off someone guilty of impiety, no matter who he happens to be. For these same people worship Zeus as the best and most righteous of the gods. They agree that he put his own father

6a in bonds for swallowing his children unjustly; yes, and that that father had in his turn castrated his father for similar reasons. Yet me they are angry at for indicting my father for his injustice. So they contradict themselves: they say one thing about the gods and another about me.

SOCRATES. I wonder if this is why I am being prosecuted, Euthyphro, because when anyone says such things about the gods, I somehow find it difficult to accept? Perhaps this is why people claim I transgress. But as it is, if even you who know such things so well accept them, people like me must apparently concede. What indeed are we to say, b we who ourselves agree that we know nothing of them. But in the name of Zeus, the God of Friendship, tell me: do you truly believe that these things happened so?

EUTHYPHRO. Yes, and things still more wonderful than these, Socrates, things the multitude does not know.

SOCRATES. Do you believe there is really war among the gods, and terrible enmities and battles, and other things of the sort our poets tell, which embellish other things sacred to us through the work of our capable painters, but especially the robe filled with embroidery that is c carried to the Acropolis at the Great Panathenaea? Are we, Euthyphro, to say those things are so?

EUTHYPHRO. Not only those, Socrates. As I just said, I shall explain many other things about religion to you if you wish, and you may rest assured that what you hear will amaze you.

SOCRATES. I should not be surprised. But explain them another time at your leisure; right now, try to answer more clearly the question I just d asked. For, my friend, you did not sufficiently teach me before, when I asked you what the holy is; you said that the thing you are doing now is holy, prosecuting your father for murder.

EUTHYPHRO. Yes, and I told the truth, Socrates.

SOCRATES. Perhaps. But, Euthyphro, are there not many other things you say are holy too?

EUTHYPHRO. Of course there are.

SOCRATES. Do you recall that I did not ask you to teach me about some one or two of the many things which are holy, but about that characteristic itself by which all holy things are holy? For you agreed, e I think, that it is by one character that unholy things are unholy and holy things holy. Or do you not recall?

EUTHYPHRO. I do.

SOCRATES. Then teach me what this very character is, so that I may look to it and use it as a standard, which, should those things which you or someone else may do be of that sort, I may affirm they are holy, but should they not be of that sort, deny it.

EUTHYPHRO. Well if you wish it so, Socrates, so shall I tell you.

SOCRATES. I do indeed wish it.

First Definition: The Holy, What Is Loved
by the Gods (6e–8b)

EUTHYPHRO. Then what is dear to the gods is holy, and what is
7a not dear to them is unholy.

SOCRATES. Excellent, Euthyphro. You have now answered as I
asked. Whether correctly, I do not yet know—but clearly you will now
go on to teach me in addition that what you say is true.

EUTHYPHRO. Of course.

SOCRATES. Come then, let us examine what it is we are saying. The
thing and the person dear to the gods is holy; the thing and the person
hateful to the gods is unholy; and the holy is not the same as the unholy,
but its utter opposite. Is that what we are saying?

EUTHYPHRO. It is.

SOCRATES. Yes, and it appears to be well said.

b EUTHYPHRO. I think so, Socrates.

SOCRATES. Now, Euthyphro, we also said, did we not, that the gods
quarrel and disagree with one another and that there is enmity among
them?

EUTHYPHRO. We did.

SOCRATES. But what is that disagreement about which causes enmity and anger, my friend? Look at it this way: If you and I disagreed
about a question of number, about which of two sums is greater, would
c our disagreement cause us to become angry with each other and make
us enemies? Or would we take to counting in a case like that, and quickly
settle our dispute?

EUTHYPHRO. Of course we would.

SOCRATES. So too if we disagreed about a question of the larger or
smaller, we would take to measurement and put an end to our disagreement quickly?

EUTHYPHRO. True.

SOCRATES. And go to the balance, I imagine, to settle a dispute
about heavier and lighter?

EUTHYPHRO. Certainly.

SOCRATES. But what sort of thing would make us enemies, angry
at each other, if we disagree about it and are unable to arrive at a decision? Perhaps you cannot say offhand, but I suggest you consider
d whether it would not be the just and unjust, beautiful and ugly, good
and evil. Are not these the things, when we disagree about them and
cannot reach a satisfactory decision, concerning which we on occasion
become enemies—you, and I, and all other men?

EUTHYPHRO. Yes, Socrates. This kind of disagreement has its source there.

SOCRATES. What about the gods, Euthyphro? If they were to disagree, would they not disagree for the same reasons?

EUTHYPHRO. Necessarily.

SOCRATES. Then by your account, my noble friend, different gods   e
must believe that different things are just—and beautiful and ugly, good
and evil. For surely they would not quarrel unless they disagreed on
this. True?

EUTHYPHRO. You are right.

SOCRATES. Now, what each of them believes to be beautiful and
good and just they also love, and the opposites of those things they hate?

EUTHYPHRO. Of course.

SOCRATES. Yes, but the same things, you say, are thought by some
gods to be just and by others unjust. Those are the things concerning
which disagreement causes them to quarrel and make war on one an-   8a
other. True?

EUTHYPHRO. Yes.

SOCRATES. Then the same things, it seems, are both hated by the
gods and loved by the gods, and would be both dear to the gods and
hateful to the gods.

EUTHYPHRO. It seems so.

SOCRATES. Then by this account, Euthyphro, the same things would
be both holy and unholy.

EUTHYPHRO. I suppose so.

SOCRATES. Then you have not answered my question, my friend.
I did not ask you what same thing happens to be both holy and unholy;
yet what is dear to the gods is hateful to the gods, it seems. And so,
Euthyphro, it would not be surprising if what you are now doing in   b
punishing your father were dear to Zeus, but hateful to Cronos and
Uranus, and loved by Hephaestus, but hateful to Hera, and if any of
the other gods disagree about it, the same will be true of them too.

First Interlude (8b–9c)

EUTHYPHRO. But Socrates, surely none of the gods disagree about
this, that he who kills another man unjustly should answer for it.

SOCRATES. Really, Euthyphro? Have you ever heard it argued
among *men* that he who kills unjustly or does anything else unjustly   c
should not answer for it?

EUTHYPHRO. Why, people never stop arguing things like that, especially in the law courts. They do a host of wrongs and then say and do everything to get off.

SOCRATES. Yes, but do they admit the wrong, Euthyphro, and admitting it, nevertheless claim they should not answer for it?

EUTHYPHRO. No!, they certainly do not do that.

SOCRATES. Then they do not do and say everything: for they do not, I think, dare to contend or debate the point that if they in fact did
d wrong they should not answer for it. Rather, I think, they deny they did wrong. Well?

EUTHYPHRO. True.

SOCRATES. So they do not contend that those who do wrong should not answer for it, but rather, perhaps about who it is that did the wrong, and what he did, and when.

EUTHYPHRO. True.

SOCRATES. Now is it not also the same with the gods, if as your account has it, they quarrel about what is just and unjust, and some claim that others do wrong and some deny it? Presumably no one, god
e or man, would dare to claim that he who does a wrong should not answer for it.

EUTHYPHRO. Yes, on the whole what you say is true, Socrates.

SOCRATES. But I imagine that those who disagree—both men and gods, if indeed the gods do disagree—disagree about particular things which have been done. They differ over given actions, some claiming they were done justly and others unjustly. True?

EUTHYPHRO. Certainly.

9a SOCRATES. Come now, my friend, teach me and make me wiser. Where is your proof that all gods believe that a man has been unjustly killed who was hired as a labourer, became a murderer, was bound by the master of the dead slave, and died of his bonds before the man who bound him could learn from the religious advisers what to do? Where is your proof that it is right for a son to indict and prosecute his father for murder in behalf of a man like that? Come, try to show me clearly
b that all the gods genuinely believe this action right. If you succeed, I shall praise you for your wisdom and never stop.

EUTHYPHRO. Well, I can certainly do it, Socrates, but it is perhaps not a small task.

SOCRATES. I see. You think I am harder to teach than the judges, for you will certainly make it clear to them that actions such as your father's are wrong, and that all the gods hate them.

EUTHYPHRO. Very clear indeed, Socrates, if they listen to what I say.

Second Definition: The Holy, What Is Loved by All the Gods (9c–11b)

SOCRATES. They will listen, if you seem to speak well. But here is c something that occurred to me while you were talking. I asked myself, "If Euthyphro were to teach me beyond any question that all the gods believe a death of this sort wrong, what more have I learned from Euthyphro about what the holy and the unholy are? The death, it seems would be hateful to the gods, but what is holy and what is unholy proved just now not to be marked off by this, for what was hateful to the gods proved dear to the gods as well." So I let you off on that point, Euthyphro: if you wish, let all the gods believe your father's action wrong and d let all of them hate it. But is this the correction we are now to make in your account, that what *all* the gods hate is unholy, and what *all* the gods love is holy, but what some love and some hate is neither or both? Do you mean for us now to mark off the holy and the unholy in that way?

EUTHYPHRO. What is to prevent it, Socrates? e

SOCRATES. Nothing, at least as far as I am concerned, Euthyphro. But, examine your account to see whether if you assume this, you will most easily teach me what you promised.

EUTHYPHRO. But I would certainly say that the holy is what all the gods love, and that the opposite, what all the gods hate, is unholy.

SOCRATES. Well, Euthyphro, should we examine this in turn to see if it is true? Or should we let it go, accept it from ourselves or anyone else without more ado, and agree that a thing is so if only someone says it is? Or should we examine what a person means when he says something?

EUTHYPHRO. Of course. I believe, though, that this time what I say is true.

SOCRATES. Perhaps we shall learn better, my friend. For consider: 10a is the holy loved by the gods because it is holy? Or is it holy because it is loved by the gods?

EUTHYPHRO. I do not know what you mean, Socrates.

SOCRATES. Then I will try to put it more clearly. We speak of carrying and being carried, or leading and being led, of seeing and being seen. And you understand in such cases, do you not, that they differ from each other, and how they differ?

EUTHYPHRO. I think I do.

SOCRATES. Now, is there such a thing as being loved, and is it different from loving?

EUTHYPHRO. Of course.

b   SOCRATES. Then tell me: if a thing is being carried, is it being carried because of the carrying, or for some other reason?

EUTHYPHRO. No, for that reason.

SOCRATES. And if a thing is being led, it is being led because of the leading? And if being seen, being seen because of the seeing?

EUTHYPHRO. Certainly.

SOCRATES. Then it is not because a thing is being seen that the seeing exists; on the contrary, it is because of the seeing that it is being seen. Nor is it because a thing is being led that the leading exists; it is because of the leading that it is being led. Nor is it because a thing is

c being carried that the carrying exists; it is because of the carrying that it is being carried. Is what I mean quite clear, Euthyphro? I mean this; if something comes to be or something is affected, it is not because it is a thing which is coming to be that the process of coming to be exists, but, because of the process of coming to be, it is a thing which is coming to be; and it is not because it is affected that the affecting exists, but because of the affecting, the thing is affected. Do you agree?

EUTHYPHRO. Yes.

SOCRATES. Now, what is being loved is either a thing coming to be something or a thing affected by something.

EUTHYPHRO. Of course.

SOCRATES. And so it is as true here as it was before: it is not because a thing is being loved that there is loving by those who love it; it is because of the loving that it is being loved.

EUTHYPHRO. Necessarily.

d   SOCRATES. Then what are we to say about the holy, Euthyphro? Is it loved by all the gods, as your account has it?

EUTHYPHRO. Yes.

SOCRATES. Because it is holy? Or for some other reason?

EUTHYPHRO. No, for that reason.

SOCRATES. Then it is loved because it is holy, not holy because it is loved?

EUTHYPHRO. It seems so.

SOCRATES. Moreover, what is loved and dear to the gods is loved because of their loving.

EUTHYPHRO. Of course.

SOCRATES. Then what is dear to the gods is not [the same as] holy, Euthyphro, nor is the holy [the same as] dear to the gods, as you claim: the two are different.

e EUTHYPHRO. But why, Socrates?

SOCRATES. Because we agreed that the holy is loved because it is holy, not holy because it is loved.

EUTHYPHRO. Yes.

SOCRATES. But what is dear to the gods is, because it is loved by the gods, dear to the gods by reason of this same loving; it is not loved because it is dear to the gods.

EUTHYPHRO. True.

SOCRATES. But if in fact what is dear to the gods and the holy were the same, my friend, then, if the holy were loved because it is holy, what is dear to the gods would be loved because it is dear to the gods; 11a but if what is dear to the gods were dear to the gods because the gods love it, the holy would be holy because it is loved. But as it is, you see, the opposite is true, and the two are completely different. For the one [what is dear to the gods] is of the sort to be loved *because* it is loved; the other [the holy], because it is of the sort to be loved, *therefore* is loved. It would seem, Euthyphro, that when you were asked what the holy is, you did not mean to make its nature and reality clear to me; you mentioned a mere affection of it—the holy has been so affected as to be loved by all the gods. But what it really is, you have not yet said. So if you b please, Euthyphro, do not conceal things from me: start again from the beginning and tell me what sort of thing the holy is. We will not quarrel over whether it is loved by the gods, or whether it is affected in other ways. Tell me in earnest: what is the holy and unholy?

Second Interlude: Socrates a Daedalus (11b–d)

EUTHYPHRO. But, Socrates, I do not know how to tell you what I mean. Somehow everything I propose goes around in circles on us and will not stand still.

SOCRATES. Your words are like the words of my ancestor, Daedalus. If I had offered them, if I had put them forward, you would perhaps c have laughed at me because my kinship to him makes my words run away and refuse to stay put. But as it is, it is you who put them forward and we must find another joke. It is for you that they refuse to stand still, as you yourself agree.

EUTHYPHRO. But, Socrates, the joke, I think, still tells. It is not me who makes them move around and not stay put. I think you are the d Daedalus. If it had been up to me, they would have stayed where they were.

SOCRATES. Then apparently, my friend, I am even more skillful than my venerated ancestor, inasmuch as he made only his own works move, whereas I, it seems, not only make my own move but other people's too. And certainly the most subtle feature of my art is that I am skilled against my will. For I really want arguments to stand still, to

e stand fixed and immovable. I want that more than the wealth of Tan-
talus and the skill of Daedalus combined. But enough of this. Since you
seem to be lazy and soft, I will come to your aid and help you teach me
about the holy. Don't give up; consider whether you do not think that
all the holy is necessarily just.

EUTHYPHRO. I do.

Requirements for Definition (11e–12e)

SOCRATES. Then is all the just holy? Or is all the holy just, but not
12a all the just holy—part of it holy, part something else?

EUTHYPHRO. I don't follow you, Socrates.

SOCRATES. And yet you are as much wiser than I am as you are
younger. As I said, you are lazy and soft because of your wealth of
wisdom. My friend, extend yourself: what I mean is not hard to understand. I mean exactly the opposite of what the poet meant when he
said that he was "Unwilling to insult Zeus, the Creator, who made all
b things; for where there is fear there is also reverence." I disagree with
him. Shall I tell you why?

EUTHYPHRO. Yes, certainly.

SOCRATES. I do not think that "where there is fear there is also
reverence." I think people fear disease and poverty and other such
things—fear them, but have no reverence for what they fear. Do you
agree?

EUTHYPHRO. Yes, certainly.

SOCRATES. Where there is reverence, however, there is also fear.
For if anyone stands in reverence and awe of something, does he not at
c the same time fear and dread the imputation of wickedness?

EUTHYPHRO. Yes, he does.

SOCRATES. Then it is not true that "where there is fear there is also
reverence," but rather where there is reverence there is also fear, even
though reverence is not everywhere that fear is: fear is broader than
reverence. Reverence is part of fear just as odd is part of number, so
that it is not true that wherever there is number there is odd, but wherever there is odd there is number. Surely you follow me now?

EUTHYPHRO. Yes, I do.

SOCRATES. Well then, that is the sort of thing I had in mind when
d I asked if, wherever there is just, there is also holy. Or is it rather that
wherever there is holy there is also just, but holy is not everywhere just
is, since the holy is part of the just. Shall we say that, or do you think
differently?

EUTHYPHRO. No, I think you are right.

SOCRATES. Then consider the next point. If the holy is part of the just, it would seem that we must find out what part of the just the holy is. Now, to take an example we used a moment ago, if you were to ask what part of number the even is, and what kind of number it is, I would say that it is number with equal rather than unequal sides. Do you agree?

EUTHYPHRO. Yes, I do.

SOCRATES. Then try in the same way to teach me what part of the e just is the holy, so that I may tell Meletus to wrong me no longer and not to indict me for impiety, since I have already learned from you what things are pious and holy and what are not.

Third Definition: The Holy, Ministry to the Gods (12e–14b)

EUTHYPHRO. Well, Socrates, I think that part of the just which is pious and holy is about ministering to the gods, and the remaining part of the just is about ministering to men.

SOCRATES. That seems excellently put, Euthyphro. But there is still one small point left; I do not yet understand what you mean by "min- 13a istering." You surely do not mean that ministering to the gods is like ministering to other things, though I suppose we do talk that way, as when we say that it is not everyone who knows how to minister to horses, but only the horse-trainer. That is true, is it not?

EUTHYPHRO. Yes, certainly.

SOCRATES. Because horse-training takes care of horses.

EUTHYPHRO. Yes.

SOCRATES. And it is not everyone who knows how to minister to dogs, but only the huntsman.

EUTHYPHRO. True.

SOCRATES. Because huntsmanship takes care of dogs.

EUTHYPHRO. Yes. b

SOCRATES. And the same is true of herdsmanship and cattle?

EUTHYPHRO. Yes, certainly.

SOCRATES. And holiness and piety minister to the gods, Euthyphro? Is that what you are saying?

EUTHYPHRO. Yes, it is.

SOCRATES. Now, is not all ministering meant to accomplish the same thing? I mean this: to take care of a thing is to aim at some good, some benefit, for the thing cared for, as you see horses benefited and improved when ministered to by horse-training. Do you not agree?

EUTHYPHRO. Yes, I do.

SOCRATES. And dogs are benefited by huntsmanship, and cattle by
c herdsmanship, and similarly with other things as well—or do you think
ministering can work harm to what is cared for?

EUTHYPHRO. No, by Zeus, not I.

SOCRATES. But rather is beneficial?

EUTHYPHRO. Of course.

SOCRATES. Now, does holiness, which is to be a kind of ministering,
benefit the gods? Does it improve them? Would you really agree that
when you do something holy you are making some god better?

EUTHYPHRO. No, by Zeus, not I.

SOCRATES. I did not think you meant that, Euthyphro. Far from
d it. That is why I asked you what you meant by ministering to the gods:
I did not believe you meant such a thing as that.

EUTHYPHRO. Yes, and you were right, Socrates. I did not mean
that.

SOCRATES. Very well. But what kind of ministering to the gods is
holiness?

EUTHYPHRO. The kind, Socrates, which slaves minister to their
masters.

SOCRATES. I see. Holiness would, it seems, be a kind of service to
gods.

EUTHYPHRO. Quite so.

SOCRATES. Now, can you tell me what sort of product service to
physicians would be likely to produce? Would it not be health?

EUTHYPHRO. Yes.

e SOCRATES. What about service to ship-builders? Is there not some
product it produces?

EUTHYPHRO. Clearly it produces a ship, Socrates.

SOCRATES. And service to house-builders produces a house?

EUTHYPHRO. Yes.

SOCRATES. Then tell me, my friend: What sort of product would
service to the gods produce? Clearly you know, for you say you know
better than anyone else about religious matters.

EUTHYPHRO. Yes; and I am telling the truth, Socrates.

SOCRATES. Then in the name of Zeus, tell me: What is that fine
product which the gods produce, using us as servants?

EUTHYPHRO. They produce many things, Socrates, excellent things.

14a SOCRATES. So do generals, my friend, but still their work can be
summed up quite easily. Generals produce victory in war. Not so?

EUTHYPHRO. Of course.

SOCRATES. And farmers too produce many excellent things, but still
their work can be summed up as producing food from the earth.

EUTHYPHRO. Of course.

SOCRATES. But what about the many excellent things the gods produce? How does one sum up their production?

EUTHYPHRO. I told you a moment ago, Socrates, that it is difficult to learn accurately how things stand in these matters. Speaking freely, b however, I can tell you that if a man knows how to say and do things acceptable to the gods in prayer and sacrifice, those things are holy; and they preserve both families and cities and keep them safe. The opposite of what is acceptable to the gods is impious, and this overturns and destroys all things.

Fourth Definition: The Holy,
an Act of Prayer and Sacrifice (14b–15c)

SOCRATES. You could have summed up the answer to my question much more briefly, Euthyphro, if you had wished. But you are not eager to instruct me; I see that now. In fact, you just came right up to the point and turned away, and if you had given me an answer, I would c by now have learned holiness from you. But as it is, the questioner must follow the answerer wherever he leads: so what do you say the holy and holiness is this time? Knowledge of how to pray and sacrifice?

EUTHYPHRO. Yes.

SOCRATES. Now, to sacrifice is to give to the gods and to pray is to ask something from them?

EUTHYPHRO. Exactly, Socrates.

SOCRATES. Then by this account, holiness is knowledge of how to d ask from and give to the gods.

EUTHYPHRO. Excellent Socrates. You have followed what I said.

SOCRATES. Yes, my friend, for I am enamoured of your wisdom and attend to it closely, so naturally what you say does not fall to the ground wasted. But tell me, what is the nature of this service we render the gods? You say it is to ask from them and give to them?

EUTHYPHRO. Yes, I do.

SOCRATES. Now, to ask rightly is to ask for things we need from them?

EUTHYPHRO. Certainly.

SOCRATES. And again, to give rightly is to give in return what they e happen to need from us? For surely there would be no skill involved in giving things to someone that he did not need.

EUTHYPHRO. You are right, Socrates.

SOCRATES. So the art of holiness would be a kind of business transaction between gods and men.

EUTHYPHRO. Yes; if it please you to call it that.

SOCRATES. Why, nothing please me unless it happens to be true. But tell me, what benefit do the gods gain from the gifts they receive from us? It is clear to everyone what they give, for we have nothing 15a good they have not given. But how are they benefited by what they get from us? Or do we claim the larger share in the transaction to such an extent that we get all good from them, and they nothing from us?

EUTHYPHRO. But, Socrates, do you think the gods benefit from the things they receive from us?

SOCRATES. Why, Euthyphro, whatever could these gifts of ours to the gods then be?

EUTHYPHRO. What do you suppose, other than praise and honour and as I just said, things which are acceptable?

b   SOCRATES. Then the holy is what is acceptable, Euthyphro, and not what is beneficial or loved by the gods?

EUTHYPHRO. I certainly think it is loved by the gods, beyond all other things.

SOCRATES. Then, on the contrary, the holy is what is loved by the gods.

EUTHYPHRO. Yes, that beyond anything.

SOCRATES. Will it surprise you if in saying this your words get up and walk? You call me a Daedalus. You say I make them walk. But I say that you are a good deal more skilful than Daedalus, for you make them walk in circles. Or are you not aware that our account has gone c round and come back again to the same place? Surely you remember in what went before that the holy appeared to us not to be the same as what is loved by the gods: the two were different. Do you recall?

EUTHYPHRO. Yes, I recall.

SOCRATES. Then do you not now realize that you are saying that what is loved by the gods is holy? But the holy in fact is something other than dear to the gods, is it not?

EUTHYPHRO. Yes.

SOCRATES. Then either we were wrong a moment ago in agreeing to that, or, if we were right in assuming it then, we are wrong in what we're saying now.

EUTHYPHRO. It seems so.

Conclusion (15c–16a)

SOCRATES. Let us begin again from the beginning, and ask what d the holy is, for I shall not willingly give up until I learn. Please do not scorn me: bend every effort of your mind and now tell me the truth. You know it if any man does, and, like Proteus, you must not be let go before you speak. For if you did not know the holy and unholy with certainty, you could not possibly undertake to prosecute your aged father for murder in behalf of a hired man. You would fear to risk the gods, lest your action be wrongful, and you would be ashamed before men. But as it is, I am confident that you think you know with certainty what is holy and what is not. So say it, friend Euthyphro. Do not conceal what it is you believe. e

EUTHYPHRO. Some other time, Socrates. Right now I must hurry somewhere and I am already late.

SOCRATES. What are you doing, my friend! You leave me and cast me down from my high hope that I should learn from you what things are holy and what are not, and escape the indictment of Meletus by showing him that, due to Euthyphro I am now wise in religious matters, 16a that I no longer ignorantly indulge in loose speech and innovation, and most especially, that I shall live better the rest of my life.

APOLOGY

I. The Speech (17a–35d)

Introduction (17a–18a)

17a   To what degree, Gentlemen of Athens, you have been affected by my accusers, I do not know. I, at any rate, was almost led to forget who I am—so convincingly did they speak. Yet hardly anything they have said is true. Among their many falsehoods, I was especially surprised by one; they said you must be on guard lest I deceive you, since I am b a clever speaker. To have no shame at being directly refuted by facts when I show myself in no way clever with words—that, I think, is the very height of shamelessness. Unless, of course, they call a man a clever speaker if he speaks the truth. If that is what they mean, why, I would even admit to being an orator—though not after *their* fashion.

These men, I claim, have said little or nothing true. But from me, Gentlemen, you will hear the whole truth. To be sure, it will not be prettily tricked out in elegant speeches like theirs, words and phrases all c nicely arranged. To the contrary, you will hear me speak naturally in the words which happen to occur to me. For I believe what I say to be just, and let no one of you expect otherwise. Besides, it would hardly be appropriate in a man of my age, Gentlemen, to come before you making up speeches like a boy.[1] So I must specifically ask one thing of you, Gentlemen. If you hear me make my defense in the same words I customarily use at the tables in the Agora, and other places where many of you have heard me, please do not be surprised or make a disturbance

---

[1] Meletus was quite young when he lodged his prosecution. See *Euthyphro* 2b.

because of it. For things stand thus: I am now come into court for the d
first time; I am seventy years old; and I am an utter stranger to this
place. If I were a foreigner, you would unquestionably make allowances 18a
if I spoke in the dialect and manner in which I was raised. In just the
same way, I specifically ask you now, and justly so, I think, to pay no
attention to my manner of speech—it may perhaps be poor, but then
perhaps an improvement—and look strictly to this one thing, whether
or not I speak justly. For that is the virtue of a judge, and the virtue of
an orator is to speak the truth.

Statement (18a–19a)

First of all, Gentlemen, it is right for me to defend myself against
the first false accusations lodged against me, and my first accusers; and
next, against later accusations and later accusers. For the fact is that
many accusers have risen before you against me; at this point they have b
been making accusations for many years, and they have told no truth.
Yet I fear them more than I fear Anytus and those around him—though
they too are clever. Still, the others are more dangerous. They took hold
of most of you in childhood, persuading you of the truth of accusations
which were in fact quite false: "There is a certain Socrates . . . Wise
man . . . Thinker on things in the Heavens . . . Inquirer into things
beneath Earth . . . Making the weaker argument stronger. . . ." Those c
men, Gentlemen of Athens, the men who spread that report, are my
dangerous accusers; for their hearers believe that those who inquire into
such things all acknowledge no gods.

Again, there have been many such accusers, and they have now
been at work for a long time; they spoke to you at a time when you
were especially credulous—some of you children, some only a little
older—and they lodged their accusations quite by default, no one ap-
pearing in defense. But the most absurd thing is that one cannot even
know or tell their names—unless perhaps in the case of a comic poet.[2] d
But those who use malicious slander to persuade you, and those who,
themselves persuaded, persuade others—all are most difficult to deal
with. For it is impossible to bring any one of them forward as a witness
and cross-examine him. I must rather, as it were, fight with shadows
in making my defense, and question where no one answers.

Please grant, then, as I say, that two sets of accusers have risen
against me: those who now lodge their accusations, and those who lodged

---

[2] A reference to Aristophanes, whose description of Socrates in the *Clouds* has in effect
just been quoted, and who will later (19c) be mentioned by name.

e accusations long since. And please accept the fact that I must defend myself against the latter first. For in fact, you heard their accusations earlier, and with far greater effect than those which came later.

Very well then. A defense is to be made, Gentlemen of Athens. I
19a am to attempt to remove from you in this short time that prejudice which you have been so long in acquiring. I might wish that this should come to pass, if it were in some way better for you and for me, wish that I might succeed in my defense. But I think the thing difficult, and its nature hardly escapes me. Still, let that go as pleases the God; the law must be obeyed, and a defense conducted.

Refutation of the Old Accusers (19a–24b)

Let us then take up from the beginning the charges which have given
b rise to the prejudice—the charges on which Meletus in fact relied in lodging his indictment. Very well, what do those who slander me say? It is necessary to read, as it were, their sworn indictment: "Socrates is guilty of needless curiosity and meddling interference, inquiring into things beneath Earth and in the Sky, making the weaker argument
c stronger, and teaching others to do the same." The charge is something like that. Indeed, you have seen it for yourselves in a comedy by Aristophanes—a certain Socrates being carried around on the stage, talking about walking on air and babbling a great deal of other nonsense, of which I understand neither much nor little. Mark you, I do not mean to disparage such knowledge, if anyone in fact has it—let me not be brought to trial by Meletus on such a charge as that! But Gentlemen,
d I have no share of it. Once again, I offer the majority of you as witnesses, and ask those of you who have heard me in conversation—there are many among you—inform each other, please, whether any of you ever heard anything of that sort. From that you will recognize the nature of the other things the multitude says about me.

The fact is that there is nothing in these accusations. And if you have heard from anyone that I undertake to educate men, and make
e money doing it, that is false too. Once again, I think it would be a fine thing to be able to educate men, as Gorgias of Leontini does, or Prodicus of Ceos, or Hippias of Elis. For each of them, Gentlemen, can enter
20a any given city and convince the youth—who might freely associate with any of their fellow citizens they please—to drop those associations and associate with them, to pay money for it, and give thanks in the bargain. As a matter of fact, there is a man here right now, a Parian, and a wise one, who as I learn has just come to town. For I happened to meet a person who has spent more money on Sophists than everyone else put

together, Callias, son of Hipponicus. So I asked him—for he has two sons—"Callias," I said, "if your two sons were colts or calves, we could get an overseer for them and hire him, and his business would be to b make them excellent in their appropriate virtue. He would be either a horse-trainer or a farmer. But as it is, since the two of them are men, whom do you intend to get as an overseer? Who has knowledge of that virtue which belongs to a man and a citizen? Since you have sons, I'm sure you have considered this. Is there such a person," I said, "or not?"

"To be sure," he said.

"Who is he?" I said. "Where is he from, and how much does he charge to teach?"

"Evenus, Socrates," he said. "A Parian. Five minae."[3]

And I counted Evenus fortunate indeed, if he really possesses that art, and teaches it so modestly. For my own part, at any rate, I would c be puffed up with vanity and pride if I had such knowledge. But I do not, Gentlemen.

Perhaps one of you will ask, "But Socrates, what is this all about? Whence have these slanders against you arisen? You must surely have been busying yourself with something out of the ordinary; so grave a report and rumor would not have arisen had you not been doing something rather different from most folk. Tell us what it is, so that we may not take action in your case unadvisedly." That, I think, is a fair re- d quest, and I shall try to indicate what it is that has given me the name I have. Hear me, then. Perhaps some of you will think I joke; be well assured that I shall tell you the whole truth.

Gentlemen of Athens, I got this name through nothing but a kind of wisdom. What kind? The kind which is perhaps peculiarly human, for it may be I am really wise in that. And perhaps the men I just e mentioned are wise with a wisdom greater than human—either that, or I cannot say what. In any case, I have no knowledge of it, and whoever says I do is lying and speaks to my slander.

Please, Gentlemen of Athens. Do not make a disturbance, even if I seem to you to boast. For it will not be my own words I utter; I shall refer you to the speaker, as one worthy of credit. For as witness to you of my own wisdom—whether it is wisdom of a kind, and what kind of wisdom it is—I shall call the God at Delphi.

You surely knew Chaerephon. He was my friend from youth, and a friend of your democratic majority. He went into exile with you.[4] and 21a with you he returned. And you know what kind of a man he was, how eager and impetuous in whatever he rushed into. Well, he once went

---

[3] Callias' answer is in the "short-answer" style of the Sophists. Cf. *Gorgias* 449b ff., *Protagoras* 334e-335c.

to Delphi and boldly asked the oracle—as I say, Gentlemen, please do not make a disturbance—he asked whether anyone is wiser than I. Now, the Pythia[5] replied that no one is wiser. And to this his brother here will testify, since Chaerephon is dead.

b Why do I mention this? I mention it because I intend to inform you whence the slander against me has arisen. For when I heard it, I reflected: "What does the God mean? What is the sense of this riddling utterance? I know that I am not wise at all; what then does the God mean by saying I am wisest? Surely he does not speak falsehood; it is not permitted to him." So I puzzled for a long time over what he meant, and then, with great reluctance, I turned to inquire into the matter in some such way as this.

I went to someone with a reputation for wisdom, in the belief that c there if anywhere I might test the meaning of the utterance and declare to the oracle that, "This man is wiser than I am, and you said I was wisest." So I examined him—there is no need to mention a name, but it was someone in political life who produced this effect on me in discussion, Gentlemen of Athens—and I concluded that though he seemed wise to many other men, and most especially to himself, he was not. I tried to show him this; and thence I became hated, by him and by many d who were present. But I left thinking to myself, "I am wiser than that man. Neither of us probably knows anything worthwhile; but he thinks he does and does not, and I do not and do not think I do. So it seems at any rate that I am wiser in this one small respect: I do not think I know what I do not." I then went to another man who was reputed to e be even wiser, and the same thing seemed true again; there too I became hated, by him and by many others.

Nevertheless, I went on, perceiving with grief and fear that I was becoming hated, but still, it seemed necessary to put the God first—so I had to go on, examining what the oracle meant by testing everyone 22a with a reputation for knowledge. And by the Dog,[6] Gentlemen—I must tell you the truth—I swear that I had some such experience as this: it seemed to me that those most highly esteemed for wisdom fell little short of being most deficient, as I carried on inquiry in behalf of the God, and that others reputedly inferior were men of more discernment.

But really, I must tell you of my wanderings, the labors I performed[7]—all to the end that I might not leave the oracle untested.

---

[4] The leading democrats in Athens were forced into exile when the Thirty Tyrants came to power in 404 B.C.

[5] The Priestess of Apollo, whose major shrine was Delphi.

[6] A humorous oath. The Dog is the Egyptian dog-headed god, Anubis.

[7] I.e., like Hercules.

From the politicians I went to the poets—tragic, dithyrambic, and the rest—thinking that there I would discover myself manifestly less wise **b** by comparison. So I took up poems over which I thought they had taken special pains, and asked them what they meant, so as also at the same time to learn from them. Now, I am ashamed to tell you the truth, Gentlemen, but still, it must be told. There was hardly anyone present who could not give a better account than they of what they had themselves produced. So presently I came to realize that poets too do not **c** make what they make by wisdom, but by a kind of native disposition or divine inspiration, exactly like seers and prophets. For the latter also utter many fine things, but know nothing of the things they speak. That is how the poets also appeared to me, while at the same time I realized that because of their poetry they thought themselves the wisest of men in other matters—and were not. Once again, I left thinking myself superior to them in just the way I was to the politicians.

Finally I went to the craftsmen. I was aware that although I knew **d** scarcely anything, I would find that they knew many things, and fine ones. In this I was not mistaken: they knew things that I did not, and in that respect were wiser. But Gentlemen of Athens, it seemed to me that the poets and our capable public craftsmen had exactly the same failing: because they practiced their own arts well, each deemed himself wise in other things, things of great importance. This mistake quite obscured **e** their wisdom. The result was that I asked myself on behalf of the oracle whether I would accept being such as I am, neither wise with their wisdom nor foolish with their folly, or whether I would accept then wisdom and folly together and become such as they are. I answered, both for myself and the oracle, that it was better to be as I am.

From this examination, Gentlemen of Athens, much enmity has risen against me, of a sort most harsh and heavy to endure, so that many **23a** slanders have arisen, and the name is put abroad that I am "wise." For on each occasion those present think I am wise in the things in which I test others. But very likely, Gentlemen, it is really the God who is wise, and by his oracle he means to say that, "Human nature is a thing **b** of little worth, or none." It appears that he does not mean this fellow Socrates, but uses my name to offer an example, as if he were saying that, "He among you, Gentlemen, is wisest, who, like Socrates, realizes that he is truly worth nothing in respect to wisdom." That is why I still go about even now on behalf of the God, searching and inquiring among both citizens and strangers, should I think some one of them is wise; and when it seems he is not, I help the God and prove it. Due to this pursuit, I have no leisure worth mentioning either for the affairs of the City or for my own estate; I dwell in utter poverty because of my service **c** to God.

Then too the young men follow after me—especially the ones with leisure, namely, the richest. They follow of their own initiative, rejoicing to hear men tested, and often they imitate me and undertake to test others; and next, I think, they find an ungrudging plenty of people who
d think they have some knowledge but know little or nothing. As a result, those whom they test become angry at me, not at themselves, and say that, "This fellow Socrates is utterly polluted, and corrupts the youth." And when someone asks them what it is this Socrates does, what it is he teaches, they cannot say because they do not know; but so as not to seem at a loss, they mutter the kind of thing that lies ready to hand against anyone who pursues wisdom: "Things in the Heavens and beneath the Earth," or, "Not acknowledging gods," or, "Making the weaker argument stronger." The truth, I suppose, they would not wish
e to state, namely, that it is become quite clear that they pretend to knowledge and know nothing. And because they are concerned for their pride, I think, and zealous, and numerous, and speak vehemently and persuasively about me, they have long filled your ears with zealous slander. It was on the strength of this that Meletus attacked me, along with Anytus and Lycon—Meletus angered on behalf of the poets, Anytus on
24a behalf of the public craftsmen and the politicians, Lycon on behalf of the orators. So the result is, as I said to begin with, that I should be most surprised were I able to remove from you in this short time a slander which has grown so great. There, Gentlemen of Athens, you have the truth, and I have concealed or misrepresented nothing in speaking it, great or small. Yet I know quite well that it is just for this that I have become hated—which is in fact an indication of the truth of
b what I say, and that this is the basis of the slander and charges against me. Whether you inquire into it now or hereafter you will find it to be so.

Refutation of Meletus (24b–28a)

Against the charges lodged by my first accusers, let this defense suffice. But for Meletus—the good man who loves his City, so he says—and for my later accusers, I shall attempt a further defense. Once more then, as before a different set of accusers, let us take up their sworn indictment.[8] It runs something like this: it says that Socrates is guilty of corrupting the youth, and not acknowledging the gods the City ac-
c knowledges, but other new divinities. Such is the charge. Let us examine its particulars.

---

[8] The exact indictment is probably preserved in Diogenes Laertius II.40; cf. Xenophon *Memorabilia* I. i. l.

It claims I am guilty of corrupting the youth. But I claim, Gentlemen of Athens, that it is Meletus who is guilty—guilty of jesting in earnest, guilty of lightly bringing men to trial, guilty of pretending a zealous concern for things he never cared about at all. I shall try to show you that this is true.

Come here, Meletus. Now tell me. Do you count it of greatest importance that the young should be as good as possible? d

"I do."

Then come and tell the jurors this: who improves them? Clearly you know, since it is a matter of concern to you. Having discovered, so you say, that I am the man who is corrupting them, you bring me before these judges to accuse me. But now come and say who makes them better. Inform the judges who he is.

You see, Meletus. You are silent. You cannot say. And yet, does this not seem shameful to you, and a sufficient indication of what I say, namely, that you never cared at all? Tell us, my friend. Who improves them?

"The laws."

But I did not ask you that, dear friend. I asked you what man im- e proves them—whoever it is who in the first place knows just that very thing, the laws.

"These men, Socrates. The judges."

Really Meletus? These men here are able to educate the youth and improve them?

"Especially they."

All of them? Or only some?

"All."

By Hera, you bring good news. An ungrudging plenty of benefactors! But what about the audience here. Do they improve them, or not? 25a

"They too."

And members of the Council?

"The Councilors too."

Well then Meletus, do the members of the Assembly, the Ecclesiasts, corrupt the young? Or do they all improve them too?

"They too."

So it seems that every Athenian makes them excellent except me, and I alone corrupt them. Is that what you are saying?

"That is exactly what I am saying."

You condemn me to great misfortune. But tell me, do you think it is so with horses? Do all men improve them, while some one man cor- b rupts them? Or quite to the contrary, is it some one man or a very few, namely horse-trainers, who are able to improve them, while the majority of people, if they deal with horses and use them, corrupt them? Is that not true, Meletus, both of horses and all other animals? Of course it is, whether you and Anytus affirm or deny it. It would be good fortune indeed for the youth if only one man corrupted them and the rest ben-

c efited. But the fact is, Meletus, that you sufficiently show that you never gave thought to the youth; you clearly indicate your own lack of concern, indicate that you never cared at all about the matters in which you bring action against me.

But again, dear Meletus, tell us this: is it better to dwell among fellow citizens who are good, or wicked? Do answer, dear friend; surely I ask nothing hard. Do not wicked men do evil things to those around them, and good men good things?

"Of course."

d Now, is there anyone who wishes to be harmed rather than benefited by those with whom he associates? Answer me, dear friend, for the law requires you to answer. Is there anyone who wishes to be harmed?

"Of course not."

Very well then, are you bringing action against me here because I corrupt the youth intentionally, or unintentionally?

"Intentionally, I say."

How can that be, Meletus? Are you at your age so much wiser than

e I at mine that you recognize that evil men always do evil things to those around them, and good men do good, while I have reached such a pitch of folly that I am unaware that if I do some evil to those with whom I associate, I shall very likely receive some evil at their hands, with the result that I do such great evil intentionally, as you claim? I do not believe you, Meletus, and I do not think anyone else does either. On the contrary: either I do not corrupt the youth, or if I do, I do so un-

26a intentionally. In either case, you lie. And if I corrupt them unintentionally, it is not the law to bring action here for that sort of mistake, but rather to instruct and admonish in private; for clearly, if I once learn, I shall stop what I unintentionally do. You, however, were unwilling to associate with me and teach me; instead, you brought action here, where it is law to bring those in need of punishment rather than instruction.

Gentlemen of Athens, what I said is surely now clear: Meletus was

b never concerned about these matters, much or little. Still, Meletus, tell us this: how do you say I corrupt the youth? Or is it clear from your indictment that I teach them not to acknowledge the gods the City acknowledges, but other new divinities? Is this what you mean by saying I corrupt by teaching?

"Certainly. That is exactly what I mean."

Then in the name of these same gods we are now discussing, Meletus, please speak a little more plainly still, both for me and for these gentlemen here. Do you mean that I teach the youth to acknowledge c that there are gods, and thus do not myself wholly deny gods, and am not in that respect guilty—though the gods are not those the City acknowledges, but different ones, and that this is the cause of my indictment, that they are different? Or are you claiming that I do not myself acknowledge any gods at all, and teach this to others?

"I mean that. You acknowledge no gods at all."

Ah, my dear Meletus, why do you say such things? Do I not at least d acknowledge Sun and Moon as gods, as other men do?

"No, no, Gentlemen and Judges, not when he says the Sun is a stone and the Moon earth."

My dear Meletus! Do you think it is Anaxagoras you are accusing? Do you so despise these judges here and think them so unlettered that they do not know it is the books of Anaxagoras of Clazomenae which teem with such statements? Are young men to learn these things specifically from me, when they can buy them sometimes in the Orchestra for a drachma, if the price is high, and laugh at Socrates if he pretends e they are his own—especially since they are so absurd? Well, dear friend, is that what you think? I acknowledge no gods at all?

"No, none whatever."

You cannot be believed, Meletus—even, I think, by yourself. Gentlemen of Athens, I think this man who stands here before you is insolent and unchastened, and has brought this suit precisely out of insolence and unchastened youth. He seems to be conducting a test by propounding a riddle: "Will Socrates, the wise man, realize how neatly 27a I contradict myself, or will I deceive him and the rest of the audience?" For certainly it seems clear that he is contradicting himself in his indictment. It is as though he were saying, "Socrates is guilty of not acknowledging gods, and acknowledges gods." Yet surely this is to jest.

Please join me, Gentlemen, in examining why it appears to me that this is what he is saying. And you answer us, Meletus. The rest of you will please remember what I asked you at the beginning, and make no b disturbance if I fashion arguments in my accustomed way.

Is there any man, Meletus, who acknowledges that there are things pertaining to men, but does not acknowledge that there are men? Let him answer for himself, Gentlemen—and let him stop interrupting. Is there any man who does not acknowledge that there are no horses, but acknowledges things pertaining to horsemanship? Or does not acknowledge that there are flutes, but acknowledges things pertaining to flute playing? There is not, my good friend. If you do not wish to answer, I'll answer for you and for the rest of these people here. But do please

answer my question, at least: Is there any man who acknowledges that
c there are things pertaining to divinities, but does not acknowledge that
there are divinities?

"There is not."

How obliging of you to answer—reluctantly, and under compulsion
from these gentlemen here. Now, you say that I acknowledge and teach
things pertaining to divinities—whether new or old, still at least I acknowledge them, by your account; indeed you swore to that in your
indictment. But if I acknowledge that there are things pertaining to divinities, must I surely not also acknowledge that there are divinities?
Isn't that so? Of course it is—since you do not answer, I count you as
d agreeing. And divinities, we surely believe, are either gods or children
of gods? Correct?

"Of course."

So if I believe in divinities, as you say, and if divinities are a kind
of god, there is the jesting riddle I attributed to you; you are saying that
I do not believe in gods, and again that I do believe in gods because I
believe in divinities. On the other hand, if divinities are children of
gods, some born illegitimately of nymphs,[9] or others of whom this is
also told,[10] who could possibly believe that there are children of gods,
but not gods? It would be as absurd as believing that there are children
of horses and asses, namely, mules, without believing there are horses
and asses. Meletus, you could not have brought this indictment except
in an attempt to test us—or because you were at a loss for any true basis
of prosecution. But as to how you are to convince anyone of even the
slightest intelligence that one and the same man can believe that there
28a are things pertaining to divinities and gods, and yet believe that there
are neither divinities nor heroes—there is no way.

Digression: Socrates' Mission to Athens (28a–34b)

Gentlemen of Athens, I do not think further defense is needed to
show that, by the very terms of Meletus' indictment, I am not guilty;
this, surely, is sufficient. But as I said before, a great deal of enmity
has risen against me among many people, and you may rest assured
this is true. And that is what will convict me, if I am convicted—not

---

[9] Aesclepius, for example, son of Apollo and the nymph Coronis. Note that nymphs
are themselves goddesses.

[10] For example, Achilles, son of the nymph Thetis and Peleus, a mortal father; or
Heracles, son of Zeus and Alcmene, a mortal mother.

Meletus, not Anytus, but the grudging slander of the multitude. It has b
convicted many another good and decent man; I think it will convict
me; nor is there any reason to fear that with me it will come to a stand.

Perhaps someone may say, "Are you not ashamed, Socrates, at having pursued such a course that you now stand in danger of being put
to death?" To him I would make a just reply: You are wrong, Sir, if
you think that a man worth anything at all should take thought for danger in living or dying. He should look when he acts to one thing: whether
what he does is just or unjust, the work of a good man or a bad one.
By your account, those demigods and heroes who laid down their lives
at Troy would be of little worth—the rest of them, and the son of Thetis. c
Achilles so much despised danger instead of submitting to disgrace that
when he was intent on killing Hector his goddess mother told him, as
I recall, "My son, if you avenge the slaying of your comrade Patroclus
with the death of Hector, you yourself shall die; for straightway with
Hector is his fate prepared for you."[11] Achilles heard, and thought little
of the death and danger. He was more afraid to live as a bad man, with d
friends left unavenged. "Straightway let me die," he said, "exacting
right from him who did the wrong, that I may not remain here as a butt
of mockery beside crook-beaked ships, a burden to the earth." Do you
suppose that he gave thought to death and danger?

Gentlemen of Athens, truly it is so: wherever a man stations himself
in belief that it is best, wherever he is stationed by his commander, there
he must I think remain and run the risks, giving thought to neither
death nor any other thing except disgrace. I should indeed have wrought
a fearful thing, Gentlemen of Athens, if, when the commanders you
chose stationed me at Potidaea and Amphipolis and Delium,[12] I there e
remained as others did, and ran the risk of death; but then, when the
God stationed me, as I thought and believed, obliging me to live in the
pursuit of wisdom, examining myself and others—if then, at that point 29a
through fear of death or any other thing, I left my post, that would have
been dreadful indeed, and then in truth might I be justly brought to
court for not acknowledging the existence of gods, for willful disobedience to the oracle, for fearing death, for thinking myself wise when I
am not.

For to fear death, Gentlemen, is nothing but to think one is wise
when one is not; for it is to think one knows what one does not. No

---

[11] This is not a wholly accurate quotation from the *Iliad*, but describes the scene at
XVIII 94ff.

[12] All battles in which Socrates fought with conspicuous bravery. See *Symposium* 220d–
221b, *Laches* 181b.

man knows death, nor whether it is not the greatest of all goods; and
b yet men fear it as though they well knew it to be the worst of evils. Yet
how is this not folly most to be reproached, the folly of believing one
knows what one does not? I, at least, Gentlemen, am perhaps superior
to most men here and just in this: that as I have no satisfactory knowledge of things in the Place of the Dead, I do not think I do. I do know
that to be guilty of disobedience to a superior, be he god or man, is
shameful evil.

So as against evils I know to be evils, I shall never fear or flee from
things which for aught I know may be good. Thus, even if you now
c dismiss me, refusing to do as Anytus bids—Anytus, who said that either
I should not have been brought to trial to begin with or, since brought,
must be put to death, testifying before you that if I were once acquitted
your sons would pursue what Socrates teaches and all be thoroughly
corrupted—if with this in view you were to say to me, "Socrates, we
shall not at this time be persuaded by Meletus, and we dismiss you. But
on this condition: that you no longer pass time in that inquiry of yours,
d or pursue philosophy. And if you are again taken doing it, you die."
If, as I say, you were to dismiss me on that condition, I would reply
that I hold you in friendship and regard, Gentlemen of Athens, but I
shall obey the God rather than you, and while I have breath and am
able I shall not cease to pursue wisdom or to exhort you, charging any
of you I happen to meet in my accustomed manner. "You are the best
of men, being an Athenian, citizen of a city honored for wisdom and
power beyond all others. Are you then not ashamed to care for the get-
e ting of money, and reputation, and public honor, while yet having no
thought or concern for truth and understanding and the greatest possible excellence of your soul?" And if some one of you disputes this,
and says he does care, I shall not immediately dismiss him and go away.
30a I shall question him and examine him and test him, and if he does not
seem to me to possess virtue, and yet says he does, I shall rebuke him
for counting of more importance things which by comparison are worthless. I shall do this to young and old, citizen and stranger, whomever I
happen to meet, but I shall do it especially to citizens, in as much as
they are more nearly related to me. For the God commands this, be
well assured, and I believe that you have yet to gain in this City a greater
good than my service to the God. I go about doing nothing but persuading you, young and old, to care not for body or money in place of,
b or so much as, excellence of soul. I tell you that virtue does not come
from money, but money and all other human goods both public and
private from virtue. If in saying this I corrupt the youth, that would be
harm indeed. But anyone who claims I say other than this speaks false-
c hood. In these matters, Gentlemen of Athens, believe Anytus, or do

not. Dismiss me, or do not. For I will not do otherwise, even if I am to die for it many times over.

Please do not make a disturbance, Gentlemen. Abide in my request and do not interrupt what I have to say, but listen. Indeed, I think you will benefit by listening. I am going to tell you certain things at which you may perhaps cry out; please do not do it. Be well assured that if you kill me, and if I am the sort of man I claim, you will harm me less than you harm yourselves. There is no harm a Meletus or Anytus can do me; it is not possible, for it does not, I think, accord with divine law that a better man be harmed by a worse. Meletus perhaps can kill me, or exile me, or disenfranchise me; and perhaps he and others too think d those things great evils. I do not. I think it a far greater evil to do what he is now doing, attempting to kill a man unjustly. And so, Gentlemen of Athens, I am far from making a defense for my own sake, as some might think; I make it for yours, lest you mistake the gift the God has given you and cast your votes against me. If you kill me, you will not e easily find such another man as I, a man who—if I may put it a bit absurdly—has been fastened as it were to the City by the God as, so to speak, to a large and well-bred horse, a horse grown sluggish because of its size, and in need of being roused by a kind of gadfly. Just so, I think, the God has fastened me to the City. I rouse you. I persuade you. I upbraid you. I never stop lighting on each one of you, everywhere, 31a all day long. Such another will not easily come to you again, Gentlemen, and if you are persuaded by me, you will spare me. But perhaps you are angry, as men roused from sleep are angry, and perhaps you will swat me, persuaded by Meletus that you may lightly kill. Then will you continue to sleep out your lives, unless the God sends someone else to look after you.

That I am just that, a gift from the God to the City, you may rec-ognize from this: it scarcely seems a human matter merely, that I should b take no thought for anything of my own and endure the neglect of my house and its affairs for these long years now, and ever attend to yours, going to each of you in private like a father or elder brother, persuading you to care for virtue. If I got something from it, if I took pay for this kind of exhortation, that would explain it. But as things are, you can see for yourselves that even my accusers, who have accused me so shamefully of everything else, could not summon shamelessness enough c to provide witnesses to testify that I ever took pay or asked for it. For it is enough, I think, to provide my poverty as witness to the truth of what I say.

Perhaps it may seem peculiar that I go about in private advising men and busily inquiring, and yet do not enter your Assembly in public to advise the City. The reason is a thing you have heard me mention

many times in many places, that something divine and godlike comes
d to me—which Meletus, indeed, mocked in his indictment.[13] I have had
it from childhood. It comes as a kind of voice, and when it comes, it
always turns me away from what I am about to do, but never toward
it. That is what opposed my entering political life, and I think it did
well to oppose. For be well assured, Gentlemen of Athens, that had I
e attempted long since to enter political affairs, I should long since have
been destroyed—to the benefit of neither you nor myself.

Please do not be angry at me for telling the simple truth. It is impossible for any man to be spared if he legitimately opposes you or any
other democratic majority, and prevents many unjust and illegal things
32a from occurring in his city. He who intends to fight for what is just, if
he is to be spared even for a little time, must of necessity live a private
rather than a public life.

I shall offer you a convincing indication of this—not words, but what
you respect, deeds. Hear, then, what befell me, so that you may know
that I will not through fear of death give way to any man contrary to
what is right, even if I am destroyed for it. I shall tell you a thing which
b is tedious—it smacks of the law courts—but true. Gentlemen of Athens,
I never held other office in the City, but I was once a member of the
Council. And it happened that our Tribe, Antiochis, held the Prytanate
when you decided to judge as a group the cases of the ten generals who
had failed to gather up the bodies of the slain in the naval battle—il-
legally, as later it seemed to all of you. But at the time, I alone of the
Prytanies opposed doing a thing contrary to law, and cast my vote
against it. And when the orators were ready to impeach me and have
c me arrested—you urging them on with your shouts—I thought that with
law and justice on my side I must run the risk, rather than concur with
you in an unjust decision through fear of bonds or death. Those things
happened while the City was still under the Democracy. But when Oligarchy came, the Thirty in turn summoned me along with four others
to the Rotunda and ordered us to bring back Leon the Salamanian from
Salamis so that he might be executed, just as they ordered many others
to do such things, planning to implicate as many people as possible in
d their own guilt. But I then showed again, not by words but deeds, that
death, if I may be rather blunt, was of no concern whatever to me; to
do nothing unjust or unholy—that was my concern. Strong as it was,
that oligarchy did not so frighten me as to do a thing unjust, and when
we departed the Rotunda, the other four went into Salamis and brought
back Leon, and I left and went home. I might have been killed for that,

---

[13] The suggestion is that Meletus lodged his accusation of acknowledging new (or
strange) gods because of the Sign. Cf. *Euthyphro* 3b.

if the oligarchy had not shortly afterward been overthrown. And of these e
things you will have many witnesses.

Now, do you think I would have lived so many years if I had been
in public life and acted in a manner worthy of a good man, defending
what is just and counting it, as is necessary, of first importance? Far
from it, Gentlemen of Athens. Not I, and not any other man. But
through my whole life I have shown myself to be that sort of man in
public affairs, the few I've engaged in; and I have shown myself the 33a
same man in private. I never gave way to anyone contrary to what is
just—not to others, and certainly not to those slanderously said to be
my pupils. In fact, I have never been teacher to anyone. If, in speaking
and tending to my own affairs, anyone wished to hear me, young or
old, I never begrudged him; nor do I discuss for a fee and not otherwise.
To rich and poor alike I offer myself as a questioner, and if anyone b
wishes to answer, he may then hear what I have to say. And if any of
them turned out to be useful men, or any did not, I cannot justly be
held responsible. To none did I promise instruction, and none did I
teach; if anyone says that he learned from me or heard in private what
others did not, you may rest assured he is not telling the truth.

Why is it, then, that some people enjoy spending so much time with
me? You have heard, Gentlemen of Athens; I told you the whole truth. c
It is because they enjoy hearing people tested who think they are wise
and are not. After all, it is not unamusing. But for my own part, as I
say, I have been ordered to do this by God—in oracles, in dreams, in
every way in which other divine apportionment orders a man to do
anything.

These things, Gentlemen of Athens, are both true and easily tested.
For if I am corrupting some of the youth, and have corrupted others, d
it must surely be that some among them, grown older, if they realize
that I counseled them toward evil while young, would now come forward to accuse me and exact a penalty. And if they were unwilling,
then some of their relatives—fathers, brothers, other kinsmen—if their
own relatives had suffered evil at my hands, would now remember, and
exact a penalty. Certainly there are many such men I see present. Here
is Crito, first, of my own age and deme,[14] father of Critobulus; then e
there is Eysanias of Sphettos, father of Aeschines[15] here. Next there is
Antiphon of Cephisus, father of Epigenes. Then there are others whose
brothers engaged in this pastime. There is Nicostratus, son of Theo-
zotides, brother of Theodotus—and Theodotus is dead, so he could not
have swayed him—and Paralus here, son of Demococus, whose brother

---

[14] Alopece. A deme was roughly the equivalent of a township.

[15] Who, like Plato, went on to write Socratic dialogues.

34a was Theages. And here is Adeimantus, son of Ariston, whose brother
is Plato here; and Aeantodorus, whose brother is Apollodorus here. I
could name many others, some of whom at least Meletus ought certainly
have provided in his speech as witnesses. If he forgot it then, let him
do it now—I yield the floor—and let him say whether he has any witnesses of the sort. You will find that quite to the contrary, Gentlemen,
every one of these men is ready to help me, I, who corrupt their relatives, as Meletus and Anytus claim. Those who are themselves cor-
b rupted might perhaps have reason to help me; but their relatives are
older men who have not been corrupted. What reason could they have
for supporting me except that it is right and just, because they know
Meletus is lying and I am telling the truth?

Peroration (34b–35d)

Very well then, Gentlemen. This, and perhaps a few other things
like it, is what I have to say in my defense. Perhaps some of you will
c remember his own conduct and be offended, if when brought to trial
on a lesser charge than this, he begged his judges with tearful supplication, and caused his children to come forward so that he might be the
more pitied, along with other relatives and a host of friends; whereas I
shall do none of these things, even though I am, as it would seem at
least, in the extremity of danger. Perhaps someone with this in mind
may become hardened against me; angered by it, he may cast his vote
d in anger. If this is true of any of you—not that I expect it, but if it is—
I think it might be appropriate to say, "I too have relatives, my friend;
for as Homer puts it, I am not 'of oak and rock,' but born of man, so
I have relatives—yes, and sons too, Gentlemen of Athens, three of them,
one already a lad and two of them children. Yet not one of them have
I caused to come forward here, and I shall not beg you to acquit me."
Why not? Not out of stubbornness, Gentlemen of Athens, nor disrespect
e for you. Whether or not I am confident in the face of death is another
story; but I think that my own honor, and yours, and that of the whole
City would suffer, if I were to behave in this way, I being of the age I
am and having the name I have—truly or falsely it being thought that
35a Socrates is in some way superior to most men. If those of you reputed
to be superior in wisdom or courage or any other virtue whatever were
men of this sort, it would be disgraceful; I have often seen such people
behave surprisingly when put on trial, even though they had a reputation to uphold, because they were persuaded that they would suffer a
terrible thing if they were put to death—as though they would be immortal if you did not kill them. I think they cloak the City in shame,

so that a stranger might think that those among the Athenians who are superior in virtue, and whom the Athenians themselves judge worthy of office and other honors, are no better than women. These are things, **b** Gentlemen of Athens, which those of you who have a reputation to uphold ought not to do; nor, if we defendants do them, ought you permit it. You ought rather make it clear that you would far rather cast your vote against a man who stages these pitiful scenes, and makes the City a butt of mockery, than against a man who shows quiet restraint.

But apart from the matter of reputation, Gentlemen, it does not seem to me just to beg a judge, or to be acquitted by begging; it is rather **c** just to teach and persuade. The judge does not sit to grant justice as a favor, but to render judgment; he has sworn no oath to gratify those whom he sees fit, but to judge according to law. We ought not accustom you, nor ought you become accustomed, to forswear yourselves; it is pious in neither of us. So do not consider it right, Gentlemen of Athens, that I do such things in your presence as I believe to be neither hon- **d** orable nor just nor holy, especially since, by Zeus, it is for impiety that I am being prosecuted by this fellow Meletus here. For clearly, if I were to persuade and compel you by supplication, you being sworn as judges, I would teach you then indeed not to believe that there are gods, and in making my defense I would in effect accuse myself of not acknowledging them. But that is far from so; I do acknowledge them, Gentlemen of Athens, as no one of my accusers does, and to you and to the God I now commit my case, to judge in whatever way will be best for me and also for you.

II. The Counterpenalty (35e–38b)

e   I am not distressed, Gentlemen of Athens, at what has happened,
36a nor angered that you have cast your votes against me. Many things
contribute to this, among them the fact that I expected it. I am much
more surprised at the number of votes either way; I did not think the
censure would be by so little, but by more. As it is, it seems, if only
thirty votes had fallen otherwise, I would have been acquitted.[16] And
so far as Meletus at least is concerned, it seems to me, I am already
acquitted—and more than acquitted, since it is clear that if Anytus and
Lycon had not come forward to accuse me, Meletus would have been
b fined a thousand drachmas for not obtaining a fifth part of the vote.

The man demands death for me. Very well. Then what counterpenalty shall I propose to you, Gentlemen of Athens?[17] Clearly something I deserve, but what? What do I deserve to pay or suffer because
I did not through life keep quiet, and yet did not concern myself, as the
multitude do, with money or property or military and public honors
and other office, or the secret societies and political clubs which keep
c cropping up in the City, believing that I was really too reasonable and
temperate a man to enter upon these things and survive. I did not go
where I could benefit neither you nor myself; instead, I went to each of
you in private, where I might perform the greatest service. I undertook
to persuade each of you not to care for anything which belongs to you
before first caring for yourselves, so as to be as good and wise as possible, nor to care for anything which belongs to the City before caring
d for the City itself, and so too with everything else in the same way. Now,
what do I deserve to suffer for being this sort of man? Some good thing,
Gentlemen of Athens, if penalty is really to be assessed according to
desert. What then is fitting for a poor man who has served his City well,
and needs leisure to exhort you? Why, Gentlemen of Athens, nothing
is more fitting for such a man than to be fed in the Prytaneum,[18] at the

---

[16] Granting that there were 500 judges, the vote must have been 280 to 220.

[17] Under Athenian law, the prosecutor proposed a penalty, and the convicted defendant a counterpenalty; the jury was required to choose between them without alteration.
The usual practice was for a convicted person to propose a penalty as heavy as he could
bear short of that which the prosecutor demanded, in hope that the jury might accept it.

[18] Public subsistence in the Prytaneum was a great honor, traditionally given to
Olympic victors in major events.

common table of the City—yes, and far more fitting than for one of you who has been an Olympic victor in the single-horse or two- or four-horse chariot races. For he makes you seem happy, whereas I make you happy in truth, and he does not need subsistence, and I do. If then I e must propose a penalty I justly deserve, I propose that—public subsistence in the Prytaneum.   37a

Perhaps some of you will think that in saying this I speak much as I spoke of tears and pleading, out of stubborn pride. That is not so, Gentlemen of Athens, though something of this sort is: I am persuaded that I have not intentionally wronged any man, but I cannot persuade you of it; we have talked so short a time. Now, I believe if you had a law, as other men do, that cases involving death shall not be decided in b a single day, that you would be persuaded; but as things are, it is not easy in so short a time to do away with slanders grown so great. Being persuaded, however, that I have wronged no one, I am quite unwilling to wrong myself, or claim that I deserve some evil and propose any penalty of the kind. What is there to fear? That I may suffer the penalty Meletus proposes, when as I say, I do not know whether it is good or evil? Shall I choose instead a penalty I know very well to be evil? Imprisonment, perhaps? But why should I live in prison, a slave to men who happen to occupy office as the Eleven? A fine, then, and prison till c I pay it? But that comes to the same thing, since I have no money to pay it. Shall I then propose exile? Perhaps you would accept that. But I must indeed love life and cling to it dearly, Gentlemen, if I were so d foolish as to think that, although you, my own fellow-citizens, cannot bear my pursuits and discussions, which have become so burdensome and hateful that you now seek to be rid of them, others will bear them lightly. No, Gentlemen. My life would be fine indeed, if at my age I went to live in exile, always moving from city to city, always driven out. For be well assured that wherever I go, the young men will listen to what I say as they do here; if I turn them away, their fathers and re- e lations will drive me out in their behalf.

Perhaps someone may say, "Would it not be possible for you to live in exile, Socrates, if you were silent and kept quiet?" But this is the hardest thing of all to make some of you believe. If I say that to do so would be to disobey the God, and therefore I cannot do it, you will not 38a believe me because you will think that I am being sly and dishonest.[19] If on the other hand I say that the greatest good for man is to fashion arguments each day about virtue and the other things you hear me discussing, when I examine myself and others, and that the unexamined life is not for man worth living, you will believe what I say still less. I

---

[19] That is, an *eiron*. "Irony" was regarded as a defect of character, not a virtue, as Theophrastus' portrait in the *Characters* of the ironical man makes clear.

b claim these things are so, Gentlemen; but it is not easy to convince you. At the same time, I am not accustomed to think myself deserving of any evil. If I had money, I would propose a fine as great as I could pay—for there would be no harm in that. But as things stand, I have no money, unless the amount I can pay is the amount you are willing to exact of me. I might perhaps be able to pay a mina of silver.[20] So I propose a penalty in that amount. But Plato here, Gentlemen of Athens, and Crito and Critobulus and Apollodorus bid me propose thirty minas, and they will stand surety. So I propose that amount. You have guarantors sufficient for the sum.

---

[20] It is useless to try to give modern money equivalents, but the ultimate fine proposed is substantial: Aristotle gives one mina as the conventional ransom for a prisoner of war (*Nicomachean Ethics* V 1134b 21). Why did Socrates propose a fine at all, or accept his friends' offer of suretyship? See 29d–30b, 30d–e.

III. Epilogue (38c–42a)

For the sake of only a little time, Gentlemen of Athens, you are to c be accused by those who wish to revile the City of having killed Socrates, a wise man—for those who wish to reproach you will say I am wise even if I am not. And if you had only waited a little, the thing would have come of its own initiative. You see my age. You see how far spent my life already is, how near to death.

I say this, not to all of you, but to those of you who voted to con- d demn me. To them I also say this. Perhaps you think, Gentlemen of Athens, that I have been convicted for lack of words to persuade you, had I thought it right to do and say anything to be acquitted. Not so. It is true I have been convicted for a lack; not a lack of words, but lack of bold shamelessness, unwillingness to say the things you would find it pleasant to hear—weeping and wailing, saying and doing many things I claim to be unworthy of me, but things of the sort you are accustomed e to hear from others. I did not then think it necessary to do anything unworthy of a free man because of danger; I do not now regret so having conducted my defense; and I would far rather die with that defense than live with the other. Neither in court of law nor in war ought I or any man contrive to escape death by any means possible. Often in battle it 39a becomes clear that a man may escape death by throwing down his arms and turning in supplication to his pursuers; and there are many other devices for each of war's dangers, so that one can avoid dying if he is bold enough to say and do anything whatever. It is not difficult to escape death, Gentlemen; it is more difficult to escape wickedness, for wicked- b ness runs faster than death. And now I am old and slow, and I have been caught by the slower runner. But my accusers are clever and quick, and they have been caught by the faster runner, namely Evil. I now take my leave, sentenced by you to death; they depart, convicted by Truth for injustice and wickedness. I abide in my penalty, and they in theirs. That is no doubt as it should be, and I think it is fit.

I desire next to prophesy to you who condemned me. For I have c now reached that point where men are especially prophetic, when they are about to die. I say to you who have decreed my death that to you there will come hard on my dying a punishment far more difficult to bear than the death you have visited upon me. You have done this thing in the belief that you would be released from submitting to examination

95

of your lives. I say that it will turn out quite otherwise. Those who come
d to examine you will be more numerous, and I have up to now restrained
them, though you perceived it not. They will be more harsh inasmuch
as they are younger, and you shall be the more troubled. If you think
by killing to hold back the reproach due you for not living rightly, you
are profoundly mistaken. That release is neither possible nor honorable.
The release which is both most honorable and most easy is not to cut
down others, but to take proper care that you will be as good as possible.
This I utter as prophecy to you who voted for my condemnation, and
take my leave.

e   But with you who voted for my acquittal, I should be glad to discuss
the nature of what has happened, now, while the authorities are busy
and I am not yet gone where, going, I must die. Abide with me, Gentlemen, this space of time; for nothing prevents our talking with each other
40a while we still can. To you, as my friends, I wish to display the meaning
of what has now fallen to my lot. A remarkable thing has occurred,
Gentlemen and Judges—and I correctly call you Judges. My accustomed oracle, which is divine, always came quite frequently before in
everything, opposing me even in trivial matters if I was about to err.
And now a thing has fallen to my lot which you also see yourselves, a
thing which some might think, and do in fact believe, to be ultimate
among evils. But the sign of the God did not oppose me early this morn-
b ing when I left my house, nor when I came up here to the courtroom,
nor at any point in my argument in anything I was about to say. And
yet frequently in other arguments, it has checked me right in the middle
of speaking; but today it has not opposed me in any way, in none of
my deeds, in none of my words. What do I take to be the reason? I will
c tell you. Very likely what has fallen to me is good, and those among us
who think that death is an evil are wrong. There has been convincing
indication of this. For the accustomed sign would surely have opposed
me, if I were not in some way acting for good.

        Let us also consider a further reason for high hope that death is
good. Death is one of two things. Either to be dead is not to exist, to
have no awareness at all, or it is, as the stories tell, a kind of alteration,
a change of abode for the soul from this place to another. And if it is
to have no awareness, like a sleep when the sleeper sees no dream, death
d would be a wonderful gain; for I suppose if someone had to pick out
that night in which he slept and saw no dream, and put the other days
and nights of his life beside it, and had to say after inspecting them how
many days and nights he had lived in his life which were better and
sweeter, I think that not only any ordinary person but even the Great
King[21] himself would find them easily numbered in relation to other

---

[21] Of Persia, a proverbial symbol of wealth and power.

days, and other nights. If death is that, I say it is gain; for the whole e
of time then turns out to last no longer than a single night. But if on
the contrary death is like taking a journey, passing from here to another
place, and the stories told are true, and all who have died are there—
what greater good might there be, my Judges? For if a man once goes
to the place of the dead, takes leave of those who claim to be judges
here, he will find the true judges who are said to sit in judgment there— 41a
Minos, Rhadamanthus, Aeacus, Triptolemus, and the other demigods
and heroes who lived just lives. Would that journey be worthless? And
again, to meet Orpheus and Musaeus, Hesiod and Homer—how much
would any of you give? I at least would be willing to die many times
over, if these things are true. I would find a wonderful pursuit there, b
when I met Palamedes, and Ajax, son of Telemon, and any others
among the ancients done to death by unjust verdicts, and compared my
experiences with theirs. It would not, I think, be unamusing. But the
greatest thing, surely, would be to test and question there as I did here:
Who among them is wise? Who thinks he is and is not? How much
might one give, my Judges, to examine the man who led the great army
against Troy, or Odysseus, or Sisyphus, or a thousand other men and
women one might mention—to converse with them, to associate with
them, to examine them—why, it would be inconceivable happiness. Es- c
pecially since they surely do not kill you for it there. They are happier
there than men are here in other ways, and they are already immortal
for the rest of time, if the stories told are true.

But you too, my Judges, must be of good hope concerning death.
You must recognize that this one thing is true: that there is not evil for d
a good man either in living or in dying, and that the gods do not neglect
his affairs. What has now come to me did not occur of its own initiative.
It is clear to me that to die now and be released from my affairs is better
for me. That is why the sign did not turn me back, and I bear no anger
whatever toward those who voted to condemn me, or toward my accusers. And yet, it was not with this in mind that they accused and
convicted me. They thought to do harm, and for that they deserve
blame. But this much would I ask of them: when my sons are grown, e
Gentlemen, exact a penalty of them; give pain to them exactly as I gave
pain to you, if it seems to you that they care more for wealth or anything
else than they care for virtue. And if they seem to be something and are
nothing, rebuke them as I rebuked you, because they do not care for
what they ought, because they think themselves something and are worth 42a
nothing. And should you do that, both I and my sons will have been
justly dealt with at your hands.

But it is now the hour of parting—I to die and you to live. Which
of us goes to the better is unclear to all but the God.

CRITO

43a   SOCRATES. Why have you come at this hour, Crito? Isn't it still early?

CRITO. Very Early.

SOCRATES. What time, exactly?

CRITO. Depth of dawn, before first light.

SOCRATES. I'm surprised the guard was willing to admit you.

CRITO. He's used to me by now, Socrates, because I come here so often. Besides, I've done him a kindness.

SOCRATES. Did you come just now, or a while ago?

CRITO. Quite a while ago.

b   SOCRATES. Then why didn't you wake me right away, instead of sitting there in silence?

CRITO. No, Socrates. I might wish I weren't in such wakeful pain myself, and I've been marvelling for some time at how sweetly you sleep. I didn't wake you on purpose, so that you could spend the time as pleasantly as possible. Often before through the whole of our lives I've thought you happy in your ways, but never more than now in the present misfortune—so cheerfully and lightly do you bear it.

c   SOCRATES. But surely, Crito, it would scarcely be appropriate in a man of my age to be distressed that he now has to die.

CRITO. Other men as old have been taken in similar misfortune, Socrates, and age did not relieve their distress at what faced them.

SOCRATES. True. But why are you here so early?

CRITO. I bring grievous news, Socrates. Not grievous to you, it appears, but grievous to me and to all your companions, and heaviest to bear, I think, for me.

d   SOCRATES. What is it? Has the ship come from Delos, on whose arrival I'm to die?

CRITO. Not yet. But I think it will come today, to judge from the report of some people who've arrived from Sunium and left it there.

From what they say, it will clearly come today, and then tomorrow, Socrates, your life must end.

SOCRATES. Well, Crito, let it be for the best. If so it pleases the Gods, let it be so. Still, I don't think it will come today.

CRITO. From what do you infer that? 44a

SOCRATES. I'll tell you. I'm to die, I think, the day after the ship arrives.

CRITO. Yes—so the authorities say, at any rate.

SOCRATES. Then I think it will come tomorrow, not today. I infer that from a dream I saw a little while ago tonight. Perhaps you chose a good time not to wake me.

CRITO. What was the dream?

SOCRATES. A woman appeared to me. She came, fair and beautiful of form, clothed in white, and she called to me and said, "Socrates, on b the third day shalt thou go to fertile Phthia."

CRITO. A strange dream, Socrates.

SOCRATES. But, Crito, I think a clear one.

CRITO Yes, too clear, it seems.

Crito's Exhortation to Escape (44b–46a)

CRITO. But, please, Socrates, my beloved friend, please let me persuade you even at this point. Save yourself. As for me, if you should die it will be a multiple misfortune. Quite apart from the loss of such friendship as I shall not find again, people who don't really know us c will think I didn't care, because I could have saved you if only I'd been willing to spend the money. Yet what could seem more shameful, than the appearance of putting money before friends? People won't believe that you refused to escape even though we were eager to help.

SOCRATES. But Crito, why should we be so concerned about what people will think? Reasonable men, who are the ones worth considering, will believe that things happened as they did.

CRITO. Surely at this point, Socrates, you see how necessary it really d is to care about what people think. The very things now happening show that they can accomplish, not the least of evils, but very nearly the greatest, if a man has been slandered among them.

SOCRATES. If only they could work the greatest evils, Crito, so that they might also work the greatest goods, it would truly be well. But as it is, they can do neither; they cannot make a man wise or foolish. They only act at random.

CRITO. Very well, let that be so. But tell me this, Socrates. Are you worried about me and the rest of your friends? Are you afraid that, if you escape, the sycophants will make trouble for us for helping you, so that we may be compelled to forfeit our estates or a great deal of money, or suffer more besides? If you're afraid of something of that sort, dismiss it. It is right for us to run that risk to save you, and still greater risk if need be. Please, let me persuade you to do as I say.

SOCRATES. Of course I'm worried about those things, Crito, and many other things too.

CRITO. Then don't be afraid. In fact, it's not a large sum which certain people are willing to take to manage your escape, and as for the sycophants, you see how cheaply they can be bought; it wouldn't take much money for them. You have mine at your disposal, and it is, I think, enough, but if you're at all worried about me and think you shouldn't spend mine, your friends from abroad are ready. One of them, Simmias of Thebes, has brought enough money just for the purpose, and Cebes and quite a few others are ready, too. So as I say, you mustn't hesitate because of that. Nor should you be troubled about what you said in court, how if you went into exile you wouldn't know what to do with yourself. There are many places for you to go where they'd welcome you warmly, but if you want to go to Thessaly, I have friends there who will honor and protect you, so that no one will cause you distress.

Furthermore, Socrates, I think the thing you're doing is wrong. You betray yourself when you could be saved. You hasten a thing for yourself of a kind your very enemies might hasten for you—and have hastened, wishing you destroyed. In addition, I think you're betraying your sons. You desert them when you could raise and educate them; so far as you're concerned, they're to take what comes, and what is likely to come is just what usually comes to orphans in the poverty of their orphanhood. No. Either a man shouldn't have children, or he should accept the burden of raising and educating them; the choice you're making is one of the most heedless indifference. Your choice should be that of a good and courageous man—especially since you say you've had a lifelong concern for virtue. I'm ashamed, Socrates, ashamed both for you and for your friends, because its going to seem that the whole business was done through a kind of cowardice in us. The case was brought to court when it needn't have been. Then there was the conduct of the trial. And now, as the final absurdity of the whole affair, it is to look as if we let slip this final opportunity because of our own badness and cowardice, whereas we could have saved you or you could have saved yourself if we were worth anything at all. These things are bad, and shameful both to you and to us. Decide. Or rather at this hour, it isn't time to decide but to have decided. This is the last chance, because everything must be done this coming night, and if we wait it won't any longer be possible. Please, Socrates, be persuaded by me and do as I ask.

Socrates' Reply to Crito (46b–49a)

SOCRATES. My dear Crito, your eagerness is worth much, if rightly b directed. But if not, the greater it is, the worse. We must consider carefully whether this thing is to be done, for I am now and always have been the sort of man who is persuaded only by the argument which on reflection proves best to me, and I cannot throw over arguments I formerly accepted merely because of what has come; they still seem much c the same to me, and I honor them as I did before. If we can't find better ones, be assured that I will not give way to you, not even if the power of the multitude were far greater than it now is to frighten us like children with its threats of confiscation, bonds, and death.

Now, how might we most fairly consider the matter? Perhaps we should first take up this argument of yours about beliefs. We often used to say that some beliefs are worth paying attention to and others not. d Was that wrong? Or was it right before I had to die, whereas it is now obviously idle nonsense put for the sake of arguing? I'd like to join with you in common inquiry, Crito. Does that appear in any way changed now that I'm here? Let us dismiss it or be persuaded by it. We often used to say, I think—and we used to think it made sense—that among e the beliefs men entertain, some are to be regarded as important and others are not. Before the Gods, Crito, were we wrong? At least insofar as it lies in human agency, you aren't about to die tomorrow, and the 47a present situation won't distort your judgment. So consider the matter. Don't you think it's satisfactory to say that one shouldn't value the beliefs of every man, but of some men and not others, and that one shouldn't value every belief of men, but some beliefs and not others? Isn't that right?

CRITO. It is.

SOCRATES. Now, it's useful beliefs which should be valued, not harmful or bad ones?

CRITO. Yes.

SOCRATES. Useful ones being those of the wise, bad ones those of the foolish?

CRITO. Of course.

SOCRATES. To continue, what did we used to say about things like this. Suppose a man goes in for athletics. Does he pay attention to the b opinions, the praise and blame, of everybody, or only the one man who is his physician or trainer?

CRITO. Only the one.

SOCRATES. Then he ought to welcome the praise and fear the blame of that one man, not of the multitude.

CRITO. Clearly.

SOCRATES. So he is to train and exercise, eat and drink, in a way that seems good to a supervisor who knows and understands, rather than anyone else.

CRITO. True.

c SOCRATES. Very well. But if he disobeys that supervisor, scorns his judgment and praises, values those of the multitude who are without understanding, won't he suffer an evil?

CRITO. Of course.

SOCRATES. What is that evil? Whither does it tend, and into what possession of the man who disobeys?

CRITO. Into the body, clearly, for it ruins that.

SOCRATES. Right. And isn't this also true in other matters, Crito? We don't need to run through them all, but isn't it especially true of what is just and unjust, honorable and shameful, good and evil—just

d the things our decision is now concerned with? Are we to fear and follow the multitude in such matters? Or is it rather the opinion of one man, if he but have knowledge, which we must reverence and fear beyond all the rest, since if we do not follow it, we will permanently damage and corrupt something we used to say becomes better by justice and is harmed by injustice. Or is there no such thing?

CRITO. I certainly think there is, Socrates.

SOCRATES. Very well then, suppose that, by disobeying the opinion of those who understand, we were to ruin what becomes better by health

e and is damaged by disease. Would life be worth living for us once it has been damaged? That is the body, of course.

CRITO. Yes.

SOCRATES. Well, would life be worth living with a wretched, damaged body?

CRITO. Surely not.

SOCRATES. Then is it worth living when there is damage to what the just benefits and the unjust corrupts? Or do we think that this—

48a whatever it is of ours to which justice and injustice pertain—is of less worth than the body?

CRITO. Surely not.

SOCRATES. Of more worth?

CRITO. Far more.

SOCRATES. Then perhaps we shouldn't give much thought to what the multitude tells us, my friend. Perhaps we should rather think of what he will say who understands things just and unjust—he being but one man, and the very Truth itself. So your first claim, that we ought to pay attention to what the multitude thinks about what is just and honorable and good, is mistaken. "But then," someone might say, "the multitude can kill us."

CRITO. Yes, Socrates, it is very clear someone might say that.   b

SOCRATES. And yet, my friend, the conclusion we've reached still seems much as it did before. Then too, consider whether this agreement still abides too: that it is not living which is of most importance, but living well.

CRITO. It does.

SOCRATES. But "well" is the same as honorably and justly—does that abide too?

CRITO. Yes.

SOCRATES. Then in light of these arguments, we must consider whether or not it would be right for me to try to escape without permission of the Athenians. If it proves right, let us try; if not, let us   c dismiss the matter. But as for these other considerations you raise about loss of money and raising children and what people think—Crito, those are really fit topics for people who lightly kill and would raise to life again without a thought if they could—the multitude. As for us, the argument has chosen: there is nothing to be considered but the things we've already mentioned—whether it is right to give money with our thanks to those who are going to manage my escape, whether in actual   d fact we shall do injustice by doing any of these things. If it proves to be unjust, then perhaps we should give thought neither to death nor to anything else except the doing of injustice.

CRITO. You are right, Socrates. Look to what we should do.

SOCRATES. Let's examine the matter together, my friend, and if you can somehow refute what I'm going to say, do so, and I'll be persuaded. But if not, then please, my dear friend, please stop returning   e over and over again to the same argument about how I ought to escape from here without permission from the Athenians. For I count it important that I act with your agreement, not against your will. So look to the starting point of the inquiry. See whether it is satisfactorily stated,   49a and try to answer what I ask as you think proper.

CRITO. I'll certainly try.

Two Premises (49a–50a)

SOCRATES. Do we say that there are any circumstances in which injustice ought willingly or wittingly be done? Or is injustice to be done in some circumstances but not others? Is the doing of injustice in no

way honorable or good, as we often in the past agreed, or have those former agreements been cast aside these last few days? Has it long es-
b caped our notice, Crito, that as old men in serious discussion with each other we were really no better than children, or is it rather precisely as we used to claim: that whether the multitude agrees or not, whether we must suffer things still worse than this or things more easy to bear, still, the doing of injustice is in every circumstance shameful and evil for him who does it. Do we affirm that, or not?

CRITO. We do.

SOCRATES. Then one must never do injustice.

CRITO. Of course not.

SOCRATES. Nor return injustice for injustice, as the multitude think, since one must never do injustice.

c CRITO. That follows.

SOCRATES. Then does this? Ought one work injury, Crito?

CRITO. No, surely not, Socrates.

SOCRATES. Then is it just to work injury in return for having suffered it, as the multitude affirms?

CRITO. Not at all.

SOCRATES. No, for surely there is no difference between doing ill to men and doing injustice.

CRITO. True.

SOCRATES. Then one ought not return injustice for injustice or do ill to any man, no matter what one may suffer at their hands. Look to
d this, Crito. Do not agree against your real opinion, for I know that few men think or will ever think it true. Between those who accept it and those who do not, there is no common basis for decision; when they view each others' counsels, they must necessarily hold each other in contempt. So consider very carefully whether you unite with me in agreeing that it can never be right to do injustice or return it, or to ward off the suffering of evil by doing it in return, or whether you recoil from
e this starting point. I have long thought it true and do still. If you think otherwise, speak and instruct me. But if you abide by our former agreements, hear what follows.

CRITO. I do abide. Please go on.

SOCRATES. I say next, or rather, I ask, whether one is to do things he agreed with someone to do, given that they are just, or is one to deceive?

CRITO. One is to do them.

SOCRATES. Then observe what follows. If I escape from here with-
50a out persuading the City, am I not injuring someone, and someone I *least* ought? And am I not failing to abide by agreements that are just?

CRITO. Socrates, I can't answer what you ask, for I don't understand.

The Speech of the Laws of Athens (50a–54d)

SOCRATES. Look at it this way. Suppose I was about to run off from here, or whatever the thing should be called. And suppose the Laws, the common constitution of the City, came and stood before me and said, "Tell us, Socrates, what you intend to do. Do you mean by this b to destroy us? To destroy, as far as in you lies, the Laws and the City as a whole? Or do you think that a city can continue to exist and not be overturned, in which legal judgments once rendered are without force, but may be rendered unauthoritative by private citizens and so corrupted?

How are we to answer that, Crito, and questions like it? A good deal might be said, especially by an orator, in behalf of that law, now to be broken, which requires that judgments judicially rendered be authoritative. Or are we to reply that the City did us an injustice and c didn't decide the case correctly. Is that what we're to say?

CRITO. Most emphatically, Socrates.

SOCRATES. Then what if the Laws were to reply, "Socrates, was that really our agreement? Or was it rather to abide by such judgments as the City might render?" And if I were surprised at the question, they might go on, "There's no reason for surprise, Socrates. Answer the question, especially since you're so used to questions and answers. Come then, what charge do you lay against us and the City, that you should d undertake to destroy us? We gave you birth. It was through us that your father took your mother to wife and begot you. Tell us, then, those of us who are the Laws of Marriage, do you find some fault in us for being incorrect?"

"No fault," I would say.

"Then what about the Laws governing the rearing of children once born, and their education—the Laws under which you yourself were educated. Did we who are the Laws established for that purpose prescribe incorrectly when we directed your father to educate you in music e and gymnastic?"

"Correctly," I'd say.

"Very well, then. We bore you, reared you, educated you. Can you then say, first of all, that you are not our offspring and our slave—you, and your fathers before you? And if that's true, do you think that justice is on a level between you and us—that it is right for you to do in return what we may undertake to do to you? Was there such an equal balance toward your father, or your master if you happened to have one, so that you might return whatever was done to you—strike back when struck, speak ill when spoken ill to, things like that? Does such a possibility 51a then exist toward your Country and its Laws, so that if we should un-

dertake to destroy you, believing it just, you in return will undertake
so far as you are able to destroy us, your Country and its Laws? Will
you claim that this is right—you, who are so profoundly concerned about
virtue? Or are you so wise that you have let it escape your notice that
Country is to be honored beyond mother and father or any forebears;
b that it is more holy, more to be revered, of greater apportionment among
both gods and men of understanding; that an angered Country must be
reverenced and obeyed and given way to even more than an angered
father; that you must either persuade it to the contrary or do what it
bids and suffer quietly what it prescribes, whether blows or bonds,
whether you are led to war for wounds or death, still, these things are
to be done. The just lies here: never to give way, never to desert, never
to leave your post, but in war or court of law or any other place, to do
c what City and Country command—that, or to persuade it of what is by
nature just. It is not holy to use force against a mother or father; and
it is far more unholy to use force against your Country."

What are we to say to that, Crito? Do the Laws speak the truth?

CRITO. Yes, I think they do.

SOCRATES. "Then consider this, Socrates," the Laws might say.
"If we speak the truth, aren't you attempting to wrong us in what you
now undertake? We gave you birth. We nurtured you. We educated
d you. We gave to you and to every other citizen a share of every good
thing we could. Nonetheless, we continue to proclaim, by giving leave
to any Athenian who wishes, that when he has been admitted to the
rights of manhood and sees things in the City and its Laws which do
not please him, he may take what is his and go either to one of our
colonies or a foreign land. No law among us stands in the way or forbids
it. You may take what is yours and go where you like, if we and the
e City do not please you. But whoever among you stays, recognizing the
way we render judgment and govern the other affairs of the City, to
him at that point we say that by his action he has entered agreement
with us to do as we bid. And if he does not obey, we say that he commits
injustice in three ways: because he disobeys us, and we gave him birth;
because he disobeys us, and we nurtured him; because he agreed to obey
us and neither obeys nor persuades us that we are doing something in-
52a correct—even though we did not rudely command him to do as we bid,
but rather set before him the alternatives of doing it or persuading us
to the contrary. Those are the charges, Socrates, which we say will be
imputable to you if you do what you're planning. To you, and to you
not least, but more than any other Athenian.

And if I were to ask, "Why is that?" they might justly assail me
with the claim that, as it happened, I more than most Athenians had
b ratified this agreement. They might say, "Socrates, we have ample in-

dication that we and the City pleased you. You would not have stayed home in it to a degree surpassing all other Athenians, unless it pleased you in surpassing degree. You never left to go on a festival, except once to the Isthmian Games. You never went anywhere else except on military service. You never journeyed abroad as other men do, nor had you any desire to gain knowledge of other cities and their laws—we and this our City sufficed for you. So eagerly did you choose us, so eagerly did you agree to live as a citizen under us, that you even founded a c family here. So much did the City please you. Even at your very trial, you could have proposed exile as a penalty, and done with the City's knowledge and permission what you're now attempting to do against her will. But at the time, you made a fine pretence of not being distressed at having to die. You'd choose death before exile—so you said. But now you feel no shame at those words, nor any concern for us, who are the Laws. You attempt to destroy us by trying to run off like the d meanest of slaves, contrary to the compacts and agreements you entered with us to live as a citizen. First of all, then, tell us this: do we or do we not speak the truth when we say that by your actions, if not your words, you have agreed to live as a citizen under us?"

What am I to say to that, Crito? Must I not agree?

CRITO. Necessarily, Socrates.

SOCRATES. "Very well then," they might say. "Aren't you trespassing against your compacts and agreements with us? You didn't agree e under constraint, you weren't misled or deceived, nor were you forced to decide in too little time. You had seventy years, during which time you could have gone abroad if we did not please you, or your agreement came to seem to you unjust. But you preferred neither Sparta nor Crete, which you often used to say were well-governed, or any other city, Greek 53a or barbarian. Quite the contrary; you traveled abroad less often than the halt, the lame, and the blind. So the City pleased you, to a degree surpassing all other Athenians. Therefore, we pleased you, too, for to whom would a city be pleasing without laws? Are you, then, now not to abide by your agreements? If you are persuaded by us, Socrates, you will. You will not make yourself a butt of mockery by escaping.

"Consider too what good you will accomplish for yourself or your friends if you transgress or offend in this way. That your friends risk prosecution themselves, with deprivation of city and confiscation of es- b tate, could hardly be more clear. But you first. If you were to go to any of the cities nearest Athens, Thebes, say, or Megara, for both are well-governed, you would go as an enemy to their polity. Those concerned for their own cities would eye you with suspicion, believing you to be a corrupter of laws. Again, you would confirm the opinion of your judges c and lead them to think they rendered judgment justly, for a corrupter of laws may surely also be thought, and emphatically, a corrupter of young and ignorant men. Will you then shun well-governed cities, and men of the more estimable sort? Or will you associate with them and without sense of shame discuss—What will you discuss, Socrates? What arguments? The ones you used to offer here, about how virtue and justice are of highest worth for men, along with prescriptive custom and

d the Laws? 'The affair of Socrates'—don't you think it will look indecent? Surely you must. Then will you keep clear of such places and go to Thessaly among Crito's friends? There is plenty of license and unchastened disorder in Thessaly, and no doubt they'd delight in hearing you tell your absurd story about how you ran off from prison dressed up in disguise—a peasant's leather coat, perhaps? Disguised like a runaway slave, just to change your looks! That you are an old man with

e probably only a little time to live, and yet cling boldly to life with such greedy desire that you will transgress the highest laws—will there be no one to say it? Perhaps not, if you give no offense. But otherwise, Socrates, you will hear many a contemptible thing said of yourself. Will you then live like a slave, fawning on every man you meet? And what will you do in Thessaly when you get there, besides eat, as if you'd

54a exiled yourself for a banquet. But as for those arguments of yours about justice and the other virtues—what will they mean to us then?

"Still, you want to live for your children's sake, so you can raise and educate them. Really? Will you take them to Thessaly and raise and educate them there, and make foreigners out of them so they can enjoy that advantage too? If you don't, will they be better reared for your being alive but not with them? Your friends will look after them. Will they look after them if you go to Thessaly, but not if you go to the

b Place of the Dead? If those who call themselves your friends are really worth anything, you cannot believe that.

"Socrates, be persuaded by us, for we nurtured you. Put not life nor children nor anything else ahead of what is just, so that when you come to the Place of the Dead you may have all this to say in your defense to those who rule there. It will not appear better here, more virtuous, more just, more holy, for you or any of those around you to do this kind of thing here. And it will not *be* better for you on your

c arrival there. You now depart, if you depart, the victim of injustice at the hands of men, not at the hands of we who are the Laws. But if you escape, if you thus shamefully return injustice for injustice and injury for injury, if you trespass against your compacts and agreements with us, and work evil on those you least ought—yourself, your friends, your Country and its laws—we shall be angered at you while you live, and those our brothers who are the Laws in the Place of the Dead will not receive you kindly, knowing that you undertook so far as in you lay to destroy us. Do not be persuaded to do what Crito bids. Be persuaded d by us.''

Crito, my dear and faithful friend, I think I hear these things as the Corybants think they hear the pipes, and the droning murmur of the words sounds within me and makes me incapable of hearing aught else. Be assured that if you speak against the things I now think true, you will speak in vain. Still, if you suppose you can accomplish anything, please speak.

CRITO. Socrates, I cannot speak.

SOCRATES. Very well, Crito. Let us so act, since so the God leads. e

X

MENO

MENO. Can you tell me Socrates—is virtue something that can be taught? Or does it come by practice? Or is it neither teaching nor practice that gives it to a man but natural aptitude or something else?

SOCRATES. Well Meno, in the old days the Thessalians had a great reputation among the Greeks for their wealth and their horsemanship. Now it seems they are philosophers as well—especially the men of Larissa, where your friend Aristippus comes from. It is Gorgias who has done it. He went to that city and captured the hearts of the foremost of the Aleuadae for his wisdom (among them your own admirer Aristippus), not to speak of other leading Thessalians. In particular he got you into the habit of answering any question you might be asked, with the confidence and dignity appropriate to those who know the answers, just as he himself invites questions of every kind from anyone in the Greek world who wishes to ask, and never fails to answer them. But here at Athens, my dear Meno, it is just the reverse. There is a dearth of wisdom, and it looks as if it had migrated from our part of the country to

71 yours. At any rate if you put your question to any of our people, they will all alike laugh and say: 'You must think I am singularly fortunate, to know whether virtue can be taught or how it is acquired. The fact is that far from knowing whether it can be taught, I have no idea what virtue itself is.'

That is my own case. I share the poverty of my fellow-countrymen in this respect, and confess to my shame that I have no knowledge about virtue at all. And how can I know a property of something when I don't even know what it is? Do you suppose that somebody entirely ignorant who Meno is could say whether he is handsome and rich and well-born or the reverse? Is that possible, do you think?

MENO. No. But is this true about yourself, Socrates, that you don't even know what virtue is? Is this the report that we are to take home about you?

SOCRATES. Not only that; you may say also that, to the best of my belief, I have never yet met anyone who did know.

MENO. What! Didn't you meet Gorgias when he was here?

SOCRATES. Yes.

MENO. And you still didn't think he knew?

SOCRATES. I'm a forgetful sort of person, and I can't say just now what I thought at the time. Probably he did know, and I expect you know what he used to say about it. So remind me what it was, or tell me yourself if you will. No doubt you agree with him.

MENO. Yes I do.

SOCRATES. Then let's leave him out of it, since after all he isn't here. What do you yourself say virtue is? I do ask you in all earnestness not to refuse me, but to speak out. I shall be only too happy to be proved wrong if you and Gorgias turn out to know this, although I said I had never met anyone who did.

MENO. But there is no difficulty about it. First of all, if it is manly virtue you are after, it is easy to see that the virtue of a man consists in managing the city's affairs capably, and so that he will help his friends and injure his foes while taking care to come to no harm himself. Or if you want a woman's virtue, that is easily described. She must be a good housewife, careful with her stores and obedient to her husband. Then there is another virtue for a child, male or female, and another for an old man, free or slave as you like; and a great many more kinds of virtue, so that no one need be at a loss to say what it is. For every act and every time of life, with reference to each separate function, there is a virtue for each one of us, and similarly, I should say, a vice. 72

SOCRATES. I seem to be in luck. I wanted one virtue and I find that you have a whole swarm of virtues to offer. But seriously, to carry on this metaphor of the swarm, suppose I asked you what a bee is, what is its essential nature, and you replied that bees were of many different kinds, what would you say if I went on to ask: 'And is it in being bees that they are many and various and different from one another? Or would you agree that it is not in this respect that they differ, but in something else, some other quality like size or beauty?'

MENO. I should say that in so far as they are bees, they don't differ from one another at all.

SOCRATES. Suppose I then continued: 'Well, this is just what I want you to tell me. What is that character in respect of which they don't differ at all, but are all the same?' I presume you would have something to say?

MENO. I should.

SOCRATES. Then do the same with the virtues. Even if they are many and various, yet at least they all have some common character which makes them virtues. That is what ought to be kept in view by anyone who answers the question: 'What is virtue?' Do you follow me?

MENO. I think I do, but I don't yet really grasp the question as I should wish.

SOCRATES. Well, does this apply in your mind only to virtue, that there is a different one for a man and a woman and the rest? Is it the same with health and size and strength, or has health the same character everywhere, if it is health, whether it be in a man or any other creature?

MENO. I agree that health is the same in a man or in a woman.

SOCRATES. And what about size and strength? If a woman is strong, will it be the same thing, the same strength, that makes her strong? My meaning is that in its character as strength, it is no different, whether it be in a man or in a woman. Or do you think it is?

MENO. No.

73 SOCRATES. And will virtue differ, in its character as virtue, whether it be in a child or an old man, a woman or a man?

MENO. I somehow feel that this is not on the same level as the other cases.

SOCRATES. Well then, didn't you say that a man's virtue lay in directing the city well, and a woman's in directing her household well?

MENO. Yes.

SOCRATES. And is it possible to direct anything well—city or household or anything else—if not temperately and justly?

MENO. Certainly not.

SOCRATES. And that means with temperance and justice?

MENO. Of course.

SOCRATES. Then both man and woman need the same qualities, justice and temperance, if they are going to be good.

MENO. It looks like it.

SOCRATES. And what about your child and old man? Could they be good if they were incontinent and unjust?

MENO. Of course not.

SOCRATES. They must be temperate and just?

MENO. Yes.

SOCRATES. So everyone is good in the same way, since they become good by possessing the same qualities.

MENO. So it seems.

SOCRATES. And if they did not share the same virtue, they would not be good in the same way.

MENO. No.

SOCRATES. Seeing then that they all have the same virtue, try to remember and tell me what Gorgias, and you who share his opinion, say it is.

MENO. It must be simply the capacity to govern men, if you are looking for one quality to cover all the instances.

SOCRATES. Indeed I am. But does this virtue apply to a child or a slave? Should a slave be capable of governing his master, and if he does, is he still a slave?

MENO. I hardly think so.

SOCRATES. It certainly doesn't sound likely. And here is another point. You speak of 'capacity to govern'. Shall we not add 'justly but not otherwise'?

MENO. I think we should, for justice is virtue.

SOCRATES. Virtue, do you say, or a virtue?

MENO. What do you mean?

SOCRATES. Something quite general. Take roundness, for instance. I should say that it is a shape, not simply that it is shape, my reason being that there are other shapes as well.

MENO. I see your point, and I agree that there are other virtues besides justice.

SOCRATES. Tell me what they are. Just as I could name other shapes 74 if you told me to, in the same way mention some other virtues.

MENO. In my opinion then courage is a virtue and temperance and wisdom and dignity and many other things.

SOCRATES. This puts us back where we were. In a different way we have discovered a number of virtues when we were looking for one only. This single virtue, which permeates each of them, we cannot find.

MENO. No, I cannot yet grasp it as you want, a single virtue covering them all, as I do in other instances.

SOCRATES. I'm not surprised, but I shall do my best to get us a bit further if I can. You understand, I expect, that the question applies to everything. If someone took the example I mentioned just now, and asked you: 'What is shape?' and you replied that roundness is shape, and he then asked you as I did, 'Do you mean it is shape or a shape?' you would reply of course that it is a shape.

MENO. Certainly.

SOCRATES. Your reason being that there are other shapes as well.

MENO. Yes.

SOCRATES. And if he went on to ask you what they were, you would tell him.

MENO. Yes.

SOCRATES. And the same with colour—if he asked you what it is, and on your replying 'White', took you up with: 'Is white colour or a colour?' you would say it is *a* colour, because there are other colours as well.

MENO. I should.

SOCRATES. And if he asked you to, you would mention other colours which are just as much colours as white is.

MENO. Yes.

SOCRATES. Suppose then he pursued the question as I did, and objected: 'We always arrive at a plurality, but that is not the kind of answer I want. Seeing that you call these many particulars by one and the same name, and say that every one of them is a shape, even though they are the contrary of each other, tell me what this is which embraces round as well as straight, and what you mean by shape when you say that straightness is a shape as much as roundness. You do say that?'

MENO. Yes.

SOCRATES. 'And in saying it, do you mean that roundness is no more round than straight, and straightness no more straight than round?'

MENO. Of course not.

SOCRATES. 'Yet you do say that roundness is no more a shape than straightness, and the other way about.'

MENO. Quite true.

SOCRATES. 'Then what is this thing which is called "shape"? Try
5 to tell me.' If when asked this question either about shape or colour you said: 'But I don't understand what you want, or what you mean,' your questioner would perhaps be surprised and say: 'Don't you see that I am looking for what is the same in all of them?' Would you even so be unable to reply, if the question was: 'What is it that is common to roundness and straightness and the other things which you call shapes?' Do your best to answer, as practice for the question about virtue.

MENO. No, you do it, Socrates.

SOCRATES. Do you want me to give in to you?

MENO. Yes.

SOCRATES. And will you in your turn give me an answer about virtue?

MENO. I will.

SOCRATES. In that case I must do my best. It's in a good cause.

MENO. Certainly.

SOCRATES. Well now, let's try to tell you what shape is. See if you accept this definition. Let us define it as the only thing which always accompanies colour. Does that satisfy you, or do you want it in some other way? I should be content if your definition of virtue were on similar lines.

MENO. But that's a naive sort of definition, Socrates.

SOCRATES. How?

MENO. Shape, if I understand what you say, is what always accompanies colour. Well and good—but if somebody says that he doesn't know what colour is, but is no better off with it than he is with shape, what sort of answer have you given him, do you think?

SOCRATES. A true one: and if my questioner were one of the clever, disputatious and quarrelsome kind, I should say to him: 'You have heard my answer. If it is wrong, it is for you to take up the argument and refute it.' However, when friendly people, like you and me, want to converse with each other, one's reply must be milder and more conducive to discussion. By that I mean that it must not only be true, but must employ terms with which the questioner admits he is familiar. So I will try to answer you like that. Tell me therefore, whether you recognize the term 'end'; I mean limit or boundary—all these words I use in the same sense. Prodicus might perhaps quarrel with us, but I assume you speak of something being bounded or coming to an end. That is all I mean, nothing subtle.

MENO. I admit the notion, and believe I understand your meaning.

SOCRATES. And again, you recognize 'surface' and 'solid', as they 76 are used in geometry?

MENO. Yes.

SOCRATES. Then with these you should by this time understand my definition of shape. To cover all its instances, I say that shape is that in which a solid terminates, or more briefly, it is the limit of a solid.

MENO. And how do you define colour?

SOCRATES. What a shameless fellow you are, Meno. You keep bothering an old man to answer, but refuse to exercise your memory and tell me what was Gorgias's definition of virtue.

MENO. I will, Socrates, as soon as you tell me this.

SOCRATES. Anyone talking to you could tell blindfold that you are a handsome man and still have your admirers.

MENO. Why so?

SOCRATES. Because you are for ever laying down the law as spoilt boys do, who act the tyrant as long as their youth lasts. No doubt you have discovered that I can never resist good looks. Well, I will give in and let you have your answer.

MENO. Do by all means.

SOCRATES. Would you like an answer à la Gorgias, such as you would most readily follow?

MENO. Of course I should.

SOCRATES. You and he believe in Empedocles's theory of effluences, do you not?

MENO. Whole-heartedly.

SOCRATES. And passages to which and through which the effluences make their way?

MENO. Yes.

SOCRATES. Some of the effluences fit into some of the passages, whereas others are too coarse or too fine.

MENO. That is right.

SOCRATES. Now you recognize the term 'sight'?

MENO. Yes.

SOCRATES. From these notions, then, 'grasp what I would tell', as Pindar says. Colour is an effluence from shapes commensurate with sight and perceptible by it.

MENO. That seems to me an excellent answer.

SOCRATES. No doubt it is the sort you are used to. And you probably see that it provides a way to define sound and smell and many similar things.

MENO. So it does.

SOCRATES. Yes, it's a high-sounding answer, so you like it better than the one on shape.

MENO. I do.

SOCRATES. Nevertheless, son of Alexidemus, I am convinced that the other is better; and I believe you would agree with me if you had not, as you told me yesterday, to leave before the mysteries, but could stay and be initiated.

MENO. I would stay, Socrates, if you gave me more answers like this.

SOCRATES. You may be sure I shan't be lacking in keenness to do so, both for your sake and mine; but I'm afraid I may not be able to do it often. However, now it is your turn to do as you promised, and try to tell me the general nature of virtue. Stop making many out of one, as the humorists say when somebody breaks a plate. Just leave virtue whole and sound and tell me what it is, as in the examples I have given you.

MENO. It seems to me then, Socrates, that virtue is, in the words of the poet, 'to rejoice in the fine and have power', and I define it as desiring fine things and being able to acquire them.

SOCRATES. When you speak of a man desiring fine things, do you mean it is good things he desires?

MENO. Certainly.

SOCRATES. Then do you think some men desire evil and others good? Doesn't everyone, in your opinion, desire good things?

MENO. No.

SOCRATES. And would you say that the others suppose evils to be good, or do they still desire them although they recognize them as evil?

MENO. Both, I should say.

SOCRATES. What? Do you really think that anyone who recognizes evils for what they are, nevertheless desires them?

MENO. Yes.

SOCRATES. Desires in what way? To possess them?

MENO. Of course.

SOCRATES. In the belief that evil things bring advantage to their possessor, or harm?

MENO. Some in the first belief, but some also in the second.

SOCRATES. And do you believe that those who suppose evil things bring advantage understand that they are evil?

MENO. No, that I can't really believe.

SOCRATES. Isn't it clear then that this class, who don't recognize evils for what they are, don't desire evil but what they think is good, though in fact it is evil; those who through ignorance mistake bad things for good obviously desire the good.

MENO. For them I suppose that is true.

SOCRATES. Now as for those whom you speak of as desiring evils, in the belief that they do harm to their possessor, these presumably know that they will be injured by them?

MENO. They must.

SOCRATES. And don't they believe that whoever is injured is, in so far as he is injured, unhappy?

MENO. That too they must believe.

SOCRATES. And unfortunate?

MENO. Yes.

SOCRATES. Well, does anybody want to be unhappy and unfortunate?

MENO. I suppose not.

SOCRATES. Then if not, nobody desires what is evil; for what else is unhappiness but desiring evil things and getting them?

MENO. It looks as if you are right, Socrates, and nobody desires what is evil.

SOCRATES. Now you have just said that virtue consists in a wish for good things plus the power to acquire them. In this definition the wish is common to everyone, and in that respect no one is better than his neighbour.

MENO. So it appears.

SOCRATES. So if one man is better than another, it must evidently be in respect of the power, and virtue, according to your account, is the power of acquiring good things.

MENO. Yes, my opinion is exactly as you now express it.

SOCRATES. Let us see whether you have hit the truth this time. You

78

may well be right. The power of acquiring good things, you say, is virtue?

MENO. Yes.

SOCRATES. And by good do you mean such things as health and wealth?

MENO. I include the gaining both of gold and silver and of high and honourable office in the State.

SOCRATES. Are these the only classes of goods that you recognize?

MENO. Yes, I mean everything of that sort.

SOCRATES. Right. In the definition of Meno, hereditary guest-friend of the Great King, the acquisition of gold and silver is virtue. Do you add 'just and righteous' to the word 'acquisition', or doesn't it make any difference to you? Do you call it virtue all the same even if they are unjustly acquired?

MENO. Certainly not.

SOCRATES. Vice then?

MENO. Most certainly.

SOCRATES. So it seems that justice or temperance or piety, or some other part of virtue, must attach to the acquisition. Otherwise, although it is a means to good things, it will not be virtue.

MENO. No, how could you have virtue without these?

SOCRATES. In fact lack of gold and silver, if it results from failure to acquire it—either for oneself or another—in circumstances which would have made its acquisition unjust, is itself virtue.

MENO. It would seem so.

SOCRATES. Then to have such goods is no more virtue than to lack them. Rather we may say that whatever is accompanied by justice is 9 virtue, whatever is without qualities of that sort is vice.

MENO. I agree that your conclusion seems inescapable.

SOCRATES. But a few minutes ago we called each of these—justice, temperance, and the rest—a part of virtue?

MENO. Yes, we did.

SOCRATES. So it seems you are making a fool of me.

MENO. How so, Socrates?

SOCRATES. I have just asked you not to break virtue up into fragments, and given you models of the type of answer I wanted, but taking no notice of this you tell me that virtue consists in the acquisition of good things with justice; and justice, you agree, is a part of virtue.

MENO. True.

SOCRATES. So it follows from your own statements that to act with a part of virtue is virtue, if you call justice and all the rest parts of virtue. The point I want to make is that whereas I asked you to give me an account of virtue as a whole, far from telling me what it is itself you say that every action is virtue which exhibits a part of virtue, as if you had already told me what the whole is, so that I should recognize it even if you chop it up into bits. It seems to me that we must put the same old question to you, my dear Meno—the question: 'What is virtue?'—if every act becomes virtue when combined with a part of virtue. That is, after all, what it means to say that every act performed with justice is virtue. Don't you agree that the same question needs to be put? Does anyone know what a part of virtue is, without knowing the whole?

MENO. I suppose not.

SOCRATES. No, and if you remember, when I replied to you about shape just now, I believe we rejected the type of answer that employs terms which are still in question and not yet agreed upon.

MENO. We did, and rightly.

SOCRATES. Then please do the same. While the nature of virtue as a whole is still under question, don't suppose that you can explain it to anyone in terms of its parts, or by any similar type of explanation. Understand rather that the same question remains to be answered; you say this and that about virtue, but what *is* it? Does this seem nonsense to you?

MENO. No, to me it seems right enough.

SOCRATES. Then go back to the beginning and answer my question. What do you and your friend say that virtue is?

MENO. Socrates, even before I met you they told me that in plain truth you are a perplexed man yourself and reduce others to perplexity. At this moment I feel you are exercising magic and witchcraft upon me and positively laying me under your spell until I am just a mass of helplessness. If I may be flippant, I think that not only in outward appearance but in other respects as well you are exactly like the flat sting-ray that one meets in the sea. Whenever anyone comes into contact with it, it numbs him, and that is the sort of thing that you seem to be doing to me now. My mind and my lips are literally numb, and I have nothing to reply to you. Yet I have spoken about virtue hundreds of times, held forth often on the subject in front of large audiences, and very well too, or so I thought. Now I can't even say what it is. In my opinion you are well advised not to leave Athens and live abroad. If you behaved like this as a foreigner in another country, you would most likely be arrested as a wizard.

SOCRATES. You're a real rascal, Meno. You nearly took me in.

MENO. Just what do you mean?

SOCRATES. I see why you used a simile about me.

MENO. Why, do you think?

SOCRATES. To be compared to something in return. All good-looking people, I know perfectly well, enjoy a game of comparisons.

They get the best of it, for naturally handsome folk provoke handsome
similes. But I'm not going to oblige you. As for myself, if the sting-ray
paralyses others only through being paralysed itself, then the comparison is just, but not otherwise. It isn't that, knowing the answers myself,
I perplex other people. The truth is rather that I infect them also with
the perplexity I feel myself. So with virtue now. I don't know what it
is. You may have known before you came into contact with me, but
now you look as if you don't. Nevertheless I am ready to carry out,
together with you, a joint investigation and inquiry into what it is.

MENO. But how will you look for something when you don't in the
least know what it is? How on earth are you going to set up something
you don't know as the object of your search? To put it another way,
even if you come right up against it, how will you know that what you
have found is the thing you didn't know?

SOCRATES. I know what you mean. Do you realize that what you
are bringing up is the trick argument that a man cannot try to discover
either what he knows or what he does not know? He would not seek
what he knows, for since he knows it there is no need of the inquiry,
nor what he does not know, for in that case he does not even know what
he is to look for.

81   MENO. Well, do you think it a good argument?

SOCRATES. No.

MENO. Can you explain how it fails?

SOCRATES. I can. I have heard from men and women who understand the truths of religion—

*(Here he presumably pauses to emphasize the solemn change of tone which
the dialogue undergoes at this point.)*

MENO. What did they say?

SOCRATES. Something true, I thought, and fine.

MENO. What was it, and who were they?

SOCRATES. Those who tell it are priests and priestesses of the sort
who make it their business to be able to account for the functions which
they perform. Pindar speaks of it too, and many another of the poets
who are divinely inspired. What they say is this—see whether you think
they are speaking the truth. They say that the soul of man is immortal:
at one time it comes to an end—that which is called death—and at another is born again, but is never finally exterminated. On these grounds
a man must live all his days as righteously as possible. For those from
whom

> Persephone receives requital for ancient doom,
> In the ninth year she restores again
> Their souls to the sun above.

> From whom rise noble kings
> And the swift in strength and greatest in wisdom;
> And for the rest of time
> They are called heroes and sanctified by men.[1]

Thus the soul, since it is immortal and has been born many times, and has seen all things both here and in the other world, has learned everything that is. So we need not be surprised if it can recall the knowledge of virtue or anything else which, as we see, it once possessed. All nature is akin, and the soul has learned everything, so that when a man has recalled a single piece of knowledge—*learned* it, in ordinary language—there is no reason why he should not find out all the rest, if he keeps a stout heart and does not grow weary of the search; for seeking and learning are in fact nothing but recollection.

We ought not then to be led astray by the contentious argument you quoted. It would make us lazy, and is music in the ears of weaklings. The other doctrine produces energetic seekers after knowledge; and being convinced of its truth, I am ready, with your help, to inquire into the nature of virtue.

MENO. I see, Socrates. But what do you mean when you say that we don't learn anything, but that what we call learning is recollection? Can you teach me that it is so?

SOCRATES. I have just said that you're a rascal, and now you ask me if I can teach you, when I say there is no such thing as teaching, only recollection. Evidently you want to catch me contradicting myself straight away.

MENO. No, honestly, Socrates, I wasn't thinking of that. It was just habit. If you can in any way make clear to me that what you say is true, please do.

SOCRATES. It isn't an easy thing, but still I should like to do what I can since you ask me. I see you have a large number of retainers here. Call one of them, anyone you like, and I will use him to demonstrate it to you.

MENO. Certainly. (*To a slave-boy.*) Come here.

SOCRATES. He is a Greek and speaks our language?

MENO. Indeed yes—born and bred in the house.

SOCRATES. Listen carefully then, and see whether it seems to you that he is learning from me or simply being reminded.

MENO. I will.

SOCRATES. Now boy, you know that a square is a figure like this?

(*Socrates begins to draw figures in the sand at his feet. He points to the square* ABCD.)

---

[1]The quotation is from Pindar.

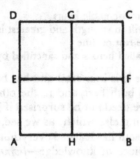

BOY. Yes.

SOCRATES. It has all these four sides equal?

BOY. Yes.

SOCRATES. And these lines which go through the middle of it are also equal? (The lines EF, GH.)

BOY. Yes.

SOCRATES. Such a figure could be either larger or smaller, could it not?

BOY. Yes.

SOCRATES. Now if this side is two feet long, and this side the same, how many feet will the whole be? Put it this way. If it were two feet in this direction and only one in that, must not the area be two feet taken once?

BOY. Yes.

SOCRATES. But since it is two feet this way also, does it not become twice two feet?

BOY. Yes.

SOCRATES. And how many feet is twice two? Work it out and tell me.

BOY. Four.

SOCRATES. Now could one draw another figure double the size of this, but similar, that is, with all its sides equal like this one?

BOY. Yes.

SOCRATES. How many feet will its area be?

BOY. Eight.

SOCRATES. Now then, try to tell me how long each of its sides will be. The present figure has a side of two feet. What will be the side of the double-sized one?

BOY. It will be double, Socrates, obviously.

SOCRATES. You see, Meno, that I am not teaching him anything, only asking. Now he thinks he knows the length of the side of the eight-feet square.

MENO. Yes.

SOCRATES. But does he?

MENO. Certainly not.

SOCRATES. He thinks it is twice the length of the other.

MENO. Yes.

SOCRATES. Now watch how he recollects things in order—the proper way to recollect.

You say that the side of double length produces the double-sized 83 figure? Like this I mean, not long this way and short that. It must be equal on all sides like the first figure, only twice its size, that is eight feet. Think a moment whether you still expect to get it from doubling the side.

BOY. Yes, I do.

SOCRATES. Well now, shall we have a line double the length of this (AB) if we add another the same length at this end (BJ)?

BOY. Yes.

SOCRATES. It is on this line then, according to you, that we shall make the eight-feet square, by taking four of the same length?

BOY. Yes.

SOCRATES. Let us draw in four equal lines (*i.e. counting* AJ, *and adding* JK, KL, *and* LA *made complete by drawing in its second half* LD), using the first as a base. Does this not give us what you call the eight-feet figure?

BOY. Certainly.

SOCRATES. But does it contain these four squares, each equal to the original four-feet one?

> (*Socrates has drawn in the lines* CM, CN *to complete the squares that he wishes to point out.*)

BOY. Yes.

SOCRATES. How big is it then? Won't it be four times as big?

BOY. Of course.

SOCRATES. And is four times the same as twice?

BOY. Of course not.

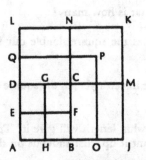

SOCRATES. So doubling the side has given us not a double but a fourfold figure?

BOY. True.

SOCRATES. And four times four are sixteen, are they not?

BOY. Yes.

SOCRATES. Then how big is the side of the eight-feet figure? This one has given us four times the original area, hasn't it?

BOY. Yes.

SOCRATES. And a side half the length gave us a square of four feet?

BOY. Yes.

SOCRATES. Good. And isn't a square of eight feet double this one and half that?

BOY. Yes.

SOCRATES. Will it not have a side greater than this one but less than that?

BOY. I think it will.

SOCRATES. Right. Always answer what you think. Now tell me: was not this side two feet long, and this one four?

BOY. Yes.

SOCRATES. Then the side of the eight-feet figure must be longer than two feet but shorter than four?

BOY. It must.

SOCRATES. Try to say how long you think it is.

BOY. Three feet.

SOCRATES. If so, shall we add half of this bit (BO, *half of* BJ) and make it three feet? Here are two, and this is one, and on this side similarly we have two plus one; and here is the figure you want.

(Socrates completes the square AOPQ.*)*

BOY. Yes.

SOCRATES. If it is three feet this way and three that, will the whole area be three times three feet?

BOY. It looks like it.

SOCRATES. And that is how many?

BOY. Nine.

SOCRATES. Whereas the square double our first square had to be how many?

BOY. Eight.

SOCRATES. But we haven't yet got the square of eight feet even from a three-feet side?

BOY. No.

SOCRATES. Then what length will give it? Try to tell us exactly. If
84 you don't want to count it up, just show us on the diagram.

BOY. It's no use, Socrates, I just don't know.

SOCRATES. Observe, Meno, the stage he has reached on the path of recollection. At the beginning he did not know the side of the square of eight feet. Nor indeed does he know it now, but then he thought he knew it and answered boldly, as was appropriate—he felt no perplexity. Now however he does feel perplexed. Not only does he not know the answer; he doesn't even think he knows.

MENO. Quite true.

SOCRATES. Isn't he in a better position now in relation to what he didn't know?

MENO. I admit that too.

SOCRATES. So in perplexing him and numbing him like the sting-ray, have we done him any harm?

MENO. I think not.

SOCRATES. In fact we have helped him to some extent towards finding out the right answer, for now not only is he ignorant of it but he will be quite glad to look for it. Up to now, he thought he could speak well and fluently, on many occasions and before large audiences, on the subject of a square double the size of a given square, maintaining that it must have a side of double the length.

MENO. No doubt.

SOCRATES. Do you suppose then that he would have attempted to look for, or learn, what he thought he knew (though he did not), before he was thrown into perplexity, became aware of his ignorance, and felt a desire to know?

MENO. No.

SOCRATES. Then the numbing process was good for him?

MENO. I agree.

SOCRATES. Now notice what, starting from this state of perplexity, he will discover by seeking the truth in company with me, though I simply ask him questions without teaching him. Be ready to catch me if I give him any instruction or explanation instead of simply interrogating him on his own opinions.

(Socrates here rubs out the previous figures and starts again.)

Tell me, boy, is not this our square of four feet? (ABCD.) You understand?

BOY. Yes.

SOCRATES. Now we can add another equal to it like this? (BCEF.)

BOY. Yes.

SOCRATES. And a third here, equal to each of the others? (CEGH.)

BOY. Yes.

SOCRATES. And then we can fill in this one in the corner? (DCHJ.)

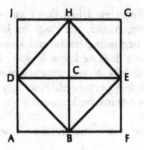

BOY. Yes.

SOCRATES. Then here we have four equal squares?

BOY. Yes.

SOCRATES. And how many times the size of the first square is the whole?

BOY. Four times.

SOCRATES. And we want one double the size. You remember?

BOY. Yes.

85   SOCRATES. Now does this line going from corner to corner cut each of these squares in half?

BOY. Yes.

SOCRATES. And these are four equal lines enclosing this area? (BEHD.)

BOY. They are.

SOCRATES. Now think. How big is this area?

BOY. I don't understand.

SOCRATES. Here are four squares. Has not each line cut off the inner half of each of them?

BOY. Yes.

SOCRATES. And how many such halves are there in this figure? (BEHD.)

BOY. Four.

SOCRATES. And how many in this one? (ABCD.)

BOY. Two.

SOCRATES. And what is the relation of four to two?

BOY. Double.

SOCRATES. How big is this figure then?

BOY. Eight feet.

SOCRATES. On what base?

BOY. This one.

SOCRATES. The line which goes from corner to corner of the square of four feet?

BOY. Yes.

SOCRATES. The technical name for it is 'diagonal'; so if we use that name, it is your personal opinion that the square on the diagonal of the original square is double its area.

BOY. That is so, Socrates.

SOCRATES. What do you think, Meno? Has he answered with any opinions that were not his own?

MENO. No, they were all his.

SOCRATES. Yet he did not know, as we agreed a few minutes ago.

MENO. True.

SOCRATES. But these opinions were somewhere in him, were they not?

MENO. Yes.

SOCRATES. So a man who does not know has in himself true opinions on a subject without having knowledge.

MENO. It would appear so.

SOCRATES. At present these opinions, being newly aroused, have a dream-like quality. But if the same questions are put to him on many occasions and in different ways, you can see that in the end he will have a knowledge on the subject as accurate as anybody's.

MENO. Probably.

SOCRATES. This knowledge will not come from teaching but from questioning. He will recover it for himself.

MENO. Yes.

SOCRATES. And the spontaneous recovery of knowledge that is in him is recollection, isn't it?

MENO. Yes.

SOCRATES. Either then he has at some time acquired the knowledge which he now has, or he has always possessed it. If he always possessed it, he must always have known; if on the other hand he acquired it at some previous time, it cannot have been in this life, unless somebody has taught him geometry. He will behave in the same way with all geometrical knowledge, and every other subject. Has anyone taught him all these? You ought to know, especially as he has been brought up in your household.

MENO. Yes, I know that no one ever taught him.

SOCRATES. And has he these opinions, or hasn't he?

MENO. It seems we can't deny it.

SOCRATES. Then if he did not acquire them in this life, isn't it im- 86 mediately clear that he possessed and had learned them during some other period?

MENO. It seems so.

SOCRATES. When he was not in human shape?

MENO. Yes.

SOCRATES. If then there are going to exist in him, both while he is and while he is not a man, true opinions which can be aroused by questioning and turned into knowledge, may we say that his soul has been for ever in a state of knowledge? Clearly he always either is or is not a man.

MENO. Clearly.

SOCRATES. And if the truth about reality is always in our soul, the soul must be immortal, and one must take courage and try to discover—that is, to recollect—what one doesn't happen to know, or (more correctly) remember, at the moment.

MENO. Somehow or other I believe you are right.

SOCRATES. I think I am. I shouldn't like to take my oath on the whole story, but one thing I am ready to fight for as long as I can, in word and act: that is, that we shall be better, braver and more active men if we believe it right to look for what we don't know than if we believe there is no point in looking because what we don't know we can never discover.

MENO. There too I am sure you are right.

SOCRATES. Then since we are agreed that it is right to inquire into something that one does not know, are you ready to face with me the question: what is virtue?

MENO. Quite ready. All the same, I would rather consider the question as I put it at the beginning, and hear your views on it; that is, are we to pursue virtue as something that can be taught, or do men have it as a gift of nature or how?

SOCRATES. If I were your master as well as my own, Meno, we should not have inquired whether or not virtue can be taught until we had first asked the main question—what it is; but not only do you make no attempt to govern your own actions—you prize your freedom, I suppose—but you attempt to govern mine. And you succeed too, so I shall let you have your way. There's nothing else for it, and it seems we must inquire into a single property of something about whose essential nature we are still in the dark. Just grant me one small relaxation of your sway and allow me, in considering whether or not it can be taught, to make use of a hypothesis—the sort of thing, I mean, that geometers often use in their inquiries. When they are asked, for example, about a given area, whether it is possible for this area to be inscribed as a triangle in 87 a given circle, they will probably reply: 'I don't know yet whether it fulfils the conditions, but I think I have a hypothesis which will help us in the matter. It is this. If the area is such that, when one has applied it [sc. as a rectangle] to the given line [i.e. the diameter] of the circle, it is deficient by another rectangle similar to the one which is applied, then,

I should say, one result follows; if not, the result is different. If you ask me, then, about the inscription of the figure in the circle—whether it is possible or not—I am ready to answer you in this hypothetical way.'[2]

Let us do the same about virtue. Since we don't know what it is or what it resembles, let us use a hypothesis in investigating whether it is teachable or not. We shall say: 'What attribute of the soul must virtue be, if it is to be teachable or otherwise?' Well, in the first place, if it is anything else but knowledge, is there a possibility of anyone teaching it—or, in the language we used just now, reminding someone of it? We needn't worry about which name we are to give to the process, but simply ask: will it be teachable? Isn't it plain to everyone that a man is not taught anything except knowledge?

MENO. That would be my view.

SOCRATES. If on the other hand virtue is some sort of knowledge, clearly it could be taught.

MENO. Certainly.

SOCRATES. So that question is easily settled; I mean, on what condition virtue would be teachable.

MENO. Yes.

SOCRATES. The next point then, I suppose, is to find out whether virtue is knowledge or something different.

MENO. That is the next question, I agree.

SOCRATES. Well then, do we assert that virtue is something good? Is that assumption a firm one for us?

MENO. Undoubtedly.

SOCRATES. That being so, if there exists any good thing different from, and not associated with, knowledge, virtue will not necessarily be any form of knowledge. If on the other hand knowledge embraces everything that is good, we shall be right to suspect that virtue is knowledge.

MENO. Agreed.

SOCRATES. First then, is it virtue which makes us good?

MENO. Yes.

SOCRATES. And if good, then advantageous. All good things are advantageous, are they not?

MENO. Yes.

SOCRATES. So virtue itself must be something advantageous?

MENO. That follows also.

---

[2]The geometrical illustration here adduced by Socrates is very loosely and obscurely expressed. Sir Thomas Heath in his *History of Greek Mathematics* (1921, vol. i, p. 298) says that C. Blass, writing in 1861, already knew of thirty different interpretations, and that many more had appeared since then. Fortunately it is not necessary to understand the example in order to grasp the hypothetical method which Socrates is expounding.

SOCRATES. Now suppose we consider what are the sort of things that profit us. Take them in a list. Health, we may say, and strength and good looks, and wealth—these and their like we call advantageous, you agree?

MENO. Yes.

88 SOCRATES. Yet we also speak of these things as sometimes doing harm. Would you object to that statement?

MENO. No, it is so.

SOCRATES. Now look here: what is the controlling factor which determines whether each of these is advantageous or harmful? Isn't it right use which makes them advantageous, and lack of it, harmful?

MENO. Certainly.

SOCRATES. We must also take spiritual qualities into consideration. You recognize such things as temperance, justice, courage, quickness of mind, memory, nobility of character and others?

MENO. Yes of course I do.

SOCRATES. Then take any such qualities which in your view are not knowledge but something different. Don't you think they may be harmful as well as advantageous? Courage for instance, if it is something thoughtless, just a sort of confidence. Isn't it true that to be confident without reason does a man harm, whereas a reasoned confidence profits him?

MENO. Yes.

SOCRATES. Temperance and quickness of mind are no different. Learning and discipline are profitable in conjunction with wisdom, but without it harmful.

MENO. That is emphatically true.

SOCRATES. In short, everything that the human spirit undertakes or suffers will lead to happiness when it is guided by wisdom, but to the opposite, when guided by folly.

MENO. A reasonable conclusion.

SOCRATES. If then virtue is an attribute of the Spirit, and one which cannot fail to be beneficial, it must be wisdom; for all spiritual qualities in and by themselves are neither advantageous nor harmful, but become advantageous or harmful by the presence with them of wisdom or folly. If we accept this argument, then virtue, to be something advantageous, must be a sort of wisdom.

MENO. I agree.

SOCRATES. To go back to the other class of things, wealth and the like, of which we said just now that they are sometimes good and sometimes harmful, isn't it the same with them? Just as wisdom when it governs our other psychological impulses turn them to advantage, and folly turns them to harm, so the mind by its right use and control of these material assets makes them profitable, and by wrong use renders them harmful.

MENO. Certainly.

SOCRATES. And the right user is the mind of the wise man, the wrong user the mind of the foolish.

MENO. That is so.

SOCRATES. So we may say in general that the goodness of nonspiritual assets depends on our spiritual character, and the goodness of that 89 on wisdom. This argument shows that the advantageous element must be wisdom; and virtue, we agree, is advantageous, so that amounts to saying that virtue, either in whole or in part, is wisdom.

MENO. The argument seems to me fair enough.

SOCRATES. If so, good men cannot be good by nature.

MENO. I suppose not.

SOCRATES. There is another point. If they were, there would probably be experts among us who could recognize the naturally good at an early stage. They would point them out to us and we should take them and shut them away safely in the Acropolis, sealing them up more carefully than bullion to protect them from corruption and ensure that when they came to maturity they would be of use to the State.

MENO. It would be likely enough.

SOCRATES. Since then goodness does not come by nature, is it got by learning?

MENO. I don't see how we can escape the conclusion. Indeed it is obvious on our assumption that, if virtue is knowledge, it is teachable.

SOCRATES. I suppose so. But I wonder if we were right to bind ourselves to that.

MENO. Well, it seemed all right just now.

SOCRATES. Yes, but to be sound it has got to seem all right not only 'just now' but at this moment and in the future.

MENO. Of course. But what has occurred to you to make you turn against it and suspect that virtue may not be knowledge?

SOCRATES. I'll tell you. I don't withdraw from the position that if it is knowledge, it must be teachable; but as for its being knowledge, see whether you think my doubts on this point are well founded. If any thing—not virtue only—is a possible subject of instruction, must there not be teachers and students of it?

MENO. Surely.

SOCRATES. And what of the converse, that if there are neither teachers nor students of a subject, we may safely infer that it cannot be taught?

MENO. That is true. But don't you think there are teachers of virtue?

SOCRATES. All I can say is that I have often looked to see if there

are any, and in spite of all my efforts I cannot find them, though I have
had plenty of fellow-searchers, the kind of men especially whom I believe to have most experience in such matters. But look, Meno, here's
a piece of luck. Anytus has just sat down beside us. We couldn't do
90 better than make him a partner in our inquiry. In the first place he is
the son of Anthemion, a man of property and good sense, who didn't
get his money out of the blue or as a gift—like Ismenias of Thebes who
has just come into the fortune of a Croesus—but earned it by his own
brains and hard work. Besides this he shows himself a decent, modest
citizen with no arrogance or bombast or offensiveness about him. Also
he brought up his son well and had him properly educated, as the Athenian people appreciate: look how they elect him into the highest offices
in the State. This is certainly the right sort of man with whom to inquire
whether there are any teachers of virtue, and if so who they are.

Please help us, Anytus—Meno, who is a friend of your family, and
myself—to find out who may be the teachers of this subject. Look at it
like this. If we wanted Meno to become a good doctor, shouldn't we
send him to the doctors to be taught?

ANYTUS. Of course.

SOCRATES. And if we wanted him to become a shoemaker, to the
shoemakers?

ANYTUS. Yes.

SOCRATES. And so on with other trades?

ANYTUS. Yes.

SOCRATES. Now another relevant question. When we say that to
make Meno a doctor we should be right in sending him to the doctors,
have we in mind that the sensible thing is to send him to those who
profess the subject rather than to those who don't, men who charge a
fee as professionals, having announced that they are prepared to teach
whoever likes to come and learn?

ANYTUS. Yes.

SOCRATES. The same is surely true of flute-playing and other accomplishments. If you want to make someone a performer on the flute
it would be very foolish to refuse to send him to those who undertake
to teach the art and are paid for it, but to go and bother other people
instead and have him try to learn from them—people who don't set up
to be teachers or take any pupils in the subject which we want our young
man to learn. Doesn't that sound very unreasonable?

ANYTUS. Sheer stupidity I should say.

91 SOCRATES. I agree. And now we can both consult together about
our visitor Meno. He has been telling me all this while that he longs to
acquire the kind of wisdom and virtue which fits men to manage an
estate or govern a city, to look after their parents, and to entertain and

send off guests in proper style, both their own countrymen and foreigners. With this in mind, to whom would it be right to send him? What we have just said seems to show that the right people are those who profess to be teachers of virtue and offer their services freely to any Greek who wishes to learn, charging a fixed fee for their instruction.

ANYTUS. Whom do you mean by that, Socrates?

SOCRATES. Surely you know yourself that they are the men called Sophists.

ANYTUS. Good heavens, what a thing to say! I hope no relative of mine or any of my friends, Athenian or foreign, would be so mad as to go and let himself be ruined by those people. That's what they are, the mainfest ruin and corruption of anyone who comes into contact with them.

SOCRATES. What, Anytus? Can they be so different from other claimants to useful knowledge that they not only don't do good, like the rest, to the material that one puts in their charge, but on the contrary spoil it—and have the effrontery to take money for doing so? I for one find it difficult to believe you. I know that one of them alone, Protagoras, earned more money from being a Sophist than an outstandingly fine craftsman like Phidias and ten other sculptors put together. A man who mends old shoes or restores coats couldn't get away with it for a month if he gave them back in worse condition than he received them; he would soon find himself starving. Surely it is incredible that Protagoras took in the whole of Greece, corrupting his pupils and sending them away worse than when they came to him, for more than forty years. I believe he was nearly seventy when he died, and had been practising for forty years, and all that time—indeed to this very day—his reputation has been consistently high; and there are plenty of others besides Protagoras, some before his time and others still alive. Are we 92 to suppose from your remark that they consciously deceive and ruin young men, or are they unaware of it themselves? Can these remarkably clever men—as some regard them—be mad enough for that?

ANYTUS. Far from it, Socrates. It isn't they who are mad, but rather the young men who hand over their money, and those responsible for them, who let them get into the Sophists' hands, are even worse. Worst of all are the cities who allow them in, or don't expel them, whether it be a foreigner or one of themselves who tries that sort of game.

SOCRATES. Has one of the Sophists done you a personal injury, or why are you so hard on them?

ANYTUS. Heavens, no! I've never in my life had anything to do with a single one of them, nor would I hear of any of my family doing so.

SOCRATES. So you've had no experience of them at all?

ANYTUS. And don't want any either.

SOCRATES. You surprise me. How can you know what is good or bad in something when you have no experience of it?

ANYTUS. Quite easily. At any rate I know *their* kind, whether I've had experience or not.

SOCRATES. It must be second sight, I suppose; for how else you know about them, judging from what you tell me yourself, I can't imagine. However, we are not asking whose instruction it is that would ruin Meno's character. Let us say that those are the Sophists if you like, and tell us instead about the ones we want. You can do a good turn to a friend of your father's house if you will let him know to whom in our great city he should apply for proficiency in the kind of virtue I have just described.

ANYTUS. Why not tell him yourself?

SOCRATES. Well, I did mention the men who in my opinion teach these things, but apparently I was talking nonsense. So you say, and you may well be right. Now it is your turn to direct him; mention the name of any Athenian you like.

ANYTUS. But why mention a particular individual? Any decent Athenian gentleman whom he happens to meet, if he follows his advice, will make him a better man than the Sophists would.

SOCRATES. And did these gentlemen get their fine qualities spontaneously—self-taught, as it were, and yet able to teach this untaught virtue to others?

ANYTUS. I suppose they in their turn learned it from forebears who were gentlemen like themselves. Would you deny that there have been many good men in our city?

SOCRATES. On the contrary, there are plenty of good statesmen here in Athens and have been as good in the past. The question is, have they also been good teachers of their own virtue? That is the point we are discussing now—not whether or not there are good men in Athens or whether there have been in past times, but whether virtue can be taught. It amounts to the question whether the good men of this and former times have known how to hand on to someone else the goodness that was in themselves, or whether on the contrary it is not something that can be handed over, or that one man can receive from another. That is what Meno and I have long been puzzling over. Look at it from your own point of view. You would say that Themistocles was a good man?

ANYTUS. Yes, none better.

SOCRATES. And that he, if anyone, must have been a good teacher of his own virtue?

ANYTUS. I suppose so, if he wanted to be.

SOCRATES. But don't you think he must have wanted others to become worthy men—above all, surely, his own son? Do you suppose he grudged him this and purposely didn't pass on his own virtue to him? You must have heard that he had his son Cleophantus so well trained in horsemanship that he could stand upright on horseback and throw a javelin from that position; and many other wonderful accomplishments the young man had, for his father had him taught and made expert in every skill that a good instructor could impart. You must have heard this from older people?

ANYTUS. Yes.

SOCRATES. No one, then, could say that there was anything wrong with the boy's natural powers?

ANYTUS. Perhaps not.

SOCRATES. But have you ever heard anyone, young or old, say that Cleophantus the son of Themistocles was a good and wise man in the way that his father was?

ANYTUS. Certainly not.

SOCRATES. Must we conclude then that Themistocles's aim was to educate his son in other accomplishments, but not to make him any better than his neighbours in his own type of wisdom—that is, supposing that virtue could be taught?

ANYTUS. I hardly think we can.

SOCRATES. So much then for Themistocles as a teacher of virtue, whom you yourself agree to have been one of the best men of former 94 times. Take another example, Aristides son of Lysimachus. You accept him as a good man?

ANYTUS. Surely.

SOCRATES. He too gave his son Lysimachus the best education in Athens, in all subjects where a teacher could help; but did he make him a better man than his neighbour? You know him, I think, and can say what he is like. Or again there is Pericles, that great and wise man. He brought up two sons, Paralus and Xanthippus, and had them taught riding, music, athletics, and all the other skilled pursuits till they were as good as any in Athens. Did he then not want to make them good men? Yes, he wanted that, no doubt, but I am afraid it is something that cannot be done by teaching. And in case you should think that only very few, and those the most insignificant, lacked this power, consider that Thucydides also had two sons, Melesias and Stephanus, to whom he gave an excellent education. Among other things they were the best wrestlers in Athens, for he gave one to Xanthias to train and the other to Eudoxus—the two who, I understand, were considered the finest wrestlers of their time. You remember?

ANYTUS. I have heard of them.

SOCRATES. Surely then he would never have had his children taught these expensive pursuits and yet refused to teach them to be good men—which would have cost nothing at all—if virtue could have been taught?

You are not going to tell me that Thucydides was a man of no account, or that he had not plenty of friends both at Athens and among the allies? He came of an influential family and was a great power both here and in the rest of Greece. If virtue could have been taught, he would have found the man to make his sons good, either among our own citizens or abroad, supposing his political duties left him no time to do it himself. No, my dear Anytus, it looks as if it cannot be taught.

ANYTUS. You seem to me, Socrates, to be too ready to run people down. My advice to you, if you will listen to it, is to be careful. I dare say that in all cities it is easier to do a man harm than good, and it is
95 certainly so here, as I expect you know yourself.

SOCRATES. Anytus seems angry, Meno, and I am not surprised. He thinks I am slandering our statesmen, and moreover he believes himself to be one of them. He doesn't know what slander really is: if he ever finds out he will forgive me.

However, tell me this yourself: are there not similar fine characters in your country?

MENO. Yes, certainly.

SOCRATES. Do they come forward of their own accord to teach the young? Do they agree that they are teachers and that virtue can be taught?

MENO. No indeed, they don't agree on it at all. Sometimes you will hear them say that it can be taught, sometimes that it cannot.

SOCRATES. Ought we then to class as teachers of it men who are not even agreed that it can be taught?

MENO. Hardly, I think.

SOCRATES. And what about the Sophists, the only people who profess to teach it? Do you think they do?

MENO. The thing I particularly admire about Gorgias, Socrates, is that you will never hear him make this claim; indeed he laughs at the others when he hears them do so. In his view his job is to make clever speakers.

SOCRATES. So you too don't think the Sophists are teachers?

MENO. I really can't say. Like most people I waver—sometimes I think they are and sometimes I think they are not.

SOCRATES. Has it ever occurred to you that you and our statesmen are not alone in this? The poet Theognis likewise says in one place that virtue is teachable and in another that it is not.

MENO. Really? Where?

SOCRATES. In the elegiacs in which he writes:

> Eat, drink, and sit with men of power and weight,
> Nor scorn to gain the favour of the great.
> For fine men's teaching to fine ways will win thee:
> Low company destroys what wit is in thee.

There he speaks as if virtue can be taught, doesn't he?

MENO. Clearly.

SOCRATES. But elsewhere he changes his ground a little:

> Were mind by art created and instilled
> Immense rewards had soon the pockets filled

of the people who could do this. Moreover

> No good man's son would ever worthless be,
> Taught by wise counsel. But no teacher's skill   96
> Can turn to good what is created ill.

Do you see how he contradicts himself?

MENO. Plainly.

SOCRATES. Can you name any other subject, in which the professed teachers are not only not recognized as teachers of others, but are thought to have no understanding of it themselves, and to be no good at the very subject they profess to teach; whereas those who are acknowledged to be the best at it are in two minds whether it can be taught or not? When people are so confused about a subject, can you say that they are in a true sense teachers?

MENO. Certainly not.

SOCRATES. Well, if neither the Sophists nor those who display fine qualities themselves are teachers of virtue, I am sure no one else can be, and if there are no teachers, there can be no students either.

MENO. I quite agree.

SOCRATES. And we have also agreed that a subject of which there were neither teachers nor students was not one which could be taught.

MENO. That is so.

SOCRATES. Now there turn out to be neither teachers nor students of virtue, so it would appear that virtue cannot be taught.

MENO. So it seems, if we have made no mistake; and it makes me wonder, Socrates, whether there are in fact no good men at all, or how they are produced when they do appear.

SOCRATES. I have a suspicion, Meno, that you and I are not much good. Our masters Gorgias and Prodicus have not trained us properly. We must certainly take ourselves in hand, and try to find someone who will improve us by hook or by crook. I say this with our recent discussion in mind, for absurdly enough we failed to perceive that it is not only under the guidance of knowledge that human action is well and rightly conducted. I believe that may be what prevents us from seeing how it is that men are made good.

MENO. What do you mean?

SOCRATES. This. We were correct, were we not, in agreeing that good men must be profitable or useful? It cannot be otherwise, can it?   97

MENO. No.

SOCRATES. And again that they will be of some use if they conduct our affairs aright—that also was correct?

MENO. Yes.

SOCRATES. But in insisting that knowledge was a *sine qua non* for right leadership, we look like being mistaken.

MENO. How so?

SOCRATES. Let me explain. If someone knows the way to Larissa, or anywhere else you like, then when he goes there and takes others with him he will be a good and capable guide, you would agree?

MENO. Of course.

SOCRATES. But if a man judges correctly which is the road, though he has never been there and doesn't know it, will he not also guide others aright?

MENO. Yes, he will.

SOCRATES. And as long as he has a correct opinion on the points about which the other has knowledge, he will be just as good a guide, believing the truth but not knowing it.

MENO. Just as good.

SOCRATES. Therefore true opinion is as good a guide as knowledge for the purpose of acting rightly. That is what we left out just now in our discussion of the nature of virtue, when we said that knowledge is the only guide to right action. There was also, it seems, true opinion.

MENO. It seems so.

SOCRATES. So right opinion is something no less useful than knowledge.

MENO. Except that the man with knowledge will always be successful, and the man with right opinion only sometimes.

SOCRATES. What? Will he not always be successful so long as he has the right opinion?

MENO. That must be so, I suppose. In that case, I wonder why knowledge should be so much more prized than right opinion, and indeed how there is any difference between them.

SOCRATES. Shall I tell you the reason for your surprise, or do you know it?

MENO. No, tell me.

SOCRATES. It is because you have not observed the statues of Daedalus. Perhaps you don't have them in your country.

MENO. What makes you say that?

SOCRATES. They too, if no one ties them down, run away and escape. If tied, they stay where they are put.

MENO. What of it?

SOCRATES. If you have one of his works untethered, it is not worth much: it gives you the slip like a runaway slave. But a tethered specimen is very valuable, for they are magnificent creations. And that, I say may, has a bearing on the matter of true opinions. True opinions are a fine thing and do all sorts of good so long as they stay in their place; but they will not stay long. They run away from a man's mind, so they are not worth much until you tether them by working out the reason. That process, my dear Meno, is recollection, as we agreed earlier. Once they are tied down, they become knowledge, and are stable. That is why knowledge is something more valuable than right opinion. What distinguishes one from the other is the tether.

MENO. It does seem something like that, certainly.

SOCRATES. Well of course, I have only been using an analogy myself, not knowledge. But it is not, I am sure, a mere guess to say that right opinion and knowledge are different. There are few things that I should claim to know, but that at least is among them, whatever else is.

MENO. You are quite right.

SOCRATES. And is this right too, that true opinion when it governs any course of action produces as good a result as knowledge?

MENO. Yes, that too is right, I think.

SOCRATES. So that for practical purposes right opinion is no less useful than knowledge, and the man who has it is no less useful than the one who knows.

MENO. That is so.

SOCRATES. Now we have agreed that the good man is useful.

MENO. Yes.

SOCRATES. To recapitulate then: assuming that there are men good and useful to the community, it is not only knowledge that makes them so, but also right opinion, and neither of these comes by nature but both are acquired—or do you think either of them *is* natural?

MENO. No.

SOCRATES. So if both are acquired, good men themselves are not good by nature.

MENO. No.

SOCRATES. That being so, the next thing we inquired was whether their goodness was a matter of teaching, and we decided that it would be, if virtue were knowledge, and conversely, that if it could be taught, it would be knowledge.

MENO. Yes.

SOCRATES. Next, that if there were teachers of it, it could be taught, but not if there were none.

MENO. That was so.

SOCRATES. But we have agreed that there are no teachers of it, and so that it cannot be taught and is not knowledge.

MENO. We did.

SOCRATES. At the same time we agreed that it is something good, and that to be useful and good consists in giving right guidance.

99   MENO. Yes.

SOCRATES. And that these two, true opinion and knowledge, are the only things which direct us aright and the possession of which makes a man a true guide. We may except chance, because what turns out right by chance is not due to human direction, and say that where human control leads to right ends, these two principles are directive, true opinion and knowledge.

MENO. Yes, I agree.

SOCRATES. Now since virtue cannot be taught, we can no longer believe it to be knowledge, so that one of our two good and useful principles is excluded, and knowledge is not the guide in public life.

MENO. No.

SOCRATES. It is not then by the possession of any wisdom that such men as Themistocles, and the others whom Anytus mentioned just now, became leaders in their cities. This fact, that they do not owe their eminence to knowledge, will explain why they are unable to make others like themselves.

MENO. No doubt it is as you say.

SOCRATES. That leaves us with the other alternative, that it is well-aimed conjecture which statesmen employ in upholding their countries' welfare. Their position in relation to knowledge is no different from that of prophets and tellers of oracles, who under divine inspiration utter many truths, but have no knowledge of what they are saying.

MENO. It must be something like that.

SOCRATES. And ought we not to reckon those men divine who with no conscious thought are repeatedly and outstandingly successful in what they do or say?

MENO. Certainly.

SOCRATES. We are right therefore to give this title to the oracular priests and the prophets that I mentioned, and to poets of every description. Statesmen, too, when by their speeches they get great things done yet know nothing of what they are saying, are to be considered as acting no less under divine influence, inspired and possessed by the divinity.

MENO. Certainly.

SOCRATES. Women, you know, Meno, do call good men "divine," and the Spartans too, when they are singing a good man's praises, say "He is divine."

MENO. And it looks as if they are right—though our friend Anytus may be annoyed with you for saying so.

SOCRATES. I can't help that. We will talk to him some other time.

If all we have said in this discussion, and the questions we have asked, have been right, virtue will be acquired neither by nature nor by teaching. Whoever has it gets it by divine dispensation without taking 100 thought, unless he be the kind of statesman who can create another like himself. Should there be such a man, he would be among the living practically what Homer said Tiresias was among the dead, when he described him as the only one in the underworld who kept his wits— "the others are mere flitting shades." Where virtue is concerned such a man would be just like that, a solid reality among shadows.

MENO. This is finely put, Socrates.

SOCRATES. On our present reasoning then, whoever has virtue gets it by divine dispensation. But we shall not understand the truth of the matter until, before asking how men get virtue, we try to discover what virtue is in and by itself. Now it is time for me to go; and my request to you is that you will allay the anger of your friend Anytus by convincing him that what you now believe is true. If you succeed, the Athenians may have cause to thank you.

XI

THE SPEECH OF SOCRATES
IN THE SYMPOSIUM

The Speech of Diotima (201d–212a)

Eros as Intermediate (201d–202d)

(201)d   And now I'll let you[1] go. But the account of Eros I once heard from a Mantinaean woman, Diotima, who was wise in this and many other things—she once caused the Athenians, when they offered sacrifices before the Plague,[2] a ten year delay in the onset of the disease, and it was she who instructed me in the things of love—well, the account she used to give I will myself try to describe to you[3] on my own, from the agreements which Agathon and I have reached, as best I can.

e   It is necessary then, Agathon, as you explained, first to recount who Eros is and of what sort, and his works afterward.[4] Now, I think I can most easily recount it as she used to do in examining me. For I used to say pretty much the same sort of thing to her that Agathon was saying now to me, that Eros would be a great god, but of beautiful things; but she refuted me by these arguments I offered him, that Eros by my account would be neither beautiful nor good.

And I said, How do you mean, Diotima? Eros then is ugly and bad?

And she said, Hush, don't blaspheme! Or do you suppose that whatever is not beautiful is necessarily ugly?

202a   Yes, of course.

And not wise, ignorant? Are you not aware that there is something intermediate between wisdom and ignorance?

From *The Dialogues of Plato*, vol. II, trans. R. E. Allen. Copyright © 1991 Yale University Press.

[1]Singular, addressed to Agathon.
[2]In 430 B.C. See Thucydides II 47.
[3]Plural. Socrates is now addressing the company.
[4]Socrates repeats loosely Agathon's formula at 195a, but with significant emphasis on who Eros is (τίς ἐστιν).

What is it?

Don't you know, she said, that right opinion without ability to render an account is not knowledge—for how could an unaccountable thing be knowledge?—nor is it ignorance—for how could what meets with what is be ignorance? Right opinion is surely that sort of thing, intermediate be-tween wisdom and ignorance.

True, I said.

Then don't compel what is not beautiful to be ugly, nor what is not b good to be bad. So too for Eros, since you yourself agree that he is neither good nor beautiful, do not any the more for that reason suppose he must be ugly and bad, she said, but rather something between these two.

And yet, I said, everybody agrees he is a great god.

You mean everybody who doesn't know, or also those who know? she said.

Why, absolutely everybody.

She laughed and said, And how would he be agreed to be a great god, Socrates, by those who say he is not even a god at all?

Who are these people? I said.   c

You're one, she said, and I'm another.

And I said, How can you say that?

Easily, she replied. For tell me: don't you claim that all gods are happy and beautiful? Or would you dare deny that any god is beautiful and happy?

Emphatically not, I said.

But you say that it is those who possess good and beautiful things who are happy?

Of course.

Moreover, you have agreed that Eros, by reason of lack of good and d beautiful things, desires those very things he lacks.

Yes, I have.

How then would what is without portion of[5] beautiful and good things be a god?

In no way, it seems.

Then you see, she said, that even you do not acknowledge Eros to be a god?

Then what is he? I said. A mortal?

Hardly.

But what, then?

As I said before, she said, intermediate between mortal and immortal.

---

[5] ἄμοιρος, an unusual word used by Agathon at 197d, cf. 181.

Eros as Daimon (202d–203a)

What is he, Diotima?

A great divinity, Socrates; for in fact, the whole realm of divinities is intermediate between god and mortal.

e   Having what power? I said.

Interpreting and conveying things from men to gods and things from gods to men, prayers and sacrifices from the one, commands and requitals in exhange for sacrifices from the other, since, being in between both, it fills the region between both so that the All is bound together with itself.

203a Through this realm moves all prophetic art and the art of priests having to do with sacrifices and rituals and spells, and all power of prophecy and enchantment. God does not mingle with man, but all intercourse and conversation of gods with men, waking and sleeping, are through this realm. He who is wise about such things as this is a divine man, but he who is wise about any other arts or crafts is a mere mechanic.[6] These divinities, then, are many and manifold, and one of them is Eros.

The Myth of Poros and Penia (102a–e)

Who is his father and mother?[7] I said.

b   It's a rather long story, she replied; nevertheless, I will tell you. When Aphrodite was born, the gods banqueted, both the others and Poros (Resourcefulness), son of Metis (Wisdom). When they dined, Penia (Want) came to beg, as one would expect when there is a feast, and hung about the doors. Well, Poros got drunk on nectar—for there was as yet no wine—and went into the garden of Zeus where, weighed down by drink, he slept. So Penia plotted to have a child by Poros by reason of her own resource-

c lessness, and lay with him and conceived Eros. This is why Eros has been a follower and servant of Aphrodite, because he was begotten on the day of her birth,[8] and at the same time it is why he is by nature a lover of beauty, since Aphrodite is beautiful.

Because then Eros is son of Poros and Penia, this is his fortune: first, he is ever poor, and far from being delicate and beautiful, as most people

d suppose,[9] he on the contrary is rough and hard and homeless and unshod, ever lying on the ground without bedding, sleeping in doorsteps and be-

---

[6] Cf. *Republic* VI 495d–e.

[7] The question arises from the fact that Eros is a 'divinity,' and so either a god or a child of gods.

[8] Dover remarks, *ad loc*: "Hesiod's injuction (*WD* 735 f.) 'do not beget offspring when you have come home from a funeral, but from a festival of the immortals,' shows the existence of a belief in some kind of connection between the character or fortunes of a child and the occasion of his or her conception."

[9] And as Agathon did, 195c 7.

side roads under the open sky. Because he has his mother's nature, he dwells ever with want. But on the other hand, by favor of his father, he ever plots for good and beautiful things, because he is courageous, eager and intense, a clever hunter ever weaving some new device, desiring under-standing and capable of it, a lover of wisdom through the whole of life, clever at enchantment, a sorcerer and a sophist.[10] And he is by nature nei- e ther mortal nor immortal, but sometimes on the same day he lives and flourishes, whenever he is full of resource, but then he dies and comes back to life again by reason of the nature of his father, though what is provided ever slips away so that Eros is never rich nor at a loss ...

Eros as Philosopher (203e–204c)

... and on the other hand he is between wisdom and ignorance. For things stand thus: no god loves wisdom or desires to become wise—for he is so, nor, if anyone else is wise, does he love wisdom. On the other hand, neither 204a do the ignorant love wisdom nor desire to become wise; for ignorance is difficult just in this, that though not beautiful and good, nor wise, it yet seems to itself to be sufficient. He who does not think himself in need does not desire what he does not think he lacks.

Then who are these lovers of wisdom, Diotima, I said, if they are nei-ther the wise nor the ignorant?

Why, at this point it's clear even to a child, she said, that they are those b intermediate between both of these, and that Eros is among them. For wis-dom is surely among the most beautiful of things, but Eros is love of the beautiful, so Eros is necessarily a philosopher, a lover of wisdom, and, be-ing a philosopher, intermediate between wisdom and ignorance. His birth is the cause of this too: for he is of a wise and resourceful father, but of an unwise and resourceless mother.

This then is the nature of the divinity, my dear Socrates; but there is c nothing surprising about what you thought Eros is. You thought, as I gather from what you say, that Eros is what is loved, not the loving. That is why, I think, Eros seemed utterly beautiful to you. In fact, it is what is beloved that is really beautiful and charming and perfect and deemed blessed; but loving has this other character, of the sort I described.

Eros as Wish for Happiness (204c–205a)

And I said: Very well then, my dear lady; you speak beautifully. But if Eros is of this sort, what usefulness does he have for men?

---

[10]Diotima is herself said to be "most wise," and her mode or reply compared to "an accomplished sophist" at 208b–c.

d   That's the next thing I will try to teach you, Socrates, she said. For since Eros is of this sort and this parentage, he is of beautiful things, as you say, But suppose someone asked us, Why is Eros of beautiful things, Socrates and Diotima? I will ask still more clearly: Why does he who loves love beautiful things?

And I replied, To possess them for himself.

But the answer still longs for the following kind of question, she said. What will he have who possesses beautiful things?

I still can't quite readily answer that question I said.

e   But suppose someone changed 'beautiful' to 'good,' she said, and then inquired: Come, Socrates, he who loves loves good things. Why does he love them?

To possess them for himself.

And what will he have who possesses good things?

This I can answer more easily, I said. He will be happy.

205a   Yes, she said, for the happy are happy by possession of good things, and there is no need in addition to ask further for what purpose he who wishes to be happy wishes it. On the contrary, the answer seems final.

True, I replied.

Diotima's Definition of Eros (205a–206a)

Do you think this wish and this love are common to all men, and that everyone wishes to possess good things for themselves forever?

Yes, I said: it is common to everyone.

b   Why is it then, Socrates, she said, that we do not say that everyone loves, if indeed everyone loves the same things, and always, but we rather say that some love and some do not?

I'm also surprised myself, I said.

Don't be, she said. It is because we subtract a certain species of eros and name it Eros, applying the name of the whole, but we use other names for the others.

As what? I said.

As this. You know that making (*poiesis*) is something manifold; for surely the cause of passing from not being into being for anything whatever is all a making, so that the productions of all the arts are makings, and the practitioners of them are all makers (*poietai*).

c   True.

But nevertheless, she said, you know that they are not called makers (*poietai*) but have other names, while from all making one single part has been subtracted, that concerned with music[11] and meter, and given the

---

[11]μουσική (sc. τέχνη) was any art over which the Muses preside, but especially poetry, which was sung. Cf. *Republic* II 376e.

name of the whole. For this alone is called poetry (*poiesis*), and those who have this part of making called poets (*poietai*).

True, I said.

So also then for Eros. In general, it is every desire for good things and happiness, "Eros most great, and wily[12] in all;" but those who turn to him in various other ways, either moneymaking or athletics or philosophy, are neither said to love nor be lovers, while those who sedulously pursue one single species get the name of the whole, Eros, and are said to love and be lovers.

Very likely true, I said.

Yes, and a certain story is told, she said, that those in love are seeking the other half of themselves. But my account is that love is of neither half nor whole, my friend, unless it happens to be actually good, since people are willing to cut off their own hands and feet if they think these possessions of theirs are bad. For they each refuse, I think, to cleave even to what is their own, unless one calls what is good kindred and his own, and what is bad alien;[13] because there is nothing else which men love than the good. Do you agree?

I most certainly do, I said.

Then one may state without qualification that men love the good? she said.

Yes, I said.

Really? Is it not to be added, she said, that they also love the good to be their own?

It must.

And not only to be theirs, she said, but also to be theirs forever?

This too is to be added.

In sum, then, she said, Eros is of the good being his own forever.

Very true, I replied.

The Works of Eros: Begetting in Beauty (206b–207a)

Then given that Eros is ever this, she said, in what way, and in what activity, would eagerness and effort among those pursuing it be called Eros? What does this work happen to be? Can you say?

No, I said. If I could, I would not admire your wisdom so much, Diotima, and keep coming to you to learn these very things.

But I will tell you, she said: this work is begetting[14] in beauty, in respect to both the body and the soul.

---

[12]δολερός. The adjective is otherwise rare in Plato, but applied at *Hippias Minor* 365c to Odysseus. See above, 203d.

[13]Cf. *Lysis* 210b–c, 221d–222e.

[14]Or, bearing children, τόκος.

What you say needs divination, I said, and I don't understand.

c   Why, I'll put it more clearly, she said. All men are pregnant in respect to both the body and the soul, Socrates, she said, and when they reach a certain age, our nature desires to beget.[15] It cannot beget in ugliness, but only in beauty. The intercourse of man and woman is a begetting. This is a divine thing, and pregnancy and procreation are an immortal element in the mortal living creature. It is impossible for birth to take place in what
d is discordant. But ugliness is in discord with all that is divine, and beauty concordant. So the Goddess of Beauty is at the birth Moira (Fate) and Eilithyia (She Who Comes in Time of Need). That is why, when what is pregnant draws near to the beautiful, it becomes tender and full of gladness and pours itself forth and begets and procreates; but when it draws near to the ugly, it shrivels in sullen grief and turns away and goes slack and does not beget, but carries with difficulty the conception within it. Whence it is that one who is pregnant and already swollen is vehemently excited over the beautiful, because it releases its possessor from great pangs. For Socrates, she said, Eros is not, as you suppose, of the beautiful.

e   But what, then?

It is of procreation and begetting of children in the beautiful.

Very well, I said.

207a   To be sure, she said. But why of procreation? Because procreation is everlasting and immortal as far as is possible for something mortal. Eros necessarily desires immortality with the good, from what has been agreed,[16] since its object is to possess the good for itself forever. It necessarily follows from this account, then, that Eros is also love of immortality.

Immortality and the Mortal Nature (207a–208b)

All these things she taught me at various times when she discoursed about matters of love. Once she asked, Socrates, what do you think is responsible for this love and desire? Or are you not aware how strangely all beasts are disposed, footed and winged, when they desire to reproduce—
b all sick and erotically disposed, first for intercourse with each other and next for the nurture of the offspring? In their behalf the weakest are ready to do battle with the strongest, to die in their behalf,[17] to be racked with hunger themselves so as to feed them, to do anything else. One might suppose, she said, that men do these things on the basis of reflection; but what is the cause of beasts being erotically disposed this way? Can you tell?

c   And I again used to say I didn't know.

---

[15]τίκτειν, verb of which τόκος is the corresponding noun.
[16]Cf. 206a.
[17]Compare Phaedrus' speech, 179b.

She said, Then do you think you'll ever become skilled in the things of love if you don't understand this?

Why, that's why I keep coming to you, Diotima, as I just now said,[18] knowing I need instruction. Please tell me the cause of this, and other things concerning matters of love.

If then you are persuaded, she said, that love is by nature of what we d have often agreed, do not be surprised. For here, in the animal world, by the same account as before, the mortal nature seeks so far as it can to exist forever and be immortal. It can do so only in this way, by giving birth, ever leaving behind a different new thing in place of the old, since even in the time in which each single living creature is said to live and to be the same— for example, as a man is said to be the same from youth to old age—though he never has the same things in himself, he nevertheless is called the same, but he is ever becoming new while otherwise perishing, in respect to hair and flesh and bone and blood and the entire body.

And not only in respect to the body but also in respect to the soul,[19] e its character and habits, opinions, desires, pleasures, pains, fears, are each never present in each man as the same, but some are coming to be, others perishing. Much more extraordinary still, not only are some kinds of 208a knowledge coming to be and others perishing in us, and we are never the same even in respect to the kinds of knowledge, but also each single one among the kinds of knowledge is affected in the same way. For what is called studying exists because knowledge leaves us; forgetting is departure of knowledge, but study, by introducing again a new memory in place of what departs, preserves the knowledge so that it seems to be the same.[20]

For it is in this way that all that is mortal is preserved: not by being b ever completely the same, like the divine, but by leaving behind, as it departs and becomes older, a different new thing of the same sort as it was. By this device, Socrates, she said, what is mortal has a share of immortality—both body and everything else; but the immortal by another device. Do not be surprised, then, if everything by nature values its own offshoot; it is for the sake of immortality that this eagerness and love attends upon all.

Creation in Respect to Body and Soul (208b–209e)

When I heard this account I was surprised and said, Why really, my most wise Diotima, are these things actually true?

---

[18]Cf. 206b.

[19]Application of the claim to the second case distinguished at 206b.

[20]Compare Aristotle's account of perception, memory, and experience at *Meta.* I 980a 29ff., *Post. An.* II 99b 35ff.

c   And she replied as the accomplished sophists do, Know it well, Socrates. Since indeed if you will look to the love of honor among men, you'd be surprised by the unreasonableness of which I've spoken, unless you keep in mind and reflect on how strangely disposed men are by Eros to make a name and "lay up store of immortal glory for everlasting time;" for

d this they are ready to run every risk, even more than for their children, to spend money, to perform labors of every sort, to die for it. Do you think, she said, that Alcestis would have died for Admetus, or Achilles after Patroclus, or our own Cadmus for his children's kingdoms, if they had not thought that the fame of their own virtue, which we now cherish, would be immortal?[21] Far from it, she said; rather, I think, it is for immortal virtue and the sort of fame which brings glory that everyone does everything, and the more in so far as they are better. For they love the immortal.

e   Some men are pregnant in respect to their bodies, she said, and turn more to women and are lovers in that way, providing in all future time, as they suppose, immortality and happiness for themselves through getting

209a children. Others are pregnant in respect to their soul—for there are those, she said, who are still more fertile in their souls than in their bodies with what pertains to soul to conceive and bear. What then so pertains? Practical wisdom and the rest of virtue—of which, indeed, all the poets are procreators, and as many craftsmen as are said to be inventors. But the greatest and most beautiful kind of practical wisdom by far, she said, is that concerned with the right ordering of cities and households, for which the name is temperance and justice.

b   On the other hand, whenever one of them is pregnant of soul from youth, being divine,[22] and reaches the age when he then desires to bear and beget, he too then, I think, goes about seeking the beautiful in which he might beget; for he will never beget in the ugly. Now, because he is fertile, he welcomes beautiful rather than ugly bodies, and should he meet with a beautiful and noble and naturally gifted soul, he welcomes the conjunction of both even more, and to this person he is straightway resourceful in speaking about virtue, and what sort of thing the good man must be concerned with and his pursuits; and he undertakes to educate him.

c   For I think that in touching the beautiful [person] and holding familiar intercourse with it [him], he bears and begets what he has long since conceived, and both present and absent he remembers and nurtures what has

---

[21]Diotima here contradicts Phaedrus' speech, 179b–180a, arguing that Alcestis and Achilles sacrificed themselves not for love, but for love of honor, in order to be remembered.

[22]Reading θεῖος with BTW Oxy., and Bury, against Parmentier's emendation, ἤθεος accepted by Burnet and Dover. The reading is supported by *Meno* 99c–d and anticipated by 206c 6.

been begotten in common with that [him],[23] so that people of this sort gain a far greater communion with each other than that of the sharing of children, and a more steadfast friendship, because they have held in common children more beautiful and more immortal. Everyone would prefer for himself to have had such children as these, rather than the human kind, d and they look to Homer and Hesiod and the rest of our good poets and envy offspring of the sort they left behind, offspring which, being such themselves, provide immortal fame and remembrance.

But if you wish, she said, look at the sort of children Lycurgus left behind in Sparta, saviors of Sparta and one might almost say of Greece.[24] Solon also is honored among you because of his begetting of the Laws,[25] and other men in other times and many other places, both in Greece and e among the Barbarians, who have displayed many beautiful deeds and begotten every sort of virtue; for whom, also, many temples and sacred rites have come into being because of children such as these, but none because of children merely human.

The Ladder of Love (209e–210e)

Into these things of love, Socrates, perhaps even you may be initiated; 210a but I do not know whether you can be initiated into the rites and revelations for the sake of which these actually exist if one pursues them correctly. Well, I will speak of them and spare no effort, she said; try to follow if you can.

It is necessary, she said, for him who proceeds rightly to this thing to begin while still young by going to beautiful bodies; and first, if his guide[26] guides rightly, to love one single body and beget there beautiful discourses; b next, to recognize that the beauty in any body whatever is akin to that in any other body, and if it is necessary to pursue the beautiful as it attaches to form, it is quite unreasonable to believe that the beauty in all bodies is not one and the same. Realizing this, he is constituted a lover of all beautiful bodies and relaxes this vehemence for one, looking down on it and believing it of small importance.

After this he must come to believe that beauty in souls is more to be

---

[23]This sentence is purposefully ambiguous: it refers to the beloved, but also anticipates what will be said in the Greater Mysteries of Eros about Beauty itself.

[24]Diotima speaks as a Mantinaean, located in the Peloponnesus and allied with Sparta. Lycurgus, like Solon in Athenas, was supposed to have given laws to Sparta, and those laws are here regarded as his children.

[25]The Laws of Athens were often referred to as the Laws of Solon, though there had been (sometimes unacknowledged) changes since his time. Plato was a direct and lineal descendent of Solon.

[26]Cf. 210c, e, 211c.

valued than that in the body, so that even if someone good of soul has but
a slight bloom, it suffices for him, and he loves and cares and begets and
c seeks those sorts of discourses which will make the young better, in order
that he may be constrained in turn to contemplate what is beautiful in
practices and laws and to see that it is in itself all akin to itself, in order
that he may believe bodily beauty a small thing.

After practices, he[27] must lead him to the various branches of knowledge, in order that he may in turn see their beauty too, and, looking now
d to the beautiful in its multitude, no longer delight like a slave, a worthless
petty-minded servant, in the beauty of one single thing, whether beauty of
a young child or man or of one practice; but rather, having been turned
toward the multitudinous ocean of the beautiful and contemplating it, he
begets many beautiful and imposing discourses and thoughts in ungrudging love of wisdom, until, having at this point grown and waxed strong, he
e beholds a certain kind of knowledge which is one, and such that it is the
following kind of beauty. Try, she said, to pay me the closest attention
possible.

The Ascent to Beauty Itself (210e–212a)

He who has been educated in the things of love up to this point, beholding beautiful things rightly and in due order, will then, suddenly, in
an instant, proceeding at that point to the end of the things of love, see
something marvelous, beautiful in nature: it is *that*, Socrates, for the sake
of which in fact all his previous labors existed.

211a   First, it ever is and neither comes to be nor perishes, nor has it growth
nor diminution.

Again, it is not in one respect beautiful but in another ugly, nor beautiful at one time but not at another, nor beautiful relative to this but ugly
relative to that, nor beautiful here but ugly there, as being beautiful to
some but ugly to others.[28]

Nor on the other hand will it appear beautiful to him as a face does,
or hands, or anything else of which body partakes, nor as any discourse or
b any knowledge does, nor as what is somewhere in something else, as in an
animal, or in earth, or in heaven, or in anything else; but it exists in itself
alone by itself, single in nature forever, while all other things are beautiful
by sharing in *that* in such manner that though the rest come to be and
perish, *that* comes to be neither in greater degree nor less and is not at all
affected.

---

[27]That is, the guide mentioned at 210a–b.
[28]Or, "As being thought beautiful by some but ugly by others."*ὡς* with participle:
Smyth 2086b, cf. 2996.

But when someone, ascending from things here through the right love of boys,[29] begins clearly to see *that*, the Beautiful, he would pretty well c touch the end. For this is the right way to proceed in matters of love, or to be led by another[30]—beginning from these beautiful things here, to ascend ever upward for the sake of *that*, the Beautiful, as though using the steps of a ladder, from one to two, and from two to all beautiful bodies, and from beautiful bodies to beautiful practices, and from practices to beautiful studies, and from studies one arrives in the end at *that* study which is nothing other than the study of *that*, the Beautiful itself, and one knows in the end, by itself, what it is to be beautiful. It is there, if anywhere, dear d Socrates, said the Mantinaean Stranger, that human life is to be lived: in contemplating the Beautiful itself. If ever you see it, it will not seem to you as gold or raiment or beautiful boys and youths, which now you look upon dumbstruck; you and many another are ready to gaze on those you love and dwell with them forever, if somehow it were possible, not to eat nor drink but only to watch and be with them.[31]

What then do we suppose it would be like, she said, if it were possible e for someone to see the Beautiful itself, pure, unalloyed, unmixed, not full of human flesh and colors, and the many other kinds of nonsense which 212a attach to mortality, but if he could behold the divine Beauty itself, single in nature? Do you think it a worthless life, she said, for a man to look *there* and contemplate *that* with that by which one must contemplate it,[32] and to be with it? Or are you not convinced, she said, that there alone it will befall him, in seeing the Beautiful with that by which it is visible, to beget, not images of virtue, because he does not touch an image, but true virtue, because he touches the truth? But in begetting true virtue and nurturing it, it is given to him to become dear to god, and if any other among men is immortal, he is too.

Socrates' Peroration (212b–c)

These then, Phaedrus and you others, are the things Diotima said, and b I am persuaded. Being persuaded, I try also to persuade others that one would not easily get a better partner for our human nature in acquiring this possession than Eros. Therefore I say that every man should honor Eros, and I myself honor and surpassingly devote myself to the things of love and summon others to do so; now and always, I praise the power and courage of Eros so far as I am able. Consider this speech then, Phaedrus, c if you will, an encomium to Eros, or if you prefer, name it what you please.

---

[29]In contradiction to Pausanias' sexualized pederasty.
[30]Cf. 210a, c, e.
[31]Diotima directly recalls the Speech of Aristophanes, 191a, 192b–d.
[32]That is, by mind or intelligence. See *Republic* VI 490a–b, VII 518c, 533c–d.

After Socrates said this, the rest praised him, but Aristophanes tried to say something, because Socrates in speaking alluded to his own speech.

And suddenly, there was a loud knocking at the courtyard door, as of revelers, and we heard the voice of a flute-girl. A moment later we heard in the courtyard the voice of Alcibiades, very drunk and shouting loudly, asking, Where is Agathon, saying, Take me to Agathon. So they led him in to us, the flute-girl supporting him, with certain others of his followers, and he stood in the doorway crowned with a bushy wreath of ivy and violets and a multitude of fillets on his head, and said, Greetings, Gentlemen. Will you accept a man already quite drunk as a drinking-companion?

XII

PHAEDO

I. Introductory Conversation

ECHECRATES. Were you there yourself, Phaedo, with Socrates on 57 the day when he drank the poison in the prison, or did you hear the story from someone else?

PHAEDO. I was there, Echecrates.

ECH. Then what was it that Socrates had to say before he died? And how did he meet his end? I should much like to hear; for nowadays hardly anyone from Phlius goes to stay in Athens, and it is a long time since any visitor from Athens has reached us who could give any reliable report, beyond the mere fact that he died by poisoning: no one could tell anything more than that.

PHAEDO. Haven't you even heard how the trial went? 58

ECH. Yes, someone told us about that; and we were surprised to find that his death came such a long time afterwards. What was really the reason, Phaedo?

PHAEDO. It was a matter of chance, Echecrates: it so happened that on the day before the trial they had crowned the stern of the ship which the Athenians sent to Delos.

ECH. Oh, what ship is that?

PHAEDO. According to the Athenian story, it is the ship in which Theseus once upon a time went off to Crete with the famous 'seven pairs,'[1] whose lives he saved as well as his own. Now the Athenians had made a vow, it is said, to Apollo that if they were saved Athens would dispatch a sacred mission to Delos every year; and ever since that time down to the present day they have sent it year by year in honour of the

---

Reprinted by permission of the publisher from R. Hackforth, trans., Plato, *Phaedo* (Cambridge University Press, 1955).

[1] The seven boys and seven girls whose lives were exacted every nine years as the Athenian tribute to Minos. Theseus slew the Minotaur, and saved himself and the other victims.

god. And in the period following the initiation of these proceedings custom ordains that the city shall be pure of bloodshed, and that no public execution shall take place until the ship has got back from its voyage to Delos. And sometimes, when the wind happens to be against them, this takes a considerable time. The period in question starts as soon as the priest of Apollo has crowned the ship's stern; and as I was saying, that happened to occur on the day before the trial, which explains the long interval which Socrates spent in prison between his trial and his death.

ECH. I see; but when it came to his actual death, Phaedo—what was said, what was done, which of his close friends were present? Or did the authorities forbid that anyone should be with him, so that he died with no one at his side?

PHAEDO. No, no: some friends were there, quite a number indeed.

ECH. Well, please do your best to give us a reliable report, unless you chance to be busy.

PHAEDO. No, I am not busy, so I will try to tell you the whole story. For indeed it is always a great delight to me to recall Socrates, whether by speaking of him myself or by hearing others do so.

ECH. And I assure you, Phaedo, that your audience feel just as you do. So see if you can give us a full and detailed account of the whole matter.

PHAEDO. Very well. When I came on the scene, I was curiously affected: on the one hand I didn't feel the pity that one usually feels at a dear friend's deathbed, because in behaviour and speech he struck me as so happy, Echecrates. What a fearless, noble ending it was! It made me realise that even as he passed to another world he had heaven's blessing; with him, if with any man, all would be well there too. That
59 is why I had hardly any feeling of pity such as might naturally be expected at a scene of mourning; nor on the other hand did I feel pleasure in the prospect of one of our regular philosophical discussions, as in fact it was. No: it was quite an extraordinary feeling that came upon me, a strange sort of blend of pleasure and pain, when I realised that he was to die forthwith. All of us, indeed, were affected much as I was, laughing at one moment, weeping at the next. This was notably true of one of our number, Apollodorus; I expect you know about him and the way he behaves.

ECH. Of course.

PHAEDO. Well, his was an extreme case; but I myself was agitated, and so were the rest of us.

ECH. Who actually were there, Phaedo?

PHAEDO. The Athenians included Apollodorus, of whom I was speaking, Critobulus and his father, Hermogenes, Epigenes, Aeschines, Antisthenes, Ctesippus of Paeane, Menexenus, and others. Plato, I believe, was sick.

ECH. And were there foreigners present?

PHAEDO. Yes: Simmias of Thebes and Cebes and Phaedondes; and the Megarians, Euclides and Terpsion.

ECH. What about Aristippus and Cleombrotus?

PHAEDO. No, they were said to be in Aegina.

ECH. Was there anyone else?

PHAEDO. I think those were about all there were.

ECH. Well now, what do you say they talked about?

II. Socrates as Poet. The Wickedness of Suicide

PHAEDO. I will try to tell you everything from the beginning. You must know that for some days before the end I and the others had been in the habit of visiting Socrates; we used to meet in the morning at the court-house in which the trial took place, as it was near the prison. Each day we used to wait chatting with each other until the prison was opened, which was not until well on in the morning. As soon as it was, we would go in to Socrates and usually spend all day with him. Well now, on this particular day we had assembled earlier than usual; for when we left the prison the evening before, we learnt that the ship was back from Delos. So we passed the word to be at the usual place as early as possible next day. When we arrived, the porter who habitually answered our knock told us to wait and not come in until he gave us the word; 'for,' he said, 'the authorities are taking Socrates's fetters off, and arranging for his death this very day.' However, we hadn't long to wait before he came back and bade us enter. On entering we found Socrates just freed from his chains, and Xanthippe, whom you know, sitting beside him 60 and holding his baby son. Xanthippe on seeing us cried out, and said the sort of thing that women always say—"Socrates, this is the last time your dear friends will speak to you and you to them.' Upon which Socrates glanced towards Crito and said, 'Crito, someone had better take her home.' So she was taken off by some of Crito's attendants, sobbing and lamenting.

Then Socrates, sitting up on his bed, began to bend his leg and rub it with his hand, and as he did so remarked, 'What a queer thing this pleasure, as they call it, seems to be, my friends! How remarkable is its relation to what we regard as its opposite, pain! Think of it: they won't both come to us at the same time, but if we run after one of them and grasp it, we are practically compelled to grasp the other too; they are like two creatures attached to a single head. I fancy that if Aesop had thought of it, he would have composed a fable telling how God wanted to put an end to their hostility, but found that he could not, and so fastened their heads together, with the result that anybody who is visited by one of them finds the other following it up afterwards. That is just what seems to be happening in my own case: the discomfort of my leg due to the fetter appears to have departed, and the pleasure following close upon it to have arrived.'

Here Cebes interrupted: 'I am grateful, Socrates, truly I am, for your reminding me of something. Do you know I have had several people asking me about those poems that you have composed, putting into verse stories by Aesop and composing the hymn to Apollo; only the other day Evenus wanted to know what induced you, after coming here, to compose these works, when you had never produced any composition before. So if you would like me to have an answer for Evenus when he repeats his question, as I am sure he will, do tell me what to say.'

'Well, Cebes,' rejoined Socrates, 'tell him the truth: it wasn't with any wish to compete with him or his work that I wrote these compositions—I knew that would not be easy; no, I was trying to get at the meaning of certain dreams which I had had, and discharging a sacred obligation, thinking that perhaps it was this sort of music they were bidding me compose. I must tell you what the dreams were like. Often in the course of my life the same dream-figure was visited me, differing in its visible form but always saying the same words, "Socrates, be diligent and make music." In the past I had supposed that it was urging and encouraging me to go on with what I was doing, just as people urge
61 on runners to run; I was to "make music" in the sense in which I was already doing so: the highest music was philosophy, and philosophy was my business. But now that my trial was over, and the festival of Apollo prevented my being put to death, it occurred to me that possibly the injunction of the dream might be to compose music in the commonly accepted sense, and that I ought to obey by so doing; it was safer, I felt, not to depart until I had fulfilled my sacred obligation by composing what the dream enjoined. Hence my first work was in honour of the god whose feast was being kept; and after that, feeling that one who means to be a real maker of music should concern himself with fancy rather than fact, and that I myself had no gift for that sort of thing, I made my poems out of the first readily available material, something that I knew by heart, namely Aesop's fables. So there, Cebes, is your reply to Evenus; say good-bye to him for me and tell him that, if he is wise, he should make all haste to follow me who am, it seems, to take my leave to-day on my country's orders.'

'What a strange piece of advice,' said Simmias, 'for Evenus! From what I know of him (and I have come across him frequently) there is very little likelihood of his obeying you, if he can help it.'

'Why not,' said Socrates, 'isn't he a philosopher?'

'Yes, I believe so,' replied Simmias.

'Well then, he will be as ready to comply as anyone else who has a proper attitude to philosophy. Yet probably he will not lay violent hands upon himself; for we are told that that is wicked.'

As he said this, Socrates let his legs down to the ground, and for the rest of the conversation remained seated.

A question then came from Cebes: 'How do you make that out, Socrates, that it is wicked to do violence to oneself, and yet that a philosopher will be ready to follow in the steps of the dying?'

'What, Cebes? Haven't you and Simmias been told about such matters in your studies with Philolaus?'

'Nothing definite, Socrates.'

'Well, of course I myself can only say what I have been told about it; however, I have no objection to repeating that; indeed I suppose it is highly suitable, now that I am on the point of passing to another place, that I should examine our ideas about it, and let fancy dwell upon our habitation yonder. What else should one do until the sun goes down?'

'Why is it then, Socrates, that they call it wicked to kill oneself? For to go back to the question you asked me just now, I did hear from Philolaus, when he was living amongst us, and indeed from other people earlier, that we ought not to do that; but from no one have I ever heard anything definite on the subject.'

'Well, we must do our best about it,' he replied; 'maybe you will 62 hear something yet. But I daresay it will strike you as surprising if in this matter, and this matter alone, we have something that holds good invariably, if (that is to say), as an exception to the general rule in human affairs, we never find that at some times and for some men death is better than life; so you think it surprising, I daresay, that it should be sinful for those for whom death *is* better to do themselves a good service, and that they should have to wait for someone else to do it for them.'

At this Cebes laughed quietly, and falling into his own dialect exclaimed 'Guid sakes, yes!'

'Put like that,' rejoined Socrates, 'it might certainly seem unreasonable; still, perhaps there is a reason for it. There is of course the reason given in mystery doctrine, that we men are in a sort of prison, and no one ought to attempt his release or run away from it; that seems to me an impressive saying, and not easy to get to the bottom of, but this much at least, I think, Cebes, is well said, that there are gods who look after us, and that we men are amongst the possessions of the gods. Do you not agree?'

'I do,' said Cebes.

'Then wouldn't you yourself be angry if one of the creatures you possessed were to put an end to itself without your signifying that it was

your wish for it to die? And if there were any punishment you could
inflict, would you not inflict it?'

'Certainly.'

'Well, perhaps that shows that it isn't unreasonable that a man ought
not to put an end to himself until God brings constraint upon him, as
he does now upon me.'

III. The Philosopher's Readiness to Die

'I think that is probably right,' said Cebes. 'But to go back to your
point, that a philosopher will be ready and willing to die, that strikes
me as astonishing, Socrates, if there is good ground for saying, as we
did just now, that there is a god who looks after us, and that we are his
possessions. That men of high intelligence should not complain at having to leave a service in which theirs were the best of all masters, the
gods, is not reasonable; they can hardly suppose that they will look after
themselves better than their former masters did. No: only an unintelligent person could possibly have the idea that he ought to escape from
his owner, not stopping to think that a good owner is not one to run
away from, but to stay with if one possibly can: hence he will only run
away because he doesn't stop to think, whereas any man of sense would
desire always to be with one better than himself. Yet that seems to point
to the opposite of what we were saying just now, Socrates: it behoves
the intelligent to complain of dying, and the unintelligent to rejoice.'

63   On hearing this Socrates seemed to me to be delighted with Cebes's
insistence; glancing at us he remarked, 'Cebes is for ever hunting up
arguments, you know: he is not exactly inclined to believe promptly
everything he is told.' At this Simmias put in a word: 'But in point of
fact I think, myself, there is something in what Cebes says this time:
for why should men who are truly wise want to run away from masters
better than themselves? Why should they lightly get rid of them? Moreover I fancy that Cebes is pointing his argument at yourself, for taking
so lightly your separation from us and from the gods whom you yourself
acknowledge as your good rulers.'

'A just remark,' he replied. 'I think what you both mean is that I
ought to defend myself on this charge as I would in a court of law.'

'Exactly,' said Simmias.

'Come then, let me attempt a more convincing defence before you
than I made before the court. If I did not believe, Simmias and Cebes,
that I shall find myself in the presence of other gods both wise and good,
and moreover of men better than those that still live on earth, then I
should be wrong not to complain of death. But as it is, rest assured that

I expect to join the company of good men, though that indeed I will not affirm with full certainty; but that I shall come to be with gods that are the best of masters, yes: you may rest assured that, if there is one thing that I will affirm in such a matter, it is that. And for that reason I am the less disposed to complain, but am of good hope that there is a future for those that have died, and, as indeed we have long been told, a far better future for the good than for the evil.'

'What then, Socrates?' said Simmias. 'Do you propose to keep these ideas to yourself, or will you let us share in them before you leave us? I really think this is a blessing in which we have a right to share: and moreover if you can persuade us of what you say, that defence you spoke of will be achieved.'

'Well, I will try. But first let us see what it is that Crito here has for some time, I fancy, been wanting to say.'

'Simply this, Socrates,' said Crito, 'that the officer who is to administer the poison has for some time been telling me that I ought to warn you to have as little conversation as possible; his point is that one gets heated by talking too much, and we mustn't let anything heating interfere with the draught; if anything of that sort happens, it is sometimes necessary to take a second or even a third dose.'

'Never mind about him,' rejoined Socrates, 'just let him make his own arrangements for administering two, or if need be, three doses.'

'I was pretty sure you would say that,' said Crito; 'only the man has been bothering me for some while.'

'Let him be. But to you, my judges, I wish now to give my grounds for thinking that a man who has truly spent his life in philosophy has good reason to be confident when he is about to die, and to be of good 64 hope that when life is over he will secure very great blessings. Now therefore, Simmias and Cebes, I will endeavour to explain how that can be so. It is probable that people in general do not realise that all those who betake themselves to philosophy in the right way are engaged in one thing only, namely training themselves for dying and being dead. Now if that is true, it would surely be absurd to devote the energy of a lifetime to that one end, and then, when it had come, to complain of that for which they had all the time been so energetically training.'

Simmias laughed at this: 'Upon my word, Socrates,' he said, 'you make me laugh, though I wasn't feeling much disposed to mirth a moment ago. I fancy that most people, hearing what you have just said, would think—and my own countrymen would emphatically agree—that it hit off the philosophers very aptly: it is a fact, they would say, that such folk want to die, and we are well aware that they deserve it.'

'Yes, and they would say that with truth, Simmias, except for the last point: for the multitude are not well aware in what sense the true philosopher wants to die, and in what sense he deserves to die, and what manner of death. Then let us not bother about the multitude, but talk it over amongst ourselves.'

IV. The Philosopher's Detachment from the Body

'Do we believe there is such a thing as death?'

'Undoubtedly,' replied Simmias.

'And by death do we not mean simply the departure of soul from body? Being dead consists, does it not, in the body having been parted from the soul and come to be by itself, and in the soul having been parted from the body, and being by itself. Can death possibly be anything other than that?'

'No, it can only be that.'

'Well now, turn your mind to this, and perhaps you will find you share my view. I think we shall make some progress in our inquiry if we start like this: Do you regard it as befitting a philosopher to devote himself to the so-called pleasures of, let us say, food and drink?'

'No indeed, Socrates', Simmias replied.

'What about the pleasures of sex?'

'Certainly not.'

'And what about all the other ministrations to bodily needs? Does that type of man set a high value on them, do you think? The possession of elegant clothes and shoes, for example, and other such bodily adornments: does he value them, or does he despise anything beyond the absolutely necessary minimum of such things?'

'The true philosopher, I should say, despises them.'

'In general terms, then, would you say that such a man's concern is not for the body, but, so far as he can detach himself from the body, is directed towards the soul?'

'Yes, I should.'

'Is it not then primarily in such things as we have mentioned that
65 the philosopher manifests his effort to release his soul from association with his body to a degree that surpasses that of the rest of mankind?'

'Evidently.'

'And may we not add, Simmias, that in the eyes of the multitude the life of one who finds no pleasure in such things, and has no part or lot in them, is not worth living? One who pays no regard to the pleasures which come by way of the body has, they would say, one foot in the grave.'

'Yes indeed, you are perfectly right.'

'And now as regards the actual attainment of intelligence: if we bring in the body as the soul's partner in our quest, is it a hindrance or not? To illustrate what I mean, is there any truth conveyed to mankind by seeing and hearing: or are not even the poets always harping on the theme that we neither hear nor see anything accurately? Yet if these two bodily senses are not accurate nor reliable, it is hardly likely that the rest are, since they are presumably inferior to these, as I expect you will agree.'

'Certainly they are.'

'Then when does the soul attain truth? For it is plain that when accompanied by the body in its attempts to inquire into things it is utterly deceived thereby.'

'True.'

'If then any part of reality is ever revealed to it, must it not be when it reasons?'

'Yes.'

'Furthermore reasoning is, I suppose, at its best when none of those senses intrudes to trouble the soul, neither hearing nor sight nor pain nor pleasure; when it is, so far as may be, alone by itself, taking leave of the body, and having as little communion and contact as possible therewith while it reaches out after reality.'

'That is so.'

'Then here again the philosopher's soul utterly despises his body and flees from it, seeking to be alone by itself.'

'Clearly so.'

'And now a further question, Simmias. We maintain, do we not, that there is such a thing as "the just itself"?'

'Yes indeed, we certainly do.'

'And a "beautiful itself" and a "good itself"?'

'Of course.'

'Well, have you ever seen anything of that sort with your eyes?'

'Of course not.'

'Then have you apprehended them with some other bodily sense? I mean the *being* of things in general, greatness, health, strength, or whatever else it may be: in short I mean the *reality* of this or that; is the full truth of them beheld through our bodies, or is it the fact that those of us that have trained ourselves to think most fully and precisely of the object in question, in and by itself, will come closest to knowing that object?'

'Yes, certainly.'

'Then the clearest knowledge will surely be attained by one who approaches the object so far as possible by thought, and thought alone, not permitting sight or any other sense to intrude upon his thinking, not dragging in any sense as accompaniment to reason: one who sets 66 himself to track down each constituent of reality purely and simply as it is by means of thought pure and simple: one who gets rid, so far as possible, of eyes and ears and, broadly speaking, of the body altogether, knowing that when the body is the soul's partner it confuses the soul and prevents it from coming to possess truth and intelligence. Is it not such a man, Simmias, that will grasp that which really is?'

'What you say, Socrates,' replied Simmias, 'is profoundly true.'

'On all these grounds then, must not genuine philosophers find themselves holding the sort of belief which will lead them to say, one to another, something like this: "It would seem that we are guided as it were along a track to our goal by the fact that, so long as we have the body accompanying our reason in its inquiries, so long as our souls are befouled by this evil admixture, we shall assuredly never fully possess that which we desire, to wit truth. For by reason of the nurture which it must have, the body makes countless demands upon us, and furthermore any sickness that may befall it hampers our pursuit of true being. Then too it fills us with desires and longings and fears and imaginations of all sorts, and such quantities of trash, that, as the common saying puts it, we really never have a moment to think about anything because of the body. Why, what else is it that causes war and faction and fighting but the body and its desires? It is always to acquire riches that men go to war, and the necessity of acquiring them is due to the servile attention that we pay to the body. And so, for all these reasons, we have no leisure for philosophy; but the worst trouble of all is that, if we do get a respite from the body's demands, and embark on some investigation, it obtrudes itself at every point of our inquiries, confusing, disturbing and alarming us, and so preventing us from discerning truth.

'However, this fact is manifest to us: if we are to have clear knowledge of anything, we must get rid of the body, and let the soul by itself behold objects by themselves. And one day, we may suppose, that intelligence which we desire and whose lovers we claim to be will be ours: not while we yet live, as our argument shows, but when we have died. For if we cannot come clearly to know anything when united to the body, there are two alternatives: either the attainment of knowledge is altogether impossible for us, or it can be ours after death; for then, and
67 only then, will our souls be by themselves, apart from our bodies. While we are alive we shall, it would seem, come nearest to knowledge if we have as little as possible to do with the body, if we limit our association therewith to absolute necessities, keeping ourselves pure and free from bodily infection until such time as God himself shall release us. And being thus made pure and rid of the body's follies we may expect to join the company of the purified, and have direct knowledge of all truth

unobscured; for that the impure should apprehend the pure heaven will hardly permit.'

'In such a strain I think, Simmias, must all those that love knowledge rightly address each other, and such must be their belief. Do you agree?'

'Unquestionably, Socrates.'

V. Moral Virtue, Genuine and Spurious

'Well then, my friend,' said Socrates, 'if that is true, I may well hope that when I have reached the place whither I am bound I shall attain in full measure, there at last, that for which I have spent the effort of a lifetime; wherefore it is with good hope that I set out upon the journey now appointed for me, as may any man who deems that his mind is made ready and purified.'

'Yes indeed,' said Simmias.

'So purification turns out, does it not, to consist in just what we have been discussing for some time past, in separating so far as may be the soul from the body, and habituating it to assemble and gather itself together from every region of the body, so as to dwell alone and apart, so far as possible, both in this present life and in the life to come, released from the body's fetters.'

'Certainly.'

'Then what we call death is a releasing or separation of soul from body?'

'Undoubtedly.'

'Moreover they that strive unceasingly for this release are, so we maintain, none other than those that pursue philosophy aright; indeed this and nothing else is the philosopher's concern, the release and separation of soul from body. Is it not so?'

'Plainly it is.'

'Hence, to repeat what I said at the outset, it would be ridiculous that a man should spend his life in a way that brought him as near as possible to being dead, and then complain of death when it came.'

'Ridiculous indeed.'

'Then it is true, Simmias, that the real philosophers train for dying, and to be dead is for them less terrible than for all other men. Look at it like this: if their continual quarrel with the body, their desire to have the soul by itself, were to result in fear and complaint when that is achieved, how unreasonable it would be! How unreasonable not to be 68 glad to go to a place where they may hope to get what they have longed for all their lives, to wit intelligence, and to be rid of the presence of their old enemy! Why, there have been not a few persons ready and willing to descend into Hades in quest of a lost wife or son or darling, led by the hope of beholding and rejoining their loved ones in another world: shall then he who truly loves not any human object, but intelligence, and has conceived this same lively hope that in that other world, and there alone, he will attain it in full measure, shall he, I say, complain when death comes? Shall he not rather depart in gladness? We must needs think so, if he is in truth, dear Simmias, a philosopher; for he will be very sure that only in that other world can he attain to intelligence in purity, and that being so, would it not, I repeat, be utterly unreasonable for such a man to fear death?'

'Yes, to be sure; utterly unreasonable.'

'Then if you see a man about to die complaining, is not that good evidence that he is not really a philosopher, a lover of wisdom, but what we may call a lover of the body? And probably he will be a lover of riches too, or of honours, or maybe of both.'

'Yes, you are quite right.'

'Tell me then, Simmias: is not what is called courage notably characteristic of the type we have been describing?'

'Assuredly.'

'And what of temperance, I mean the quality which is so named in common parlance, the sober attitude of one who disdains to be excited by his desires? Isn't that also characteristic of these men alone, these who utterly disdain the body and live in the pursuit of wisdom?'

'It must be.'

'Yes: and if you will give a moment's thought to the courage and temperance of other people, you will find them astonishing.'

'How so, Socrates?'

'You know, do you not, that all other people count death as a great evil?'

'Yes indeed.'

'And isn't it because they fear some greater evil that those of them who are brave face death firmly, when they do?'

'Yes.'

'Then it is through fear, through being afraid, that anyone who is not a philosopher is brave: yet surely it is illogical that a man should be brave through fear and cowardice?'

'It certainly is.'

'Again, doesn't the same thing hold good of such as are of sober conduct, doesn't their temperance spring from a sort of profligacy? Of course people say that is impossible: nevertheless it is a fact that something like that does happen to those who are temperate in the naïve fashion we refer to; they abstain from one sort of pleasure simply because the longing for another sort, and the fear of losing it, are too strong for them to resist. Of course to be mastered by pleasures is what they call profligacy: nevertheless the fact is that they master one kind 69 of pleasure only because they are mastered by another; which amounts to what we said just now, namely that in a sense they have attained temperance as the result of profligacy.'

'So it seems.'

'Yes, my dear good Simmias: for I fancy that that is not the right way to exchange things for virtue, that exchanging of pleasures for pleasures, pains for pains, fears for fears, small ones for great and great ones for small, as though they were coins; no, there is, I suggest, only one right sort of coin for which we ought to exchange all these things, and that is intelligence; and if all our buying and selling is done *for* intelligence and *with* its aid, then we have real courage, real temperance, real justice; and true virtue in general is that which is accompanied by intelligence, no matter whether pleasures and fears and all the rest of such things be added or subtracted. But to keep these apart from intelligence and merely exchange them for each other results, I fear, in a sort of illusory façade of virtue, veritably fit for slaves, destitute of all sound substance and truth; whereas the true virtue, whether it be of temperance, of justice, or of courage, is in fact a purging of all such things, intelligence itself being a sort of purge. And it may well be that those persons to whom we owe the institution of mystery-rites are not to be despised, inasmuch as they have in fact long ago hinted at the truth by declaring that all such as arrive in Hades uninitiated into the rites shall lie in mud, while he that comes there purified and initiated shall dwell with the gods. For truly, as their authorities tell us, there are

Many that carry the wand; but Bacchants few are amongst them;

where by "Bacchants" I understand them to mean simply those who have pursued philosophy aright; to be numbered amongst whom I have bent all the effort of a lifetime, leaving nothing undone that was within my power. Whether that effort was well directed and has had any success I shall know for certain, if God will, when I come to the place to which I am going; and I think that will be very soon.

'There then is my defence, Simmias and Cebes, to show that it is not unreasonable for me to leave you and my masters in this world without misgiving or complaint, inasmuch as I believe that I shall find good masters and friends yonder, just as I have found them here. So now, if you find my defence more convincing than the Athenian court did, I shall be well content.'

VI. The First Argument for Immortality. The Cycle of Opposites

To this speech of Socrates Cebes replied as follows:

'Most of what you have been saying, Socrates, seems to me excellent, but your view about the soul is one that people find it very hard to accept; they suspect that, when it has left the body, it no longer exists anywhere; on the day when a man dies his soul is destroyed and annihilated; immediately upon its departure, its exit, it is dispersed like breath or smoke, vanishing into thin air, and thereafter not existing anywhere at all. Of course if it could exist somewhere gathered together by itself, and quit of all the troubles which you were enumerating a while ago, then, Socrates, one might confidently cherish the hope that what you say is true; but to show that the soul exists when the man has died, and possesses some power and intelligence—well, that, I feel, needs a great deal of persuasive argument.'

'You are right, Cebes,' replied Socrates, 'but what then are we to do? Would you like to talk over this particular point amongst ourselves, and see whether or not the thing is likely?'

'At all events,' said Cebes, 'I should like to hear your opinion about it.'

'Well,' said Socrates, 'I don't think that anyone listening to me now, even were he a comic poet, could maintain that I am a vain babbler who talks about matters that don't concern him. If you agree then, we had better have a discussion; and we may put our question like this: do the souls of men that have departed this life exist in Hades or do they not? Now there is an ancient doctrine that comes into my mind, that souls which have come from this world exist in the other, and conversely souls come and are born into this world from the world of the dead. If that is so, if the living are reborn from those that have died, presumably our souls must exist yonder; for they could hardly be born again if they did not exist; and there you have good evidence for what we have been saying, if it could be clearly demonstrated as a fact that the living originate from the dead, and only from the dead. But if that is not so, we shall need another argument.'

'Just so,' said Cebes.

'Well now, if you would grasp my point more readily don't think only of mankind, but of the whole animal and vegetable world, in short of everything that comes into being: and let us put the general question:

isn't it always a case of opposite coming to be from opposite whenever the relation in question exists? Take for example the opposition of beautiful to ugly, or of just to unjust, out of the thousands of similar instances; and then let us ask ourselves whether it is not necessary that, when a thing has an opposite, it can come to be only from that opposite; for instance, when something comes to be bigger it must (I suggest) necessarily pass to the later state of being bigger from the earlier state of being smaller.'

'Yes.'

'And conversely, when it becomes smaller it must pass to being now smaller from being then bigger?'

'That is so.'

71

'And of course there is the same transition from stronger to weaker, and from slower to faster?'

'Quite so.'

'Again, anything that becomes worse must have been better, anything that becomes more just must have been more unjust?'

'Of course.'

'Are we satisfied then that all coming-to-be means the coming to be of an opposite thing from its opposite?'

'Quite satisfied.'

'To proceed then: is there not a further fact involved, namely that between any and every pair of opposites there are two "becomings" or processes, from this to that and conversely from that to this: thus between bigger thing and smaller there are increase and decrease, so that we say that this is increasing and that decreasing?'

'Yes.'

'And similarly with separating and combining, cooling and heating, and so on and so forth: we may sometimes have no name for the process, but the actual occurrence must conform to our principle: they all come into being from each other, and there is a process in which each becomes the other.'

'Quite so.'

'Well now, is there an opposite to living, corresponding to sleeping as the opposite of being awake?'

'Certainly.'

'And what is it?'

'Being dead.'

'Then if these are opposites, they must come to be from each other, and between the two of them there must be two processes.'

'Of course.'

'Now I will tell you one of the pairs that I was mentioning just now, together with its processes; and you must tell me the other one. My pair is sleeping and being awake: the latter comes into being from the former, and the former from the latter: and the processes here are going to sleep and waking up. Is that satisfactory?'

'Perfectly.'

'Then do you give me a similar account of life and death. You allow that being dead is the opposite of being alive?'

'I do.'

'And that they come into being from each other?'

'Yes.'

'Then what is it that comes to be from that which is alive?'

'What is dead.'

'And from what is dead?'

'I am bound to admit that the answer must be "What is alive".'

'Then, Cebes, living things and living people come into being from dead things and dead people.'

'Evidently.'

'Hence our souls do exist in Hades?'

'Apparently.'

'Now of the two processes here involved one is really obvious; for dying is an obvious fact, is it not?'

'Yes, of course.'

'Then what is our next step? Shall we not supply the opposite process to balance dying? Is Nature to be lame on one side, or must we needs supply her with an opposite process to this one?'

'Certainly we must.'

'And what is it?'

'Coming to life again.'

'Well then, if there is such a thing as coming to life again, the process from dead to living must be that.'

'Quite so.'

'Hence we have another ground for agreeing that the living come into being from the dead no less surely than the dead from the living. And we felt, I believe, that if this were so we should have a satisfactory indication that the souls of the dead must exist somewhere, and thence be reborn.'

'Yes, Socrates: I think that what we have agreed necessarily leads to that conclusion.'

'And here's another point, Cebes, which will show, I think, that we are not at fault in our agreement. If this circular process of one opposite coming into being to balance the other were not always going on, if instead of that there were only a one-way process in a straight line, with no bending back, no turning in the other direction, you will realise that ultimately all things would arrive at the same state, would undergo the same experience, and the coming into being of things would be at an end.'

'How do you mean?'

'My point is easy enough to understand. Suppose we had the process of going to sleep, but no balancing process of waking up again from sleep, you will realise that the ultimate state of things would make the story of Endymion pointless: he would turn out to be a nobody, since his experience of sleeping would be the universal experience. Again, if everything were to be combined and nothing separated, we should soon have that condition of "all things together" which Anaxagoras describes. And similarly, my dear Cebes, if everything endowed with life were to die, and having died were to remain in the state of death and not come to life again, it is not beyond dispute that ultimately there would be a universal absence of life, a universal death? Even supposing that the living had some other origin than the dead, yet if they were to die what escape could there possibly be from the whole stock of things being exhausted and dying out?'

'None whatever that I can see, Socrates. I think what you say is perfectly true.'

'Yes, Cebes, I feel quite certain that it is so: in agreeing on this particular point we are not deceiving ourselves. These are real facts: coming to life again, coming-to-be of the living from the dead, existence of the souls of those that have died.'

VII. A Complementary Argument.
The Theory of Recollection

To this Cebes rejoined: 'There is also another theory which, if true, points the same way, Socrates: the one that you are constantly asserting, namely that learning is really just recollection, from which it follows presumably that what we now call to mind we have learnt at some previous time; which would not be possible unless our souls existed somewhere before being born in this human frame. Hence we seem to have another indication that the soul is something immortal.'

Simmias now intervened to ask: 'But how is that proved, Cebes? Please remind me, as I can't quite remember at the moment.'

'First,' replied Cebes, 'by the excellent argument that when people are asked questions they can produce the right answers to anything of their own accord, provided that the questioning is done properly. Of course they wouldn't be able to do so unless they had knowledge and correct views within them. Secondly, if you confront people with anything in the nature of a diagram, you have the plainest proof of the point in question.'

'And if that doesn't convince you, Simmias,' said Socrates, 'I will suggest another consideration to which you may perhaps agree. You are evidently sceptical about the possibility of what is called learning being recollection.'

'Not sceptical,' said Simmias; 'what I need is just what are we talking about, namely to recollect. In point of fact, thanks to Cebes's setting out of the arguments I do already almost remember, and am almost convinced; all the same, I should like now to hear how you yourself have set them out.'

'I will tell you. We agree, I take it, that to be reminded of something implies having at some previous time known it?'

'Certainly.'

'And can we further agree that recollection may take the form of acquiring knowledge in a particular way, I mean like this: a man who has seen or heard or by some other sense perceived something may come to know something other than that, may think of something else besides that, something that is the object of a different knowledge. When this happens are we not justified in saying that he recollects or is reminded of the new object that he has thought of?'

'How do you mean?'

'To give an example, the knowledge of a man is different from that of a lyre.'

'Of course.'

'Well, you know how a lover feels when he sees a lyre or a cloak of some other object commonly used by his beloved: he apprehends the lyre, but he also conceives in his mind the form of the boy to whom it belongs; and that is reminder. Similarly one who sees Simmias is often reminded of Cebes, and we could think of any number of similar cases.'

'Yes indeed, any number,' agreed Simmias emphatically.

'Reminder then may take that form: but it is most apt to occur in connexion with things that we have forgotten owing to the lapse of time and our not having thought about them. Isn't that so?'

'Yes, certainly.'

'Another point: is it possible to see the picture of a horse or a lyre and be reminded of their owner: or again to see a picture of Simmias and be reminded of Cebes?'

'Certainly.'

'Or alternatively to see a picture of Simmias and be reminded of Simmias?'

'Yes, that is possible.'

'And from all this it follows, doesn't it, that we may be reminded of things either by something like them or by something unlike them?'

'It does.'

'Moreover, when it is by something like the other thing, are we not certain to find ourselves doing something else besides, namely asking ourselves whether the similarity between the object and the thing it reminds us of is defective or not?'

'Certainly we shall.'

'Well now, see if you agree with my next point. We maintain, do we not, that there is such a thing as equality, not the equality of one log to another, or one stone to another, but something beyond all these cases, something different, equality itself. May we maintain that that exists, or may we not?'

'Most assuredly we may,' answered Simmias: 'not a doubt of it.'

'And have we knowledge of it, and by itself?'

'Certainly we have.'

'Then where do we get that knowledge from? Mustn't it be from the objects we mentioned just now, the equal logs or stones or whatever they were that we saw? Didn't they lead us to conceive of that other something? You do regard it as something other than those things, don't you? Look at it like this: two stones or two logs equal in length sometimes seem equal to one man, but not to another, though they haven't changed.'

'Yes certainly.'

'But now, what about equals themselves? Have they ever appeared to you to be unequal, or equality to be inequality?'

'Never, Socrates.'

'Then those equal objects are not the same as the equal itself.'

'Far from it, I should say.'

'And yet it is from those equal objects, different as they are from this equal, that you have conceived and acquired knowledge of the latter?'

'That is perfectly true.'

'This latter being either like those others or unlike?'

'Just so.'

'However, that point is immaterial; but so long as the sight of one thing leads you to conceive another, whether like it or unlike, a case of reminder must have occurred.'

'Yes, to be sure.'

'And to continue: in the instance of those equal logs and other equal objects that we mentioned just now, is it our experience that they appear equal to the same degree as the equal itself? Is there some deficiency in respect of the likeness of the former to the latter, or is there none?'

'Yes, a considerable deficiency.'

'Then when someone sees a certain object and says to himself "The thing I am looking at wants to be like something else, but can resemble that other thing only defectively, as an inferior copy", may we agree that what he is saying necessarily implies a previous knowledge of that which he finds the object seen to resemble thus defectively?'

'That is necessarily implied.'

'Well then, is our own experience of the equal objects and the equal itself that just described, or is it not?'

'Undoubtedly it is.'

'So it necessarily follows that we knew the equal at a time previous
75 to that first sight of equal objects which led us to conceive all these as striving to be like *the* equal, but defectively succeeding.'

'That is so.'

'And we agree moreover on a further point, that the conception referred to has arisen only, and could have arisen only, from seeing or touching, or some other form of sense-perception: what I am saying applies to them all alike.'

'And alike they are, Socrates, in respect of the point that our argument seeks to establish.'

'But the fact is that these very sense-perceptions must lead us to conceive that all those objects of perception are striving for that which *is* equal, but defectively attaining it. Is that right?'

'Yes.'

'Hence before we ever began to see or hear or otherwise perceive things we must, it seems, have possessed knowledge of the equal itself, if we were going to refer the equal things of our sense-perceptions to that standard, conceiving that all such objects are doing their best to resemble it, yet are in fact inferior to it.'

'That must follow from what we said before, Socrates.'

'Well, we have been seeing and hearing things, and employing our other senses from the very moment we were born, have we not?'

'Certainly.'

'And before doing so we must, so we maintain, have possessed knowledge of the equal?'

'Yes.'

'Then it seems that we must have possessed it before we were born.'

'It does.'

'Then if we were born with this knowledge, having acquired it before birth, must we not have had knowledge, both before birth and immediately afterwards, not only of the equal, the greater and the smaller, but of all things of that sort? For our argument applies not merely to the equal, but with the same force to the beautiful itself, the good itself, the just, the holy, in fact, as I have just said, to everything upon which we affix our seal and mark as being "the thing itself", when we put our questions and give our answers. Of all these then we must have possessed the knowledge before we were born.'

'That is so.'

'And if we do not each time forget what we have acquired, we must be possessed of knowledge always, we must have it throughout our whole life; for to know means to have acquired knowledge of something and not have lost it. The losing of knowledge is what we mean by forgetting, isn't it, Simmias?'

'Undoubtedly, Socrates.'

'But if on the other hand we lost at the moment of birth what we had acquired before birth, but afterwards by directing our senses to the relevant object recover that old knowledge, then, I take it, what is called learning will consist in recovering a knowledge which belongs to us; and should we not be right in calling this recollection?'

'Certainly.'

'The reason being that we found that it was possible for a person 76 who had seen or heard or otherwise perceived an object to go on to conceive another object which he had forgotten, something with which the first object was connected, whether by resemblance or contrast. Hence my two alternatives: either we are all of us born knowing the things in question, and retain the knowledge throughout our life, or else those who are said to learn are simply recollecting, and learning will consist in recollection.'

'I am quite sure you are right, Socrates.'

'Then which do you choose, Simmias? Are we born with that knowledge, or do we recollect a knowledge which we once possessed?'

'At the moment, Socrates, I don't know which to choose.'

'Well, here is something about which perhaps you can choose, and give me your view. If a man knows certain things, will he be able to give an account of them, or will he not?'

'Unquestionably he will, Socrates.'

'And do you think that everybody could give an account of those objects we were speaking of just now?'

'I only wish I did,' replied Simmias; 'alas, on the contrary I fear that by this time to-morrow there will be no man left alive capable of doing so adequately.'

'So you don't think that everybody knows those objects, Simmias.'

'By no means.'

'Can they then recollect what they once learnt?'

'It must be so.'

'But when did our souls acquire this knowledge? Evidently not since our birth as human beings.'

'No indeed.'

'Before that, then?'

'Yes.'

'Then, Simmias, our souls did exist before they were within this human form, apart from our bodies and possessed of intelligence.'

'Unless possibly it was at the actual moment of birth that we acquired the knowledge in question, Socrates; there is that moment still left.'

'Yes yes, my friend; but at what moment, may I ask, do we lose it? We are not born with the knowledge: that we agreed a moment ago: do we then lose it at the very moment that we acquire it, or is there some other moment that you can suggest?'

'No indeed, Socrates; I see now that I was talking nonsense.'

'Then may our position be put like this, Simmias? If those objects exist which are always on our lips, a beautiful and a good and all reality of that sort, and if it is to that that we refer the content of our sense-perceptions, thereby recovering what was ours aforetime, and compare our percepts thereto, it must follow that as surely as those objects exist so surely do our souls exist before we are born; but if the former do not exist, all our arguments will have gone for nothing. Is that our position? Does the existence of our souls before birth stand or fall with the existence of those objects?'

'I am utterly convinced, Socrates,' replied Simmias, 'that it does so stand or fall: our argument is happily reduced to this, that it is equally certain that our souls exist before birth as that the reality of which you now speak exists. I say happily, because there is nothing so plainly true to my mind as that all that sort of thing most assuredly does exist, a beautiful and a good and all those other things that you were speaking of just now. So I think we have had a satisfactory proof.'

XIV. Refutation of Simmias's Theory of Soul

(91)   'And now to proceed,' said Socrates. 'First of all remind me of what you were saying, in case I prove not to have remembered. Simmias, I think, is sceptical, and fears that the soul, despite its being a fairer and more divine thing than the body, may nevertheless perish before it, because it is a sort of attunement. Cebes, on the other hand, seemed to agree with me on that point: he thought that the soul is longer-lasting than the body, but that nobody could be sure that it might not wear out a whole series of bodies, yet itself perish with the last one left behind: death might really be just this destruction of the soul, not of the body, for of course the body is incessantly and always perishing. Am I right, Simmias and Cebes, in thinking these to be the points for our consideration?'

They both agreed that they were.

'Well now, do you reject all the previous arguments, or only some of them?'

'Only some,' they replied.

'Then what have you to say about our assertion that learning is recollection, together with its corollary, that our souls must have existed somewhere else before being imprisoned in our bodies?'   92

'For my part,' said Cebes, 'I found it wonderfully convincing at the time; and I still abide by it as outstandingly true.'

'And let me assure you,' said Simmias, 'that that is my position too, and I should be much surprised if we ever changed our belief on that point.'

To this Socrates rejoined: 'My Theban friend, you will have to change your belief if you continue to think that an attunement is something composite, and that the soul is a sort of attunement resulting from the corporeal components held in tension; for you would hardly permit yourself to say that the attunement existed as a composite whole before the parts from which it was to be composed were in existence; or would you?'

'No indeed, Socrates.'

'Then do you realise that that is what you are in effect maintaining, when you say that the soul exists before entering the human frame or body, and yet that it exists as a whole composed of parts not yet existent? The fact is, of course, that an attunement is not the same sort of thing as that to which you are comparing it: lyre and strings and notes can be there as yet untuned: the attunement comes into existence last of all, and perishes first of all. So how is this theory of yours going to harmonise with the other one?'

'It never can,' said Simmias.

'But surely, if there is any theory that ought to be in tune, it is a theory about attunement.'

'It certainly ought.'

'Well, this one of yours isn't. But which of the two theories, on reflexion, do you prefer? That learning is recollection, or that the soul is an attunement?'

'I find the former far preferable, Socrates; the latter I have adopted without any proof, merely because it seemed likely and plausible, which is indeed the general ground for its acceptance. I am well aware that theories which rest their proofs on a basis of what is likely are tricksters; unless one is careful about them they cheat one completely, whether it be in geometry or anything else. But the theory about recollection and learning has proceeded from a postulate that deserves acceptance; we said, I think, that the existence of our souls before their entry into the body was just as certain as the existence of that very reality which bears the title of "the thing itself". That is a postulate which, I feel sure, I am fully justified in accepting; and consequently I am bound, it seems, to refuse to accept the theory, whether advanced by myself or anyone else, that the soul is an attunement.'

93 'Now look at it from another angle, Simmias. Do you consider it befits an attunement or any other compound to be otherwise qualified than the elements of which it is the product?'

'Certainly not.'

'Nor, I imagine, to do anything, or have anything done to it, other than that which those elements do or have done to them.'

He assented.

'Hence it doesn't befit an attunement to direct its elements: it must follow them.'

He agreed.

'Then it is out of the question for an attunement to have a movement or produce a sound, or do anything else, contrary to its own parts.'

'Utterly out of the question.'

'Now another point: will not any attunement naturally correspond to the way in which the tuning has been done?'

'I don't understand.'

'If the tuning has been done more completely, more fully (supposing that to be possible), won't there be more of an attunement, a fuller attunement; whereas if it has been done less completely, there will be less of an attunement; don't you agree?'

'Quite so.'

'Well, will that apply to a soul? Can there possibly be such a distinction between two souls that one is, even to a fractional extent, more or more fully itself, that is to say more or more fully soul, while the other is less or less fully soul?'

'No, that is quite impossible.'

'Then look here, will you please! We speak of one soul as possessing wisdom and virtue, and being good, and of another as possessing folly and wickedness, and being bad; and we are, I suppose, right in so speaking.'

'Certainly we are.'

'Well, how will an adherent of the attunement doctrine conceive of this soul-content, this virtue and vice? Will he say that they are respectively a second attunement and a non-attunement? Will the good soul be tuned, and have a second attunement within the first one, that is to say within itself, while the bad soul is itself untuned and devoid of any attunement within itself?'

'I really can't answer, Socrates: but plainly he would have to have some such theory.'

'But we are already agreed that one soul cannot be more or less a soul than another; and that amounts to agreeing that, on the theory under discussion, one cannot be more or more fully, or again less or less fully, an attunement than another; does it not?'

'Certainly.'

'And that what is not more or less of an attunement cannot be more or less tuned. Is that so?'

'It is.'

'And what is neither more or less tuned than something else cannot partake of attunement to a greater or less degree than that other, but only to an equal degree.'

'Yes, to an equal degree.'

'Then since one soul cannot be more or less itself, that is to say more or less soul, than another, it clearly cannot be either more or less tuned.'

'No.'

'And that being the case, it cannot partake either of attunement or of non-attunement to a greater degree than another.'

'No, it cannot.'

'Then in that case again, and if we allow that virtue is an attunement and vice a non-attunement, one soul cannot partake of virtue or vice to a greater degree than another.'

'No.'

'But indeed it would be more logical surely to say that, if soul is an 94
attunement, no soul will ever partake of vice: for of course an attunement that is really and truly an attunement can never partake of non-attunement.'

'No indeed.'

'And similarly, I imagine, a soul that is really and truly soul can never partake of vice.'

'Not on our premisses, certainly.'

'So we reach the conclusion that inasmuch as it is the nature of every soul to be just as much of a soul as every other, all souls of all living beings will be equally good.'

'That seems to me to be our conclusion, Socrates.'

'And does it seem to you a satisfactory one? Do you think we should have reached this position if the suggestion that soul is an attunement were correct?'

'I certainly do not.'

'And now for another point. Is it a man's soul that controls every part of him, more especially if it be intelligent, or can you point to something else?'

'I cannot.'

'And does it do so by conforming to the feelings of the body, or by opposing them? For instance, when a man feels hot and thirsty, don't we find his soul pulling him away from drinking, when he feels hungry pulling him away from eating; and don't we observe countless other instances of the soul opposing the bodily feelings?'

'Yes indeed.'

'But then didn't we agree just now that the soul, if it is an attunement, could never utter a note that was opposed to the tension or relaxation or the manner of striking the strings or anything else that was done to those alleged sources from which it sprang? Didn't we agree that it must follow them and could never dominate them?'

'To be sure, we did.'

'Well now, don't we find the soul in fact achieving the exact opposite of this? Dominating all these alleged sources of its existence, opposing them almost incessantly for a whole lifetime, mastering them in this way and that, sometimes inflicting severe and painful punishment in the course of physical training or medical treatment, sometimes proceeding more gently; threatening here and admonishing there; speaking to a man's desires and passions and fears after the fashion of a visitor from without, a fashion reminding us of Homer's description of Odysseus:

Then did he smite his breast, and spake to his heart with a chiding:
'Heart, I bid thee endure: worse ills ere now thou enduredst.'

'Do you suppose that the poet would have written thus if he had regarded the heart as an attunement, as something that could be guided by the feelings of the body, instead of guiding those feelings and mastering them, being much too divine a thing to be conceived as an attunement?'

'Upon my word, I think you are right, Socrates.'

'Then, my good friend, we by no means approve the doctrine that the soul is a kind of attunement: it would involve, it seems, contra-
95 dicting both the divine Homer and ourselves.'

'That is so.'

XV. Socrates as Student of Natural Science

'Very well, then,' said Socrates; 'we seem to have more or less propitiated the tuneful goddess of Thebes; but now comes the question of Cadmus: What sort of argument shall we use to propitiate him, Cebes?'

'I expect you will discover one,' replied Cebes; 'at all events your argument against the tuneful lady came as a wonderful surprise to me; for while Simmias was telling us of his difficulties I was wondering very much whether anyone would be able to cope with his argument, and so

I was quite taken aback by his apparent inability to withstand your first attack for a moment. Hence it wouldn't surprise me if the theory of Cadmus were to suffer the same fate.'

'No boasting, please, my good sir,' rejoined Socrates, 'or we shall find some malign power making havoc of our next argument. However, that possibility must be left to heaven; what we must do is to come to close quarters, in Homeric fashion, with your contention, and try to see whether there is anything in it. Now your problem may be summed up like this: you require it to be proved that our souls are indestructible and immortal, if the confidence shown by a philosopher at the point of death, who believes that he will be far better off in the other world than if he had lived a different sort of life, is not to be an irrational, foolish confidence. To show that the soul is something strong and godlike, and that it existed even before we were born as men—all that, you urge, may well be a revelation not of its immortality, but of its being long-lasting, of its having existed somewhere for ever so long, knowing much and doing much; but that leaves it as far as ever from being immortal, and indeed its very entry into a human body was the beginning of a sickness which would end in its destruction; its life here is a life of distress, and it finally perishes in what men call death. And in respect of our individual fears it makes no difference, you argue, whether it enters a body once or many times; anyone who is not a fool will naturally be afraid if he doesn't know, and cannot give a ground for believing, that it is immortal.

'That, I think, Cebes, is more or less what you maintain: and I am deliberately going over it again and again in order that no point may escape us, and that you may add or subtract anything that you wish.'

To this Cebes replied, 'There is nothing that I want to subtract or add at the moment; my contention is what you have said.'

At this point Socrates paused for a long time in meditation; finally he resumed: 'The problem you raise, Cebes, is no light one: we have got to have a thorough inquiry into the general question of the cause of coming into being and perishing. I will therefore, if you like, narrate 96 my own experiences bearing on the matter; and then, if anything I have to say should appear to you helpful, you can make use of it to settle the points you have been raising.'

'Why of course,' said Cebes, 'I should like that.'

'Then listen and I will tell you. When I was young, Cebes, I had a remarkable enthusiasm for the kind of wisdom known as natural science; it seemed to me magnificent to know the causes of everything, why a thing comes into being, why it perishes, why it exists. Often I used to shift backwards and forwards trying to answer questions like this, to start with: Is it when the conjunction of the hot and the cold results in putrefaction that living creatures develop? Is it blood that we think with, or air or fire? Or is thought due to something else, namely the brain's providing our senses of hearing, sight and smell, which give rise to memory and judgement, and ultimately, when memory and judgement have acquired stability, to knowledge?

'Next I tried to investigate how things perish, and what went on in the heavens and on the earth, until in the end I decided that I had simply no gift whatever for this sort of investigation. To show how right I was about that, I may tell you that, whereas there were some things which up till then I had, as I thought myself and other people thought too, definitely understood, I was now smitten with such complete blindness as the result of my investigations that I unlearnt even what I previously thought I knew, including more particularly the cause of a human being's growth. I had supposed that to be obvious to anybody: he grew because he ate and drank; on taking food flesh was added to flesh, bone to bone, and similarly the appropriate matter was added to each part of a man, until in the end his small bulk had become a large one, and so the little child had become a big man. That was what I used to believe: reasonably enough, wouldn't you say?'

'I would,' said Cebes.

'Now see what you think about this. I used to find it perfectly satisfactory when a tall man standing beside a short one appeared to be taller just by a head; similarly with two horses. And to take an even plainer case, I thought that ten was more than eight because of the addition of two, and that an object two yards long was greater than one only one yard long because the one extended by half its own length beyond the other.'

'And what do you think about it all now?'

'I assure you I am very far from supposing that I know the cause of any of these things; why, I am dubious even about saying that, when we add one to one, either the one to which the addition is made becomes two, or that the one and the other together become two by reason of the addition of this to that. What puzzles me is that when the units were
97 apart from each other each was one, and there was as yet no two, whereas as soon as they had approached each other there was the cause of the coming into being of two, namely the union in which they were put next to each other. Nor again can I any longer persuade myself that if we divide one it is the division this time that causes two to come into being; for then the cause of two would be the opposite of that just suggested: a moment ago it was because the units were brought into close proximity each to each, and now it is because they are kept away and separated each from each. And for that matter I no longer feel sure that by ad-

hering to the old method I can understand how a unit comes into being or perishes or exists: that method has lost all attraction for me, and in its place I am gaily substituting a new sort of hotch-potch of my own.

'One day, however, I heard someone reading an extract from what he said was a book by Anaxagoras, to the effect that it is Mind that arranges all things in order and causes all things; now there was a cause that delighted me, for I felt that in a way it was good that Mind should be the cause of everything; and I decided that if this were true Mind must do all its ordering and arranging in the fashion that is best for each individual thing. Hence if one wanted to discover the cause for anything coming into being or perishing or existing, the question to ask was how it was best for that thing to exist or to act or be acted upon. On this principle then the only thing that a man had to think about, whether in regard to himself or anything else, was what is best, what is the highest good; though of course he would also have to know what is bad, since knowledge of good involves knowledge of bad. With these reflexions I was delighted to think I had found in Anaxagoras an instructor about the cause of things after my own heart; I expected him to tell me in the first place whether the earth is flat or round, and then go on to explain the cause why it must be the one or the other, using the term "better", and showing how it was better for it to be as it is; and then if he said the earth is in the centre of the universe, he would proceed to explain how it was better for it to be there. If he could make all these 98 things plain to me, I was ready to abandon the quest of any other sort of cause. Indeed I was ready to go further, applying the same principle of inquiry to sun, moon and stars, their relative velocities and turnings and so forth: I would ask which is the better way for these bodies to act or be acted upon. For I never supposed that when Anaxagoras had said that they are ordered by Mind he would bring in some other cause for them, and not be content with showing that it is best for them to be as they are; I imagined that in assigning the cause of particular things and of things in general he would proceed to explain what was the individual best and the general good; and I wouldn't have sold my hopes for a fortune. I made all haste to get hold of the books, and read them as soon as ever I could, in order to discover without delay what was best and what was worst.

'And then, my friend, from my marvellous height of hope I came hurtling down; for as I went on with my reading I found the man making no use of Mind, not crediting it with any causality for setting things in order, but finding causes in things like air and aether and water and a host of other absurdities. It seemed to me that his position was like that of a man who said that all the actions of Socrates are due to his

mind, and then attempted to give the causes of my several actions by saying that the reason why I am now sitting here is that my body is composed of bones and sinews, and the bones are hard and separated by joints, while the sinews, which can be tightened or relaxed, envelop the bones along with the flesh and skin which hold them together; so that when the bones move about in their sockets, the sinews, by lessening or increasing the tension, make it possible for me at this moment to bend my limbs, and that is the cause of my sitting here in this bent position. Analogous causes might also be given of my conversing with you, sounds, air-currents, streams of hearing and so on and so forth, to the neglect of the true causes, to wit that, inasmuch as the Athenians have thought it better to condemn me, I too in my turn think it better to sit here, and more right and proper to stay where I am and submit to such punishment as they enjoin. For, by Jingo, I fancy these same sinews and bones would long since have been somewhere in Megara or
99 Boeotia, impelled by their notion of what was best, if I had not thought it right and proper to submit to the penalty appointed by the State rather than take to my heels and run away.

'No: to call things like that causes is quite absurd; it would be true to say that if I did not possess things like that—bones and sinews and so on—I shouldn't be able to do what I had resolved upon; but to say that I do what I do because of them—and that too when I am acting with my mind—and not because of my choice of what is best, would be to use extremely careless language. Fancy not being able to distinguish between the cause of a thing and that without which the cause would not be a cause! It is evidently this latter that most people, groping in the dark, call by the name of cause, a name which doesn't belong to it. Hence we find one man making the earth be kept in position by the heavens, encompassing it with a rotatory movement; and another treating it as a flat lid supported on a base of air; but the power thanks to which heaven and earth are now in the position that it was the best possible position for them to be set in, *that* they never look for, and have no notion of its amazing strength; instead they expect to discover one day a stronger and more immortal Atlas, better able to hold things together; for they don't believe in any good, binding force which literally binds things together and holds them fast.

'Well, I for my part should be most happy to be instructed by anybody about a cause of this sort; but I was baulked of it: I failed to discover it for myself, and I couldn't learn of it from others; and so I have had recourse to a second-best method to help my quest of a cause; would you like me to give a formal account of it, Cebes?'

'Yes, indeed; I should like that immensely.'

XVI. The New Method of Hypothesis

'Well, at that point, when I had wearied of my investigations, I felt that I must be careful not to meet the fate which befalls those who observe and investigate an eclipse of the sun; sometimes, I believe, they ruin their eyesight, unless they look at its image in water or some other medium. I had the same sort of idea: I was afraid I might be completely blinded in my mind if I looked at things with my eyes and attempted to apprehend them with one or other of my senses; so I decided I must take refuge in propositions, and study the truth of things in them. Perhaps, however, my comparison in one aspect does not hold good: for I don't altogether admit that studying things in propositions is more of 100 an image-study than studying them in external objects. Anyhow, it was on this path I set out: on each occasion I assume the proposition which I judge to be the soundest, and I put down as true whatever seems to me to be in agreement with this, whether the question is about causes or anything else; what does not seem to be in agreement I put down as false. But I should like to make my meaning clearer to you; I fancy you don't as yet understand.'

'Indeed no,' said Cebes, 'not very well.'

'Well, here is what I mean; it is nothing new, but what I have constantly spoken of both in the talk we have been having and at other times too. I am going to attempt a formal account of the sort of cause that I have been concerned with and I shall go back to my well-worn theme and make it my starting point; that is, I shall assume the existence of a beautiful that is in and by itself, and a good, and a great, and so on with the rest of them; and if you grant me them and admit their existence, I hope they will make it possible for me to discover and expound to you the cause of the soul's immortality.'

'Why of course I grant you that,' said Cebes: 'so pray lose no time in finishing your story.'

'Now consider whether you think as I do about the next point. It appears to me that if anything else is beautiful besides the beautiful itself the sole reason for its being so is that it participates in that beautiful; and I assert that the same principle applies in all cases. Do you assent to a cause of that sort?'

'Yes, I do.'

'It follows that I can no longer understand nor recognize those other learned causes which they speak of; if anyone tells me that the reason why such-and-such a thing is beautiful is that it has a bright colour or a certain shape or something of that kind, I take no notice of it all, for

I find it all confusing, save for one fact, which is my simple, naïve and maybe foolish fashion I hug close: namely that what makes a thing beautiful is nothing other than the presence or communion of that beautiful itself—if indeed these are the right terms to express how it comes to be there; for I won't go so far as to dogmatize about that, but merely affirm that all beautiful things are beautiful because of the beautiful itself. That seems to me the safest answer for me to give whether to myself or to another; if I hold fast to that I feel I am not likely to come to grief; yes, the safe course is to tell myself or anybody else that beautiful things are beautiful because of the beautiful itself. Do you not agree?'

'I do.'

'Similarly big things are big, and bigger things are bigger, because of bigness, while smaller things are smaller because of smallness.'

'Yes.'

'Then you would reject, as I do, the assertion that one man is bigger than another by, or because of, his head, and that the latter is smaller
101 by, or because of, that same thing; you would protest that the only thing you could say is that anything bigger than another thing is so solely because of bigness, that bigness is the reason for its being bigger; and again that a smaller thing is smaller because of smallness, and smallness is the reason for its being smaller. You would, I fancy, be afraid that if you said that someone was bigger or smaller "by a head", you would be met with the objection that in the first place it would be by the same thing that the bigger is bigger and the smaller smaller, and in the second place that the head by which the bigger man is bigger is itself small; and that, it would be objected, is monstrous, for a big man to be big by, or because of, something small. Or wouldn't you be afraid of that?'

'Yes, I should,' replied Cebes with a laugh.

'Then would you be afraid to say that ten is more than eight by two, and that two is the cause of the excess, instead of saying by quantity and because of quantity? Or that a length of two yards is greater than a length of one yard by half its own length, rather than by greatness? Surely you should have the same qualms as before.'

'Quite so.'

'Or again, wouldn't you hesitate to say that when one is added to one the addition is the cause of there coming to be two, or that when one is divided the division is the cause? Would you not loudly protest that the only way you know of, by which anything comes to be, is by its participating in the special being in which it does participate; and that in the case just mentioned you know of no other cause of there coming to be two save coming to participate in duality, in which everything that is to be two must participate, just as anything that is to be one must participate in unity; all these divisions and additions and suchlike subtleties you would have nothing to do with; you would leave questions about them to be answered by wiser folk; conscious of your inexperience you would shy, as the phrase goes, at your own shadow, cling to the safety of your hypothesis, and answer accordingly. And if anyone were to fasten upon the hypothesis itself, you would disregard him, and refuse to answer until you could consider the consequences of it, and see whether they agree or disagree with each other. But when the time came for you to establish the hypothesis itself, you would pursue the same method; you would assume some more ultimate hypothesis, the best you could find, and continue until you reached something satisfactory. But you wouldn't muddle matters as contentious people do, by simultaneously discussing premiss and consequences, that is if you wanted to discover a truth. Such discovery is perhaps a matter of complete unconcern to the contentious, whose wisdom enables them to jumble everything up together, and nevertheless to be well pleased with themselves. But you, I fancy, if you are a philosopher, will do as I have 102 said.'

'What you say,' replied Simmias and Cebes together, 'is perfectly true.'

XVII. The Exclusion of Opposites

ECH. Upon my word, Phaedo, they had good reason to say so. As I see it, Socrates made matters wonderfully clear even to a feeble intelligence.

PHAEDO. Just so, Echecrates; that is what everyone there thought.

ECH. As do we who were not there, your present audience. But how did the conversation proceed?

PHAEDO. It was like this, I think. When Socrates had gained their assent, and it was agreed that every Form was a real existent, and that other things bore their names by virtue of participating in those Forms, he then put this question:

'If,' he said, 'that is your view, then when you say that Simmias is taller than Socrates and shorter than Phaedo, are you not saying that both tallness and shortness are in Simmias?'

'Yes, I am.'

'But of course you admit that the words "Simmias overtops Socrates" do not express the truth of the matter. For surely it isn't part of the nature of Simmias to overtop him: he doesn't do so by being Simmias, but by tallness which he happens to possess. Again, you will admit that he doesn't overtop Socrates because Socrates is Socrates, but because Socrates possesses shortness over against Simmias's tallness.'

'True.'

'Once again, Simmias is not overtopped by Phaedo because Phaedo is Phaedo, but because Phaedo has tallness over against Simmias's shortness.'

'Yes.'

'So that is how Simmias comes to be spoken of as both short and tall, being as he is between the two others; he offers his shortness to the tallness of Phaedo to be overtopped, and presents his tallness to Socrates to overtop the shortness of Socrates.'

Socrates smiled as he said this, and added: 'That sounds as if I were going to talk like a book; however, what I have said surely is true.' Simmias agreed, and Socrates continued: 'My purpose in saying this is to get you to share my view: which is this, that not only will tallness itself never consent to be simultaneously tall and short, but the tallness in us can never admit shortness, and never consent to be overtopped; instead, one of these two things must happen: it must either retreat and withdraw when its opposite, shortness, advances, or it must perish at that advance; what it won't consent to is to endure and admit shortness, and so to be something other than it was. For example, I have admitted and endured shortness, and am short without ceasing to be what I am; but the Form that is tall can never bring itself to be short; and similarly shortness, even the shortness in us, can never consent to be or become tall; nor can any other opposite, while still being what it was, simul-
103 taneously become or be its own opposite; when that threatens, it either takes its departure or perishes.'

'I agree entirely,' said Cebes.

On hearing this one of the company (I am not sure who it was) intervened: 'Look here,' he said, 'did we not agree a while ago to the exact opposite of what is now asserted? Didn't we say that the greater comes into being from the smaller, and the smaller from the greater? Was not the coming-to-be of an opposite agreed to be just this coming out of its opposite? Whereas now apparently it is maintained that that can never happen.'

Socrates inclined his head towards the speaker, and having listened to him remarked: 'A courageous reminder; but you don't realise the difference between what we said then and what we say now. Then we said that of two opposite *things* the one comes into being from the other; now we say that an opposite *itself* can never become its own opposite, whether the opposite in question be in us or in the world of true being. Previously, my friend, we were speaking of things that *have* opposites, and calling them by the names of those opposites which they possessed; but now we are speaking of the opposites themselves from whose im-manence the things called after them derive their names: these opposites themselves, we maintain, could never consent to originate from one another.'

With these words he glanced at Cebes, and added: 'Can it be, Cebes, that you too were disturbed by anything our friend here said?'

'No,' said Cebes, 'I don't feel like that on this occasion; yet I won't deny that many matters do disturb me.'

'We agree then, without reserve, on this point, that no opposite will ever be its own opposite.'

'Absolutely.'

'Now please consider whether you will agree to my next point. Do you speak of "hot" and "cold"?'

'I do.'

'Meaning by them the same as "snow" and "fire"?'

'Why no, of course not.'

'That is to say, the hot is different from fire, and the cold from snow.'

'Yes.'

'But I think you would agree that what starts as snow cannot ever, as we were saying just now, admit the hot and still be what it was: still be snow and also hot; on the approach of the hot it will either withdraw or perish.'

'Quite so.'

'Again fire, when the cold approaches it, will either get out of its way or perish; it will never bring itself to admit coldness and still be what it was, still be fire and also cold.'

'That is true.'

'Then in some of these cases we find that it is not only the form itself that is entitled to its own name for all time, but something else too which, though not being that form, yet always bears that form's character, whenever it exists. Here's an example which will perhaps make my meaning clearer: the odd, I presume, must ways have this name which we now give it, mustn't it?'

'Of course.'

'But will it be the only thing in the world to have it—that is what I am asking—or is there something else which, though not identical with 104 the odd, nevertheless must be called by the name "odd" as well as by its own name, owing to the fact that its nature is such that it can never be apart from the odd? What I mean may be illustrated by the case of the number three, to take one of many instances. Consider the number three: wouldn't you say that it must always be designated both by its own name and also by the name "odd", though it is not identical with the odd? Not identical: nevertheless such is the nature of three and five and half the entire number-series that every one of these numbers is odd. Correspondingly two and four and the whole of the other column of numbers are not identical with the even, but nevertheless each of them is for ever even. Do you agree?'

'Certainly.'

'Then mark what I want to show; it is this, that not only do we find the opposites that we spoke of refusing to admit each other, but all things which, while not being mutually opposed, always possess opposites, themselves likewise appear not to admit the character which is opposite to that contained in themselves; when that character advances upon them they either perish or withdraw. Thus shall we not affirm that three will sooner perish, sooner allow anything to happen to it, than endure, while still being three, to become even?'

'Indeed we shall,' said Cebes.

['And similarly shall we not affirm that two will sooner perish, sooner allow anything to happen to it than endure, while still being two, to become odd?'

'Indeed we shall.']

'Nevertheless two is not the opposite of three.'

'No, it is not.'

'Hence it is not only two opposite forms that won't endure an onset by one on the other: there are others also that won't endure the onset of opposites.'

'Very true.'

'Then would you like us, if we can, to specify what sort of forms these are?'

'Certainly.'

'Must they not be those which compel the object which they come to occupy to have not only its own character, but also the character of a certain opposite, which it will never lose?'

'How do you mean?'

'Remember what we said just now. You know presumably that anything occupied by the character of three must be not only three but also odd.'

'Certainly.'

'Well, what we maintain is that such a thing can never be visited by the character that is opposite to the form which brings that about.'

'No.'

'And what brought it about was the form of odd?'

'Yes.'

'Whose opposite is the form of even?'

'Yes.'

'Then the character of even will never visit three.'

'No, it will not.'

'That is to say, three has nothing to do with even.'

'Nothing.'

'In fact three is non-even.'

'Yes.'

'Now I was saying that we must specify what sort of things they are which, while not the opposite of a given thing, nevertheless will not admit that thing; our example just now was the refusal of the number three to admit the even, despite its not being the opposite of even; the reason being that three always brings up the opposite of even, just as two brings up the opposite of odd, fire the opposite of cold, and so on and so forth. Well, I wonder if you would specify them in this way: it 105 is not only two opposites that refuse to admit each other, but if any form brings up one of two opposites into that which it itself enters, that form itself will never admit the character opposite to the one brought up. Let me refresh your memory; it does no harm to hear a thing more than once; five will not admit the character of even, nor ten, its double, the character of odd. Of course the double is also in itself opposite to something else: nevertheless ten will not admit the character of odd. Again the fraction 3/2 and all the other members of the series of halves will not admit the character of wholeness, and the same is true of 1/3 and all the terms of that series. I hope you go along with me here and share my view.'

'I do so most emphatically.'

XVIII. The Argument Concluded.
Soul Is Both Deathless and Indestructible

'Well now, go back to the beginning, will you? And please don't meet my questions with that safe answer we spoke of, but copy my example. I say that because the course of our argument has led me to discern a different kind of safety from that which I mentioned originally. Thus, if you were to ask me what must come to be present in a thing's body to make it hot, I should not give you that safe, stupid answer "heat", but a cleverer one now at my disposal, namely "fire". Again, if you ask what must come to be present in a body to make it sick, I shall not say "sickness" but "fever". Similarly, what must be present in a number for it to be odd? Not oddness, but a unit; and so on. I wonder if you see clearly by now what I want?'

'Oh yes, quite clearly.'

'Then tell me, what must come to be present in a body for it to be alive?'

'Soul.'

'Does that hold good always?'

'Certainly.'

'Then soul always brings life along with it to anything that it occupies?'

'Yes indeed.'

'And is there an opposite to life, or is there none?'

'There is.'

'What?'

'Death.'

'Now soul will assuredly never admit the opposite of what it introduces: that has been agreed already, hasn't it?'

'Emphatically so.'

'Well now: what name did we give just now to the thing that won't admit the character of even?'

'Non-even.'

'And to that which won't admit "just" or "musical"?'

' "Unjust" and "unmusical".'

'All right: then what name shall we give to that which won't admit death?'

'Deathless.'

'And isn't it soul that won't admit death?'

'Yes.'

'Then soul is deathless.'

'Very well; may we say that that has been proved? Or how do you feel about it?'

'Yes, and very adequately proved, Socrates.'

106 'Now a further point, Cebes: if the non-even were necessarily imperishable, presumably three would be imperishable.'

'Undoubtedly.'

'Or again, if the non-hot were necessarily imperishable, then when you confront snow with something hot, the snow would retreat out of its way, intact and unmelted; for it couldn't perish, nor could it endure to admit heat.'

'That is true.'

'Similarly, I suppose, if the non-coolable were imperishable, then when a cold object approached fire, the fire could never be extinguished, or perish, but would take itself off intact.'

'It would have to do so.'

'Then must we not apply the same principle in the case of what is deathless? That is to say, if the deathless is also imperishable, it is impossible for a soul to perish when death approaches it, for it follows from what we have said that the soul will not admit death, will never be dead, any more than three, and of course oddness, will ever be even, or fire, and of course the heat in fire, ever be cold. But it may be objected, ''Granting that the odd cannot become even when the even approaches, what is to prevent it perishing, and an even taking its place?'' In reply, we could not contend that the odd cannot perish, for the non-even is not imperishable. Of course, if that had been admitted to be so, we could easily now contend that on the approach of the even oddness and three take their departure; and we could have maintained the same thing about fire and the hot, and the rest of them, couldn't we?'

'Yes indeed.'

'Then similarly in our present instance of the deathless, if that is admitted to be also imperishable, soul would be imperishable in addition to being deathless; but if that is not admitted, we shall need a further argument.'

'Oh but, so far as that goes, we need nothing further: for if the deathless, which lasts for ever, is to admit destruction, it is hardly likely that anything else will escape destruction.'

'Yes, and I suppose it would be agreed by everyone that God, and the Form of life itself, and any other deathless entity there may be, can never perish.'

'Why yes, to be sure: agreed by every human being; and the gods, I expect, would be even more inclined to agree.'

'Then inasmuch as the deathless is also indestructible, I presume that soul, if it really is deathless, must be indestructible too.'

'There can be no question of that.'

'So when death approaches a man his mortal part, it seems, dies, but his immortal part gets out of the way of death and takes its departure intact and indestructible.'

'Evidently.'

'Beyond all doubt then, Cebes, soul is deathless and imperishable, 107 and our souls will in truth exist in Hades.'

'I for my part, Socrates,' replied Cebes, cannot dispute that, nor can I feel any doubt about our arguments. But if Simmias here or anyone else has anything to say, it is desirable that he should not suppress it; any further discussion of these matters that may be desired can hardly, I think, be put off for a later occasion.'

XXII. The Last Scene

To this Crito replied, 'Very well, Socrates; but what instructions (115) have you for our friends here or for me about the children, or about any other matter? We want to do just what would be of most service to you.'

'Only what I am always telling you, Crito, nothing very new. Look after yourselves: then anything you do will be of service to me and mine, and to yourselves too, even if at this moment you make no promises to that effect; but if you neglect yourselves, and refuse to follow that path of life which has been traced out in this present conversation and in others that we have had before, then, plentiful and vehement though your present promises may be, all you do will be fruitless.'

'Then,' said Crito, 'we shall strive to do as you bid us. But how are we to bury you?'

'However you like,' said Socrates, 'provided you can catch me and prevent my escaping you.' Then with a quiet laugh and a look in our direction he remarked, 'You know, I can't persuade Crito that I am the Socrates here present, the person who is now talking to you and arranging the topics of our conversation; he imagines that I am the dead body which he will shortly be looking at, and so he asks how he is to bury me. As for all I have been maintaining this long while, to wit that when I have drunk the poison I shall no longer be with you, but shall have taken my departure to some happy land of blest, that, I suppose, he regards as idle talk, intended to console you all and myself as well. That being so, I want you to stand surety for me with Crito, but for the precise opposite of that for which he sought to stand surety with the court. His pledge then, offered under oath, was that I would stay where I was; but I want you to pledge yourselves under oath that I will not stay where I am after I have died, but will take my departure; that will make it easier for Crito; when he sees my body being burnt or put under the ground he won't have to distress himself on my behalf, as though I were being outraged, and won't have to say at the funeral that it is Socrates whom he is laying out or carrying to the grave or burying.'

Then turning to Crito, 'My best of friends,' he continued, 'I would assure you that misuse of language is not only distasteful in itself, but actually harmful to the soul. So you must be of good cheer, and say that you are burying my body; and do that in whatever fashion you please and deem to be most conformable to custom.'

116 With these words he rose and went into another room to take his bath. Crito went with him, and told us to stay where we were. This we did, discussing amongst ourselves and meditating upon all that had been said, or sometimes talking of the great sorrow that had come upon us; for truly we felt like children who had lost a father, condemned to live henceforth as orphans. However, when Socrates had had his bath his children—two little boys and one bigger—were brought in to him, and those women relatives of his appeared; to these he addressed some words in the presence of Crito, with certain directions as to his wishes. He

then told the women and children to withdraw, and himself came over
to us.

By this time it was near to sunset, for he had spent a long time in
the inner room. So he came and sat with us after his bath, and did not
talk much more. And now the agent of the prison authorities had arrived, and stepping up to him said, 'Socrates, I shan't have my usual
ground for complaint in your case; many people get angry and abusive
when I instruct them, at the behest of the authorities, to drink the poison; but I have always known you, while you have been here, for the
most generous, the best tempered and the finest man of any that have
entered this place; and in particular I feel sure now that you are not
angry with me, but with those whom you know to be responsible for
this. Well, you know what I have come to tell you; so now good-bye,
and try to bear as best you may what must be borne.' As he said this,
he burst into tears, and turned to leave us. Socrates looked up at him
and said, 'Good-bye to you. I will do as you say'; and then to us, 'What
a delightful person! All these weeks he has been coming to see me, and
talking with me now and then, like the excellent fellow he is; and now
see how generously he weeps for me! Well, come now, Crito, let us do
his bidding. If the draught has been prepared, will someone please bring
it me; if not, tell the man to prepare it.'

'Oh, but I think, Socrates,' said Crito, 'that the sun is still upon
the mountains; it has not set yet. Besides, I know of people who have
taken the draught long after they were told to do so, and had plenty to
eat and drink, and even in some cases had intercourse with those whom
they desired. Don't hurry: there is still plenty of time.'

'It is quite natural, Crito,' he replied, 'that the people you speak of
should do that: they think it brings them some advantage; and it is
equally natural that I should not do so; I don't think I should get any
advantage out of taking the poison a little later on; I should merely make   117
myself ridiculous in my own eyes by clinging to life and eking out its
last dregs. No, no: don't hamper me: do as I say.'

At this Crito nodded to his slave who stood close by; whereupon the
latter went out, and after a considerable time came back with the man
who was to administer the poison, which he was carrying in a cup ready
to drink. On seeing him Socrates exclaimed, 'All right, good sir: you
know about this business: what must I do?'

'Simply drink it,' he replied, 'and then walk about until you have
a feeling of heaviness in your legs; then lie down, and it will act of itself.'
And as he spoke he offered Socrates the cup. And I tell you, Echecrates,
he took it quite calmly, without a tremor or any change of complexion
or expression. He just fixed the man with his well-known glare and

asked, 'What do you say to using the drink for a libation? Or is that not allowed?' The man replied, 'We only mix what we judge to be the right dose, Socrates.'

'I see', he rejoined. 'Well, at all events it is allowed to pray to the gods, as indeed we must, for a happy journey to our new dwelling-place; and that is my prayer; so may it be.' With these words he put the cup to his lips and drained it with no difficulty or distaste whatever.

So far most of us had more or less contrived to hold back our tears, but now, when we saw him drinking, and the cup emptied, it became impossible; for myself, despite my efforts the tears were pouring down my cheeks, so that I had to cover my face; but I was weeping not for him, no, but for myself and my own misfortune in losing such a friend. Crito had got up and withdrawn already, finding that he could not restrain his tears; as for Apollodorus, he had even before this been weeping continuously, and at this last moment he burst into sobs, and his tears of distress were heart-breaking to all of us, except to Socrates himself, who exclaimed, 'My dear good people, what a way to behave! Why, it was chiefly to avoid such a lapse that I sent the women away; for I was always told that a man ought to die in peace and quiet. Come, calm yourselves and do not give way.'

At that we felt ashamed, and ceased to weep. He walked round the room until, as he told us, his legs came to feel heavy, and then lay on his back, as he had been bidden. Thereupon the man who had brought the poison felt his body, and after a while examined his feet and legs, and then squeezed his foot tightly, asking if he felt anything. Socrates said no; next he felt his legs again, and moving his hand gradually up 118 he showed us that he was becoming cold and rigid. Touching him once more, he told us that when the cold reached the heart all would be over.

By this time it had reached somewhere about the pit of the stomach, when he removed the covering which he had put over his face, and uttered his final words: 'Crito, we owe a cock to Asklepios; pray do not forget to pay the debt.' 'It shall be done,' said Crito. 'Is there anything else you can think of?' There was no reply to this question; a moment afterwards he shuddered; the attendant uncovered his face again, and his gaze had become rigid; seeing which Crito closed his mouth and his eyes.

'And that, Echecrates, was the end of our friend, the finest man— so we should say—of all whom we came to know in his generation; the wisest too, and the most righteous.'

XIII

REPUBLIC

BOOK IV

(435) Now . . . if two things, one large, the other small, are called by the same name, they will be alike in that respect to which the common name applies. Accordingly, in so far as the quality of justice is concerned, there will be no difference between a just man and a just society.

No.

Well, but we decided that a society was just when each of the three types of human character it contained performed its own function; and again, it was temperate and brave and wise by virtue of certain other affections and states of mind of those same types.

True.

Reprinted by permission of the publisher from F. M. Cornford, *The Republic of Plato* (The Clarendon Press, Oxford, 1941).

Accordingly, my friend, if we are to be justified in attributing those same virtues to the individual, we shall expect to find that the individual soul contains the same three elements and that they are affected in the same way as are the corresponding types in society.

That follows.

Here, then, we have stumbled upon another little problem: Does the soul contain these three elements or not?

Not such a very little one, I think. It may be a true saying, Socrates, that what is worth while is seldom easy.

Apparently; and let me tell you, Glaucon, it is my belief that we shall never reach the exact truth in this matter by following our present methods of discussion; the road leading to that goal is longer and more laborious. However, perhaps we can find an answer that will be up to the standard we have so far maintained in our speculations.

Is not that enough? I should be satisfied for the moment.

Well, it will more than satisfy me, I replied.

436 Don't be disheartened, then, but go on.

Surely, I began, we must admit that the same elements and characters that appear in the state must exist in every one of us; where else could they have come from? It would be absurd to imagine that among peoples with a reputation for a high-spirited character, like the Thracians and Scythians and northerners generally, the states have not derived that character from their individual members; or that it is otherwise with the love of knowledge, which would be ascribed chiefly to our own part of the world, or with the love of money, which one would specially connect with Phoenicia and Egypt.

Certainly.

So far, then, we have a fact which is easily recognized. But here the difficulty begins. Are we using the same part of ourselves in all these three experiences, or a different part in each? Do we gain knowledge with one part, feel anger with another, and with yet a third desire the pleasures of food, sex, and so on? Or is the whole soul at work in every impulse and in all these forms of behaviour? The difficulty is to answer that question satisfactorily.

I quite agree.

Let us approach the problem whether these elements are distinct or identical in this way. It is clear that the same thing cannot act in two opposite ways or be in two opposite states at the same time, with respect to the same part of itself, and in relation to the same object. So if we find such contradictory actions or states among the elements concerned, we shall know that more than one must have been involved.

Very well.

Consider this proposition of mine, then. Can the same thing, at the same time and with respect to the same part of itself, be at rest and in motion?

Certainly not.

We had better state this principle in still more precise terms, to guard against misunderstanding later on. Suppose a man is standing still, but moving his head and arms. We should not allow anyone to say that the same man was both at rest and in motion at the same time, but only that part of him was at rest, part in motion. Isn't that so?

Yes.

An ingenious objector might refine still further and argue that a peg-top, spinning with its peg fixed at the same spot, or indeed any body that revolves in the same place, is both at rest and in motion as a whole. But we should not agree, because the parts in respect of which such a body is moving and at rest are not the same. It contains an axis and a circumference; and in respect of the axis it is at rest inasmuch as the axis is not inclined in any direction, while in respect of the circumference it revolves; and if, while it is spinning, the axis does lean out of the perpendicular in all directions, then it is in no way at rest.

That is true.

No objection of that sort, then, will disconcert us or make us believe that the same thing can ever act or be acted upon in two opposite ways, or be two opposite things, at the same time, in respect of the same part 43 of itself, and in relation to the same object.

I can answer for myself at any rate.

Well, anyhow, as we do not want to spend time in reviewing all such objections to make sure they are unsound, let us proceed on this assumption, with the understanding that, if we ever come to think otherwise, all the consequences based upon it will fall to the ground.

Yes, that is a good plan.

Now, would you not class all appetites such as hunger and thirst, and again willing and wishing, with the affirmative members of those pairs I have just mentioned? For instance, you would say that the soul of a man who desires something is striving after it, or trying to draw to itself the thing it wishes to possess, or again, in so far as it is willing to have its want satisfied, it is giving its assent to its own longing, as if to an inward question.

Yes.

And on the other hand, disinclination, unwillingness, and dislike, we should class on the negative side with acts of rejection or repulsion.

Of course.

That being so, shall we say that appetites form one class, the most conspicuous being those we call thirst and hunger?

Yes.

Thirst being desire for drink, hunger for food?

Yes.

Now, is thirst, just in so far as it is thirst, a desire in the soul for anything more than simply drink? Is it, for instance, thirst for hot drink or for cold, for much drink or for little, or in a word for drink of any particular kind? Is it not rather true that you will have a desire for cold drink only if you are feeling hot as well as thirsty, and for hot drink only if you are feeling cold; and if you want much drink or little, that will be because your thirst is a great thirst or a little one? But, just in itself, thirst or hunger is a desire for nothing more than its natural object, drink or food, pure and simple.

Yes, he agreed, each desire, just in itself, is simply for its own natural object. When the object is of such and such a particular kind, the desire will be correspondingly qualified.

438   We must be careful here, or we might be troubled by the objection that no one desires mere food and drink, but always wholesome food and drink. We shall be told that what we desire is always something that is good; so if thirst is a desire, its object must be, like that of any other desire, something—drink or whatever it may be—that will be good for one.

Yes, there might be something in that objection.

But surely, wherever you have two correlative terms, if one is qualified, the other must always be qualified too; whereas if one is unqualified, so is the other.

I don't understand.

Well, 'greater' is a relative term; and the greater is greater than the less; if it is much greater, then the less is much less; if it is greater at some moment, past or future, then the less is less at that same moment. The same principle applies to all such correlatives, like 'more' and 'fewer', 'double' and 'half'; and again to terms like 'heavier' and 'lighter', 'quicker' and 'slower', and to things like hot and cold.

Yes.

Or take the various branches of knowledge: is it not the same there? The object of knowledge pure and simple is the knowable—if that is the right word—without any qualification; whereas a particular kind of knowledge has an object of a particular kind. For example, as soon as men learnt how to build houses, their craft was distinguished from others under the name of architecture, because it had a unique character, which was itself due to the character of its object; and all other branches of craft and knowledge were distinguished in the same way.

True.

This, then, if you understand me now, is what I meant by saying that, where there are two correlatives, the one is qualified if, and only if, the other is so. I am not saying that the one must have the same quality as the other—that the science of health and disease is itself healthy and diseased, or the knowledge of good and evil is itself good and evil—but only that, as soon as you have a knowledge that is restricted to a particular kind of object, namely health and disease, the knowledge itself becomes a particular kind of knowledge. Hence we no longer call it merely knowledge, which would have for its object whatever can be known, but we add the qualification and call it medical science.

I understand now and I agree.

Now, to go back to thirst: is not that one of these relative terms? It 439 is essentially thirst for something.

Yes, for drink.

And if the drink desired is of a certain kind, the thirst will be correspondingly qualified. But thirst which is just simply thirst is not for drink of any particular sort—much or little, good or bad—but for drink pure and simple.

Quite so.

We conclude, then, that the soul of a thirsty man, just in so far as he is thirsty, has no other wish than to drink. That is the object of its craving, and towards that it is impelled.

This is clear.

Now if there is ever something which at the same time pulls it the opposite way, that something must be an element in the soul other than the one which is thirsting and driving it like a beast to drink; in accordance with our principle that the same thing cannot behave in two opposite ways at the same time and towards the same object with the same part of itself. It is like an archer drawing the bow: it is not accurate to say that his hands are at the same time both pushing and pulling it. One hand does the pushing, the other the pulling.

Exactly.

Now, is it sometimes true that people are thirsty and yet unwilling to drink?

Yes, often.

What, then, can one say of them, if not that their soul contains something which urges them to drink and something which holds them back, and that this latter is a distinct thing and overpowers the other?

I agree.

And is it not true that the intervention of this inhibiting principle in such cases always has its origin in reflection; whereas the impulses driving and dragging the soul are engendered by external influences and abnormal conditions?

Evidently.

We shall have good reason, then, to assert that they are two distinct principles. We may call that part of the soul whereby it reflects, rational; and the other, with which it feels hunger and thirst and is distracted by sexual passion and all the other desires, we will call irrational appetite, associated with pleasure in the replenishment of certain wants.

Yes, there is good ground for that view.

Let us take it, then, that we have now distinguished two elements in the soul. What of that passionate element which makes us feel angry and indignant? Is that a third, or identical in nature with one of those two?

It might perhaps be identified with appetite.

I am more inclined to put my faith in a story I once heard about Leontius, son of Aglaion. On his way up from the Piraeus outside the north wall, he noticed the bodies of some criminals lying on the ground, with the executioner standing by them. He wanted to go and look at them, but at the same time he was disgusted and tried to turn away. 440 He struggled for some time and covered his eyes, but at last the desire was too much for him. Opening his eyes wide, he ran up to the bodies and cried, 'There you are, curse you; feast yourselves on this lovely sight!'

Yes, I have heard that story too.

The point of it surely is that anger is sometimes in conflict with appetite, as if they were two distinct principles. Do we not often find a man whose desires would force him to go against his reason, reviling himself and indignant with this part of his nature which is trying to put constraint on him? It is like a struggle between two factions, in which indignation takes the side of reason. But I believe you have never observed, in yourself or anyone else, indignation make common cause with appetite in behaviour which reason decides to be wrong.

No, I am sure I have not.

Again, take a man who feels he is in the wrong. The more generous his nature, the less can he be indignant at any suffering, such as hunger and cold, inflicted by the man he has injured. He recognizes such treatment as just, and, as I say, his spirit refuses to be roused against it.

That is true.

But now contrast one who thinks it is he that is being wronged. His spirit boils with resentment and sides with the right as he conceives it. Persevering all the more for the hunger and cold and other pains he suffers, it triumphs and will not give in until its gallant struggle has ended in success or death; or until the restraining voice of reason, like a shepherd calling off his dog, makes it relent.

An apt comparison, he said; and in fact it fits the relation of our

Auxiliaries to the Rulers: they were to be like watch-dogs obeying the shepherds of the commonwealth.

Yes, you understand very well what I have in mind. But do you see how we have changed our view? A moment ago we were supposing this spirited element to be something of the nature of appetite; but now it appears that, when the soul is divided into factions, it is far more ready to be up in arms on the side of reason.

Quite true.

Is it, then, distinct from the rational element or only a particular form of it, so that the soul will contain no more than two elements, reason and appetite? Or is the soul like the state, which had three orders to hold it together, traders, Auxiliaries, and counsellors? Does the spirited element make a third, the natural auxiliary of reason, when not 441 corrupted by bad upbringing?

It must be a third.

Yes, I said, provided it can be shown to be distinct from reason, as we saw it from appetite.

That is easily proved. You can see that much in children: they are full of passionate feelings from their very birth; but some, I should say, never become rational, and most of them only late in life.

A very sound observation, said I, the truth of which may also be seen in animals. And besides, there is the witness of Homer in that line I quoted before: 'He smote his breast and spoke, childing his heart.' The poet is plainly thinking of the two elements as distinct, when he makes the one which has chosen the better course after reflection rebuke the other for its unreasoning passion.

I entirely agree.

The Virtues in the Individual

And so, after a stormy passage, we have reached the land. We are fairly agreed that the same three elements exist alike in the state and in the individual soul.

That is so.

Does it now follow at once that state and individual will be wise or brave by virtue of the same element in each and in the same way? Both will possess in the same manner any quality that makes for excellence.

That must be true.

Then it applies to justice: we shall conclude that a man is just in the same way that a state was just. And we have surely not forgotten that justice in the state meant that each of the three orders in it was doing its own proper work. So we may henceforth bear in mind that each of us likewise will be a just person, fulfilling his proper function, only if the several parts of our nature fulfil theirs.

Certainly.

And it will be the business of reason to rule with wisdom and forethought on behalf of the entire soul; while the spirited element ought to act as its subordinate and ally. The two will be brought into accord, as we said earlier, by that combination of mental and bodily training which will tune up one string of the instrument and relax the other, nourishing the reasoning part on the study of noble literature and allaying the oth-442 er's wildness by harmony and rhythm. When both have been nurtured and trained to know their own true functions, they must be set in command over the appetites, which form the greater part of each man's soul and are by nature insatiably covetous. They must keep watch lest this part, by battening on the pleasures that are called bodily, should grow so great and powerful that it will no longer keep to its own work, but will try to enslave the others and usurp a dominion to what it has no right, thus turning the whole of life upside down. At the same time, those two together will be the best of guardians for the entire soul and for the body against all enemies from without: the one will take counsel, while the other will do battle, following its ruler's commands and by its own bravery giving effect to the ruler's designs.

Yes, that is all true.

And so we call an individual brave in virtue of this spirited part of his nature, when, in spite of pain or pleasure, it holds fast to the injunctions of reason about what he ought or ought not to be afraid of.

True.

And wise in virtue of that small part which rules and issues these injunctions, possessing as it does the knowledge of what is good for each of the three elements and for all of them in common.

Certainly.

And, again, temperate by reason of the unanimity and concord of all three, when there is no internal conflict between the ruling element and its two subjects, but all are agreed that reason should be ruler.

Yes, that is an exact account of temperance, whether in the state or in the individual.

Finally, a man will be just by observing the principle we have so often stated.

Necessarily.

Now is there any indistinctness in our vision of justice, that might make it seem somehow different from what we found it to be in the state?

I don't think so.

Because, if we have any lingering doubt, we might make sure by comparing it with some commonplace notions. Suppose, for instance, that a sum of money were entrusted to our state or to an individual of corresponding character and training, would anyone imagine that such a person would be specially likely to embezzle it? 443

No.

And would he not be incapable of sacrilege and theft, or of treachery to friend or country; never false to an oath or any other compact; the last to be guilty of adultery or of neglecting parents or the due service of the gods?

Yes.

And the reason for all this is that each part of his nature is exercising its proper function, of ruling or of being ruled.

Yes, exactly.

Are you satisfied, then, that justice is the power which produces states or individuals of whom that is true, or must we look further?

There is no need; I am quite satisfied.

And so our dream has come true—I mean the inkling we had that, by some happy chance, we had lighted upon a rudimentary form of justice from the very moment when we set about founding our commonwealth. Our principle that the born shoemaker or carpenter had better stick to his trade turns out to have been an adumbration of justice; and that is why it has helped us. But in reality justice, though evidently analogous to this principle, is not a matter of external behaviour, but of the inward self and of attending to all that is, in the fullest sense, a man's proper concern. The just man does not allow the several elements in his soul to usurp one another's functions; he is indeed one who sets his house in order, by self-mastery and discipline coming to be at peace with himself, and bringing into tune those three parts, like the terms in the proportion of a musical scale, the highest and lowest notes and the mean between them, with all the intermediate intervals. Only when he has linked these parts together in well-tempered harmony and has made himself one man instead of many, will he be ready to go about whatever he may have to do, whether it be making money and satisfying bodily wants, or business transactions, or the affairs of state. In all these fields when he speaks of just and honourable conduct, he will mean the behaviour that helps to produce and to preserve this habit of mind; and by wisdom he will mean the knowledge which presides over such con- 444 duct. Any action which tends to break down this habit will be for him unjust: and the notions governing it he will call ignorance and folly.

That is perfectly true, Socrates.

Good, said I. I believe we should not be thought altogether mistaken, if we claimed to have discovered the just man and the just state, and wherein their justice consists.

Indeed we should not.

Shall we make that claim, then?

Yes, we will.

So be it, said I. Next, I suppose, we have to consider injustice.

Evidently.

This must surely be a sort of civil strife among the three elements, whereby they usurp and encroach upon one another's functions and some one part of the soul rises up in rebellion against the whole, claiming a supremacy to which it has no right because its nature fits it only to be the servant of the ruling principle. Such turmoil and aberration we shall, I think, identify with injustice, intemperance, cowardice, ignorance, and in a word with all wickedness.

Exactly.

And now that we know the nature of justice and injustice, we can be equally clear about what is meant by acting justly and again by unjust action and wrongdoing.

How do you mean?

Plainly, they are exactly analogous to those wholesome and unwholesome activities which respectively produce a healthy or unhealthy condition in the body; in the same way just and unjust conduct produce a just or unjust character. Justice is produced in the soul, like health in the body, by establishing the elements concerned in their natural relations of control and subordination, whereas injustice is like disease and means that this natural order is inverted.

Quite so.

It appears, then, that virtue is as it were the health and comeliness and well-being of the soul, as wickedness is disease, deformity, and weakness.

True.

And also that virtue and wickedness are brought about by one's way of life, honourable or disgraceful.

That follows.

So now it only remains to consider which is the more profitable 445 course: to do right and live honourably and be just, whether or not anyone knows what manner of man you are, or to do wrong and be unjust, provided that you can escape the chastisement which might make you a better man.

But really, Socrates, it seems to me ridiculous to ask that question now that the nature of justice and injustice has been brought to light. People think that all the luxury and wealth and power in the world cannot make life worth living when the bodily constitution is going to rack and ruin; and are we to believe that, when the very principle whereby we live is deranged and corrupted, life will be worth living so long as a man can do as he will, and wills to do anything rather than to free himself from vice and wrongdoing and to win justice and virtue?

BOOK V

Philosophers Must Be Kings

472 . . . Well, said I, let me begin by reminding you that what brought us to this point was our inquiry into the nature of justice and injustice.

True; but what of that?

Merely this: suppose we do find out what justice is, are we going to demand that a man who is just shall have a character which exactly corresponds in every respect to the ideal of justice? Or shall we be satisfied if he comes as near to the ideal as possible and has in him a larger measure of that quality than the rest of the world?

That will satisfy me.

If so, when we set out to discover the essential nature of justice and injustice and what a perfectly just and a perfectly unjust man would be like, supposing them to exist, our purpose was to use them as ideal patterns: we were to observe the degree of happiness or unhappiness that each exhibited, and to draw the necessary inference that our own destiny would be like that of the one we most resembled. We did not set out to show that these ideals would exist in fact.

That is true.

Then suppose a painter has drawn an ideally beautiful figure complete to the last touch, would you think any the worse of him, if he could not show that a person as beautiful as that could exist?

No, I should not.

Well, we have been constructing in discourse the pattern of an ideal state. Is our theory any the worse, if we cannot prove it possible that a state so organized should be actually founded?

Surely not.

That, then, is the truth of the matter. But if, for your satisfaction, I am to do my best to show under what conditions our ideal would have the best chance of being realized, I must ask you once more to admit that the same principle applies here. Can theory ever be fully realized
473 in practice? Is it not in the nature of things that action should come less close to truth than thought? People may not think so; but do you agree or not?

I do.

Then you must not insist upon my showing that this construction we have traced in thought could be reproduced in fact down to the last detail. You must admit that we shall have found a way to meet your demand for realization, if we can discover how a state might be constituted in the closest accordance with our description. Will not that content you? It would be enough for me.

And for me too.

Then our next attempt, it seems, must be to point out what defect in the working of existing states prevents them from being so organized, and what is the least change that would effect a transformation into this type of government—a single change if possible, or perhaps two; at any rate let us make the changes as few and insignificant as may be.

By all means.

Well, there is one change which, as I believe we can show, would bring about this revolution—not a small change, certainly, nor an easy one, but possible.

What is it?

I have now to confront what we called the third and greatest wave. But I must state my paradox, even though the wave should break in laughter over my head and drown me in ignominy. Now mark what I am going to say.

Go on.

Unless either philosophers become kings in their countries or those who are now called kings and rulers come to be sufficiently inspired with a genuine desire for wisdom; unless, that is to say, political power and philosophy meet together, while the many natures who now go their several ways in the one or the other direction are forcibly debarred from doing so, there can be no rest from troubles, my dear Glaucon, for states, nor yet, as I believe, for all mankind; nor can this commonwealth which we have imagined ever till then see the light of day and grow to its full stature. This is what I have so long hung back from saying; I knew what a paradox it would be, because it is hard to see that there is no other way of happiness either for the state or for the individual.

Socrates, exclaimed Glaucon, after delivering yourself of such a pronouncement as that, you must expect a whole multitude of by no means contemptible assailants to fling off their coats, snatch up the handiest 474 weapon, and make a rush at you, breathing fire and slaughter. If you cannot find arguments to beat them off and make your escape, you will learn what it means to be the target of scorn and derision.

Well, it was you who got me into this trouble.

Yes, and a good thing too. However, I will not leave you in the lurch. You shall have my friendly encouragement for what it is worth; and perhaps you may find me more complaisant than some would be in answering your questions. With such backing you must try to convince the unbelievers.

I will, now that I have such a powerful ally.

The Philosopher Defined

Now, I continued, if we are to elude those assailants you have described, we must, I think, define for them whom we mean by these lovers of wisdom who, we have dared to assert, ought to be our rulers. Once we have a clear view of their character, we shall be able to defend our position by pointing to some who are naturally fitted to combine philosophic study with political leadership, while the rest of the world should accept their guidance and let philosophy alone.

Yes, this is the moment for a definition.

Here, then, is a line of thought which may lead to a satisfactory explanation. Need I remind you that a man will deserve to be called a lover of this or that, only if it is clear that he loves that thing as a whole, not merely in parts?

You must remind me, it seems; for I do not see what you mean.

That answer would have come better from someone less susceptible to love than yourself, Glaucon. You ought not to have forgotten that any boy in the bloom of youth will arouse some sting of passion in a man of your amorous temperament and seem worthy of his attentions. Is not this your way with your favourites? You will praise a snub nose as piquant and a hooked one as giving a regal air, while you call a straight nose perfectly proportioned; the swarthy, you say, have a manly look, the fair are children of the gods; and what do you think is that word 'honey-pale', if not the euphemism of some lover who had no fault 475 to find with sallowness on the cheek of youth? In a word, you will carry pretence and extravagance to any length sooner than reject a single one that is in the flower of his prime.

If you insist on taking me as an example of how lovers behave, I will agree for the sake of argument.

Again, do you not see the same behaviour in people with a passion for wine? They are glad of any excuse to drink wine of any sort. And there are the men who covet honour, who, if they cannot lead an army, will command a company, and if they cannot win the respect of important people, are glad to be looked up to by nobodies, because they must have someone to esteem them.

Quite true.

Do you agree, then, that when we speak of a man as having a passion for a certain kind of thing, we mean that he has an appetite for
everything of that kind without discrimination?

Yes.

So the philosopher, with his passion for wisdom, will be one who
desires all wisdom, not only some part of it. If a student is particular
about his studies, especially while he is too young to know which are
useful and which are not, we shall say he is no lover of learning or of
wisdom; just as, if he were dainty about his food, we should say he was
not hungry or fond of eating, but had a poor appetite. Only the man
who has a taste for every sort of knowledge and throws himself into
acquiring it with an insatiable curiosity will deserve to be called a philosopher. Am I not right?

That description, Glaucon replied, would include a large and ill-
assorted company. It is curiosity, I suppose, and a delight in fresh experience that gives some people a passion for all that is to be seen and
heard at theatrical and musical performances. But they are a queer set
to reckon among philosophers, considering that they would never go
near anything like a philosophical discussion, though they run round at
all the Dionysiac festivals in town or country as if they were under con-
tract to listen to every company of performers without fail. Will curiosity
entitle all these enthusiasts, not to mention amateurs of the minor arts,
to be called philosophers?

Certainly not; though they have a certain counterfeit resemblance.

And whom do you mean by the genuine philosophers?

Those whose passion it is to see the truth.

That must be so; but will you explain?

It would not be easy to explain to everyone; but you, I believe, will
grant my premiss.

Which is ——?

That since beauty and ugliness are opposite, they are two things; 476
and consequently each of them is one. The same holds of justice and
injustice, good and bad, and all the essential Forms: each in itself is
one; but they manifest themselves in a great variety of combinations,
with actions, with material things, and with one another, and so each
seems to be many.

That is true.

On the strength of this premiss, then, I can distinguish your amateurs of the arts and men of action from the philosophers we are concerned with, who are alone worthy of the name.

What is your distinction?

Your lovers of sights and sounds delight in beautiful tones and colours and shapes and in all the works of art into which these enter; but

they have not the power of thought to behold and to take delight in the nature of Beauty itself. That power to approach Beauty and behold it as it is in itself, is rare indeed.

Quite true.

Now if a man believes in the existence of beautiful things, but not of Beauty itself, and cannot follow a guide who would lead him to a knowledge of it, is he not living in a dream? Consider: does not dreaming, whether one is awake or asleep, consist in mistaking a semblance for the reality it resembles?

I should certainly call that dreaming.

Contrast with him the man who holds that there is such a thing as Beauty itself and can discern that essence as well as the things that partake of its character, without ever confusing the one with the other—is he a dreamer or living in a waking state?

He is very much awake.

So may we say that he knows, while the other has only a belief in appearances; and might call their states of mind knowledge and belief?

Certainly.

But this person who, we say, has only belief without knowledge may be aggrieved and challenge our statement. Is there any means of soothing his resentment and converting him gently, without telling him plainly that he is not in his right mind?

We surely ought to try.

Come then, consider what we are to say to him. Or shall we ask him a question, assuring him that, far from grudging him any knowledge he may have, we shall be only too glad to find that there is something he knows? But, we shall say, tell us this: When a man knows, must there not be something that he knows? Will you answer for him, Glaucon?

My answer will be, that there must.

Something real or unreal?

477 Something real; how could a thing that is unreal ever be known?

Are we satisfied, then, on this point, from however many points of view we might examine it: that the perfectly real is perfectly knowable, and the utterly unreal is entirely unknowable?

Quite satisfied.

Good. Now if there is something so constituted that it both *is* and *is not*, will it not lie between the purely real and the utterly unreal?

It will.

Well then, as knowledge corresponds to the real, and absence of knowledge necessarily to the unreal, so, to correspond to this intermediate thing, we must look for something between ignorance and knowledge, if such a thing there be.

Certainly.

Is there not a thing we call belief?

Surely.

A different power from knowledge, or the same?

Different.

Knowledge and belief, then, must have different objects, answering to their respective powers.

Yes.

And knowledge has for its natural object the real—to know the truth about reality. However, before going further, I think we need a definition. Shall we distinguish under the general name of 'faculties' those powers which enable us—or anything else—to do what we can do? Sight and hearing, for instance, are what I call faculties, if that will help you to see the class of things I have in mind.

Yes, I understand.

Then let me tell you what view I take of them. In a faculty I cannot find any of those qualities, such as colour or shape, which, in the case of many other things, enable me to distinguish one thing from another. I can only look to its field of objects and the state of mind it produces, and regard these as sufficient to identify it and to distinguish it from faculties which have different fields and produce different states. Is that how you would go to work?

Yes.

Let us go back, then, to knowledge. Would you class that as a faculty?

Yes; and I should call it the most powerful of all.

And is belief also a faculty?

It can be nothing else, since it is what gives us the power of believing.

But a little while ago you agreed that knowledge and belief are not the same thing.

Yes; there could be no sense in identifying the infallible with the fallible.

Good. So we are quite clear that knowledge and belief are different 478 things?

They are.

If so, each of them, having a different power, must have a different field of objects.

Necessarily.

The field of knowledge being the real; and its power, the power of knowing the real as it is.

Yes.

Whereas belief, we say, is the power of believing. Is its object the same as that which knowledge knows? Can the same things be possible objects of knowledge and of belief?

Not if we hold to the principles we agreed upon. If it is of the nature of a different faculty to have a different field, and if both knowledge and belief are faculties and, as we assert, different ones, it follows that the same things cannot be possible objects of both.

So if the real is the object of knowledge, the object of belief must be something other than the real.

Yes.

Can it be the unreal? Or is that an impossible object even for belief? Consider: if a man has a belief, there must be something before his mind; he cannot be believing nothing, can he?

No.

He is believing something, then; whereas the unreal could only be called nothing at all.

Certainly.

Now we said that ignorance must correspond to the unreal, knowledge to the real. So what he is believing cannot be real nor yet unreal.

True.

Belief, then, cannot be either ignorance or knowledge.

It appears not.

Then does it lie outside and beyond these two? Is it either more clear and certain than knowledge or less clear and certain than ignorance?

No, it is neither.

It rather seems to you to be something more obscure than knowledge, but not so dark as ignorance, and so to lie between the two extremes?

Quite so.

Well, we said earlier that if some object could be found such that it both *is* and at the same time *is not*, that object would lie between the perfectly real and the utterly unreal; and that the corresponding faculty would be neither knowledge nor ignorance, but a faculty to be found situated between the two.

Yes.

And now what we have found between the two is the faculty we call belief.

True.

It seems, then, that what remains to be discovered is that object which can be said both to be and not to be and cannot properly be called either purely real or purely unreal. If that can be found, we may justly call it the object of belief, and so give the intermediate faculty the intermediate object, while the two extreme objects will fall to the extreme faculties.

Yes.

On these assumptions, then, I shall call for an answer from our friend 479
who denies the existence of Beauty itself or of anything that can be called
an essential Form of Beauty remaining unchangeably in the same state
for ever, though he does recognize the existence of beautiful things as
a plurality—that lover of things seen who will not listen to anyone who
says that Beauty is one, Justice is one, and so on. I shall say to him,
Be so good as to tell us: of all these many beautiful things is there one
which will not appear ugly? Or of these many just or righteous actions,
is there one that will not appear unjust or unrighteous?

No, replied Glaucon, they must inevitably appear to be in some way
both beautiful and ugly; and so with all the other terms your question
refers to.

And again the many things which are doubles are just as much halves
as they are doubles. And the things we call large or heavy have just as
much right to be called small or light.

Yes; any such thing will always have a claim to both opposite des-
ignations.

Then, whatever any one of these many things may be said to be,
can you say that it absolutely *is* that, any more than that it *is not* that?

They remind me of those punning riddles people ask at dinner parties, or the child's puzzle about what the eunuch threw at the bat and
what the bat was perched on. These things have the same ambiguous
character, and one cannot form any stable conception of them either as
being or as not being, or as both being and not being, or as neither.

Can you think of any better way of disposing of them than by plac-
ing them between reality and unreality? For I suppose they will not
appear more obscure and so less real than unreality, or clearer and so
more real than reality.

Quite true.

It seems, then, we have discovered that the many conventional notions of the mass of mankind about what is beautiful or honourable or
just and so on are adrift in a sort of twilight between pure reality and
pure unreality.

We have.

And we agreed earlier that, if any such object were discovered, it
should be called the object of belief and not of knowledge. Fluctuating
in that half-way region, it would be seized upon by the intermediate
faculty.

Yes.

So when people have an eye for the multitude of beautiful things or
of just actions or whatever it may be, but can neither behold Beauty or
Justice itself nor follow a guide who would lead them to it, we shall say
that all they have is belief, without any real knowledge of the objects of
their belief.

That follows.

But what of those who contemplate the realities themselves as they are for ever in the same unchanging state? Shall we not say that they have, not mere belief, but knowledge?

That too follows.

480 And, further, that their affection goes out to the objects of knowledge, whereas the others set their affections on the objects of belief; for it was they, you remember, who had a passion for the spectacle of beautiful colours and sounds, but would not hear of Beauty itself being a real thing.

I remember.

So we may fairly call them lovers of belief rather than of wisdom—not philosophical, in fact, but philodoxical. Will they be seriously annoyed by that description?

Not if they will listen to my advice. No one ought to take offence at the truth.

The name of philosopher, then, will be reserved for those whose affections are set, in every case, on the reality.

By all means.

BOOK VI: The Sun

[The guardian of the commonwealth and its laws] will have to take (504) the longer way and work as hard at learning as at training his body; otherwise he will never reach the goal of the highest knowledge, which most of all concerns him.

Why, are not justice and the other virtues we have discussed the highest? Is there something still higher to be known?

There is; and of those virtues themselves we have as yet only a rough outline, where nothing short of the finished picture should content us. If we strain every nerve to reach precision and clearness in things of little moment, how absurd not to demand the highest degree of exactness in the things that matter most.

Certainly. But what do you mean by the highest kind of knowledge and with what is it concerned? You cannot hope to escape that question.

I do not; you may ask me yourself. All the same, you have been told many a time; but now either you are not thinking or, as I rather suspect, you mean to put me to some trouble with your insistence. For you have often been told that the highest object of knowledge is the essential nature of the Good, from which everything that is good and right derives its value for us. You must have been expecting me to speak 505 of this now, and to add that we have no sufficient knowledge of it. I need not tell you that, without that knowledge, to know everything else, however well, would be of no value to us, just as it is of no use to possess anything without getting the good of it. What advantage can there be in possessing everything except what is good, or in understanding everything else while of the good and desirable we know nothing?

None whatever.

Well then, you know too that most people identify the Good with pleasure, whereas the more enlightened think it is knowledge.

Yes, of course.

And further that these latter cannot tell us what knowledge they mean, but are reduced at last to saying, 'knowledge of the Good'.

That is absurd.

It is; first they reproach us with not knowing the Good, and then tell us that it is knowledge of the Good, as if we did after all understand the meaning of that word 'Good' when they pronounce it.

217

Quite true.

What of those who define the Good as pleasure? Are they any less confused in their thoughts? They are obliged to admit that there are bad pleasures; from which it follows that the same things are both good and bad.

Quite so.

Evidently, then, this is a matter of much dispute. It is also evident that, although many are content to do what seems just or honourable without really being so, and to possess a mere semblance of these qualities, when it comes to good things, no one is satisfied with possessing what only seems good: here all reject the appearance and demand the reality.

Certainly.

A thing, then, that every soul pursues as the end of all her actions, dimly divining its existence, but perplexed and unable to grasp its nature with the same clearness and assurance as in dealing with other things, and so missing whatever value those other things might have—

506 a thing of such supreme importance is not a matter about which those chosen Guardians of the whole fortunes of our commonwealth can be left in the dark.

Most certainly not.

At any rate, institutions or customs which are desirable and right will not, I imagine, find a very efficient guardian in one who does not know in what way they are good. I should rather guess that he will not be able to recognize fully that they are right and desirable.

No doubt.

So the order of our commonwealth will be perfectly regulated only when it is watched over by a Guardian who does possess this knowledge.

That follows. But, Socrates, what is your own account of the Good? Is it knowledge, or pleasure, or something else?

There you are! I exclaimed; I could see all along that you were not going to be content with what other people think.

Well, Socrates, it does not seem fair that you should be ready to repeat other people's opinions but not to state your own, when you have given so much thought to this subject.

And do you think it fair of anyone to speak as if he knew what he does not know?

No, not as if he knew, but he might give his opinion for what it is worth.

Why, have you never noticed that opinion without knowledge is always a shabby sort of thing? At the best it is blind. One who holds a true belief without intelligence is just like a blind man who happens to take the right road, isn't he?

No doubt.

Well, then, do you want me to produce one of these poor blind cripples, when others could discourse to you with illuminating eloquence?

No really, Socrates, said Glaucon, you must not give up within sight of the goal. We should be quite content with an account of the Good like the one you gave us of justice and temperance and the other virtues.

So should I be, my dear Glaucon, much more than content! But I am afraid it is beyond my powers; with the best will in the world I should only disgrace myself and be laughed at. No, for the moment let us leave the question of the real meaning of good; to arrive at what I at any rate believe it to be would call for an effort too ambitious for an inquiry like ours. However, I will tell you, though only if you wish it, what I picture to myself as the offspring of the Good and the thing most nearly resembling it.

Well, tell us about the offspring, and you shall remain in our debt for an account of the parent.

I only wish it were within my power to offer, and within yours to 507 receive, a settlement of the whole account. But you must be content now with the interest only; and you must see to it that, in describing this offspring of the Good, I do not inadvertently cheat you with false coin.

We will keep a good eye on you. Go on.

First we must come to an understanding. Let me remind you of the distinction we drew earlier and have often drawn on other occasions, between the multiplicity of things that we call good or beautiful or whatever it may be and, on the other hand, Goodness itself or Beauty itself and so on. Corresponding to each of these sets of many things, we postulate a single Form or real essence, as we call it.

Yes, that is so.

Further, the many things, we say, can be seen, but are not objects of rational thought; whereas the Forms are objects of thought, but invisible.

Yes, certainly.

And we see things with our eyesight, just as we hear sounds with our ears, to speak generally, perceive any sensible thing with our sense-faculties.

Of course.

Have you noticed, then, that the artificer who designed the senses has been exceptionally lavish of his materials in making the eyes able to see and their objects visible?

That never occurred to me.

Well, look at it in this way. Hearing and sound do not stand in need of any third thing, without which the ear will not hear nor sound be heard; and I think the same is true of most, not to say all, of the other senses. Can you think of one that does require anything of the sort?

No, I cannot.

But there is this need in the case of sight and its objects. You may have the power of vision in your eyes and try to use it, and colour may be there in the objects; but sight will see nothing and the colours will remain invisible in the absence of a third thing peculiarly constituted to serve this very purpose.

By which you mean ——?

Naturally I mean what you call light; and if light is a thing of value, 508 the sense of sight and the power of being visible are linked together by a very precious bond, such as unites no other sense with its object.

No one could say that light is not a precious thing.

And of all the divinities in the skies is there one whose light, above all the rest, is responsible for making our eyes see perfectly and making objects perfectly visible?

There can be no two opinions: of course you mean the Sun.

And how is sight related to this deity? Neither sight nor the eye which contains it is the Sun, but of all the sense-organs it is the most sun-like; and further, the power it possesses is dispensed by the Sun, like a stream flooding the eye. And again, the Sun is not vision, but it is the cause of vision and also is seen by the vision it causes.

Yes.

It was the Sun, then, that I meant when I spoke of that offspring which the Good has created in the visible world, to stand there in the same relation to vision and visible things as that which the Good itself bears in the intelligible world to intelligence and to intelligible objects.

How is that? You must explain further.

You know what happens when the colours of things are no longer irradiated by the daylight, but only by the fainter luminaries of the night: when you look at them, the eyes are dim and seem almost blind, as if there were no unclouded vision in them. But when you look at things on which the Sun is shining, the same eyes see distinctly and it becomes evident that they do contain the power of vision.

Certainly.

Apply this comparison, then, to the soul. When its gaze is fixed upon an object irradiated by truth and reality, the soul gains understanding and knowledge and is manifestly in possession of intelligence. But when it looks towards that twilight world of things that come into existence and pass away, its sight is dim and it has only opinions and beliefs which shift to and fro, and now it seems like a thing that has no intelligence.

That is true.

This, then, which gives to the objects of knowledge their truth and to him who knows them his power of knowing, is the Form or essential nature of Goodness. It is the cause of knowledge and truth; and so, while you may think of it as an object of knowledge, you will do well to regard it as something beyond truth and knowledge and, precious as these both are, of still higher worth. And, just as in our analogy light and vision were to be thought of as like the Sun, but not identical with it, so here 509 both knowledge and truth are to be regarded as like the Good, but to identify either with the Good is wrong. The Good must hold a yet higher place of honour.

You are giving it a position of extraordinary splendour, if it is the source of knowledge and truth and itself surpasses them in worth. You surely cannot mean that it is pleasure.

Heaven forbid, I exclaimed. But I want to follow up our analogy still further. You will agree that the Sun not only makes the things we see visible, but also brings them into existence and gives them growth and nourishment; yet he is not the same thing as existence. And so with the objects of knowledge: these derive from the Good not only their power of being known, but their very being and reality; and Goodness is not the same thing as being, but even beyond being, surpassing it in dignity and power.

Glaucon exclaimed that some amusement at my exalting Goodness in such extravagant terms.

It is your fault, I replied; you forced me to say what I think.

Yes, and you must not stop there. At any rate, complete your comparison with the Sun, if there is any more to be said.

There is a great deal more, I answered.

Let us hear it, then; don't leave anything out.

I am afraid much must be left unspoken. However, I will not, if I can help it, leave out anything that can be said on this occasion.

Please do not.

Four Stages of Cognition: The Line

Conceive, then, that there are these two powers I speak of, the Good reigning over the domain of all that is intelligible, the Sun over the visible world—or the heaven as I might call it; only you would think I was showing off my skill in etymology. At any rate you have these two orders of things clearly before your mind: the visible and the intelligible?

I have.

Now take a line divided into two unequal parts, one to represent the visible order, the other the intelligible; and divide each part again in the same proportion, symbolizing degrees of comparative clearness or obscurity. Then (A) one of the two sections in the visible world will stand for images. By images I mean first shadows, and then reflections 510 in water or in close-grained, polished surfaces, and everything of that kind, if you understand.

Yes, I understand.

Let the second section (B) stand for the actual things of which the first are likenesses, the living creatures about us and all the works of nature or of human hands.

So be it.

Will you also take the proportion in which the visible world has been divided as corresponding to degrees of reality and truth, so that the likeness shall stand to the original in the same ratio as the sphere of appearances and belief to the sphere of knowledge?

Certainly.

Now consider how we are to divide the part which stands for the intelligible world. There are two sections. In the first (C) the mind uses as images those actual things which themselves had images in the visible world; and it is compelled to pursue its inquiry by starting from assumptions and travelling, not up to a principle, but down to a conclusion. In the second (D) the mind moves in the other direction, from an assumption up towards a principle which is not hypothetical; and it makes no use of the images employed in the other section, but only of Forms, and conducts its inquiry solely by their means.

I don't quite understand what you mean.

Then we will try again; what I have just said will help you to understand. (C) You know, of course, how students of subjects like geometry and arithmetic begin by postulating odd and even numbers, or the various figures and the three kinds of angle, and other such data in each subject. These data they take as known; and, having adopted them as assumptions, they do not feel called upon to give any account of them to themselves or to anyone else, but treat them as self-evident. Then, starting from these assumptions, they go on until they arrive, by a series of consistent steps, at all the conclusions they set out to investigate.

Yes, I know that.

You also know how they make use of visible figures and discourse about them, though what they really have in mind is the originals of which these figures are images: they are not reasoning, for instance, about this particular square and diagonal which they have drawn, but about *the* Square and *the* Diagonal; and so in all cases. The diagrams they draw and the models they make are actual things, which may have their shadows or images in water; but now they serve in their turn as images, while the student is seeking to behold those realities which only thought can apprehend.   511

True.

This, then, is the class of things that I spoke of as intelligible, but with two qualifications: first, that the mind, in studying them, is compelled to employ assumptions, and, because it cannot rise above these, does not travel upwards to a first principle; and second, that it uses as images those actual things which have images of their own in the section below them and which, in comparison with those shadows and reflections, are reputed to be more palpable and valued accordingly.

I understand: you mean the procedure of geometry and of the kindred arts.

(D) Then by the second section of the intelligible world you may understand me to mean all that unaided reasoning apprehends by the power of dialectic, when it treats its assumptions, not as first principles, but as *hypotheses* in the literal sense, things 'laid down' like a flight of steps up which it may mount all the way to something that is not hypothetical, the first principle of all; and having grasped this, may turn back and, holding on to the consequences which depend upon it, descend at last to a conclusion, never making use of any sensible object, but only of Forms, moving through Forms from one to another, and ending with Forms.

I understand, he said, though not perfectly; for the procedure you describe sounds like an enormous undertaking. But I see that you mean to distinguish the field of intelligible reality studied by dialectic as having a greater certainty and truth than the subject-matter of the 'arts', as they are called, which treat their assumptions as first principles. The students of these arts are, it is true, compelled to exercise thought in contemplating objects which the senses cannot perceive; but because they start from assumptions without going back to a first principle, you do not regard them as gaining true understanding about those objects, although the objects themselves, when connected with a first principle, are intelligible. And I think you would call the state of mind of the students of geometry and other such arts, not intelligence, but thinking, as being something between intelligence and mere acceptance of appearances.

You have understood me quite well enough, I replied. And now you may take, as corresponding to the four sections, these four states of mind: *intelligence* for the highest, *thinking* for the second, *belief* for the third, and for the last *imagining*. These you may arrange as the terms in a proportion, assigning to each a degree of clearness and certainty corresponding to the measure in which their objects possess truth and reality.

I understand and agree with you. I will arrange them as you say.

BOOK VII

The Allegory of the Cave

514   Next, said I, here is a parable to illustrate the degrees in which our nature may be enlightened or unenlightened. Imagine the condition of men living in a sort of cavernous chamber underground, with an entrance open to the light and a long passage all down the cave. Here they have been from childhood, chained by the leg and also by the neck, so that they cannot move and can see only what is in front of them, because the chains will not let them turn their heads. At some distance higher up is the light of a fire burning behind them; and between the prisoners and the fire is a track with a parapet built along it, like the screen at a puppet-show, which hides the performers while they show their puppets over the top.

I see, said he.

Now behind this parapet imagine persons carrying along various 515 artificial objects, including figures of men and animals in wood or stone or other materials, which project above the parapet. Naturally, some of these persons will be talking, others silent.

It is a strange picture, he said, and a strange sort of prisoners.

Like ourselves, I replied; for in the first place prisoners so confined would have seen nothing of themselves or of one another, except the shadows thrown by the fire-light on the wall of the Cave facing them, would they?

Not if all their lives they had been prevented from moving their heads.

And they would have seen as little of the objects carried past.

Of course.

Now, if they could talk to one another, would they not suppose that their words referred only to those passing shadows which they saw?

Necessarily.

And suppose their prison had an echo from the wall facing them? When one of the people crossing behind them spoke, they could only suppose that the sound came from the shadow passing before their eyes.

No doubt.

In every way, then, such prisoners would recognize as reality nothing but the shadows of those artificial objects.

Inevitably.

Now consider what would happen if their release from the chains and the healing of their unwisdom should come about in this way. Suppose one of them set free and forced suddenly to stand up, turn his head, and walk with eyes lifted to the light; all these movements would be painful, and he would be too dazzled to make out the objects whose shadows he had been used to see. What do you think he would say, if someone told him that what he had formerly seen was meaningless illusion, but now, being somewhat nearer to reality and turned towards more real objects, he was getting a truer view? Suppose further that he were shown the various objects being carried by and were made to say, in reply to questions, what each of them was. Would he not be perplexed and believe the objects now shown him to be not so real as what he formerly saw?

Yes, not nearly so real.

And if he were forced to look at the fire-light itself, would not his eyes ache, so that he would try to escape and turn back to the things which he could see distinctly, convinced that they really were clearer than these other objects now being shown to him?

Yes.

And suppose someone were to drag him away forcibly up the steep and rugged ascent and not let him go until he had hauled him out into the sunlight, would he not suffer pain and vexation at such treatment, 516 and, when he had come out into the light, find his eyes so full of its radiance that he could not see a single one of the things that he was now told were real?

Certainly he would not see them all at once.

He would need, then, to grow accustomed before he could see things in that upper world. At first it would be easiest to make out shadows, and then the images of men and things reflected in water, and later on the things themselves. After that, it would be easier to watch the heavenly bodies and the sky itself by night, looking at the light of the moon and stars rather than the Sun and the Sun's light in the day-time.

Yes, surely.

Last of all, he would be able to look at the Sun and contemplate its nature, not as it appears when reflected in water or any alien medium, but as it is in itself in its own domain.

No doubt.

And now he would begin to draw the conclusion that it is the Sun that produces the seasons and the course of the year and controls everything in the visible world, and moreover is in a way the cause of all that he and his companions used to see.

Clearly he would come at last to that conclusion.

Then if he called to mind his fellow prisoners and what passed for wisdom in his former dwelling-place, he would surely think himself happy in the change and be sorry for them. They may have had a practice of honouring and commending one another, with prizes for the man who had the keenest eye for the passing shadows and the best memory for the order in which they followed or accompanied one another, so that he could make a good guess as to which was going to come next. Would our released prisoner be likely to covet those prizes or to envy the men exalted to honour and power in the Cave? Would he not feel like Homer's Achilles, that he would far sooner 'be on earth as a hired servant in the house of a landless man' or endure anything rather than go back to his old beliefs and live in the old way?

Yes, he would prefer any fate to such a life.

Now imagine what would happen if he went down again to take his former seat in the Cave. Coming suddenly out of the sunlight, his eyes would be filled with darkness. He might be required once more to deliver his opinion on those shadows, in competition with the prisoners who had never been released, while his eyesight was still dim and unsteady; and it might take some time to become used to the darkness. They would laugh at him and say that he had gone up only to come back with his sight ruined; it was worth no one's while even to attempt the ascent. If they could lay hands on the man who was trying to set them free and lead them up, they would kill him.

Yes, they would.

Every feature in this parable, my dear Glaucon, is meant to fit our earlier analysis. The prison dwelling corresponds to the region revealed to us through the sense of sight, and the fire-light within it to the power of the Sun. The ascent to see the things in the upper world you may take as standing for the upward journey of the soul into the region of the intelligible; then you will be in possession of what I surmise, since that is what you wish to be told. Heaven knows whether it is true; but this, at any rate, is how it appears to me. In the world of knowledge, the last thing to be perceived and only with great difficulty is the essential Form of Goodness. Once it is perceived, the conclusion must follow that, for all things, this is the cause of whatever is right and good; in the visible world it gives birth to light and to the lord of light, while it is itself sovereign in the intelligible world and the parent of intelligence and truth. Without having had a vision of this Form no one can act with wisdom, either in his own life or in matters of state.

So far as I can understand, I share your belief.

Then you may also agree that it is no wonder if those who have reached this height are reluctant to manage the affairs of men. Their souls long to spend all their time in that upper world—naturally enough, if here once more our parable holds true. Nor, again, is it at all strange that one who comes from the contemplation of divine things to the miseries of human life should appear awkward and ridiculous when, with eyes still dazed and not yet accustomed to the darkness, he is compelled, in a law-court or elsewhere, to dispute about the shadows of justice or the images that cast those shadows, and to wrangle over the notions of what is right in the minds of men who have never beheld Justice itself.

It is not at all strange.

No; a sensible man will remember that the eyes may be confused 518 in two ways—by a change from light to darkness or from darkness to light; and he will recognize that the same thing happens to the soul. When he sees it troubled and unable to discern anything clearly, instead of laughing thoughtlessly, he will ask whether, coming from a brighter existence, its unaccustomed vision is obscured by the darkness, in which case he will think its condition enviable and its life a happy one; or whether, emerging from the depths of ignorance, it is dazzled by excess of light. If so, he will rather feel sorry for it; or, if he were inclined to laugh, that would be less ridiculous than to laugh at the soul which has come down from the light.

That is a fair statement.

If this is true, then, we must conclude that education is not what it is said to be by some, who profess to put knowledge into a soul which does not possess it, as if they could put sight into blind eyes. On the contrary, our own account signifies that the soul of every man does possess the power of learning the truth and the organ to see it with; and that, just as one might have to turn the whole body round in order that the eye should see light instead of darkness, so the entire soul must be turned away from this changing world, until its eye can bear to contemplate reality and that supreme splendour which we have called the Good. Hence there may well be an art whose aim would be to effect this very thing, the conversion of the soul, in the readiest way; not to put the power of sight into the soul's eye, which already has it, but to ensure that, instead of looking in the wrong direction, it is turned the way it ought to be.

Yes it may well be so.

It looks, then, as though wisdom were different from those ordinary virtues, as they are called, which are not far removed from bodily qualities, in that they can be produced by habituation and exercise in a soul which has not possessed them from the first. Wisdom, it seems, is cer-

tainly the virtue of some diviner faculty, which never loses its power,
519 though its use for good or harm depends on the direction towards which
it is turned. You must have noticed in dishonest men with a reputation
for sagacity the shrewd glance of a narrow intelligence piercing the objects to which it is directed. There is nothing wrong with their power
of vision, but it has been forced into the service of evil, so that the keener
its sight, the more harm it works.

Quite true.

And yet if the growth of a nature like this had been pruned from
earliest childhood, cleared of those clinging overgrowths which come of
gluttony and all luxurious pleasure and, like leaden weights charged
with affinity to this mortal world, hang upon the soul, bending its vision
downwards; if, freed from these, the soul were turned round towards
true reality, then this same power in these very men would see the truth
as keenly as the objects it is turned to now.

Yes, very likely.

Is it not also likely, or indeed certain after what has been said, that
a state can never be properly governed either by the uneducated who
know nothing of truth or by men who are allowed to spend all their days
in the pursuit of culture? The ignorant have no single mark before their
eyes at which they must aim in all the conduct of their own lives and
of affairs of state; and the others will not engage in action if they can
help it, dreaming that, while still alive, they have been translated to the
Islands of the Blest.

Quite true.

It is for us, then, as founders of a commonwealth, to bring compulsion to bear on the noblest natures. They must be made to climb the
ascent to the vision of Goodness, which we called the highest object of
knowledge; and, when they have looked upon it long enough, they must
not be allowed, as they now are, to remain on the heights, refusing to
come down again to the prisoners or to take any part in their labours
and rewards, however much or little these may be worth.

Shall we not be doing them an injustice, if we force on them a worse
life than they might have?

You have forgotten again, my friend, that the law is not concerned
to make any one class specially happy, but to ensure the welfare of the
commonwealth as a whole. By persuasion or constraint it will unite the
520 citizens in harmony, making them share whatever benefits each class
can contribute to the common good; and its purpose in forming men of
that spirit was not that each should be left to go his own way, but that
they should be instrumental in binding the community into one.

True, I had forgotten.

You will see, then, Glaucon, that there will be no real injustice in compelling our philosophers to watch over and care for the other citizens. We can fairly tell them that their compeers in other states may quite reasonably refuse to collaborate: there they have sprung up, like a self-sown plant, in despite of their country's institutions; no one has fostered their growth, and they cannot be expected to show gratitude for a care they have never received. 'But', we shall say, 'it is not so with you. We have brought you into existence for your country's sake as well as for your own, to be like leaders and king-bees in a hive; you have been better and more thoroughly educated than those others and hence you are more capable of playing your part both as men of thought and as men of action. You must go down, then, each in his turn, to live with the rest and let your eyes grow accustomed to the darkness. You will then see a thousand times better than those who live there always; you will recognize every image for what it is and know what it represents, because you have seen justice, beauty, and goodness in their reality; and so you and we shall find life in our commonwealth no mere dream, as it is in most existing states, where men live fighting one another about shadows and quarrelling for power, as if that were a great prize; whereas in truth government can be at its best and free from dissension only where the destined rulers are least desirous of holding office.'

Quite true.

Then will our pupils refuse to listen and to take their turns at sharing in the work of the community, though they may live together for most of their time in a purer air?

No; it is a fair demand, and they are fair-minded men. No doubt, unlike any ruler of the present day, they will think of holding power as an unavoidable necessity.

Yes, my friend; for the truth is that you can have a well-governed society only if you can discover for your future rulers a better way of 521 life than being in office; then only will power be in the hands of men who are rich, not in gold, but in the wealth that brings happiness, a good and wise life. All goes wrong when, starved for lack of anything good in their own lives, men turn to public affairs hoping to snatch from thence the happiness they hunger for. They set about fighting for power, and this internecine conflict ruins them and their country. The life of true philosophy is the only one that looks down upon offices of state; and access to power must be confined to men who are not in love with it; otherwise rivals will start fighting. So whom else can you compel to undertake the guardianship of the commonwealth, if not those who, besides understanding best the principles of government, enjoy a nobler life than the politician's and look for rewards of a different kind?

There is indeed no other choice.

Shall we next consider how men of this quality are to be produced and how they may be led upward to the light, as some are fabled to have ascended from the underworld to the gods?

By all means.

It is a question of 'night or day', to be determined not, as in the children's game, by spinning a shell, but by the turning about of the soul from a day that is like night to the veritable day, that journey up to the real world which we shall call the true pursuit of wisdom. We have to ask what studies will have this effect.

Yes.

What form of study is there, Glaucon, that would draw the soul from the world of change to reality? At this moment it occurs to me that our young men were to be trained warriors; so the study we are looking for ought to be not without use in warfare as well.

Yes, if possible.

Now, of the two branches of their earlier education, physical training is certainly concerned with perishable things, for bodily strength grows and decays. So this cannot be the study we are in search of. Can 522 it be education in poetry and music carried to the point we laid down earlier?

No, he replied; that, if you remember, was the counterpart of bodily training. It educated our Guardians by the influence of habit, imparting no real knowledge, but only a kind of measure and harmony by means of melody and rhythm, and forming the character in similar ways through the content of the literature, fabulous or true. It taught nothing useful for so high a purpose as you now have in view.

Quite true; your memory is very exact. But where shall we find what we want? The manual crafts, we agreed, were all rather degrading.

Yes, of course. But if you exclude them as well as all that early education, what is there left to study?

Well, if we cannot find anything over and above these subjects, suppose we take something that has a bearing upon them all. There is one, for instance, which is universally useful in all crafts and in every form of knowledge and intellectual operation—the first thing everyone has to learn.

What do you mean?

A simple matter: learning to tell the difference between one, two, and three, or, to put it shortly, number and calculation. Is it not true that this is something which no art or science can dispense with?

Certainly.

Including the art of war. On the stage, at any rate, Agamemnon is made to look a very ridiculous sort of general. You must remember how often the tragedians make Palamedes claim to have invented number and by that means to have marshalled the ranks of the army at Troy and counted the ships and everything. Apparently nothing could be counted before, and Agamemnon could not even tell how many feet he had—an odd kind of general, don't you think?

Very odd, if that is really true.

So we may conclude that a soldier must know how to count and calculate?

He must, or he could not be a human being at all, to say nothing of marshalling an army.

Does it strike you, then, that this study is one of those we are looking for, which naturally awaken the power of thought, though no one makes a right use of its tendency to draw us towards reality? 523

How do you mean?

I will try to explain how I distinguish in my own mind the things which have that tendency. If you will consider them too and say whether or not you agree, we shall see if I am right in my surmise.

Please explain.

Take our perceptions, then. I can point to some of these which do not provoke thought to reflect upon them, because we are satisfied with the judgement of the senses. But in other cases perception seems to yield no trustworthy result, and reflection is instantly demanded.

You mean objects seen from a great distance, or illusory effects in scene-painting.

No, you have not understood me. I mean that reflection is provoked when perception yields a contradictory impression, presenting two opposite qualities with equal clearness, no matter whether the object be distant or close at hand. When there is no such contradiction, we are not encouraged to reflect. Let me illustrate what I mean. Here are three fingers, the middle finger, the third, and the little one. I am assuming that you have a close view of them. The point is this. Each one of them presents itself equally as a finger, and in this respect it makes no difference whether we see it at either end of the row or in the middle, as fair or dark, thick or thin, and so on. In any case we see it as a finger, and the ordinary mind is not driven to call in its power of reflection and ask for a definition of 'finger', because at no stage has the sense of sight intimated that the finger is at the same moment the opposite of a finger. So an impression of this kind naturally has no tendency to arouse reflection.

Naturally.

But now take the size of these fingers. Can sight satisfactorily distinguish their bigness and smallness, and does it make no difference whether any particular one of them is at the end of the row or in between? Or can touch discriminate between thick and thin or hard and

soft? In reporting on qualities like these all the senses are deficient. They
524 seem to work in this way. The sense which takes cognizance of hardness
must also take cognizance of softness, and it reports to the mind that it
feels the same thing as both hard and soft.

That is true.

In such cases, then, the mind must be at a loss to know what this
sensation means by hard, since it declares the same thing to be also soft;
or what sensations of lightness and heaviness mean by light and heavy,
if they intimate that what is light is heavy and what is heavy is light.

Yes; these reports strike the mind as paradoxical and they do call
for reflection.

So it is natural in these circumstances for the mind to invoke the
help of reason with its power of calculation, to consider whether any
given message it receives refers to a single thing or to two. If there appear to be two things, each of them will appear as one thing, distinct
from the other; and accordingly, each being one and both together making two, the mind will conceive them as separate; otherwise it would
think of them not as two, but as one.

Quite so.

Now sight, too, as we said, perceives both big and little; only not
as separate, but in a confused impression. In order to clear up this confusion, intelligence was driven to look at bigness and smallness in the
opposite way, as distinct things. It is some such experience as this that
first prompts us to ask what is meant by bigness or smallness. And that
is how we came to distinguish what we call the object of intelligence
from the thing seen.

Exactly.

Well then, that is the distinction I was trying to express just now,
when I defined as provocative of thought impressions of sense in which
opposites are combined; whereas, if there is no contradictory impression, there is nothing to awaken reflection.

I understand now and I agree.

Now what about unity and number? To which of those two classes
do they belong?

I cannot be sure.

What we have just said should help you to a conclusion. If unity
can be satisfactorily apprehended, just by itself, by sight or any other
sense, as we said of the finger, then it will not have the quality of drawing the mind towards reality. But if it is always seen in some contradictory combination, so as to appear no more one than the opposite of
one, then a judge will be needed to decide; the mind will be forced to

seek a way out of the difficulty, setting thought in motion and asking what unity means. In this way the study of unity would be one of those which convert the soul and lead it to the contemplation of reality. 525

Well, unity is a case in which sight certainly does present a contradiction. We see the same thing as both one and also indefinitely many.

Then if that is true of unity, all number has the same property, hasn't it?

Yes.

Well now, number is the subject of the whole art of calculation and of the science of number; and since the properties of number appear to have the power of leading us towards reality, these must be among the studies we are in search of. The soldier must learn them in order to marshal his troops; the philosopher, because he must rise above the world of change and grasp true being, or he will never become proficient in the calculations of reason. Our Guardian is both soldier and philosopher; so this will be a suitable study for our law to prescribe. Those who are to take part in the highest functions of state must be induced to approach it, not in an amateur spirit, but perseveringly, until, by the aid of pure thought, they come to see the real nature of number. They are to practise calculation, not like merchants or shopkeepers for purposes of buying and selling, but with a view of war and to help in the conversion of the soul itself from the world of becoming to truth and reality.

Excellent.

Moreover, talking of this study, it occurs to me now what a fine thing it is and in how many ways it will further our intentions, if it is pursued for the sake of knowledge and not for commercial ends. As we were saying, it has a great power of leading the mind upwards and forcing it to reason about pure numbers, refusing to discuss collections of material things which can be seen and touched. Good mathematicians, as of course you know, scornfully reject any attempt to cut up the unit itself into parts: if you try to break it up small, they will multiply it up again, taking good care that the unit shall never lose its oneness and appear as a multitude of parts.

Quite true.

And if they are asked what are these numbers they are talking about, in which every unit, as they claim, is exactly equal to every other and contains no parts, what would be their answer? 526

This, I should say: that the numbers they mean can only be conceived by thought: there is no other way of dealing with them.

You see, then, that this study is really indispensable for our purpose, since it forces the mind to arrive at pure truth by the exercise of pure thought.

Yes, it has a powerful effect of that kind. . . .

(526) It is settled, then, that arithmetic is to be one of our subjects. Have we any use for the one that comes next?

You mean geometry?

I do.

Obviously, so much of it as bears on warlike operations will concern us. For pitching a camp, occupying a position, closing up or deploying troops, and for other formations in battle or on the march, a knowledge of geometry will be an advantage.

But still, I replied, for such purposes a small amount of geometry and arithmetic will be enough. We have to ask whether a much more advanced study will help towards a comprehension of the essential Form of Goodness. Any study, as we said, will have that tendency, if it forces the soul to turn towards the region of that beatific reality, which it must by all means behold. So geometry will be suitable or not, according as it makes us contemplate reality or the world of change.

That is our view.

527 In this respect, then, no one who has even a slight acquaintance with geometry will deny that the nature of this science is in flat contradiction with the absurd language used by mathematicians, for want of better terms. They constantly talk of 'operations' like 'squaring', 'applying', 'adding', and so on, as if the object were to *do* something, whereas the true purpose of the whole subject is knowledge—knowledge, moreover, of what eternally exists, not of anything that comes to be this or that at some time and ceases to be.

Yes, that will be readily agreed: geometry is knowledge of the eternally existent.

If so, it will tend to draw the soul towards truth and to direct upwards the philosophic intelligence which is now wrongly turned earthwards.

There is no doubt about that.

Then there can be no doubt that geometry must by no means be neglected by the citizens of your Callipolis. It has incidental advantages, too, which are not to be despised. There are its uses in war, which you mentioned; and also we know that a training in geometry makes all the difference in preparing the mind for any kind of study.

It does indeed.

Then we will make this the second subject of study for our young men.

We will.

Shall we put astronomy third? Do you agree?

Certainly I do. It is important for military purposes, no less than for agriculture and navigation, to be able to tell accurately the times of the month or year.

I am amused by your evident fear that the public will think you are recommending useless knowledge. True, it is quite hard to realize that every soul possesses an organ better worth saving than a thousand eyes, because it is our only means of seeing the truth; and that when its light is dimmed or extinguished by other interests, these studies will purify the hearth and rekindle the sacred fire. Those who believe in this faculty will approve of your proposals without reserve; all who are unaware of its existence will of course think them nonsense, because they can see in such knowledge no ulterior profit worth mentioning. So you had bet- 528 ter decide at once which party you mean to reason with. Or you may ignore both and carry on the discussion chiefly for your own satisfaction, though anyone who can benefit by it may be welcome to do so.

I would rather go on with the conversation for my own sake in the main.

Well then, we must retrace our steps. We made a mistake just now about the subject that comes next after geometry. From plane geometry we went straight on to the study of solid bodies in circular motion. We ought first to take solid bodies in themselves; for the third dimension should come after the second, and that brings us to the cube and all the figures which have depth.

That is so. But this subject, Socrates, seems not to have been investigated.

There are two reasons for that. These inquiries, difficult as they are, languish because no state thinks them worth encouraging. Secondly, students are not likely to make discoveries without a director, who is hard to find, and supposing him found, as matters now stand, the men with a gift for these researches would be too proud to accept his guidance. They would be amenable only if a whole community were to conceive a respect for such work and give a director its support. The problems might then be solved by continuous and energetic investigation. Even now, despised as the subject is by the public and curtailed by students who do not take account of its true utility, in spite of everything it is gaining ground, thanks to its inherent charm; and it would not be surprising if inquiry should succeed in bringing the truth to light.

Yes, he agreed, it has a remarkable charm. But please explain further. Just now you spoke of geometry as the study of plane surfaces, and you put astronomy next. But then you went back on that.

Yes, I was in too great a hurry to cover all the ground; more haste less speed. The study of solids should have come next; I passed it over because it is in such a pitiable state, and went on to astronomy, which studies the motion of solid bodies.

True.

Then let us put astronomy fourth, assuming the subject now neglected to have been established, provided that the state will take it up.

That may well happen. And now, Socrates, I will praise astronomy
on your own principles, instead of commending its usefulness in the
529 vulgar spirit for which you upbraided me. Anyone can see that this subject forces the mind to look upwards, away from this world of ours to
higher things.

Anyone except me, perhaps, I replied. I do not agree.

Why not?

As it is now handled by those who are trying to lead us up to philosophy, I think it simply turns the mind's eye downwards.

What do you mean?

You put a too generous construction on the study of 'higher things'.
Apparently you would think a man who threw his head back to contemplate the decorations on a ceiling was using his reason, not his eyes,
to gain knowledge. Perhaps you are right and my notion is foolish; but
I cannot think of any study as making the mind look upwards, except
one which has to do with unseen reality. No one, I should say, can ever
gain knowledge of any sensible object by gaping upwards any more than
by shutting his eyes and searching for it on the ground, because there
can be no knowledge of sensible things. His mind will be looking downwards, though he may pursue his studies lying on his back or floating
on the sea.

I deserve to be rebuked, he answered. But how did you mean the
study of astronomy to be reformed, so as to serve our purposes?

In this way. These intricate traceries in the sky are, no doubt, the
loveliest and most perfect of material things, but still part of the visible
world, and therefore they fall far short of the true realities—the real
relative velocities, in the world of pure number and all perfect geometrical figures, of the movements which carry round the bodies involved in them. These, you will agree, can be conceived by reason and
thought, not seen by the eye.

Exactly.

Accordingly, we must use the embroidered heaven as a model to
illustrate our study of those realities, just as one might use diagrams
exquisitely drawn by some consummate artist like Daedalus. An expert
in geometry, meeting with such designs, would admire their finished
workmanship, but he would think it absurd to study them in all earnest
530 with the expectation of finding in their proportions the exact ratio of
any one number to another.

Of course it would be absurd.

The genuine astronomer, then, will look at the motions of the stars
with the same feelings. He will admit that the sky with all that it contains

has been framed by its artificer with the highest perfection of which such works are capable. But when it comes to the proportions of day to night, of day and night to month, of month to year, and of the periods of other stars to Sun and Moon and to one another, he will think it absurd to believe that these visible material things go on for ever without change or the slightest deviation, and to spend all his pains on trying to find exact truth in them.

Now you say so, I agree.

If we mean, then, to turn the soul's native intelligence to its proper use by a genuine study of astronomy, we shall proceed, as we do in geometry, by means of problems, and leave the starry heavens alone.

That will make the astronomer's labour many times greater than it is now.

Yes; and if we are to be of any use as lawgivers, the other tasks we set will be no less burdensome.

And now, I went on, have you any further suitable study to suggest?

Not at the moment.

Yet there is more than one variety of motion, I fancy. An expert would be able to name them all; but even people like us can distinguish two.

What are they?

Besides the motion studied in astronomy, there is its counterpart, the harmonious movement for which our ears are framed, as our eyes are for the study of the stars. These are sister sciences, so the Pythagoreans say, and we may agree with them. This is a large subject and we will ask what they have to tell us about it, and perhaps about some other questions. Only we must constantly hold by our own principle, not to let our pupils take up any study in an imperfect form, stopping short of that higher region to which all studies should attain, as we said just now in speaking of astronomy. As you will know, the students of 531 harmony make the same sort of mistake as the astronomers: they waste their time in measuring audible concords and sounds one against another.

Yes, said Glaucon, they are absurd enough, with their talk of 'groups of quarter-tones' and all the rest of it. They lay their ears to the instrument as if they were trying to overhear the conversation from next door. One says he can still detect a note in between, giving the smallest possible interval, which ought to be taken as the unit of measurement, while another insists that there is now no difference between the two notes. Both prefer their ears to their intelligence.

You are thinking of those worthy musicians who tease and torture the strings, racking them on the pegs. I will not push the metaphor so far as to picture the musician beating them with the plectrum and charging them with faults which the strings deny or brazen out. I will drop the comparison and tell you that I am thinking rather of those Pythagoreans whom we were going to consult about harmony. They are just like the astronomers—intent upon the numerical properties embodied in these audible consonances: they do not rise to the level of formulating problems and inquiring which numbers are inherently consonant and which are not, and for what reasons.

That sounds like a superhuman undertaking.

I would rather call it a 'useful' study; but useful only when pursued as a means to the knowledge of beauty and goodness.

No doubt. . . .

Further, I continued, this whole course of study will, I believe, contribute to the end we desire and not be labour wasted, only if it is carried to the point at which reflection can take a comprehensive view of the mutual relations and affinities which bind all these sciences together.

So I suspect; but it is an enormous task, Socrates.

What do you refer to? The prelude? Do we not know that all this is no more than an introduction to the main theme which has yet to be learnt? Surely you would not regard experts in mathematics as masters of dialectic.

Certainly not, except a very few of those I have met.

Well, can the knowledge we are demanding ever be attained by people who cannot give a rational account of their statements or make others give an account of theirs?

532 Once more I should say No.

Here at last, then, we come to the main theme, to be developed in philosophic discussion. It falls within the domain of the intelligible world; but its progress is like that of the power of vision in the released prisoner of our parable. When he had reached the stage of trying to look at the living creatures outside the Cave, then at the stars, and lastly at the Sun himself, he arrived at the highest object in the visible world. So here, the summit of the intelligible world is reached in philosophic discussion by one who aspires, through the discourse of reason unaided by any of the senses, to make his way in every case to the essential reality and perseveres until he has grasped by pure intelligence the very nature of Goodness itself. This journey is what we call Dialectic.

Yes, certainly.

There was also that earlier stage when the prisoner, set free from his chains, turned from the shadows to the images which cast them and to the fire-light, and climbed up out of the cavern into the sunshine. When there, he was still unable to look at the animals and plants and

the sunlight; he could only see the shadows of things and their reflections
in water, though these, it is true, are works of divine creation and come
from real things, not mere shadows of images thrown by the light of the
fire, which was itself only an image as compared with the Sun. Now the
whole course of study in the arts we have reviewed has the corresponding effect of leading up the noblest faculty of the soul towards the contemplation of the highest of all realities, just as in our allegory the bodily
organ which has the clearest perceptions was led up towards the bright-
est of visible things in the material world.

I agree to what you are saying, Glaucon replied: I find it very hard
to accept, but in another way no less hard to deny. However, there will
be many other opportunities to reconsider it; so let us assume for the
moment that it is true, and go on to develop what you call the main
theme as fully as we have treated the prelude. I want you to describe
the function of philosophic discussion, into what divisions it falls, and
what are its methods; for here, it seems, we have come to the procedure
which should lead to the resting-place at our journey's end.

My dear Glaucon, said I, you will not be able to follow me farther, 533
though not for want of willingness on my part. It would mean that,
instead of illustrating the truth by an allegory, I should be showing you
the truth itself, at least as it appears to me. I cannot be sure whether
or not I see it as it really is; but we can be sure that there is some such
reality which it concerns us to see. Is not that so?

No doubt.

And also that it can be revealed only to one who is trained in the
studies we have discussed, and to him only by the power of dialectic?

That also we can assert.

At any rate, no one will maintain against us that there is any other
method of inquiry which systematically attempts in every case to grasp
the nature of each thing as it is in itself. The other arts are nearly all
concerned with human opinions and desires, or with the production of
natural and artificial things, or with the care of them when produced.
There remain geometry and those other allied studies which, as we said,
do in some measure apprehend reality; but we observe that they cannot
yield anything clearer than a dream-like vision of the real so long as
they leave the assumptions they employ unquestioned and can give no
account of them. If your premiss is something you do not really know
and your conclusion and the intermediate steps are a tissue of things
you do not really know, your reasoning may be consistent with itself,
but how can it ever amount to knowledge?

It cannot.

So, said I, the method of dialectic is the only one which takes this
course, doing away with assumptions and travelling up to the first prin-

ciple of all, so as to make sure of confirmation there. When the eye of the soul is sunk in a veritable slough of barbarous ignorance, this method gently draws it forth and guides it upwards, assisted in this work of conversion by the arts we have enumerated. From force of habit we have several times spoken of these as branches of knowledge; but they need some other name implying something less clear than knowledge, though not so dim as the apprehension of appearances. 'Thinking', I believe, was the term we fixed on earlier; but in considering matters of such high importance we shall not quarrel about a name.

Certainly not.

534 We shall be satisfied, then, with the names we gave earlier to our four divisions: first, knowledge; second, thinking; third, belief; and fourth, imagining. The last two taken together constitute the apprehension of appearances in the world of Becoming; the first two, intelligence concerned with true Being. Finally, as Being is to Becoming, so is intelligence to the apprehension of appearances; and in the same relation again stand knowledge to belief, and thinking to imagining. We had better not discuss the corresponding objects, the intelligible world and the world of appearance, or the twofold division of each of those provinces and the proportion in which the divisions stand. We might be involved in a discussion many times as long as the one we have already had.

Well, I certainly agree on those other points, so far as I can follow you.

And by a master of dialectic do you also mean one who demands an account of the essence of each thing? And would you not say that, in so far as he can render no such account to himself or to others, his intelligence is at fault?

I should.

And does not this apply to the Good? He must be able to distinguish the essential nature of Goodness, isolating it from all other Forms; he must fight his way through all criticisms, determined to examine every step by the standard, not of appearances and opinions, but of reality and truth, and win through to the end without sustaining a fall. If he cannot do this, he will know neither Goodness itself nor any good thing; if he does lay hold upon some semblance of good, it will be only a matter of belief, not of knowledge; and he will dream away his life here in a sleep which has no awakening on this side of that world of Death where he will sleep at last for ever.

I do most earnestly agree with you.

Well then, if you should ever be charged in actual fact with the upbringing and education of these imaginary children of yours, you will not allow them, I suppose, to bear rule in your commonwealth so long as their minds are, as a mathematician might say, irrational quantities, not commensurate with the highest responsibilities. So you will make a law that they must devote themselves especially to the discipline which will make them masters of the technique of asking and answering questions.

Yes, I will, with your collaboration.

May we conclude, then, that our account of the subjects of study is now complete? Dialectic will stand as the coping-stone of the whole structure; there is no other study that deserves to be put above it.   535

Yes, I agree.

It only remains, then, to draw up a scheme showing how, and to whom, these studies are to be allotted.

Clearly.

You remember what sort of people we chose earlier to be Rulers?

Of course I do.

In most respects, then, natures of that quality are to be selected: we shall prefer the steadiest, the bravest, and, so far as possible, the handsomest persons. But, besides that, we must look not only for generous and virile characters, but for gifts fitting them for this sort of education. They must be eager students and learn with ease, because the mind is more apt to shrink from severe study than from hard physical exercise, in which part of the burden falls upon the body. Also we must demand a good memory and a dogged appetite for hard work of every kind. How else can you expect a man to undergo all the hardships of bodily training and, on the top of that, to carry through such a long course of study?

He will certainly need every natural advantage.

At any rate, this explains what is wrong now with the position of Philosophy and why she has fallen into disrepute: as I said before, she ought never to have been wooed by the base-born, who are unworthy of her favours. To begin with, the genuine aspirant should not be one-sided in his love of work, liking one half of it and neglecting the other; as happens with one who throws himself into athletics and hunting and all sorts of bodily exertion, but hates the trouble of learning anything from others or of thinking for himself. His industry goes halting on one foot; and so it does too if it takes the opposite direction.

Quite true.

Also with regard to truth, we shall count as equally crippled a mind which, while it hates deliberate falsehood, cannot bear to tell lies, and is very angry when others do so, yet complacently tolerates involuntary error and is in no way vexed at being caught wallowing in swinish ig-   536
norance. We must be no less on the watch to distinguish the base metal from the true in respect of temperance, courage, highmindedness, and every kind of virtue. A state which chooses its rulers, or a man who

chooses his friends, without a searching eye for these qualities will find
themselves, in respect of one or another of them, cheated by a counterfeit or leaning on a broken reed. So all such precautions are very
much our concern. If we can find, for this long course of training and
study, men who are at all points sound of limb and sound in mind, then
Justice herself will have no fault to find with us and we shall ensure the
safety of our commonwealth and its institutions. We should only ruin
it by choosing pupils of a different stamp; and moreover we should bring
down upon philosophy an even greater storm of ridicule.

That would be a discreditable result.

It would. But at the moment I seem to be inviting ridicule myself.

In what way?

By speaking with so much warmth and forgetting that these speculations are only an amusement for our leisure. As I spoke, I seemed
to see Philosophy suffering undeserved insults, and was so vexed with
her persecutors that I lost my temper and became too vehement.

I did not think so as I listened.

No, but I felt it myself. However, here is something we must not
forget. When we spoke earlier of selecting Rulers, we said we should
choose old men; but that will not do for the selection we are making
now. We must not let Solon persuade us that a man can learn many
things as he grows old; he could sooner learn to run. Youth is the time
for hard work of all sorts.

Undoubtedly.

Arithmetic, then, and geometry and all branches of the preliminary
education which is to pave the way for Dialectic should be introduced
in childhood; but not in the guise of compulsory instruction, because
for the free man there should be no element of slavery in learning. Enforced exercise does no harm to the body, but enforced learning will not
537 stay in the mind. So avoid compulsion, and let your children's lessons
take the form of play. This will also help you to see what they are naturally fitted for.

That is a reasonable plan.

You remember, too, our children were to be taken to the wars on
horseback to watch the fighting, and, when it was safe, brought close
up like young hounds to be given a taste of blood.

I remember.

Then we must make a select list including everyone who shows for-
wardness in all these studies and exercises and dangers.

At what age?

As soon as they are released from the necessary physical training.
This may take two or three years, during which nothing else can be
done; for weariness and sleep are unfavourable to study. And at the

same time, these exercises will provide not the least important test of character.

No doubt.

When that time is over, then, some of those who are now twenty years old will be selected for higher privileges. The detached studies in which they were educated as children will now be brought together in a comprehensive view of their connexions with one another and with reality.

Certainly that is the only kind of knowledge which takes firm root in the mind.

Yes, and the chief test of a natural gift for Dialectic, which is the same thing as the ability to see the connexions of things.

I agree.

You will keep an eye, then, on these qualities and make a further selection of those who possess them in the highest degree and show most steadfastness in study as well as in warfare and in their other duties. When they reach thirty they will be promoted to still higher privileges and tested by the power of Dialectic, to see which can dispense with sight and the other senses and follow truth into the region of pure reality. And here, my friend, you will need the greatest watchfulness.

Why in particular?

You must have seen how much harm is done now by philosophical discussion—how it infects people with a spirit of lawlessness.

Yes, I have.

Does that surprise you? Can you not make allowances for them? Imagine a child brought up in a rich family with powerful connexions and surrounded by a host of flatterers; and suppose that, when he comes 538 to manhood, he learns that he is not the son of those who call themselves his parents and his true father and mother are not to be found. Can you guess how he would feel towards his supposed parents and towards his flatterers before he knew about his parentage and after learning the truth? Or shall I tell you what I should expect?

Please do.

I should say that, so long as he did not know the truth, he would have more respect for his reputed parents and family than for the flatterers, and be less inclined to neglect them in distress or to be insubordinate in word or deed; and in important matters the flatterers would have less influence with him. But what he learnt the facts, his respect would be transferred to them; their influence would increase, and he would openly associate with them and adopt their standards of behaviour, paying no heed to his reputed father and family, unless his disposition were remarkably good.

Yes; all that would be likely to happen. But how does your illustration apply to people who are beginning to take part in philosophical discussions?

In this way. There are certain beliefs about right and honourable conduct, which we have been brought up from childhood to regard with the same sort of reverent obedience that is shown to parents. In opposition to these, other courses attract us with flattering promises of pleasure; though a moderately good character will resist such blandishments and remain loyal to the beliefs of his fathers. But now suppose him confronted by the question, What does 'honourable' mean? He gives the answer he has been taught by the lawgiver, but he is argued out of his position. He is refuted again and again from many different points of view and at last reduced to thinking that what he called honourable might just as well be called disgraceful. He comes to the same conclusion about justice, goodness, and all the things he most revered. What will become now of his old respect and obedience?

Obviously they cannot continue as before.

And when he has disowned these discredited principles and failed to find the true ones, naturally he can only turn to the life which flatters his desires; and we shall see him renounce all morality and become a
539 lawless rebel. If this is the natural consequence of plunging the young into philosophical discussion, ought we not to make allowances, as I said before?

Yes, and be sorry for them too.

Then, if you do not want to be sorry for those pupils of yours who have reached the age of thirty, you must be very careful how you introduce them to such discussions. One great precaution is to forbid their taking part while they are still young. You must have seen how youngsters, when they get their first taste of it, treat argument as a form of sport solely for purposes of contradiction. When someone has proved them wrong, they copy his methods to confute others, delighting like puppies in tugging and tearing at anyone who comes near them. And so, after a long course of proving others wrong and being proved wrong themselves, they rush to the conclusion that all they once believed is false; and the result is that in the eyes of the world they discredit, not themselves only, but the whole business of philosophy. An older man will not share this craze for making a sport of contradiction. He will prefer to take for his model the conversation of one who is bent on seeking truth, and his own reasonableness will bring credit on the pursuit. We meant to ensure this result by all that we said earlier against the present practice of admitting anybody, however unfit, to philosophic discussions, and about the need for disciplined and steadfast character.

Certainly.

If a man, then, is to devote himself to such discussion as continuously and exclusively as he gave himself up earlier to the corresponding training of his body, will twice as long a time be enough?

Do you mean six years or four?

No matter; let us say five. For after that they must be sent down again into that Cave we spoke of and compelled to take military commands and other offices suitable to the young, so that they may not be behind their fellow citizens in experience. And at this stage they must once more be tested to see whether they will stand firm against all seductions. 540

How much time do you allow for this?

Fifteen years. Then, when they are fifty, those who have come safely through and proved the best at all points in action and in study must be brought at last to the goal. They must lift up the eye of the soul to gaze on that which sheds light on all things; and when they have seen the Good itself, take it as a pattern for the right ordering of the state and of the individual, themselves included. For the rest of their lives, most of their time will be spent in study; but they will all take their turn at the troublesome duties of public life and act as Rulers for their country's sake, not regarding it as a distinction, but as an unavoidable task. And so, when each generation has educated others like themselves to take their place as Guardians of the commonwealth, they will depart to dwell in the Islands of the Blest. The state will set up monuments for them and sacrifices, honouring them as divinities, if the Pythian Oracle approves, or at least as men blest with a godlike spirit.

XIV

PHAEDRUS

The Immortality of Soul

(245)   All soul is immortal; for that which is ever in motion is immortal. But that which while imparting motion is itself moved by something else can cease to be in motion, and therefore can cease to live; it is only that which moves itself that never intermits its motion, inasmuch as it cannot abandon its own nature; moreover this self-mover is the source and first principle of motion for all other things that are moved. Now a first principle cannot come into being: for while anything that comes to be must come to be from a first principle, the latter itself cannot come to be from anything whatsoever: if it did, it would cease any longer to be a first principle. Furthermore, since it does not come into being, it must be imperishable: for assuredly if a first principle were to be destroyed, nothing could come to be out of it, nor could anything bring the principle itself back into existence, seeing that a first principle is needed for anything to come into being.

The self-mover, then, is the first principle of motion: and it is as impossible that it should be destroyed as that it should come into being: were it otherwise, the whole universe, and the whole of that which comes to be, would collapse into immobility, and never find another source of motion to bring it back into being.

And now that we have seen that that which is moved by itself is immortal, we shall feel no scruple in affirming that precisely that is the essence and definition of soul, to wit self-motion. Any body that has an external source of motion is soulless; but a body deriving its motion from a source within itself is animate or *besouled*, which implies that the nature of soul is what has been said.

And if this last assertion is correct, namely that 'that which moves

---

Reprinted by permission of the publisher from R. Hackforth, trans., Plato, *Phaedrus* (Cambridge University Press, 1952).

itself' is precisely identifiable with soul, it must follow that soul is not 246
born and does not die.

Myth of the Soul: The Charioteer and Two Horses

As to soul's immortality then we have said enough, but as to its
nature there is this that must be said: what manner of thing it is would
be a long tale to tell, and most assuredly a god alone could tell it; but
what it resembles, that a man might tell in briefer compass: let this
therefore be our manner of discourse. Let it be likened to the union of
powers in a team of winged steeds and their winged charioteer. Now all
the gods' steeds and all their charioteers are good, and of good stock;
but with other beings it is not wholly so. With us men, in the first place,
it is a pair of steeds that the charioteer controls; moreover one of them
is noble and good, and of good stock, while the other has the opposite
character, and his stock is opposite. Hence the task of our charioteer is
difficult and troublesome.

And now we must essay to tell how it is that living beings are called
mortal and immortal. All soul has the care of all that is inanimate, and
traverses the whole universe, though in ever-changing forms. Thus when
it is perfect and winged it journeys on high and controls the whole world;
but one that has shed its wings sinks down until it can fasten on something solid, and settling there it takes to itself an earthy body which
seems by reason of the soul's power to move itself. This composite structure of soul and body is called a living being, and is further termed
'mortal': 'immortal' is a term applied on no basis of reasoned argument
at all, but our fancy pictures the god whom we have never seen, nor
fully conceived, as an immortal living being, possessed of a soul and a
body united for all time. Howbeit let these matters, and our account
thereof, be as god pleases; what we must understand is the reason why
the soul's wings fall from it, and are lost. It is on this wise.

The natural property of a wing is to raise that which is heavy and
carry it aloft to the region where the gods dwell; and more than any
other bodily part it shares in the divine nature, which is fair, wise and
good, and possessed of all other such excellences. Now by these excellences especially is the soul's plumage nourished and fostered, while by
their opposites, even by ugliness and evil, it is wasted and destroyed.
And behold, there in the heaven Zeus, mighty leader, drives his winged
team: first of the host of gods and daemons he proceeds, ordering all
things and caring therefor: and the host follows after him, marshalled
in eleven companies. For Hestia abides alone in the gods' dwelling- 247

place; but for the rest, all such as are ranked in the number of the twelve as ruler gods lead their several companies, each according to his rank.

Now within the heavens are many spectacles of bliss upon the high-ways whereon the blessed gods pass to and fro, each doing his own work; and with them are all such as will and can follow them: for jealousy has no place in the choir divine. But at such times as they go to their feasting and banquet, behold they climb the steep ascent even unto the summit of the arch that supports the heavens; and easy is that ascent for the chariots of the gods, for that they are well-balanced and readily guided; but for the others it is hard, by reason of the heaviness of the steed of wickedness, which pulls down his driver with his weight, except that driver have schooled him well.

And now there awaits the soul the extreme of her toil and struggling. For the souls that are called immortal, so soon as they are at the summit, come forth and stand upon the back of the world: and straightway the revolving heaven carries them round, and they look upon the regions without.

Of that place beyond the heavens none of our earthly poets has yet sung, and none shall sing worthily. But this is the manner of it, for assuredly we must be bold to speak what is true, above all when our discourse is upon truth. It is there that true Being dwells, without colour or shape, that cannot be touched; reason alone, the soul's pilot, can behold it, and all true knowledge is knowledge thereof. Now even as the mind of a god is nourished by reason and knowledge, so also is it with every soul that has a care to receive her proper food; wherefore when at last she has beheld Being she is well content, and contemplating truth she is nourished and prospers, Until the heaven's revolution brings her back full circle. And while she is borne round she discerns justice, its very self, and likewise temperance, and knowledge, not the knowledge that is neighbour to Becoming and varies with the various objects to which we commonly ascribe being, but the veritable knowledge of Being that veritably is. And when she has contemplated likewise and feasted upon all else that has true being, she descends again within the heavens and comes back home. And having so come, her charioteer sets his steeds at their manger, and puts ambrosia before them and draught of nectar to drink withal.

Such is the life of gods: of the other souls that which best follows a god and becomes most like thereunto raises her charioteer's head into the outer region, and is carried round with the gods in the revolution, but being confounded by her steeds she has much ado to discern the things that are; another now rises, and now sinks, and by reason of her unruly steeds sees in part, but in part sees not. As for the rest, though all are eager to reach the heights and seek to follow, they are not able: sucked down as they travel they trample and tread upon one another, this one striving to outstrip that. Thus confusion ensues, and conflict and grievous sweat: whereupon, with their charioteers powerless, many are lamed, and many have their wings all broken; and for all their toiling they are baulked, every one, of the full vision of Being, and departing therefrom, they feed upon the food of semblance.

Now the reason wherefore the souls are fain and eager to behold the Plain of Truth, and discover it, lies herein: to wit, that the pasturage that is proper to their noblest part comes from that Meadow, and the plumage by which they are borne aloft is nourished thereby.

Hear now the ordinance of Necessity. Whatsoever soul has followed in the train of a god, and discerned something of truth, shall be kept from sorrow until a new revolution shall begin; and if she can do this always, she shall remain always free from hurt. But when she is not able so to follow, and sees none of it, but meeting with some mischance comes to be burdened with a load of forgetfulness and wrongdoing, and because of that burden sheds her wings and falls to the earth, then thus runs the law: in her first birth she shall not be planted in any brute beast, but the soul that hath seen the most of Being shall enter into the human babe that shall grow into a seeker after wisdom or beauty, a follower of the Muses and a lover; the next, having seen less, shall dwell in a king that abides by law, or a warrior and ruler; the third in a statesman, a man of business or a trader; the fourth in an athlete, or physical trainer or physician; the fifth shall have the life of a prophet or a mystery-priest; to the sixth that of a poet or other imitative artist shall be fittingly given; the seventh shall live in an artisan or farmer, the eighth in a sophist or demagogue, the ninth in a tyrant.

Now in all these incarnations he who lives righteously has a better lot for his portion, and he who lives unrighteously a worse. For a soul does not return to the place whence she came for ten thousand years, since in no lesser time can she regain her wings, save only his soul who 249 has sought after wisdom unfeignedly, or has conjoined his passion for a loved one with that seeking. Such a soul, if with three revolutions of a thousand years she has thrice chosen this philosophic life, regains thereby her wings, and speeds away after three thousand years; but the rest, when they have accomplished their first life, are brought to judgment, and after the judgment some are taken to be punished in places of chastisement beneath the earth, while others are borne aloft by Justice to a certain region of the heavens, there to live in such manner as is merited by their past life in the flesh. And after a thousand years these and those alike come to the allotment and choice of their second life, each choosing according to her will; then does the soul of a man enter into the life of a beast, and the beast's soul that was aforetime in a man goes back to a man again. For only the soul that has beheld truth may enter into this our human form: seeing that man must needs understand the language of Forms, passing from a plurality of perceptions to a unity gathered together by reasoning; and such understanding is a recollection of those things which our souls beheld aforetime as they journeyed with their god, looking down upon the things which now we suppose to be, and gazing up to that which truly is.

Therefore is it meet and right that the soul of the philosopher alone should recover her wings: for she, so far as may be, is ever near in memory to those things a god's nearness whereunto makes him truly god. Wherefore if a man makes right use of such means of remembrance, and ever approaches to the full vision of the perfect mysteries, he and he alone becomes truly perfect. Standing aside from the busy doings of mankind, and drawing nigh to the divine, he is rebuked by the multitude as being out of his wits, for they know not that he is possessed by a deity.

Mark therefore the sum and substance of all our discourse touching the fourth sort of madness: to wit, that this is the best of all forms of divine possession, both in itself and in its sources, both for him that has it and for him that shares therein; and when he that loves beauty is touched by such madness he is called a lover. Such an one, as soon as he beholds the beauty of this world, is reminded of true beauty, and his wings begin to grow; then is he fain to lift his wings and fly upward; yet he has not the power, but inasmuch as he gazes upward like a bird, and cares nothing for the world beneath, men charge it upon him that he is demented.

Now, as we have said, every human soul has, by reason of her nature, had contemplation of true Being: else would she never have entered into this human creature; but to be put in mind thereof by things here is not easy for every soul; some, when they had the vision, had it but for a moment; some when they had fallen to earth consorted unhappily with such as led them to deeds of unrighteousness, wherefore they forgot the holy objects of their vision. Few indeed are left that can still remember much: but when these discern some likeness of the things yonder, they are amazed, and no longer masters of themselves, and know not what is come upon them by reason of their perception being dim.

Now in the earthly likeness of justice and temperance and all other prized possessions of the soul there dwells no lustre; nay, so dull are the organs wherewith men approach their images that hardly can a few behold that which is imaged; but with beauty it is otherwise. Beauty it was ours to see in all its brightness in those days when, amidst that happy company, we beheld with our eyes that blessed vision, ourselves in the train of Zeus, others following some other god; then we were all initiated into that mystery which is rightly accounted blessed beyond all others; whole and unblemished were we that did celebrate it, untouched by the evils that awaited us in days to come; whole and unblemished likewise, free from all alloy, steadfast and blissful were the spectacles on which we gazed in the moment of final revelation; pure was the light that shone around us, and pure were we, without taint of that prison-house which now we are encompassed withal, and call a body, fast bound therein as an oyster in its shell.

There let it rest then, our tribute to a memory that has stirred us to linger awhile on those former joys for which we yearn. Now beauty, as we said, shone bright amidst these visions, and in this world below we apprehend it through the clearest of our senses, clear and resplendent. For sight is the keenest mode of perception vouchsafed us through the body; wisdom, indeed, we cannot see thereby—how passionate had been our desire for her, if she had granted us so clear an image of herself to gaze upon—nor yet any other of those beloved objects, save only beauty; for beauty alone this has been ordained, to be most manifest to sense and most lovely of them all.

Now he whose vision of the mystery is long past, or whose purity has been sullied, cannot pass swiftly hence to see Beauty's self yonder, when he beholds that which is called beautiful here; wherefore he looks upon it with no reverence, and surrendering to pleasure he essays to go after the fashion of a four-footed beast, and to beget offspring of the flesh; or consorting with wantonness he has no fear nor shame in running after unnatural pleasure. But when one who is fresh from the mystery, and saw much of the vision, beholds a godlike face or bodily form that truly expresses beauty, first there comes upon him a shuddering and a measure of that awe which the vision inspired, and then reverence as at the sight of a god: and but for fear of being deemed a very madman he would offer sacrifice to his beloved, as to a holy image of deity. Next, with the passing of the shudder, a strange sweating and fever seizes him: for by reason of the stream of beauty entering in through his eyes there comes a warmth, whereby his soul's plumage is fostered; and with that warmth the roots of the wings are melted, which for long had been so hardened and closed up that nothing could grow; then as the nourishment is poured in the stump of the wing swells and hastens to grow from the root over the whole substance of the soul: for aforetime the whole soul was furnished with wings. Meanwhile she throbs with ferment in every part, and even as a teething child feels an aching and pain in its gums when a tooth has just come through, so does the soul of him who is beginning to grow his wings feel a ferment and painful irritation. Wherefore as she gazes upon the boy's beauty, she admits a flood of particles streaming therefrom—that is why we speak of a "flood of passion"—whereby she is warmed and fostered; then has she respite from her anguish, and is filled with joy. But when she has been parted from him and become parched, the openings of those outlets at which the wings are sprouting dry up likewise and are closed, so that the wing's germ is barred off; and behind its bars, together with the flood aforesaid, it throbs like a fevered pulse, and pricks at its proper outlet; and thereat the whole soul round about is stung and goaded into anguish; howbeit she remembers the beauty of her beloved, and rejoices again. So between joy and anguish she is distraught at being in such strange case, perplexed and frenzied; with madness upon her she can neither sleep by night nor keep still by day, but runs hither and thither, yearning for him in whom beauty dwells, if haply she may behold him. At last she does behold him, and lets the flood pour in upon her, releasing the imprisoned waters; then has she refreshment and respite from her stings and sufferings, and at that moment tastes a pleasure that is sweet beyond compare. Nor will she willingly give it up: above all others does she esteem her beloved in his beauty: mother, brother, friends, she forgets them all: naught does she reck of losing worldly possessions through neglect: all the rules of conduct, all the graces of life, of which aforetime she was proud, she now disdains, welcoming a slave's estate and any couch where she may be suffered to lie down close beside her darling; for besides her reverence for the possessor of beauty she has found in him the only physician for her grievous suffering.

Hearken, fair boy to whom I speak: this is the experience that men term love (*Eros*), but when you hear what the gods call it, you will probably smile at its strangeness. There are a couple of verses on love quoted by certain Homeric scholars from the unpublished works, the second of which is remarkably bold and a trifle astray in its quantities: they run as follows:

> Eros, cleaver of air, in mortals' speech is he named;
> But, since he must grow wings, Pteros the celestials call him.

You may believe that or not, as you please; at all events the cause and the nature of the lover's experience are in fact what I have said.

Now if he whom Love has caught be amongst the followers of Zeus, he is able to bear the burden of the winged one with some constancy; but they that attend upon Ares, and did range the heavens in his train, when they are caught by Love and fancy that their beloved is doing them some injury, will shed blood and not scruple to offer both themselves and their loved ones in sacrifice. And so does each lover live, after the manner of the god in whose company he once was, honouring him and copying him so far as may be, so long as he remains uncorrupt and is still living in his first earthly period; and in like manner does he comport himself towards his beloved and all his other associates. And so each selects a fair one for his love after his disposition, and even as if the beloved himself were a god he fashions for himself as it were an image, and adorns it to be the object of his veneration and worship.

Thus the followers of Zeus seek a beloved who is Zeus-like in soul; wherefore they look for one who is by nature disposed to the love of wisdom and the leading of men, and when they have found him and come to love him they do all in their power to foster that disposition. And if they have not aforetime trodden this path, they now set out upon it, learning the way from any source that may offer or finding it for themselves; and as they follow up the trace within themselves of the nature of their own god their task is made easier, inasmuch as they are 253 constrained to fix their gaze upon him; and reaching out after him in memory they are possessed by him, and from him they take their ways and manners of life, in so far as a man can partake of a god. But all this, mark you, they attribute to the beloved, and the draughts which they draw from Zeus they pour out, like Bacchants, into the soul of the beloved, thus creating in him the closest possible likeness to the god they worship.

Those who were in the train of Hera look for a royal nature, and when they have found him they do unto him all things in like fashion. And so it is with the followers of Apollo and each other god: every love is fain that his beloved should be of a nature like to his own god; and when he has won him, he leads him on to walk in the ways of their god, and after his likeness, patterning himself thereupon and giving counsel and discipline to the boy. There is no jealousy nor petty spitefulness in his dealings, but his every act is aimed at bringing the beloved to be every whit like unto himself and unto the god of their worship.

So therefore glorious and blissful is the endeavour of true lovers in that mystery-rite, if they accomplish that which they endeavour after the fashion of which I speak, when mutual affection arises through the madness inspired by love. But the beloved must needs be captured: and the manner of that capture I will now tell.

In the beginning of our story we divided each soul into three parts, two being like steeds and the third like a charioteer. Well and good. Now of the steeds, so we declare, one is good and the other is not; but we have not described the excellence of the one nor the badness of the other, and that is what must now be done. He that is on the more honourable side is upright and clean-limbed, carrying his neck high, with something of a hooked nose: in colour he is white, with black eyes: a lover of glory, but with temperance and modesty: one that consorts with genuine renown, and needs no whip, being driven by the word of command alone. The other is crooked of frame, a massive jumble of a creature, with thick short neck, snub nose, black skin, and grey eyes; hot-blooded, consorting with wantonness and vainglory; shaggy of ear, deaf, and hard to control with whip and goad.

Now when the driver beholds the person of the beloved, and causes a sensation of warmth to suffuse the whole soul, he begins to experience a tickling or pricking of desire; and the obedient steed, constrained now as always by modesty, refrains from leaping upon the beloved; but his fellow, heeding no more the river's goad or whip, leaps and dashes on, sorely troubling his companion and his driver, and forcing them to approach the loved one and remind him of the delights of love's commerce. For a while they struggle, indignant that he should force them to a monstrous and forbidden act; but at last, finding no end to their evil plight, they yield and agree to do his bidding. And so he draws them on, and now they are quite close and behold the spectacle of the beloved flashing upon them. At that sight the driver's memory goes back to that form of Beauty, and he sees her once again enthroned by the side of Temperance upon her holy seat; then in awe and reverence he falls upon his back, and therewith is compelled to pull the reins so violently that he brings both steeds down on their haunches, the good one willing and unresistant, but the wanton sore against his will. Now that they are a little way off, the good horse in shame and horror drenches the whole soul with sweat, while the other, contriving to recover his wind after the pain of the bit and his fall, bursts into angry abuse, railing at the charioteer and his yoke-fellow as cowardly treacherous deserters. Once again he tries to force them to advance, and when they beg him to delay awhile he grudgingly consents. But when the time appointed is come, and they feign to have forgotten, he reminds them of it, struggling and neighing and pulling until he compels them a second time to approach the beloved and renew their offer; and when they have come close, with head down and tail stretched out he takes the bit between his teeth and shamelessly plunges on. But the driver, with resentment even stronger than before, like a racer recoiling from the starting-rope, jerks back the bit in the mouth of the wanton horse with an even stronger pull, bespatters his railing tongue and his jaws with blood, and forcing him down on legs and haunches delivers him over to anguish.

And so it happens time and again, until the evil steed casts off his wantonness; humbled in the end, he obeys the counsel of his driver, and when he sees the fair beloved is like to die of fear. Wherefore at long last the soul of the lover follows after the beloved with reverence and awe.

Thus the loved one receives all manner of service, as peer of the 255 gods, from a lover that is no pretender but loves in all sincerity; of his own nature, too, he is kindly disposed to him who pays such service. Now it may be that in time past he has been misled, by his school-fellows or others, who told him that it is shameful to have commerce with a lover, and by reason of this he may repel his advances; nevertheless as time goes on ripening age and the ordinance of destiny together lead him to welcome the other's society; for assuredly fate does not suffer one evil man to be friend to another, nor yet one good man to lack the friendship of another.

And now that he has come to welcome his lover and to take pleasure in his company and converse, it comes home to him what a depth of kindliness he has found, and he is filled with amazement, for he perceives that all his other friends and kinsmen have nothing to offer in comparison with this friend in whom there dwells a god. So as he continues in this converse and society, and comes close to his lover in the gymnasium and elsewhere, that flowing stream which Zeus, as the lover of Ganymede, called the 'flood of passion', pours in upon the lover; and part of it is absorbed within him, but when he can contain no more the rest flows away outside him; and as a breath of wind or an echo, rebounding from a smooth hard surface, goes back to its place of origin, even so the stream of beauty turns back and re-enters the eyes of the fair beloved; and so by the natural channel it reaches his soul and gives it fresh vigour, watering the roots of the wings and quickening them to growth: whereby the soul of the beloved, in its turn, is filled with love. So he loves, yet knows not what he loves: he does not understand, he cannot tell what has come upon him; like one that has caught a disease of the eye from another, he cannot account for it, not realising that his lover is as it were a mirror in which he beholds himself. And when the other is beside him, he shares his respite from anguish; when he is absent, he likewise shares his longing and being longed for; since he possesses that counter-love which is the image of love, though he supposes it to be friendship rather than love, and calls it by that name. He feels a desire, like the lover's yet not so strong, to behold, to touch, to kiss him, to share his couch: and now ere long the desire, as one might guess, leads to the act.

So when they lie side by side, the wanton horse of the lover's soul would have a word with the charioteer, claiming a little guerdon for all his trouble. The like steed in the soul of the beloved has no word to say, 256 but swelling with desire for he knows not what embraces and kisses the lover, in grateful acknowledgment of all his kindness. And when they lie by one another, he is minded not to refuse to do his part in gratifying his lover's entreaties; yet his yoke-fellow in turn, being moved by reverence and heedfulness, joins with the driver in resisting. And so, if the victory be won by the higher elements of mind guiding them into the ordered rule of the philosophic life, their days on earth will be blessed with happiness and concord; for the power of evil in the soul has been subjected, and the power of goodness liberated: they have won self-mastery and inward peace. And when life is over, with burden shed and wings recovered they stand victorious in the first of the three rounds in that truly Olympic struggle; nor can any nobler prize be secured whether by the wisdom that is of man or by the madness that is of god.

But if they turn to a way of life more ignoble and unphilosophic, yet covetous of honour, then mayhap in a careless hour, or when the wine is flowing, the wanton horses in their two souls will catch them off their guard, bring the pair together, and choosing that part which the multitude account blissful achieve their full desire. And this once done, they continue therein, albeit but rarely, seeing that their minds are not wholly set thereupon. Such a pair as this also are dear friends, but not so dear as that other pair, one to another, both in the time of their love and when love is past; for they feel that they have exchanged the most binding pledges, which it were a sin to break by becoming enemies. When death comes they quit the body wingless indeed, yet eager to be winged, and therefore they carry off no mean reward for their lovers' madness: for it is ordained that all such as have taken the first steps on the celestial highway shall no more return to the dark pathways beneath the earth, but shall walk together in a life of shining bliss, and be furnished in due time with like plumage the one to the other, because of their love.

XV

PARMENIDES

Introductory Conversation (126a–127a)

The narrator is Cephalus of Clazomenae.

When we arrived at Athens from our home in Clazomenae, we met 126a
Adeimantus and Glaucon in the Agora. Adeimantus took my hand and
said, Welcome, Cephalus. If you need anything here that we can provide, please say so.

Well really, I replied, we are here for just that very purpose—to ask
something of you.

You have only to state it, he said.

What was the name, I said, of your half-brother on your mother's
side? I do not remember. He was just a boy, the last time I came here b
from Clazomenae, but that was a long time ago now. His father's name,
I think, was Pyrilampes.

Quite so, he said, and his own is Antiphon, but why do you ask?

These gentlemen here, I said, are fellow-citizens of mine, much interested in philosophy. They have heard that your Antiphon used to
associate with a certain Pythodorus, a companion of Zeno's, and that
he can relate from memory the arguments that once were discussed by c
Socrates, Zeno, and Parmenides, having heard them from Pythodorus.

True, he said.

Well, I replied, that is what we want, to hear those arguments.

No difficulty there, he said. When Antiphon was young he used to
rehearse them diligently, though now, like his grandfather of the same
name, he spends most of his time on horses. But if you will, let us call
on him. He just left here for home, but he lives nearby, in Melite.

So we set out to walk, and found Antiphon at home giving directions 127a
to a smith for making some sort of bit. But when he dismissed the fellow,
his brothers told him why we were there, and he recognized me from
my previous visit and greeted me warmly. When we asked him to go

through the arguments, he at first hesitated—he said it was a difficult task. But finally, he complied.

Characters and Setting (127a–d)

According to Antiphon, Pythodorus said that Zeno and Parmenides
b once came to Athens for the Great Panathenaea. Parmenides was then well along in years and quite grey, a distinguished-looking man of perhaps sixty-five. Zeno was about forty, handsome and tall. It was said
c that he had been Parmenides' favorite. They stayed at Pythodorus' house in Ceramicus, outside the city walls, and Socrates came there with a number of other people, eager to hear a reading of Zeno's treatise, which Zeno and Parmenides had brought to Athens for the first time. Socrates was then quite young. Zeno himself read to them, but Par-
d menides, as it happened, was out. Pythodorus said he came in with Parmenides and Aristoteles, who was later one of the Thirty Tyrants, when the reading of the arguments was very nearly finished, and they heard only a small part of the treatise remaining. As for himself, however, he had heard Zeno read it before.

PART I. Zeno's Paradox and the Theory of Forms (127d–130a)

Zeno's Paradox (127d–128e)

When the reading was finished, Socrates asked to hear the hypothesis of the first argument again. When it was read, he asked, What does that mean, Zeno? If things are many, then it follows that the same things must be both like and unlike; but that is impossible; for unlike things cannot be like or like things unlike. Isn't that your claim?

It is, said Zeno.

Now, if it is impossible for unlike things to be like and like things unlike, it is also impossible for there to be many things; for if there were, things would undergo impossible qualifications. Isn't that the point of your arguments, to contend, contrary to everything generally said, that there is no plurality? And don't you suppose that each of your arguments is a proof of just that, so that you believe that you have given precisely as many proofs that there is no plurality as there are arguments in your treatise? Is that what you mean, or have I failed to understand you?

No, said Zeno, you have grasped the point of the whole treatise. 128a

I gather, Parmenides, said Socrates, that Zeno here wishes to associate himself with you not only by other marks of friendship, but also by his book. He has written to much the same effect as you, but by changing tactics he tries to mislead us into thinking he is saying something different. In your poem, you say that the All is one, and for this b you provide fine and excellent proofs. He, on the other hand, says it is not many, and he also provides proofs of great multitude and magnitude. So you say unity, he says no plurality, and each so speaks that, though there is no difference in what you mean, what you say hardly seems the same at all. That is why what you've said appears to mean something quite beyond the rest of us.

Yes, Socrates, said Zeno. But you have not wholly perceived the truth about my treatise. To be sure, you pick up the scent of the arguments and follow their trail like a young Spartan hound, but you c overlook this at the outset: the book is not so thoroughly pretentious as

259

to have been written with the motive you allege, disguised for the public as a great achievement. What you mention is incidental. The real truth is that it is a kind of defense of Parmenides' argument, directed against

d those who ridicule it on the ground that, if it is one, many absurd and inconsistent consequences follow. This book is a retort to those who assert plurality, and pays them back in kind with interest; its purpose is to make clear that their own hypothesis, that plurality is, when followed out far enough, suffers still more absurd consequences than the hypothesis of there being one. I wrote it when I was young, in a spirit of controversy, and when it was written someone stole it, so that I was

e not allowed to decide whether or not it should see the light of day. That is what you overlook, Socrates: you suppose it was written by an older man zealous of reputation, not by a young man fond of controversy. Though as I said, you did not misrepresent it.

Socrates' Solution to Zeno's Paradox (128e–130a)

I accept that, said Socrates. What you say is no doubt true. But tell me: do you not believe that there exists, alone by itself, a certain char-

129a acter of likeness, and again, another character opposite to it, what it is to be unlike; and that you and I and the other things we call many get a share of these two things? Things that get a share of likeness become like in the respect and to the degree that they get a share; things that get a share of unlikeness become unlike; and things that get a share of both become both. Even if all things get a share of both, opposite as they are, and by reason of having a share of both it is possible for them to be both like and unlike themselves, what is surprising in that? If someone were to show that things that are *just* like become unlike, or

b *just* unlike like, no doubt that would be a portent. But I find nothing strange, Zeno, if he shows that things which get a share of both undergo both qualifications, nor if he shows that all things are by reason of having a share of the one, and that those very same things are also in turn many by reason of having a share of multitude. But if he shows that what it is to be one is many, and the many in turn one, that *will* surprise

c me. The same is true in like manner of all other things. If someone should show that the kinds and characters in themselves undergo these opposite qualifications, there is reason for surprise. But what is surprising if someone shows that I am one and many? When he wishes to show that I am many, he says that my right side is one thing and my left another, that my front is different from my back, and my upper body in like manner different from my lower; for I suppose I have a share of multitude. To show that I am one, he says I am one man among the seven of us, since I also have a share of the one. The result is that he shows that both are true. Now, if someone should undertake to show that sticks and stones and things like that are many, and the same things one, we shall grant that he has proved that something is many and one, but not that the one is many or the many one; he has said nothing out of the ordinary, but a thing on which we all agree. But I should be filled with admiration, Zeno, said Socrates, if someone were first to distinguish separately alone by themselves the characters I just mentioned—likeness and unlikeness, for example, multitude and the one, rest and motion, and all such similar things—and then show that these things in themselves can be combined and distinguished. You have no doubt dealt manfully with the former issue. But as I say, I should admire it much more if someone should show that this same perplexity is interwoven in all kinds of ways in the characters themselves—that just as you and Parmenides have explained in the things we see, so it proves too in what we apprehend by reflection.

PART II. Parmenides' Criticisms of the Theory of Forms (130a–135d)

The Extent of Separate Ideas (130a–e)

As Socrates was speaking, Pythodorus said he expected Parmenides and Zeno to be annoyed at every word. Instead, they paid close attention, and from time to time glanced at each other and smiled as if in admiration. When Socrates finished, Parmenides expressed this. Soc-
b rates, he said, your impulse toward argument is admirable: Now tell me: do you yourself thus distinguish, as you say, certain characters themselves separately, and separately in turn the things that have a share of them? And do you think that likeness itself is something separate from the likeness that we have, and one and many, and all the others you just heard Zeno mention?

Yes, I do, said Socrates.

And characters of this sort too? said Parmenides. For example, a certain character of just, alone by itself, and of beautiful and good, and all such as those in turn?

Yes, he said.

c Well, is there a character of man separate from us and all such as we are, a certain character of man itself, or fire, or even water?

I have often been in perplexity, Parmenides, he said, about whether one should speak about them as about the others, or not.

And what about these, Socrates—they would really seem ridiculous: hair and mud and dirt, for example, or anything else which is utterly worthless and trivial. Are you perplexed whether one should say that
d there is a separate character for each of them too, a character that again is other than the sorts of things we handle?

Not at all, said Socrates. Surely those things actually are just what we see them to be, and it would be quite absurd to suppose that something is a character of them. Still, I sometimes worry lest what holds in one case may not hold in all; but when I take that stand, I retreat, for fear of tumbling undone into depths of nonsense. So I go back to the things we just said have characters, and spend my time dealing with them.

You are still young, Socrates, said Parmenides, and philosophy has e not yet taken hold of you as I think it one day will. You will despise none of these things then. But as it is, because of your youth, you still pay attention to what people think. Now tell me this: do you think, as you say, that there are certain characters, and that these others here, by reason of having a share of them, get their names from them? As 131a for example, things that get a share of likeness become like, of largeness large, of beauty and justice beautiful and just?

Yes, certainly, said Socrates.

The Dilemma of Participation (131a–c)

Then does each thing that gets a share get a share of the whole character, or of a part? Or could there be any kind of sharing separate from these?

Surely not, Socrates replied.

Well, does it seem to you that the whole character, being one, is in each of the many?

What prevents it, Parmenides? said Socrates.

Therefore, being one and the same, it will be present at once and b as a whole in things that are many and separate, and thus it would be separate from itself.

No, it would not, he said, at least if it were like one and the same day, which is in many different places at once and nonetheless not separate from itself. If it were in fact that way, each of the characters could be in everything at once as one and the same.

Very neat, Socrates, he said. You make one and the same thing be in many different places at once, as if you'd spread a sail over a number of men and then claimed that one thing as a whole was over many. Or isn't that the sort of thing you mean to say?

Perhaps, he said.

Now, would the whole sail be over each man, or part of it over one c and part over another?

Part.

Therefore, Socrates, he said, the characters themselves are divisible, and things that have a share of them have a share of parts of them; whole would no longer be in each, but part of each in each.

Yes, so it appears.

Well, Socrates, are you willing to say that the one character is in truth divided for us, and yet that it will still be one?

Not at all, he said.

The Paradox of Divisibility (131c–e)

No, for consider, he said: if you divide largeness itself, and each of
d the many large things is to be large by a part of largeness smaller than largeness itself, won't that appear unreasonable?

Of course, he said.

Well then, suppose something has a given small part of the equal. Will the possessor be equal to anything by what is smaller than the equal itself?

Impossible.

But suppose that one of us is to have a part of the small. The small will be larger than this part of itself, because it is part of it, and thus
e the small itself will be larger. But that to which the part subtracted is added will be smaller, not larger, than before.

Surely that could not happen, he said.

Then in what way, Socrates, will the others get a share of characters for you, since they cannot get a share part by part or whole by whole?

Such a thing, it seems to me, is difficult, emphatically difficult, to determine, he said.

The Largeness Regress (131e–132b)

Really! Then how do you deal with this?

What is that?

132a I suppose you think that each character is one for some such reason as this: when some plurality of things seem to you to be large, there perhaps seems to be some one characteristic that is the same when you look over them all, whence you believe that the large is one.

True, he said.

What about the large itself and the other larges? If with your mind you should look over them all in like manner, will not some one large again appear, by which they all appear to be large?

It seems so.

Therefore, another character of largeness will have made its appearance alongside largeness itself and the things that have a share of it; and over and above all those, again, a different one, by which they

will all be large. And each of the characters will no longer be one for b
you, but unlimited in multitude.

Ideas as Thoughts (132b–c)

But Parmenides, said Socrates, may it not be that each of these
characters is a thought, and that it pertains to it to come to be nowhere
else except in minds? For in that way, each would still be one, and no
longer undergo what was just now said.

Well, he said, is each of the thoughts one, but a thought of nothing?

No, that is impossible, he said.

A thought of something, then?

Yes.

Of something that is, or is not?

Of something that is.   c

Of some one thing which that thought thinks as being over all, that
is, of some one characteristic?

Yes.

Then that which is thought to be one will be a character, ever the
same over all?

Again, it appears it must.

Really! Then what about this, said Parmenides: in virtue of the necessity by which you say that the others have a share of characters, does
it not seem to you that either each is composed of thoughts and all think,
or that being thoughts they are unthought?

But that, he said, is hardly reasonable.

Ideas as Paradigms (132d–133a)

Still, Parmenides, he said, this much is quite clear to me: these characters stand, as it were, as paradigms fixed in the nature of things, and d
the others resemble them and are likenesses of them; this sharing that
the others come to have of characters is nothing other than being a resemblance of them.

Well, Parmenides said, if something resembles a character, is it possible for that character not to be like what has come to resemble it,
insofar as it has become like it? Is there any way in which what is like
is not like what is like it?

There is not.

Rather, what is like must have a share of one and the same character
e as what it is like?

True.

But will not that of which like things have a share so as to be like
be the character itself?

Certainly.

Then it is not possible for anything to be like the character, or the
character like anything else. For otherwise, another character will always appear alongside it, and should that character be like something,
133a a different one again. Continual generation of a new character will never
stop, if the character comes to be like what has a share of it.

You are quite right.

Then the others do not get a share of characters by likeness. It is
necessary to look for something else by which they get a share.

So it seems.

Separation and Unknowability (133a–134e)

Do you see, then, Socrates, how great the perplexity is, if someone
should distinguish as characters things that are alone by themselves?

Yes indeed.

Rest assured, he said, that you hardly even have yet begun to grasp
b how great the perplexity is, if you are going to assume that each character of things that are is one, ever marking it off as something.

How so? he said.

There are many other difficulties, he said, but the greatest is this.
If someone said that it does not even pertain to the characters to be
known if they are such as we say they must be, one could not show him
that he was mistaken unless the disputant happened to be a man of wide
experience and natural ability, willing to follow many a remote and la-
c borious demonstration. Otherwise, the man who compels them to be
unknowable would be left unconvinced.

Why is that, Parmenides? said Socrates.

Because, Socrates, I suppose that you and anyone else who assumes
that the nature and reality of each thing exists as something alone by
itself would agree, first of all, that none of them is in us.

No, for how would it still be alone by itself? said Socrates.

You are right, he said. And further, as many of the characteristics
as are what they are relative to each other have their nature and reality
relative to themselves, but not relative to things among us—likenesses,
d or whatever one assumes they are—of which we have a share and in
each case are called by their names. But things among us, in turn,

though they are of the same name as those, are relative to themselves but not to the characters, and it is to themselves but not to those that as many as are so named refer.

How do you mean? said Socrates.

Take an example, said Parmenides. If one of us is master or slave *of* someone, he is surely not a slave of master itself, what it is to be master, nor is a master the master of slave itself, what it is to be slave. Being a man, we are either of the two of another man. But mastership e itself is what it is *of* slavery itself, and slavery in like manner slavery *of* mastership. Things in us do not have their power and significance relative to things there, nor things there relative to us. Rather, as I say, things there are themselves of and relative to themselves, and in like manner things among us are relative to themselves. Or don't you see 134a what I mean?

Of course I do, said Socrates.

And furthermore, he said, knowledge itself, what it is to be knowledge, would be knowledge of what is there, namely, what it is to be real and true?

Of course.

And each of the branches of knowledge in turn would be knowledge of what it is to be each of the things that are. Not so?

Yes.

But knowledge among us would be knowledge of the truth and reality among us? And does it not in turn follow that each branch of knowledge among us is knowledge of each of the things that are among us? b

Necessarily.

Moreover, as you agree, we surely do not have the characters themselves, nor can they be among us.

No.

But the kinds themselves, what it is to be each thing, are known, I take it, by the character of knowledge?

Yes.

Which we do not have.

No.

Then none of the characters is known by us, since we have no share of knowledge itself.

It seems not.

Therefore, what it is to be beautiful itself, and the good, and everything we at this point accept as characteristics themselves, is for us un- c knowable.

Very likely.

Consider then whether the following is not still more remarkable.

What is it?

You would say, I take it, that if there is a certain kind of knowledge itself, it is much more exact than knowledge among us. So too of beauty, and all the rest.

Yes.

Now, if anything has a share of knowledge itself, would you say that no one but god has the most exact knowledge?

Necessarily.

d   Then will it be possible for the god, having knowledge itself, to know things among us?

Why shouldn't it be?

Because, Socrates, said Parmenides, we agreed that those characters do not have the power they have relative to things among us, nor things among us relative to those, but each relative to themselves.

Yes, we agreed to that.

Now, if the most exact mastership and most exact knowledge is in the god's realm, mastership there would never master us here, nor

e   knowledge there know us or anything where we are. In like manner, we do not rule there by our authority here, and know nothing divine by our knowledge. By the same account again, those there are not our masters, and have no knowledge of human things, being gods.

But surely, said Socrates, it would be too strange an account, if one were to deprive the gods of knowing.

Conclusion (134e–135d)

And yet, Socrates, said Parmenides, these difficulties and many more
135a   in addition necessarily hold of the characters, if these characteristics of things that are exist, and one is to distinguish each character as something by itself. The result is that the hearer is perplexed, and contends that they do not exist, and that even if their existence is conceded, they are necessarily unknowable by human nature. In saying this, he thinks he is saying something significant, and as we just remarked, it is astonishingly hard to convince him to the contrary. Only a man of considerable natural gifts will be able to understand that there is a certain kind
b   of each thing, a nature and reality alone by itself, and it will take a man more remarkable still to discover it and be able to instruct someone else who has examined all these difficulties with sufficient care.

I agree with you, Parmenides, said Socrates. You are saying very much what I think too.

Nevertheless, said Parmenides, if, in light of all the present difficulties and others like them, one will not allow that there are characters of things that are, and refuses to distinguish as something a character of each single thing, he will not even have anything to which to turn his mind, since he will not allow that there is a characteristic, ever the same, of each of the things that are; and so he will utterly destroy the c power and significance of thought and discourse. I think you are even more aware of that sort of consequence.

True, he replied.

What will you do about philosophy, then? Which way will you turn while these things are unknown?

For the moment, at least, I am not really sure I see.

No, because you undertake to mark off as something beauty and justice and goodness, and each of the characters, too soon, before being d properly trained. I realized that yesterday when I heard you discussing with Aristoteles here. Believe me, your impulse toward argument is noble, and indeed divine. But train yourself more thoroughly while you are still young; drag yourself through what is generally regarded as useless, and condemned by the multitude as idle talk. Otherwise, the truth will escape you.

XVI

TIMAEUS

The Motive of Creation

(29)   TIM. Let us, then, state for what reason becoming and this universe
were framed by him who framed them. He was good; and in the good
no jealousy in any matter can ever arise. So, being without jealousy,
he desired that all things should come as near as possible to being like
himself. That this is the supremely valid principle of becoming and of
the order of the world, we shall most surely be right to accept from men
30 of understanding. Desiring, then, that all things should be good and,
so far as might be, nothing imperfect, the god took over all that is visible—not at rest, but in discordant and unordered motion—and brought
it from disorder into order, since he judged that order was in every way
the better.

Now it was not, nor can it ever be, permitted that the work of the
supremely good should be anything but that which is best. Taking
thought, therefore, he found that, among things that are by nature visible, no work that is without intelligence will ever be better than one
that has intelligence, when each is taken as a whole, and moreover that
intelligence cannot be present in anything apart from soul. In virtue of
this reasoning, when he framed the universe, he fashioned reason within
soul and soul within body, to the end that the work he accomplished
might be by nature as excellent and perfect as possible. This, then, is
how we must say, according to the likely account, that this world came
to be, by the god's providence, in very truth a living creature with soul
and reason.

The Creator's Model

This being premised, we have now to state what follows next: What
was the living creature in whose likeness he framed the world? We must

Reprinted by permission of the publishers from F. M. Cornford, *Plato's Cosmology*
(Humanities Press, Inc., Atlantic Highlands, N.J. 07716, and Routledge & Kegan Paul
Ltd, 1952).

not suppose that it was any creature that ranks only as a species; for no copy of that which is incomplete can ever be good. Let us rather say that the world is like, above all things, to that Living Creature of which all other living creatures, severally and in their families, are parts. For that embraces and contains within itself all the intelligible living creatures, just as this world contains ourselves and all other creatures that have been formed as things visible. For the god, wishing to make this world most nearly like that intelligible thing which is best and in every way complete, fashioned it as a single visible living creature, containing within itself all living things whose nature is of the same order. 31

One World, Not Many

Have we, then, been right to call it one Heaven, or would it have been true rather to speak of many and indeed of an indefinite number? One we must call it, if we are to hold that it was made according to its pattern. For that which embraces all the intelligible living creatures that there are, cannot be one of a pair; for then there would have to be yet another Living Creature embracing those two, and they would be parts of it; and thus our world would be more truly described as a likeness, not of them, but of that other which would embrace them. Accordingly, to the end that this world may be like the complete Living Creature in respect of its uniqueness, for that reason its maker did not make two worlds nor yet an indefinite number; but this Heaven has come to be and is and shall be hereafter one and unique.

The Body of the World: Why This Consists of Four Primary Bodies

Now that which comes to be must be bodily, and so visible and tangible; and nothing can be visible without fire, or tangible without something solid, and nothing is solid without earth. Hence the god, when he began to put together the body of the universe, set about making it of fire and earth: But two things alone cannot be satisfactorily united without a third; for there must be some bond between them drawing them together. And of all bonds the best is that which makes itself and the terms it connects a unity in the fullest sense; and it is of the nature of a continued geometrical proportion to effect this most per- 32 fectly. For whenever, of three numbers, the middle one between any two that are either solids (cubes?) or squares is such that, as the first is to it, so is it to the last, and conversely as the last is to the middle, so is the middle to the first, then since the middle becomes first and last, and again the last and first become middle, in that way all will necessarily come to play the same part towards one another, and by so doing they will all make a unity.

Now if it had been required that the body of the universe should be a plane surface with no depth, a single mean would have been enough to connect its companions and itself; but in fact the world was to be solid in form, and solids are always conjoined, not by one mean, but by two. Accordingly the god set water and air between fire and earth, and made them, so far as was possible, proportional to one another, so that as fire is to air, so is air to water, and as air is to water, so is water to earth, and thus he bound together the frame of a world visible and tangible.

For these reasons and from such constituents, four in number, the body of the universe was brought into being, coming into concord by means of proportion, and from these it acquired Amity, so that coming into unity with itself it became indissoluble by any other save him who bound it together.

The World's Body Contains the Whole of All the Four Primary Bodies

Now the frame of the world took up the whole of each of these four; he who put it together made it consist of all the fire and water and air and earth, leaving no part or power of any one of them outside. This was his intent: first, that it might be in the fullest measure a living being
33 whole and complete, of complete parts; next, that it might be single, nothing being left over, out of which such another might come into being; and moreover that it might be free from age and sickness. For he perceived that, if a body be composite, when hot things and cold and all things that have strong powers beset that body and attack it from without, they bring it to untimely dissolution and cause it to waste away by bringing upon it sickness and age. For this reason and so considering, he fashioned it as a single whole consisting of all these wholes, complete and free from age and sickness.

It Is a Sphere, Without Organs or Limbs, Rotating on Its Axis

And for shape he gave it that which is fitting and akin to its nature. For the living creature that was to embrace all living creatures within itself, the fitting shape would be the figure that comprehends in itself all the figures there are; accordingly, he turned its shape rounded and spherical, equidistant every way from centre to extremity—a figure the

most perfect and uniform of all; for he judged uniformity to be im-
measurably better than its opposite.

And all round on the outside he made it perfectly smooth, for several
reasons. It had no need of eyes, for nothing visible was left outside; nor
of hearing, for there was nothing outside to be heard. There was no
surrounding air to require breathing, nor yet was it in need of any organ
by which to receive food into itself or to discharge it again when drained
of its juices. For nothing went out or came into it from anywhere, since
there was nothing: it was designed to feed itself on its own waste and
to act and be acted upon entirely by itself and within itself; because its
framer thought that it would be better self-sufficient, rather than dependent upon anything else.

It had no need of hands to grasp with or to defend itself, nor yet of
feet or anything that would serve to stand upon; so he saw no need to
attach to it these limbs to no purpose. For he assigned to it the motion
proper to its bodily form, namely that one of the seven which above all   34
belongs to reason and intelligence; accordingly, he caused it to turn
about uniformly in the same place and within its own limits and made
it revolve round and round; he took from it all the other six motions
and gave it no part in their wanderings. And since for this revolution
it needed no feet, he made it without feet or legs.

All this, then, was the plan of the god who is for ever for the god
who was sometime to be. According to this plan he made it smooth and
uniform, everywhere equidistant from its centre, a body whole and complete, with complete bodies for its parts. And in the centre he set a soul
and caused it to extend throughout the whole and further wrapped its
body round with soul on the outside; and so he established one world
alone, round and revolving in a circle, solitary but able by reason of its
excellence to bear itself company, needing no other acquaintance or
friend but sufficient to itself. On all these accounts the world which he
brought into being was a blessed god. . . .

Soul Is Prior to Body

Now this soul, though it comes later in the account we are now   (34)
attempting, was not made by the god younger than the body; for when
he joined them together, he would not have suffered the elder to be ruled
by the younger. There is in us too much of the casual and random,
which shows itself in our speech; but the god made soul prior to body
and more venerable in birth and excellence, to be the body's mistress
and governor.

The World's Body Fitted to Its Soul

(36)   When the whole fabric of the soul had been finished to its maker's mind, he next began to fashion within the soul all that is bodily, and brought the two together, fitting the centre to centre. And the soul, being everywhere inwoven from the centre to the outermost heaven and enveloping the heaven all round on the outside, revolving within its own limit, made a divine beginning of ceaseless and intelligent life for all time. . . .

(37)   When the father who had begotten it saw it set in motion and alive, a shrine brought into being for the everlasting gods, he rejoiced and being well pleased he took thought to make it yet more like its pattern. So as that pattern is the Living Being that is for ever existent, he sought to make this universe also like it, so far as might be, in that respect. Now the nature of that Living Being was eternal, and this character it was impossible to confer in full completeness on the generated thing. But he took thought to make, as it were, a moving likeness of eternity; and, at the same time that he ordered the Heaven, he made, of eternity that abides in unity, an everlasting likeness moving according to number—that to which we have given the name Time.

For there were no days and nights, months and years, before the Heaven came into being; but he planned that they should now come to be at the same time that the Heaven was framed. All these are parts of Time, and 'was' and 'shall be' are forms of time that have come to be; we are wrong to transfer them unthinkingly to eternal being. We say that it was and is and shall be; but 'is' alone really belongs to it and describes it truly; 'was' and 'shall be' are properly used of becoming which proceeds in time, for they are motions. But that which is for ever in the same state immovably cannot be becoming older or younger by lapse of time, nor can it ever become so; neither can it now have been, nor will it be in the future; and in general nothing belongs to it of all that Becoming attaches to the moving things of sense; but these have come into being as forms of time, which images eternity and revolves according to number. And besides we make statements like these: that what is past *is* past, what happens now *is* happening now, and again that what will happen *is* what will happen, and that the non-existent *is* non-existent: no one of these expressions is exact. But this, perhaps, may not be the right moment for a precise discussion of these matters.

Be that as it may, Time came into being together with the Heaven, in order that, as they were brought into being together, so they may be dissolved together, if ever their dissolution should come to pass; and it is made after the pattern of the ever-enduring nature, in order that it may be as like that pattern as possible; for the pattern is a thing that has being for all eternity, whereas the Heaven has been and is and shall be perpetually throughout all time.

The Planets as Instruments of Time

In virtue, then, of this plan and intent of the god for the birth of (38) Time, in order that Time might be brought into being, Sun and Moon and five other stars—'wanderers', as they are called—were made to define and preserve the numbers of Time. Having made a body for each of them, the god set them in the circuits in which the revolution of the Different was moving—in seven circuits seven bodies: the Moon in the circle nearest the Earth; the Sun in the second above the Earth; the Morning Star (Venus) and the one called sacred to Hermes (Mercury) in circles revolving so as, in point of speed, to run their race with the Sun, but possessing the power contrary to his; whereby the Sun and the star of Hermes and the Morning Star alike overtake and are overtaken by one another. As for the remainder, where he enshrined them and for what reasons—if one should explain all these, the account, though only by the way, could be a heavier task than that for the sake of which it was given. Perhaps these things may be duly set forth later at our leisure.

Necessity. The Errant Cause

Now our foregoing discourse, save for a few matters, has set forth (47) the works wrought by the craftsmanship of Reason; but we must now set beside them the things that come about of Necessity. For the generation of this universe was a mixed result of the combination of Ne- 48 cessity and Reason. Reason overruled Necessity by persuading her to guide the greatest part of the things that become towards what is best; in that way and on that principle this universe was fashioned in the beginning by the victory of reasonable persuasion over Necessity. If, then, we are really to tell how it came into being on this principle, we must bring in also the Errant Cause—in what manner its nature is to cause motion. So we must return upon our steps thus, and taking, in its turn, a second principle concerned in the origin of these same things, start once more upon our present theme from the beginning, as we did upon the theme of our earlier discourse.

We must, in fact, consider in itself the nature of fire and water, air and earth, before the generation of the Heaven, and their condition before the Heaven was. For to this day no one has explained their generation, but we speak as if men knew what fire and each of the others is, positing them as original principles, elements (as it were, letters) of the universe; whereas one who has ever so little intelligence should not rank them in this analogy even so low as syllables. On this occasion, however, our contribution is to be limited as follows. We are not now to speak of the 'first principle' or 'principles'—or whatever name men choose to employ—of all things, if only on account of the difficulty of explaining what we think by our present method of exposition. You, then, must not demand the explanation of me; nor could I persuade myself that I should be right in taking upon myself so great a task; but holding fast to what I said at the outset—the worth of a probable account—I will try to give an explanation of all these matters in detail, no less probable than another, but more so, starting from the beginning in the same manner as before. So now once again at the outset of our discourse let us call upon a protecting deity to grant us safe passage through a strange and unfamiliar exposition to the conclusion that probability dictates; and so let us begin once more.

The Receptacle of Becoming

Our new starting-point in describing the universe must, however, be a fuller classification than we made before. We then distinguished two things; but now a third must be pointed out. For our earlier discourse the two were sufficient: one postulated as model, intelligible and always unchangingly real; second, a copy of this model, which becomes
49 and is visible. A third we did not then distinguish, thinking that the two would suffice; but now, it seems, the argument compels us to attempt to bring to light and describe a form difficult and obscure. What nature must we, then, conceive it to possess and what part does it play? This, more than anything else: that it is the Receptacle—as it were, the nurse—of all Becoming.

Fire, Air, etc., Are Names of Qualities, Not of Substances

True, however, as this statement is, it needs to be put in clearer language; and that is hard, in particular because to that end it is necessary to raise a previous difficulty about fire and the things that rank with fire. It is hard to say, with respect to any one of these, which we ought to call really water rather than fire, or indeed which we should call by any given name rather than by all the names together or by each severally, so as to use language in a sound and trustworthy way. How, then, and in what terms are we to speak of this matter, and what is the previous difficulty that may be reasonably stated?

In the first place, take the thing we now call water. This, when it is compacted, we see (as we imagine) becoming earth and stones, and this same thing, when it is dissolved and dispersed, becoming wind and air; air becoming fire by being inflamed; and, by a reverse process, fire, when condensed and extinguished, returning once more to the form of air, and air coming together again and condensing as mist and cloud; and from these, as they are yet more closely compacted, flowing water; and from water once more earth and stones: and thus, as it appears, they transmit in a cycle the process of passing into one another. Since, then, in this way no one of these things ever makes its appearance as the *same* thing, which of them can we steadfastly affirm to be *this*—whatever it may be—and not something else, without blushing for ourselves? It cannot be done; but by far the safest course is to speak of them in the following terms. Whenever we observe a thing perpetually changing—fire, for example—in every case we should speak of fire, not as 'this', but as 'what is of such and such a quality', nor of water as 'this', but always as 'what is of such and such a quality'; nor must we speak of anything else as having some permanence, among all the things we indicate by the expressions 'this' or 'that', imagining we are pointing out some definite thing. For they slip away and do not wait to be described as 'that' or 'this' or by any phrase that exhibits them as having permanent being. We should not use these expressions of any of them, but 'that which is of a certain quality and has the same sort of quality as it perpetually recurs in the cycle'—that is the description we should use in the case of each and all of them. In fact, we must give the name 'fire' to that which is at all times of such and such a quality; and so with anything else that is in process of becoming. Only in speaking of that *in* which all of them are always coming to be, making their appearance and again vanishing out of it, may we use the words 'this' or 'that'; we must not apply any of these words to that which is of some quality— hot or cold or any of the opposites—or to any combination of these opposites. But I must do my best to explain this thing once more in still clearer terms.

Suppose a man had moulded figures of all sorts out of gold, and were unceasingly to remould each into all the rest: then, if you should point to one of them and ask what it was, much the safest answer in respect of truth would be to say 'gold', and never to speak of a triangle or any of the other figures that were coming to be in it as things that have being, since they are changing even while one is asserting their existence. Rather one should be content if they so much as consent to accept the description 'what is of such and such a quality' with any certainty. Now the same thing must be said of that nature which receives all bodies. It must be called always the same; for it never departs at all from its own character; since it is always receiving all things, and never in any way whatsoever takes on any character that is like any of the things that enter it: by nature it is there as a matrix for everything, changed and diversified by the things that enter it, and on their account it *appears* to have different qualities at different times; while the things that pass in and out are to be called copies of the eternal things, impressions taken from them in a strange manner that is hard to express: we will follow it up on another occasion.

The Receptacle Has No Qualities of Its Own

Be that as it may, for the present we must conceive three things: that which becomes; that in which it becomes; and the model in whose likeness that which becomes is born. Indeed we may fittingly compare the Recipient to a mother, the model to a father, and the nature that arises between them to their offspring. Further we must observe that, if there is to be an impress presenting all diversities of aspect, the thing itself in which the impress comes to be situated, cannot have been duly prepared unless it is free from all those characters which it is to receive from elsewhere. For if it were like any one of the things that come in upon it, then, when things of contrary or entirely different nature came, in receiving them it would reproduce them badly, intruding its own features alongside. Hence that which is to receive in itself all kinds must be free from all characters; just like the base which the makers of scented ointments skilfully contrive to start with: they make the liquids that are to receive the scents as odourless as possible. Or again, anyone who sets about taking impressions of shapes in some soft substance, allows no shape to show itself there beforehand, but begins by making the surface as smooth and level as he can. In the same way, that which is duly to 51 receive over its whole extent and many times over all the likenesses of the intelligible and eternal things ought in its own nature to be free of all the characters. For this reason, then, the mother and Receptacle of what has come to be visible and otherwise sensible must not be called earth or air or fire or water, nor any of their compounds or components; but we shall not be deceived if we call it a nature invisible and characterless, all-receiving, partaking in some very puzzling way of the intelligible and very hard to apprehend. So far as its nature can be arrived at from what has already been said, the most correct amount of it would be this: that part of it which has been made fiery appears at any time as fire; the part that is liquefied as water; and as earth or air such parts as receive likeness of these.

Ideal Models of Fire, Air, Water, Earth

But in pressing our inquiry about them, there is a question that must rather be determined by argument: Is there such a thing as 'Fire just in itself' or any of the other things which we are always describing in such terms, as things that 'are just in themselves'? Or are the things we see or otherwise perceive by the bodily senses the only things that have such reality, and has nothing else, over and above these, any sort of being at all? Are we talking idly whenever we say that there is such a thing as an intelligible Form of anything? Is this nothing more than a word?

Now it does not become us either to dismiss the present question without trial or verdict, simply asseverating that it is so, nor yet to insert a lengthy digression into a discourse that is already long. If we could see our way to draw a distinction of great importance in few words, that would best suit the occasion. My own verdict, then, is this. If intelligence and true belief are two different kinds, then these things—Forms that we cannot perceive but only think of—certainly exist in themselves; but if, as some hold, true belief in no way differs from intelligence, then all the things we perceive through the bodily senses must be taken as the most certain reality. Now we must affirm that they are two different things, for they are distinct in origin and unlike in nature. The one is produced in us by instruction, the other by persuasion; the one can always give a true account of itself, the other can give none; the one cannot be shaken by persuasion, whereas the other can be won over; and true belief, we must allow, is shared by all mankind, intelligence only by the gods and a small number of men.

This being so, we must agree that there is, first, the unchanging Form, ungenerated and indestructible, which neither receives anything 52 else into itself from elsewhere nor itself enters into anything else anywhere, invisible and otherwise imperceptible; that, in fact, which thinking has for its object.

Second is that which bears the same name and is like that Form; is sensible; is brought into existence; is perpetually in motion, coming to be in a certain place and again vanishing out of it; and is to be apprehended by relief involving perception.

Third is Space, which is everlasting, not admitting destruction; providing a situation for all things that come into being, but itself apprehended without the senses by a sort of bastard reasoning, and hardly an object of belief.

This, indeed, is that which we look upon as in a dream and say that anything that is must needs be in some place and occupy some room, and that what is not somewhere in earth or heaven is nothing. Because of this dreaming state, we prove unable to rouse ourselves and to draw all these distinctions and others akin to them, even in the case of the waking and truly existing nature, and so to state the truth: namely that, whereas for an image, since not even the very principle on which it has come into being belongs to the image itself, but it is the ever moving semblance of something else, it is proper that it should come to be *in* something else, clinging in some sort to existence on pain of being nothing at all, on the other hand that which has real being has the support of the exactly true account, which declares that, so long as the two things are different, neither can ever come to be in the other in such a way that the two should become at once one and the same thing and two.

Description of Chaos

Let this, then, be given as the tale summed according to my judgment: that there are Being, Space, Becoming—three distinct things—even before the Heaven came into being. Now the nurse of Becoming, being made watery and fiery and receiving the characters of earth and air, and qualified by all the other affections that go with these, had every sort of diverse appearance to the sight; but because it was filled with powers that were neither alike nor evenly balanced, there was no equipoise in any region of it; but it was everywhere swayed unevenly and shaken by these things, and by its motion shook them in turn. And they, being thus moved, were perpetually being separated and carried in different directions; just as when things are shaken and winnowed by means of winnowing-baskets and other instruments for cleaning corn, the dense
53 and heavy things go one way, while the rare and light are carried to another place and settle there. In the same way at that time the four kinds were shaken by the Recipient, which itself was in motion like an instrument for shaking, and it separated the most unlike kinds farthest apart from one another, and thrust the most alike closest together; whereby the different kinds came to have different regions, even before the ordered whole consisting of them came to be. Before that, all these kinds were without proportion or measure. Fire, water, earth, and air possessed indeed some vestiges of their own nature, but were altogether in such a condition as we should expect for anything when deity is absent from it. Such being their nature at the time when the ordering of the universe was taken in hand, the god then began by giving them a distinct configuration by means of shapes and numbers. That the god framed them with the greatest possible perfection, which they had not before, must be taken, above all, as a principle we constantly assert; what I must now attempt to explain to you is the distinct formation of each and their origin. The account will be unfamiliar; but you are schooled in those branches of learning which my explanations require, and so will follow me.

Care of the Soul

(89)   Let this suffice for the treatment of the living creature as a whole and of its bodily part, and the way in which a man may best lead a rational life, both governing and being governed by himself. Still more

should precedence be given to the training of the part that is destined to govern, so that it may be as perfectly equipped as possible for its work of governance. To treat of this matter in detail would in itself be a sufficient task; but, as a side issue, it may not be out of place to determine the matter in conformity with what has gone before, with these observations. As we have said more than once, there dwell in us three distinct forms of soul, each having its own motions. Accordingly, we may say now as briefly as possible that whichever of these lives in idleness and inactivity with respect to its proper motions must needs become the weakest, while any that is in constant exercise will be strongest; hence we must take care that their motions be kept in due proportion 90 one to another.

As concerning the most sovereign form of soul in us we must conceive that heaven has given it to each man as a guiding genius—that part which we say dwells in the summit of our body and lifts us from earth towards our celestial affinity, like a plant whose roots are not in earth, but in the heavens. And this is most true, for it is to the heavens, whence the soul first came to birth, that the divine part attaches the head or root of us and keeps the whole body upright. Now if a man is engrossed in appetites and ambitions and spends all his pains upon these, all his thoughts must needs be mortal and, so far as that is possible, he cannot fall short of becoming mortal altogether, since he has nourished the growth of his mortality. But if his heart has been set on the love of learning and true wisdom and he has exercised that part of himself above all, he is surely bound to have thoughts immortal and divine, if he shall lay hold upon truth, nor can he fail to possess immortality in the fullest measure that human nature admits; and because he is always devoutly cherishing the divine part and maintaining the guardian genius that dwells with him in good estate, he must needs be happy above all. Now there is but one way of caring for anything, namely to give it the nourishment and motions proper to it. The motions akin to the divine part in us are the thoughts and revolutions of the universe; these, therefore, every man should follow, and correcting those circuits in the head that were deranged at birth, by learning to know the harmonies and revolutions of the world, he should bring the intelligent part, according to its pristine nature, into the likeness of that which intelligence discerns, and thereby win the fulfilment of the best life set by the gods before mankind both for this present time and for the time to come.

ARISTOTLE

XVII

CATEGORIES

Chapter I

Things are said equivocally which have only a name in common, but 1a
the definition of being answering to the name is different; for example,
both man and picture are animal. For of these name alone is common, but
the definition of being answering to the name is different. For should one
give what it is for each of the two to be animal, one will render an account
peculiar to each of them.

Things are said univocally which have the name in common and the
definition of being answering to the name is the same; for example, man
and ox are animal. For man and ox are called by a common name, animal,
and the definition of being is the same. For if one renders account of what
it is for each of the two of them to be animal, one will render the same
account.

Things are said paronymously which are named after something else,
with difference in ending; for example, the grammarian after grammar,
the courageous after courage.

Chapter II

Of things said, some are said in combination, some without combination. Things said in combination: man runs, man wins. Things said without
combination: man, ox, runs wins.

Of things which are, some are said of a substrate but not present in a
substrate; for example, man is said of a substrate, but present in no substrate. Some are present in a substrate, but said of no substrate (by in a
substrate I mean what is in something, not as a part, and cannot exist separately from what it is in); for example, a given knowledge of grammar is
in the soul as substrate, but said of no substrate, and a given white is in
the body as substrate (for all color is in body), but said of no substrate. 1b
Some things are both said of some substrate and present in a substrate; for
example, knowledge is in the soul as substrate, but said of grammar as a

substrate. Some things are neither present in a substrate nor said of some substrate; for example, a given man, a given horse. For nothing of this sort is either present in a substrate or said of a substrate. Things indivisible and one in number are not said simply of any substrate, but nothing prevents some of them from being present in a substrate: for a given knowledge of grammar is present in a substrate.

Chapter III

When one thing is predicated of another as of a substrate, everything said of what is predicated will also be said of the substrate; for example, man is predicated of a given man, but animal of man, so animal will also be predicated of a given man. For a given man and man are both animal.

Of genera different and not subordinate to each other, differentiae are different in kind; for example, animal and knowledge. Footed, two-footed, winged, aquatic are differentiae of animal, but not of knowledge. For knowledge does not differ from knowledge in being two footed.

Of genera subordinate to each other, nothing prevents the same differentiae: for the superior are predicated of the genera below them, so that there will be as many differentiae of substrate as there are of what is predicated.

Chapter IV

Of things said without combination, each indicates either substance or quantity or quality or relation or place or time or position or possession or action or being acted on. To speak in outline: *Substance* is for example 2a man, horse. *Quantity*: two cubits, three cubits. *Quality*: white, grammatical. *Relation*: double, half, greater than. *Place*: in the Lyceum, in the Agora. *Time*: Yesterday, a year ago. *Position*: sits, lies. *Possession*: has shoes on, has armor on. *Action*, to cut, to burn. *Being acted on*: to be cut, to be burned.

None among things said is said alone by itself in any affirmation; affirmation and denial occur by combination of them relative to each other. For it seems that all affirmation and denial is either true or false. But things said without combination are neither true nor false; for example, man, white, runs, wins.

Chapter V

Substance, in the most determinative and primary and strict sense of the term, is neither said of a substrate nor present in a substrate; for example, this given man, this given horse. But secondary substances, both the species which substances in the primary sense are in and the genera of those species, are said of a substrate; for example, this particular man is in the species man, and animal is the genus of the species. These substances then are said to be secondary; for example, man and animal.

It is evident from what has been said that of things said of a substrate, both the name and the definition are necessarily predicated of the substrate; for example, man is said of a substrate, a given man, and the name is predicated. For you will predicate man of a given man. And the definition of man will be predicated of the individual man; for a man and man are both animal. So that both the name and the definition will be predicated of the substrate.

But of things present in a substrate, for the most part neither the name nor the definition will be predicated of the substrate. In some cases nothing prevents the name from being predicated of the substrate, but it is impossible to predicate the definition; for example, white, being present in a substrate, is predicted of the substrate (for a body is called white), but the definition of white will never be predicated of body.

All other things are said of primary substances as substrates or are present in them as substrates. This is evident from grasping particular instances. For example, animal is predicated of man; so animal will also be predicated of this particular man; for if of no particular man, then not of man generally. Again, color is in body, therefore also in some given body; 2b for if not in a given body, then not in body generally. So that all other things are either said of primary substances or in them as substates. If there were no primary substances, then, it would be impossible for anything else to be.

Of secondary substances, the species or form is more substance than the genus: for it is closer to the primary substance. For if someone should render an account of what the primary substance is, he will render it more intelligibly and more properly in giving the species rather than the genus; for example, he would render an account of the individual man more intelligibly by giving man rather than animal—for the one is more proper to this individual man, the other more common. And he will give what a particular tree is by giving tree rather than plant.

Again, primary substances are said especially to be substances because they are substrates for all other things; all other things are predicated of them or present in them, because they underlie all other things, and all other things are predicated of them or present in them. But as primary substances are to other things, so also is species to genus. For species is substrate to genus. For the genus is predicated of species, but species not in turn of genera. So that from this too, the species is more substance than the genus.

Of species themselves, as many as are not genera, none is more substance than another: for one will not give man as more proper to this particular man than horse to this particular horse. In like manner, one primary substance is not more substance than another: for a given man is not more substance than a given ox.

After primary substances, species and genera alone are reasonably said to be secondary substances. For it is clear that they alone are predicated of primary substance. For if someone renders what a particular man is, he will properly render the species or the genus, and he will make it more intelligible by rendering man or animal. For example, white or runs or anything of that sort will have been rendered as more alien. So that only these among the rest are reasonably said to be substances.

Again, primary substances are said to be substances in the most determinative sense. But as primary substances are to all other things, so the species and genera of primary substances are to all the rest; for all the rest are predicated of them. For you will say that a given man is grammatical; therefore you will also say that man and animal are grammatical. And so similarly for the rest.

It is common to all substance not to be present in a substrate. For primary substance is neither said of a substrate nor present in a substrate. But it is evident of secondary substances as well that they are not present in a substrate. For man is said of a substrate, this particular man, but is not present in a substrate. For man is not present in a given man. In like manner, animal is said of a substrate, a given man, but animal is not persent in a given man.

Gain, of things present in a substrate, nothing prevents the name being sometimes predicated of the substrate, but it is impossible for the definition. But of secondary substances, both the definition and the name are predicated of the substrate. For you will predicate the definition of man of this particular man, and that of animal; so that substance would not be present in a subject.

This is not peculiar to substances; differentia also is not present in a substrate. For footed or two-footed is said of a substrate, the man, but not present in a substrate—for neither two-footed nor footed is present in man—and the definition of the differentia is predicated of that of which the differentia is said; for example, if footed is said of man, the definition of footed is also predicated of man, for man is footed.

Let us not be worried that the parts of substances are in wholes as in substrates, lest we ever be compelled to say they are not substances. For it was said of things present in a substrate that they are not in something as a part.

All things said of substances and of their differentiae are said univocaly. For all predications of them are either of individuals or of species. For of primary substances, none is predicate, for said of no substrate; but of secondary substances, the species and form is predicated of the individual, and the genus of both the species and of the individual. In like manner 3b also, differentiae are predicated of species and of individuals. And primary substances admit the definition of the species and genera, and species of the genus: for everything said of what is predicated will also be said of the substrate. In like manner, species and individuals admit the definition of their differentiae. But things are univocal of which the name is common and the definition the same, so that all things said from substances and from differentiae are said univocally.

Every substance seems to signify a this. Now in respect to primary substances, it is indisputably true that they signify a this: for what is made evident is individual and one in number. But in respect to secondary substances, though it likewise appears that they signify a this by the form of statement when one says man or animal, this is not really true. Rather, it signifies something of a certain sort; for the substrate is not one as the primary substance is, but man is said of many things, as is animal. But it does not signify something of a certain quality simply, as white does; for white signifies nothing other than a certain quality. But the species and genus mark off a certain quality with respect to substance; for they signify some sort of substance. But more is marked off by the genus than the species; for saying animal encompasses more things than saying man.

Substances have no opposite. For what would be opposite to primary substance? For example, nothing is opposite to a given man; again, nothing is opposite to man, or animal. This is not peculiar to substance, but to many other things too; for example, quantity. For nothing is opposite to two cubits or three cubits or ten or anything of that sort, unless one says more is opposite to fewer, or large to small. But of determinate quantities, none is opposite to any other.

It seems substance does not admit the more and less. I do not mean that a substance is not more substance than a substance, and less substance (for it has been said this is possible), but rather that each substance is not said to be more or less that which it is. For example, if this substance is a man, it will not be more and less man, either compared to itself or to 4a another. For one man is not more man than another, as one white is more and less white than another, and one beautiful thing said to be more and less beautiful than another. The same thing is said to be more and less than itself; for example the white body is said to be more white now than before, and being warm is said to be more warm and less. But substance is not said to be more and less; for a man is not said to be more man now than before, nor anything else in so far as it is substance. So that substance does not admit the more and less, admit of degree.

It seems especially peculiar to substance that, being one and the same in number, it is able to accept opposites. One could not put forward anything else which, being one in number, can accept opposites; for example, color, which is one and the same in number, will not be white and black; the same action, also one in number, will not be good and bad, and so in like manner for as many things as are not substances. But substance, being one and the same in number, is able to accept opposites; for example, a given man, being one and the same, sometimes becomes pale and sometimes dark, and hot and cold, good and bad.

With respect to nothing else does this sort of thing appear, unless one were to object by claiming that statement and opinion are of this sort: for the same statement seems to be both true and false. For example, if the statement that someone is sitting is true, this same statement will be false when he stands up, and so in like manner with opinion. For if one has the opinion that someone is sitting, the same opinion about him will be false when he stands up.

But even if one accepts this, there is difference in manner. Substances are able to admit opposites by changing: what becomes cold after being hot changes, for it changes quality; and dark after pale, good after bad, and so in like manner of each of the others, substance is able to accept opposites by admitting change. But statement and opinion remain unmoved in any and every way; but when the thing changes, the opposite 4b becomes true of it. For the statement that someone is sitting remains the same, but the thing is changed when it becomes true and when it becomes false. So in like manner with opinion. The result is that it would be peculiar to substance to be able in a manner to accept opposites by changing.

Suppose then one should decide that statement and opinion are able to receive opposites: this is not true. For statement and opinion are not said to be able to admit opposites because they can themselves admit something, but because something different has been affected. For the statement is said to be true or false because of the fact being or not being, not because it itself is able to admit opposites. For neither statement nor opinion is changed by anything *simpliciter*, so that they could not admit opposites by anything coming to be in them. But substance itself admits opposites, by reason of which it is said to be able to receive opposite affections; it admits disease and health, paleness and darkness, and, receiving each of such things as these, it is said to be able to admit opposites. So that it would be peculiar to substance that, being the same and one in number, it can admit opposites. Let so much be said, then about substance.

Chapter VI

20   Of quantity, some is discrete, some continuous; some composed of parts having position relative to each other, others not composed of parts having position.

Number and language are discrete; line, plane, and body are continuous, as are time and place. For the parts of number have no common 25
boundary at which they touch; for example, if five is part of ten, five and
five do not touch at a common boundary but are discrete; and three and
seven do not touch at any common boundary. In general, you cannot have
a common boundary of the part of any number; they are always discrete, 30
so number is discrete quantity.

So is language a discrete quantity. That language is a quantity is evident: syllables are measured long and short—I mean spoken language. For
its parts do not touch at any common boundary. There is no common 35
boundary at which syllables touch; each is discrete, alone by itself.

But the line is continuous. For you have a common boundary at which 5a
its parts touch, a point, and for a surface, a line; for the parts of a plane
also touch at a common boundary. In like manner you have a common
boundary for a body—line or surface—at which the parts of the body 5
touch. Time and place are of this sort. Present time, the now, touches past
and future. Place again is continuous, for the parts of the body contain
some place which touches at some common boundary. So also the parts of
place which each of the parts of the body contain touch the same boundary 10
the parts of the body touch. So place is continuous, for its parts touch at
one common boundary.

XVIII

ON THE SOUL

Book III

I. One may be satisfied that there are no senses apart from the five
(I mean vision, hearing, smell, taste and touch) from the following arguments. We may assume that we actually have perception of everything which is apprehended by touch (for by touch we perceive all those
things which are qualities of the tangible object, *qua* tangible). Again,
if we lack some sense, we must lack some sense organ; and, again, all
the things which we perceive by direct contact are perceptible by touch,
a sense which we in fact possess; but all those things which are perceived
through media, and not by direct contact, are perceptible by means of
the elements, *viz.*, air and water. Again, the facts are such that, if objects
of more than one kind are perceived through one medium, the possessor
of the appropriate sense organ will apprehend both (for instance, if the
sense organ is composed of air, and air is the medium both of sound
and of colour), but if there is more than one medium of the same thing,
as for instance both air and water are media of colour (for both are
transparent), then he that has either of these will perceive what is perceptible through both. But sense organs are composed of only two of
these elements, air and water (for the pupil of the eye is composed of
water, and the hearing organ of air, while the organ of smell is composed
of one or other of these). But fire is the medium of no perception, or
else is common to them all (for there is no possibility of perception without heat), and earth is the medium of no sense perception, or else is
connected in a special way with the sense of touch. So we are left to
suppose that there is no sense organ apart from water and air; and some
animals actually have organs composed of these. The conclusion is that
all the senses are possessed by all such animals as are neither undevel-

424 B

425 A

Reprinted by permission of the publishers and The Loeb Classical Library from Aristotle, *On the Soul,* translated by W. S. Hett, Cambridge, Mass.: Harvard University
Press, 1957.

oped nor maimed; even the mole, we find, has eyes under the skin. If then there is no other body, and no property other than those which belong to the bodies of this world, there can be no sense perception omitted from our list.

But, again, it is impossible that there should be a special sense organ to perceive common sensibles, which we perceive incidentally by each sense, such, I mean, as motion, rest, shape, magnitude, number and unity; for we perceive all these things by movement; for instance we perceive magnitude by movement, and shape also; for shape is a form of magnitude. What is at rest is perceived by absence of movement; number by the negation of continuity, and by the special sensibles; for each sense perceives one kind of object. Thus it is clearly impossible for there to be a special sense of any of these common sensibles, e.g., movement; if there were, we should perceive them in the same way as we now perceive what is sweet by sight. But we do this because we happen to have a sense for each of these qualities, and so recognize them when they occur together; otherwise we should never perceive them except incidentally, as, e.g., we perceive of Cleon's son, not that he is Cleon's son, but that he is white; and this white object is incidentally Cleon's son. But we have already a common faculty which apprehends common sensibles directly. Therefore there is no special sense for them. If there were, we should have no perception of them, except as we said that we saw Cleon's son. The senses perceive each other's proper objects incidentally, not in their own identity, but acting together as one, when sensation occurs simultaneously in the case of the same object, as for instance of bile, that it is bitter and yellow; for it is not the part of any single sense to state that both objects are one. Thus sense may be deceived, and, if an object is yellow, may think that it is bile. One might ask why we have several senses and not one only. It may be in order that the accompanying common sensibles, such as movement, size and number, may escape us less; for if vision were our only sense, and it perceived mere whiteness, they would be less apparent; indeed all sensibles would be indistinguishable, because of the concomitance of, e.g., colour and size. As it is, the fact that common sensibles inhere in the objects of more than one sense shows that each of them is something distinct. 425 B

II. Since we can perceive that we see and hear, it must be either by sight itself, or by some other sense. But then the same sense must perceive both sight and colour, the object of sight. So that either two senses perceive the same object, or sight perceives itself. Again, if there is a separate sense perceiving sight, either the process will go on *ad infinitum*, or a sense must perceive itself. So we may assume that this occurs with the first sense. But here is a difficulty; for if perception by vision is seeing, and that which is seen either is colour or has colour, then if one is to see that which sees, it follows that what primarily sees will possess colour. It is therefore obvious that the phrase "perceiving by vision" has not merely one meaning; for, even when we do not see, we discern darkness and light by vision, but not in the same way. Moreover that which sees does in a sense possess colour; for each sense organ is receptive of the perceived object, but without its matter. This is why, even when the objects of perception are gone, sensations and mental images are still present in the sense organ.

The activity of the sensible object and of the sensation is one and the same, though their essence is not the same; in saying that they are the same, I mean the actual sound and the actual hearing; for it is possible for one who possesses hearing not to hear, and that which has sound is not always sounding. But when that which has the power of hearing is exercising its power, and that which can sound is sounding, 426 A then the active hearing and the active sound occur together; we may call them respectively audition and sonance.

If then the movement, that is, the acting and being acted upon, takes place in that which is acted upon, then the sound and the hearing in a state of activity must reside in the potential hearing; for the activity of what is moving and active takes place in what is being acted upon. Hence that which causes motion need not be moved. The activity, then, of the object producing sound is sound, or sonance, and of that producing hearing is hearing or audition, for hearing is used in two senses, and so is sound. The same argument applies to all other senses and sensible objects. For just a acting and being acted upon reside in that which is acted upon, and not in the agent, so also the activity of the sensible object and that of the sensitive subject lie in the latter. In some cases we have names for both, such as sonance and audition, but in others one of the terms has no name; for the activity of vision is called seeing, but that of colour has no name; the activity of taste is called tasting, but that of flavour has no name. But since the activity of the sensible and of the sensitive is the same, though their essence is different, it follows that hearing in the active sense must cease or continue simultaneously with the sound, and so with flavour and taste and the rest; but this does not apply to their potentialities. The earlier natural philosophers were at fault in this, supposing that white and black have no existence without vision, nor flavour without taste. In one sense they were right, but in another wrong; for the terms sensation and sensible being used in two senses, that is potentially and actually, their statements apply to the latter class, but not to the former. These thinkers did not distinguish the meanings of terms which have more than one meaning.

If harmony is a species of voice, and voice and hearing are in one sense one and the same, and if harmony is a ratio, then it follows that hearing must be in some sense a ratio. That is why both high and low pitch, if excessive, destroy hearing; in the same way in flavours excess destroys taste, and in colours the over-brilliant or over-dark destroys 426 B vision, and in smelling the strong scent, whether sweet or bitter, destroys smell; which implies that sense is some kind of ratio. That is also why things are pleasant when they enter pure and unmixed into the ratio, *e.g.*, acid, sweet or salt; for in that case they are pleasant. But generally speaking a mixed constitution produces a better harmony than the high or low pitch, and to the touch that is more pleasant which can be warmed or cooled; the sense is the ratio, and excess hurts or destroys.

Each sense then relates to its sensible subject-matter; it resides in the sense organ as such, and discerns differences in the said subject-matter; *e.g.*, vision discriminates between white and black, and taste between sweet and bitter; and similarly in all other cases. But, since we also distinguish white and sweet, and compare all objects perceived with each other, by what sense do we perceive that they differ? It must evidently be by some sense that we perceive the difference; for they are objects of sense. Incidentally it becomes clear that flesh is not the ultimate sense organ; for, if it were, judgment would depend on being in contact. Nor, again, is it possible to judge that sweet and white are different by separate senses, but both must be clearly presented to a single sense. For, in the other case, if you perceived one thing and I another, it would be obvious that they differed from each other. That which asserts the difference must be one; for sweet differs from white. It is the same faculty, then, that asserts this; hence as it asserts, so it thinks and perceives. Evidently, therefore, it is impossible to pass judgement on separate objects by separate faculties; and it is also obvious from the following considerations that they are not judged at separate times. For just as the same faculty declares that good and evil are different, so also when it declares that one is different and the other different, the "time when" is not merely incidental (as when, *e.g.*, I *now* say that there is a difference, but do not say that there is *now* a difference). The faculty says now, and also that the difference is now; hence both are different at once. So the judging sense must be undivided, and also must judge without an interval. But, again, it is impossible that the same faculty should be moved at the same time with contrary movements, in so far as it is indivisible, and in indivisible time. For if the object is sweet it excites sensation or thought in one way, but if bitter, in the contrary way, and if white, in a different way altogether. Are we, 427 A then, to suppose that the judging faculty is numerically indivisible and inseparable, but is divided in essence? Then in one sense it is what is divided that perceives divided things, but in sense it does this *qua* indivisible. For it is divisible in essence, but indivisible spatially and numerically. Or is this impossible? For although the same indivisible thing may be both contraries potentially, it is not so in essence, but it becomes divisible in actualization; the same thing cannot be at once white and black, and so the same thing cannot be acted upon by the forms of these, if this is what happens in perception and thought. The fact is that just as what some thinkers describe as a point is, as being both one and two, in this sense divisible, so too in so far as the judging faculty is indivisible, it is one and instantaneous in action; but in so far as it is divisible, it uses the same symbol twice at the same time. In so far, then, as it treats the limit as two, it passes judgement on two distinct things, as being itself in a sense distinct; but in so far as it judges of it as only one, it judges by one faculty and at one time.

Concerning the principle in virtue of which we call a living creature sentient, let this account suffice.

III. Now there are two special characteristics which distinguish soul, *viz.*, (1) movement in space, and (2) thinking, judging and perceiving. Thinking, both speculative and practical, is regarded as a form of perceiving; for in both cases the soul judges and has cognizance of something which is. Indeed the older philosophers assert that thinking and perceiving are identical. For instance Empedocles has said "Understanding grows with a man according to what appears to him," and in another passage "whence it befalls them ever to think different thoughts." Homer's phrase, again, "Such is the nature of man's mind" implies the same thing. For all these authors suppose the process of thinking to be a bodily function like perceiving, and that men both perceive and recognize like by like, as we have explained at the beginning 427 B of this treatise. And yet they ought to have made some mention of error at the same time; for error seems to be more natural to living creatures, and the soul spends more time in it. From this belief it must follow either that, as some say, all appearances are true, or that error is contact with the unlike; for this is the opposite to recognizing like by like. But it appears that in the case of contraries error, like knowledge, is one and the same. Now it is quite clear that perceiving and practical thinking are not the same; for all living creatures have a share in the former, but only a few in the latter. Nor again is speculative thinking, which involves being right or wrong—"being right" corresponding to intelligence and knowledge and true opinion, and "being wrong" to their contraries—the same thing as perceiving; for the perception of proper objects is always true, and is a characteristic of all living creatures, but it is possible to think falsely, and thought belongs to no animal which has not reasoning power; for imagination is different from both perception and thought; imagination always implies perception, and is itself implied by judgement. But clearly imagination and judgement are different modes of thought. For the former is an affection which lies in our power whenever we choose (for it is possible to call up mental pictures, as those do who employ images in arranging their ideas under a mnemonic system), but it is not in our power to form opinions as we will; for we must either hold a false opinion or a true one. Again, when we form an opinion that something is threatening or frightening, we are immediately affected by it, and the same is true of our opinion of something that inspires courage; but in imagination we are like spectators looking at something dreadful or encouraging in a picture. Judgement itself, too, has various forms—knowledge, opinion, prudence, and their opposites, but their differences must be the subject of another discussion.

As for thought, since it is distinct from perception, and is held to comprise imagination and judgement, it will be best to discuss it after having completed our analysis of imagination. If imagination is (apart 428 A from any metaphorical sense of the word) the process by which we say that an image is presented to us, it is one of those faculties or states of mind by which we judge and are either right or wrong. Such are sensation, opinion, knowledge and intelligence. It is clear from the following considerations that imagination is not sensation. Sensation is either potential or actual, *e.g.*, either sight or seeing, but imagination occurs when neither of these is present, as when objects are seen in dreams. Secondly, sensation is always present but imagination is not. If sensation and imagination were identical in actuality, then imagination would be possible for all creatures; but this appears not to be the case; for instance it is not true of the ant, the bee, or the grub. Again, all sensations are true, but most imaginations are false. Nor do we say "I imagine that it is a man" when our sense is functioning accurately with regard to its object, but only when we do not perceive distinctly. And, as we have said before, visions are seen by men even with their eyes shut. Nor is imagination any one of the faculties which are always right, such as knowledge or intelligence; for imagination may be false. It remains, then, to consider whether it is opinion; for opinion may be either true or false. But opinion implies belief (for one cannot hold opinions in which one does not believe); and no animal has belief, but many have imagination. Again, every opinion is accompanied by belief, belief by conviction, and conviction by rational discourse; but although some creatures have imagination, they have no reasoning power. It is clear, then, that imagination cannot be either opinion in conjunction with sensation, or opinion based on sensation, or a blend of opinion and sensation, both for the reasons given, and because the opinion relates to nothing else but the object of sensation: I mean that imagination is the blend of the perception of white with the opinion that it is white—not, surely, of the perception of white with the opinion that it is good. To imagine, then, is to form an opinion exactly corresponding to a direct perception. But things about which we have at the same time a true belief may have a false appearance; for instance the sun appears to measure a foot across, but we are convinced that it is greater than the inhabited globe; it follows, then, that either the percipient, without any alteration in the thing itself, and without forgetting or changing his mind, has rejected the true opinion which he had, or, if he still holds that opinion, it must be at once true and false. But a true opinion only becomes false when the fact changes unnoticed. Imagination, then, is not one of these things, nor a compound of them.

But since when a particular thing is moved another thing may be moved by it, and since imagination seems to be some kind of movement, and not to occur apart from sensation, but only to men when perceiving, and in connexion with what is perceptible, and since movement may be caused by actual sensation, and this movement may be caused by actual sensation, and this movement must be similar to the sensation, this movement cannot exist without sensation, or when we are not perceiving; in virtue of it the possessor may act and be acted upon in various ways; and the movement may be true or false. The reason for this last fact is as follows. The perception of proper objects is true, or is only capable of error to the least possible degree. Next comes perception that they are attributes, and here a possibility of error at once arises; for perception does not err in perceiving that an object is white; but only as to whether the white object is one thing or another. Thirdly comes perception of the common attributes which accompany the concomitants to which the proper sensibles belong (I mean, *e.g.*, motion and magnitude); it is about these that error is most likely to occur. But the movement produced by the sense-activity will differ from the actual sensation in each of these three modes of perception. The first is true whenever the sensation is present, but the others may be false both when it is present and when it is absent, and especially when the sensible object is at a distance. If, then, imagination involves nothing else than we have stated, and is as we have described it, then imagination must be a movement produced by sensation actively operating. Since sight is the chief sense, the name *phantasia* (imagination) is derived from *phaos* (light), because without light it is impossible to see. Again, because imaginations persist in us and resemble sensations, living creatures frequently act in accordance with them, some, *viz.*, the brutes, because they have no mind, and some, *viz.*, men, because the mind is temporarily clouded over by emotion, or disease, or sleep. Let this suffice about the nature and cause of imagination.

IV. Concerning that part of the soul (whether it is separable in extended space, or only in thought) with which the soul knows and thinks, we have to consider what is its distinguishing characteristic, and how thinking comes about. If it is analogous to perceiving, it must be either a process in which the soul is acted upon by what is thinkable, or something else of a similar kind. This part, then, must (although impassive) be receptive of the form of an object, *i.e.*, must be potentially the same as its object, although not identical with it: as the sensitive is to the sensible, so must mind be to the thinkable. It is necessary then that mind, since it thinks all things, should be uncontaminated, as Anaxagoras says, in order that it may be in control, that is, that it may know; for the intrusion of anything foreign hinders and obstructs it. Hence the mind, too, can have no characteristic except its capacity to receive. That part of the soul, then, which we call mind (by mind I mean that part by which the soul thinks and forms judgements) has no actual existence until it thinks. So it is unreasonable to suppose that it is mixed with the body; for in that case it would become somehow qualitative, *e.g.*, hot or cold, or would even have some organ, as the sensitive faculty has; but in fact it has none. It has been well said that the soul is the place of forms, except that this does not apply to the soul as a whole, but only in its thinking capacity, and the forms occupy it not actually but only potentially. But that the perceptive and thinking faculties are not alike in their impassivity is obvious if we consider the sense organs and sensation. For the sense loses sensation under the stimulus of a too violent sensible object; *e.g.*, of sound immediately after loud sounds, and neither seeing nor smelling is possible just after strong colours and scents; but when mind thinks the highly intelligible, it is not less able to think of slighter things, but even more able; for the faculty of sense is not apart from the body, whereas the mind is separable. But when the mind has become the several groups of its objects, as the learned man when active is said to do (and this happens, when he can exercise his function by himself), even then the mind is in a sense potential, though not quite in the same way as before it learned and discovered; moreover the mind is then capable of thinking itself.

Since magnitude is not the same as the essence of magnitude, nor water the same as the essence of water (and so too in many other cases, but not in all, because in some cases there is no difference), we judge flesh and the essence of flesh either by different faculties, or by the same faculty in different relations; for flesh cannot exist without its matter, but like "snub-nosed" implies a definite form in a definite matter. Now

429 B

it is by the sensitive faculty that we judge hot and cold, and all qualities whose due proportion constitutes flesh; but it is by a different sense, either quite distinct, or related to it in the same way as a bent line to itself when pulled out straight, that we judge the essence of flesh. Again, among abstract objects "straight" is like "snub-nosed," for it is always combined with extension; but its essence, if "straight" and "straightness" are not the same, is something different; let us call it duality. Therefore we judge it by another faculty, or by the same faculty in a different relation. And speaking generally, as objects are separable from their matter so also are the corresponding faculties of the mind.

One might raise the question: if the mind is a simple thing, and not liable to be acted upon, and has nothing in common with anything else, as Anaxagoras says, how will it think, if thinking is a form of being acted upon? For it is when two things have something in common that we regard one as acting and the other as acted upon. And our second problem is whether the mind itself can be an object of thought. For either mind will be present in all other objects (if, that is, mind is an object of thought in itself and not in virtue of something else, and what is thought is always identical in form), or else it will contain some common element, which makes it an object of thought like other things. Or there is the explanation which we have given before of the phrase "being acted upon in virtue of some common element," that mind is potentially identical with the objects of thought but is actually nothing, until it thinks. What the mind thinks must be in it in the same sense as letters are on a tablet which bears no actual writing; this is just what happens in the case of the mind. It is also itself thinkable, just like other objects of thought. For in the case of things without matter that which thinks and that which is thought are the same; for speculative knowledge is the same as its object. (We must consider why mind does not always think.) In things which have matter, each of the objects of thought is only potentially present. Hence while material objects will not have mind in them (for it is apart from their matter that mind is potentially identical with them) mind will still have the capacity of being thought.

V. Since in every class of objects, just as in the whole of nature, there is something which is their matter, *i.e.,* which is potentially all the individuals, and something else which is their cause or agent in that it makes them all—the two being related as an art to its material—these distinct elements must be present in the soul also. Mind in the passive sense is such because it becomes all things, but mind has another aspect in that it makes all things; this is a kind of positive state like light; for in a sense light makes potential into actual colours. Mind in this sense is separable, impassive and unmixed, since it is essentially an activity;

430 A

for the agent is always superior to the patient, and the originating cause to the matter. Actual knowledge is identical with its object. Potential is prior in time to actual knowledge in the individual, but in general it is not prior in time. Mind does not think intermittently. When isolated it is its true self and nothing more, and this alone is immortal and everlasting (we do not remember because, while mind in this sense cannot be acted upon, mind in the passive sense is perishable), and without this nothing thinks.

VI. The thinking of indivisible objects of thought occurs among things concerning which there can be no falsehood; where truth and falsehood are possible there is implied a compounding of thoughts into a fresh unity, as Empedocles said, "where without necks the heads of many grew," and then were joined together by Love—, so also these separate entities are combined, as for instance "incommensurable" and "diagonal." But if the thinking is concerned with things past or future, then we take into account and include the notion of time. For falsehood always lies in the process of combination, for if a man calls white notwhite, he has combined the notion not-white. It is equally possible to say that all these cases involve division. At any rate it is not merely true or false to say that Cleon is white, but also that he was or will be. The principle which unifies is in every case the mind. 430 B

Since the term indivisible has two senses—potential or actual—there is nothing to prevent the mind from thinking of the indivisible when it thinks of length (which is in actuality undivided), and that in indivisible time. Time is also both divisible and indivisible in the same sense as length. So it is impossible to say what it was thinking in each half of the time; for the half has no existence, except potentially, unless the whole is divided. But by thinking each half separately, mind divides the time as well; in which case the halves are treated as separate units of length. But if the line is thought of as the sum of two halves, it is also thought of in a time which covers both half periods.

But when the object of thought is not quantitatively but qualitatively indivisible, the mind thinks of it in indivisible time, and by an indivisible activity of the soul; but incidentally this whole is divisible, not in the sense in which the activity and the time are divisible, but in the sense in which they are indivisible; for there is an indivisible element even in these, though perhaps incapable of separate existence, which makes the time and the length one. And this is equally true of every continuous thing whether time or length. Points and all divisions and everything indivisible in this sense are apprehended in the same way as privations. And the same explanation applies in all other cases; e.g., how the mind cognizes evil or black; for it recognizes them, in a sense, by their contraries. The cognizing agent must be potentially one contrary, and contain the other. But if there is anything which has no contrary, it is self-cognizant, actual and separately existent. Assertion, like affirmation, states an attribute of a subject, and is always either true or false; but this is not always so with the mind: the thinking of the definition in the sense of the essence is always true and is not an instance of predication; but just as while the seeing of a proper object is always true, the judgement whether the white object is a man or not is not always true, so it is with every object abstracted from its matter.

431 A　　VII. Knowledge when actively operative is identical with its object. In the individual potential knowledge has priority in time, but generally it is not prior even in time; for everything comes out of that which actually is. And clearly the sensible object makes the sense-faculty actually operative from being only potential; it is not acted upon, nor does it undergo change of state; and so, if it is motion, it is motion of a distinct kind; for motion, as we saw, is an activity of the imperfect, but activity in the absolute sense, that is activity of the perfected, is different. Sensation, then, is like mere assertion and thinking; when an object is pleasant or unpleasant, the soul pursues or avoids it, thereby making a sort of assertion or negation. To feel pleasure or pain is to adopt an attitude with the sensitive mean towards good or bad as such. This is what avoidance or appetite, when actual, really means, and the faculties of appetite or avoidance are not really different from each other, or from the sensitive faculty, though their actual essence is different. Now for the thinking soul images take the place of direct perceptions; and when it asserts or denies that they are good or bad, it avoids or pursues them. Hence the soul never thinks without a mental image. The process is just like that in which air affects the eye in a particular way, and the eye again affects something else; and similarly with hearing. The last thing to be affected is a single entity and a single mean, although it has more than one aspect.

We have explained before what part of the soul distinguishes between sweet and hot, but some further details must now be added. It is a unity, but in the sense just described, i.e., as a point of connexion. The faculties which it connects, being analogically and numerically one, are related to one another just as their sensible objects are. It makes no difference whether we ask how the soul distinguishes things which are not of the same class, or contraries like white and black. Suppose that as A (white) is to B (black), so is C to D. Then *alternando* C is to A as D is to B. If then C and D belong to one subject, they will stand in the same relation as A and B; A and B are one and the same, though their being has different aspects, and so it is with C and D. The same holds

431 B　good if we take A as sweet and B as white.

So the thinking faculty thinks the forms in mental images, and just as in the sphere of sense what is to be pursued and avoided is defined for it, so also outside sensation, when it is occupied with mental images, is moved. For instance in perceiving a beacon a man recognizes that it is fire; then seeing it moving he knows that it signifies an enemy. But sometimes by means of the images or thoughts in the soul, just as if it were seeing, it calculates and plans for the future in view of the present; and when it makes a statement, as in sensation it asserts that an object is pleasant or unpleasant, in this case it avoids or pursues; and so generally in action. What does not involve action, *i.e.*, the true or false, belongs to the same sphere as what is good or evil; but they differ in having respectively a universal and a particular reference. Abstract objects, as they are called, the mind thinks as if it were thinking the snub-nosed; *qua* snub-nosed, it would not be thought of apart from flesh, but *qua* hollow, if it were actually so conceived, it would be thought of apart from the flesh in which the hollowness resides. So when mind thinks the objects of mathematics, it thinks them as separable though actually they are not. In general, the mind when actively thinking is identical with its objects. Whether it is possible for the mind to think of unextended objects when it is not itself unextended, must be considered later.

VIII. Now summing up what we have said about the soul, let us assert once more that in a sense the soul is all existing things. What exists is either sensible or intelligible; and in a sense knowledge is the knowable and sensation the sensible. We must consider in what sense this is so. Both knowledge and sensation are divided to correspond to their objects, the potential to the potential, and the actual to the actual. The sensitive and cognitive faculties of the soul are potentially these objects, *viz.*, the sensible and the knowable. These faculties, then, must be identical either with the objects themselves or with their forms. Now they are not identical with the objects; for the stone does not exist in the soul, but only the form of the stone. The soul, then, acts like a hand; 432 A for the hand is an instrument which employs instruments, and in the same way the mind is a form which employs forms, and sense is a form which employs the forms of sensible objects. But since apparently nothing has a separate existence, except sensible magnitudes, the objects of thought—both the so-called abstractions of mathematics and all states and affections of sensible things—reside in the sensible forms. And for this reason as no one could ever learn or understand anything without the exercise of perception, so even when we think speculatively, we must have some mental picture of which to think; for mental images are similar to objects perceived except that they are without matter. But imagination is not the same thing as assertion and denial; for truth and falsehood involve a combination of notions. How then will the simplest notions differ from mental pictures? Surely neither these simple notions nor any others are mental pictures, but they cannot occur without such mental pictures.

IX. The soul in living creatures is distinguished by two functions, the judging capacity which is a function of the intellect and of sensation combined, and the capacity for exciting movement in space. We have completed our account of sense and mind, and must now consider what it is in the soul that excites movement; whether it is a part separable from the soul itself, either in extension or only in definition, or whether it is the whole soul; and if it is a part, whether it is a special part beyond those usually described, and of which we have given an account, or whether it is one of them. A problem at once arises: in what sense should we speak of parts of the soul, and how many are there? For in one sense they seem to be infinite, and not confined to those which some thinkers describe, when they attempt analysis, as calculative, emotional, and desiderative, or, as others have it, rational and irrational. When we consider the distinctions according to which they classify, we shall find other parts exhibiting greater differences than those of which we have already spoken; for instance the nutritive part, which belongs both to plants and to all living creatures, and the sensitive part, which one could not easily 432 B assign either to the rational or irrational part; and also the imaginative part, which appears to be different in essence from them all, but which is extremely difficult to identify with, or to distinguish from any one of them, if we are to suppose that the parts of the soul are separate. Beyond these again is the appetitive part, which in both definition and capacity would seem to be different from them all. And it is surely unreasonable to split this up; for there is will in the calculative, and desire and passion in the irrational part; and if the soul is divided into three, appetite will be found in each.

Moreover, to come to the point with which our inquiry is now concerned, what is it that makes the living creature move in space? The generative and nutritive faculties, which all share, would seem responsible for movement in the sense of growth and decay, as this movement belongs to them all; later on we shall have to consider inspiration and expiration, and sleep and waking; for these also present considerable difficulty. But now, about movement in space, we must consider what it is that causes the living animal to exhibit a travelling movement. Obviously it is not the nutritive faculty; for this movement always has an object in view, and is combined with imagination or appetite; for nothing moves except under compulsion, unless it is seeking or avoiding something. Besides, plants would be capable of locomotion, and would have some part instrumental towards this movement. Nor is it the sensitive faculty; for there are many living creatures which have feeling, but are stationary, and do not move throughout their existence. Then seeing that nature does nothing in vain, and omits nothing essential, except in maimed or imperfect animals (and the sort of animal under consideration is perfect and not maimed; this is proved by the fact that they propagate their species and have a prime and decline), they would also have parts instrumental to progression. Nor is the calculative faculty, which is called mind, the motive principle, for the speculative mind thinks of nothing practical, and tells us nothing about what is to be avoided or pursued; but movement is characteristic of one who is either avoiding or pursuing something. Even when the mind contemplates such an object, it does not directly suggest avoidance or pursuit; e.g., it often thinks of something fearful or pleasant without suggesting fear. It is the heart which is moved,—or if the object is pleasant, some other part. 433 A Further, even when the mind orders and thought urges avoidance or pursuit, there is no movement, but action is prompted by desire, e.g., in the absence of self-control. Speaking generally, we see that the man, possessing knowledge of the healing art is not always healing, so that there is some other factor which causes action in accordance with knowledge, and not knowledge itself. Finally, it is not appetite which is responsible for movement; for the self-controlled, though they may crave and desire, do not do these things for which they have an appetite, but follow their reason. . . .

XII. Every living thing, then, must have the nutritive soul, and in (434 A) fact has a soul from its birth until its death; for what has been born must have growth, a highest point of development, and decay, and these things are impossible without food. The nutritive faculty must then exist in all things which grow and decay. But sensation is not necessarily present in all living things. Those whose bodies are uncompounded cannot have a sense of touch, nor can those which are incapable of receiving forms without their matter. But an animal must have sensation, if it is a fact that nature does nothing in vain. For all provisions of nature are means to an end, or must be regarded as coincidental to such means. Any body capable of moving from place to place, if it had no sensation, 434 B would be destroyed, and would not reach the end which is its natural function; for how could it be nourished? Stationary living things can draw their food from the source from which they were born, but it is not possible for a body to possess a soul and a mind capable of judgement without also having sensation, if that body is not stationary but produced by generation; nor even if it is ungenerated. For why should it not have sensation? Either for the good of the soul or for that of the body, but in fact neither alternative is true; for the soul will not think any better, and the body will be no better, for not having sensation. No, body, then, which is not stationary possesses a soul without sensation.

Further, if it does possess sensation, the body must be either simple or compound. But it cannot be simple; for in that case it will have no sense of touch, and this is indispensable to it. This is obvious from the following considerations. For since the living animal is a body possessing soul, and every body is tangible, and tangible means perceptible by touch, it follows that the body of the animal must have the faculty of touch if the animal is to survive. For the other senses, such as smell, vision and hearing, perceive through the medium of something else; but the animal when it touches, if it has no sensation, will not be able to avoid some things and seize others. In that case it will be impossible for the animal to survive. This is why taste is a kind of touch; for it relates to food, and food is a tangible body. Sound, colour and smell supply no food, nor do they produce growth and decay. Hence taste must be some kind of touch, because it is the perception of what is tangible and nutritive. These two senses then, are essential to the animal, and it is obvious that an animal cannot exist without a sense of touch.

The other senses are means to well-being; they do not belong to any class of living creatures taken at random, but only to certain ones, *e.g.*, they are essential to the animal which is capable of locomotion; for if it is to survive, not only must it perceive when in contact, but also from a distance. And this will occur only if it can perceive through a medium, the medium being affected and set in motion by the sensible object, and the animal itself by the medium. For just as that which produces movement in space causes change up to a certain point, and that which has given an impulse causes something else to give one also, and the movement takes place through a medium; and as the first mover impels without being impelled, while the last in the series is impelled without impelling, but the medium both impels and is impelled, and there may 435 A be many media: so it is in the case of alteration, except that the subject suffers alteration without changing place. If one were to dip something into wax, the movement would occur in the wax just so far as one dipped it; stone would not be moved at all, but water would be to a great distance. But it is air that is moved, acting and being acted upon to the greatest extent, so long as it remains a constant unity. This is why in the case of reflection it is better to suppose, not that sight proceeds from the eye and is reflected, but rather than the air, so long as it remains a unity, is affected by the shape and colour. Now on a smooth surface it is a unity; and so it in its turn sets the sight in motion, just as if the impression on the wax extended right through to the other side. . . .

XIX

METAPHYSICS

Book I

I. All men naturally desire knowledge. An indication of this is our 980 A
esteem for the senses: for apart from their use we esteem them for their
own sake, and most of all the sense of sight. Not only with a view to
action, but even when no action is contemplated, we prefer sight, generally speaking, to all the other senses. The reason of this is that of all
the senses sight best helps us to know things, and reveals many distinctions.

Now animals are by nature born with the power of sensation, and
from this some acquire the faculty of memory, whereas others do not.
Accordingly the former are more intelligent and capable of learning than 980 B
those which cannot remember. Such as cannot hear sounds (as the bee,
and any other similar type of creature) are intelligent, but cannot learn;
those only are capable of learning which possess this sense in addition
to the faculty of memory.

Thus the other animals live by impressions and memories, and have
but a small share of experience; but the human race lives also by art
and reasoning. It is from memory that men acquire experience, because
the numerous memories of the same thing eventually produce the effect 981 A
of a single experience. Experience seems very similar to science and art,
but actually it is through experience that men acquire science and art;
for as Polus rightly says, "experience produces art, but inexperience
chance." Art is produced when from many notions of experience a single universal judgement is formed with regard to like objects. To have
a judgement that when Callias was suffering from this or that disease
this or that benefitted him, and similarly with Socrates and various other
individuals, is a matter of experience; but to judge that it benefits all

Reprinted by permission of the publishers and The Loeb Classical Library from Aristotle, *Metaphysics*, translated by Hugh Tredennick, Cambridge, Mass.: Harvard University Press, 1935.

persons of a certain type, considered as a class, who suffer from this or that disease (*e.g.* the phlegmatic or bilious when suffering from burning fever) is a matter of art.

It would seem that for practical purposes experience is in no way inferior to art; indeed we see men of experience succeeding more than those who have theory without experience. The reason of this is that experience is knowledge of particulars, but art of universals; and actions and the effects produced are all concerned with the particular. For it is not man that the physician cures, except incidentally, but Callias or Socrates or some other person similarly named, who is incidentally a man as well. So if a man has theory without experience, and knows the universal, but does not know the particular contained in it, he will often fail in his treatment; for it is the particular that must be treated. Nevertheless we consider that knowledge and proficiency belong to art rather than to experience, and we assume that artists are wiser than men of mere experience (which implies that in all cases wisdom depends rather upon knowledge); and this is because the former know the cause, whereas the latter do not. For the experienced know the fact, but not the wherefore; but the artists know the wherefore and the cause. For the same reason we consider that the master craftsmen in every profession are more estimable and know more and are wiser than the artisans, 981 B because they know the reasons of the things which are done; but we think that the artisans, like certain inanimate objects, do things, but without knowing what they are doing (as, for instance, fire burns); only whereas inanimate objects perform all their actions in virtue of a certain natural quality, artisans perform theirs through habit. Thus the master craftsmen are superior in wisdom, not because they can do things, but because they possess a theory and know the causes.

In general the sign of knowledge or ignorance is the ability to teach, and for this reason we hold that art rather than experience is scientific knowledge; for the artists can teach, but the others cannot. Further, we do not consider any of the senses to be Wisdom. They are indeed our chief sources of knowledge about particulars, but they do not tell us the reason for anything, as for example why fire is hot, but only that it *is* hot.

It is therefore probable that at first the inventor of any art which went further than the ordinary sensations was admired by his fellow-men, not merely because some of his inventions were useful, but as being a wise and superior person. And as more and more arts were discovered, some relating to the necessities and some to the pastimes of life, the inventors of the latter were always considered wiser than those of the former, because their branches of knowledge did not aim at utility. Hence when all the discoveries of this kind were fully developed, the sciences which relate neither to pleasure nor yet to the necessities of life were invented, and first in those places where men had leisure. Thus the mathematical sciences originated in the neighbourhood of Egypt, because there the priestly class was allowed leisure.

The difference between art and science and the other kindred mental activities has been stated in the *Ethics;* the reason for our present discussion is that it is generally assumed that what is called Wisdom is concerned with the primary causes and principles, so that, as has been already stated, the man of experience is held to be wiser than the mere possessors of any power of sensation, the artist than the man of experience, the master craftsman than the artisan; and the speculative sciences to be more learned than the productive. Thus it is clear that Wisdom is knowledge of certain principles and causes. 982 A

II. Since we are investigating this kind of knowledge, we must consider what these causes and principles are whose knowledge is Wisdom. Perhaps it will be clearer if we take the opinions which we hold about the wise man. We consider first, then, that the wise man knows all things, so far as it is possible, without having knowledge of every one of them individually; next, that the wise man is he who can comprehend difficult things, such as are not easy for human comprehension (for sense-perception, being common to all, is easy, and has nothing to do with Wisdom); and further that in every branch of knowledge a man is wiser in proportion as he is more accurately informed and better able to expound the causes. Again among the sciences we consider that that science which is desirable in itself and for the sake of knowledge is more nearly Wisdom than that which is desirable for its results, and that the superior is more nearly Wisdom than the subsidiary; for the wise man should give orders, not receive them; nor should he obey others, but the less wise should obey him.

Such in kind and in number are the opinions which we hold with regard to Wisdom and the wise. Of the qualities there described the knowledge of everything must necessarily belong to him who in the highest degree possesses knowledge of the universal, because he knows in a sense all the particulars which it comprises. These things, viz. the most universal, are perhaps the hardest for man to grasp, because they are furthest removed from the senses. Again, the most exact of the sciences are those which are most concerned with the first principles; for those which are based on fewer principles are more exact than those which include additional principles; *e.g.,* arithmetic is more exact than geometry. Moreover, the science which investigates causes is more instructive than one which does not, for it is those who tell us the causes of any particular thing who instruct us. Moreover, knowledge and understanding which are desirable for their own sake are most attainable in the knowledge of that which is most knowable. For the man who desires knowledge for its own sake will most desire the most perfect knowledge, and this is the knowledge of the most knowable, and the

982 B things which are most knowable are first principles and causes; for it is through these and from these that other things come to be known, and not these through the particulars which fall under them. And that science is supreme, and superior to the subsidiary, which knows for what end each action is to be done; *i.e.* the Good in each particular case, and in general the highest Good in the whole of nature.

Thus as a result of all the above considerations the term which we are investigating falls under the same science, which must speculate about first principles and causes; for the Good, *i.e.* the *end*, is one of the causes.

That it is not a productive science is clear from a consideration of the first philosophers. It is through wonder that men now begin and originally began to philosophize; wondering in the first place at obvious perplexities, and then by gradual progression raising questions about the greater matters too, *e.g.* about the changes of the moon and of the sun, about the stars and about the origin of the universe. Now he who wonders and is perplexed feels that he is ignorant (thus the myth-lover is in a sense a philosopher, since myths are composed of wonders); therefore if it was to escape ignorance that men studied philosophy, it is obvious that they pursued science for the sake of knowledge, and not for any practical utility. The actual course of events bears witness to this; for speculation of this kind began with a view to recreation and pastime, at a time when practically all the necessities of life were already supplied. Clearly then it is for no extrinsic advantage that we seek this knowledge; for just as we call a man independent who exists for himself and not for another, so we call this the only independent science, since it alone exists for itself.

For this reason its acquisition might justly be supposed to be beyond human power, since in many respects human nature is servile; in which case, as Simonides says, "God alone can have this privilege," and man should only seek the knowledge which is within his reach. Indeed if the

983 A poets are right and the Deity is by nature jealous, it is probable that in this case He would be particularly jealous, and all those who excel in knowledge unfortunate. But it is impossible for the Deity to be jealous (indeed, as the proverb says, "poets tell many a lie"), nor must we suppose that any other form of knowledge is more precious than this; for what is most divine is most precious. Now there are two ways only in which it can be divine. A science is divine if it is peculiarly the possession of God, or if it is concerned with divine matters. And this science

alone fulfills both these conditions; for (*a*) all believe that God is one of the causes and a kind of principle, and (*b*) God is the sole or chief possessor of this sort of knowledge. Accordingly, although all other sciences are more necessary than this, none is more excellent.

The acquisition of this knowledge, however, must in a sense result in something which is the reverse of the outlook with which we first approached the inquiry. All begin, as we have said, by wondering that things should be as they are, *e.g.* with regard to marionettes, or the solstices, or the incommensurability of the diagonal of a square; because it seems wonderful to everyone who has not yet perceived the cause that a thing should not be measurable by the smallest unit. But we must end with the contrary and (according to the proverb) the better view, as men do even in these cases when they understand them; for a geometrician would wonder at nothing so much as it the diagonal were to become measurable.

Thus we have stated what is the nature of the science which we are seeking, and what is the object which our search and our whole investigation must attain.

III. It is clear that we must obtain knowledge of the primary causes, because it is when we think that we understand its primary cause that we claim to know each particular thing. Now there are four recognized kinds of cause. Of these we hold that one is the essence or essential nature of the thing (since the "reason why" of a thing is ultimately reducible to its formula, and the ultimate "reason why" is a cause and principle); another is the matter or substrate; the third is the source of motion; and the fourth is the cause which is opposite to this, namely the purpose or "good"; for this is the end of every generative or motive   983 B
process. We have investigated these sufficiently in the *Physics;* however, let us avail ourselves of the evidence of those who have before us approached the investigation of reality and philosophized about Truth. For clearly they too recognize certain principles and causes, and so it will be of some assistance to our present inquiry if we study their teaching; because we shall either discover some other kind of cause, or have more confidence in those which we have just described.

Most of the earliest philosophers conceived only of material principles as underlying all things. That of which all things consist, from which they first come and into which on their destruction they are ultimately resolved, of which the essence persists although modified by its affections—this, they say, is an element and principle of existing things. Hence they believe that nothing is either generated or destroyed, since this kind of primary entity always persists. Similarly we do not say that Socrates comes into being *absolutely* when he becomes handsome or cultured, nor that he is destroyed when he loses these qualities; because the substrate, Socrates himself, persists. In the same way nothing else is generated or destroyed; for there is some one entity (or more than one) which always persists and from which all other things are generated. All are not agreed, however, as to the number and character of these principles. Thales, the founder of this school of philosophy, says the permanent entity is water (which is why he also propounded that the earth floats on water). Presumably he derived this assumption from seeing that the nutriment of everything is moist, and that heat itself is generated from moisture and depends upon it for its existence (and that from which a thing is generated is always its first principle). He derived his assumption, then, from this; and also from the fact that the seeds of everything have a moist nature, whereas water is the first principle of the nature of moist things.

There are some who think that the men of very ancient times, long before the present era, who first speculated about the gods, also held this same opinion about the primary entity. For they represented Oceanus and Tethys to be the parents of creation, and the oath of the gods to be by water—Styx, as they call it. Now what is most ancient is most revered, and what is most revered is what we swear by. Whether 984 A this view of the primary entity is really ancient and time-honoured may perhaps be considered uncertain; however, it is said that this was Thales' opinion concerning the first cause. (I say nothing of Hippo, because no one would presume to include him in this company, in view of the paltriness of his intelligence.)

Anaximenes and Diogenes held that air is prior to water, and is of all corporeal elements most truly the first principle. Hippasus of Metapontum and Heraclitus of Ephesus hold this of fire; and Empedocles—adding earth as a fourth to those already mentioned—takes all four. These, he says, always persist, and are only generated in respect of multitude and paucity, according as they are combined into unity or differentiated out of unity.

Anaxagoras of Clazomenae—prior to Empedocles in point of age, but posterior in his activities—says that the first principles are infinite in number. For he says that as a general rule all things which are, like fire and water, homoeomerous, are generated and destroyed in this sense only, by combination and differentiation; otherwise they are neither generated nor destroyed, but persist eternally.

From this account it might be supposed that the only cause is of the kind called "material." But as men proceeded in this way, the very circumstances of the case led them on and compelled them to seek further; because if it is really true that all generation and destruction is out of some one entity or even more than one, *why* does this happen, and what is the cause? It is surely not the substrate itself which causes itself to change. I mean, *e.g.,* that neither wood nor bronze is responsible for changing itself; wood does not make a bed, nor bronze a statue, but something else is the cause of the change. Now to investigate this is to investigate the second type of cause: the *source of motion,* as we should say.

Those who were the very first to take up this inquiry, and who maintained that the substrate is one thing, had no misgivings on the subject; but some of those who regard it as one thing, being baffled, as it were, by the inquiry, say that that one thing (and indeed the whole physical world) is immovable in respect not only of generation and destruction (this was a primitive belief and was generally admitted) but of all other change. This belief is peculiar to them. 984 B

None of those who maintained that the universe is a unity achieved any conception of this type of cause, except perhaps Parmenides; and him only in so far as he admits, in a sense, not one cause only but two. But those who recognize more than one entity, *e.g.* hot and cold, or fire and earth, are better able to give a systematic explanation, because they avail themselves of fire as being of a kinetic nature, and of water, earth, etc., as being the opposite.

After these thinkers and the discovery of these causes, since they were insufficient to account for the generation of the actual world, men were again compelled (as we have said) by truth itself to investigate the next first principle. For presumably it is unnatural that either fire or earth or any other such element should cause existing things to be or become well and beautifully disposed; or indeed that those thinkers should hold such a view. Nor again was it satisfactory to commit so important a matter to spontaneity and chance. Hence when someone said that there is Mind in nature, just as in animals, and that this is the cause of all order and arrangement, he seemed like a sane man in contrast with the haphazard statements of his predecessors. We know definitely that Anaxagoras adopted this view; but Hermotimus of Clazomenae is credited with having stated it earlier. Those thinkers, then, who held this view assumed a principle in things which is the cause of beauty, and the sort of cause by which motion is communicated to things.

IV. It might be inferred that the first person to consider this question was Hesiod, or indeed anyone else who assumed Love or Desire as a first principle in things; *e.g.* Parmenides. For he says, where he is describing the creation of the universe,

Love she created first of all the gods.

And Hesiod says,

> First of all things was Chaos made, and then
> Broad-bosomed Earth . . .
> And Love, the foremost of immortal beings,

thus implying that there must be in the world some cause to move things and combine them.

The question of arranging these thinkers in order of priority may be decided later. Now since it was apparent that nature also contains the opposite of what is good, *i.e.* not only order and beauty, but disorder and ugliness; and that there are more bad and common things than there are good and beautiful; in view of this another thinker introduced Love and Strife as the respective causes of these things—because if one follows up and appreciates the statements of Empedocles with a view to his real meaning and not to his obscure language, it will be found that Love is the cause of good, and Strife of evil. Thus it would perhaps be correct to say that Empedocles in a sense spoke of evil and good as first principles, and was the first to do so—that is, if the cause of all good things is absolute good.

These thinkers then, as I say, down to the time of Empedocles, seem to have grasped two of the causes which we have defined in the *Physics:* the material cause and the source of motion; but only vaguely and indefinitely. They are like untrained soldiers in a battle, who rush about and often strike good blows, but without science; in the same way these thinkers do not seem to understand their own statements, since it is clear that upon the whole they seldom or never apply them. Anaxagoras avails himself of Mind as an artificial device for producing order, and drags it in whenever he is at a loss to explain some necessary result; but otherwise he makes anything rather than Mind the cause of what happens. Again, Empedocles does indeed use causes to a greater degree than Anaxagoras, but not sufficiently; nor does he attain to consistency in their use. At any rate Love often differentiates and Strife combines; because whenever the universe is differentiated into its elements by Strife, fire and each of the other elements are agglomerated into a unity; and whenever they are all combined together again by Love, the particles of each element are necessarily again differentiated.

Empedocles, then, differed from his predecessors in that he first introduced the division of this cause, making the source of motion not one but two contrary forces. Further, he was the first to maintain that the so-called material elements are four—not that he uses them as four, but as two only, treating fire on the one hand by itself, and the elements opposed to it—earth, air and water—on the other, as a single nature. This can be seen from a study of his writings. Such, then, as I say, is his account of the nature and number of the first principles.

Leucippus, however, and his disciple Democritus hold that the ele-

ments are the Full and the Void—calling the one "what is" and the
other "what is not." Of these they identify the full or solid with "what
is," and the void or rare with "what is not" (hence they hold that what
is not is no less real than what is, because Void is as real as Body); and
they say that these are the material causes of things. And just as those
who make the underlying substance a unity generate all other things by
means of its modifications, assuming rarity and density as first principles of these modifications, so these thinkers hold that the "differences"
are the causes of everything else. These differences, they say, are three:
shape, arrangement, and position; because they hold that what is differs
only in *contour, inter-contact,* and *inclination.* (Of these contour means
shape, inter-contact arrangement, and inclination position.) Thus, *e.g.*,
A differs from N in shape, AN from NA in arrangement, and Z from
N in position. As for motion, whence and how it arises in things, they
casually ignored this point, very much as the other thinkers did. Such,
then, as I say, seems to be the extent of the inquiries which the earlier
thinkers made into these two kinds of cause.

V. At the same time, however, and even earlier the so-called Pythagoreans applied themselves to mathematics, and were the first to develop this science; and through studying it they came to believe that its
principles are the principles of everything. And since *numbers* are by
nature first among these principles, and they fancied that they could
detect in numbers, to a greater extent than in fire and earth and water,
many analogues of what is and comes into being—such and such a property of number being *justice,* and such and such *soul* or *mind,* another
opportunity, and similarly, more or less, with all the rest—and since they
saw further that the properties and ratios of the musical scales are based
on numbers, and since it seemed clear that all other things have their
whole nature modelled upon numbers, and that numbers are the ulti-   986 A
mate things in the whole physical universe, they assumed the elements
of numbers to be the elements of everything, and the whole universe to
be a proportion or number. Whatever analogues to the processes and
parts of the heavens and to the whole order of the universe they could
exhibit in numbers and proportions, these they collected and correlated;
and if there was any deficiency anywhere, they made haste to supply it,
in order to make their system a connected whole. For example, since
the decad is considered to be a complete thing and to comprise the whole
essential nature of the numerical system, they assert that the bodies
which revolve in the heavens are ten; and there being only nine that
are visible, they make the "antichthon" the tenth. We have treated this
subject in greater detail elsewhere; but the object of our present review
is to discover from these thinkers too what causes they assume and how
these coincide with our list of causes. Well, it is obvious that these thinkers too consider number to be a first principle, both as the material of

things and as constituting their properties and states. The elements of number, according to them, are the Even and the Odd. Of these the former is limited and the latter unlimited; Unity consists of both (since it is both odd and even); number is derived from Unity; and numbers, as we have said, compose the whole sensible universe.

Others of this same school hold that there are ten principles, which they enunciate in a series of corresponding pairs: (i.) Limit and the Unlimited; (ii.) Odd and Even; (iii.) Unity and Plurality; (iv.) Right and Left; (v.) Male and Female; (vi.) Rest and Motion; (vii.) Straight and Crooked; (viii.) Light and Darkness; (ix.) Good and Evil; (x.) Square and Oblong. Apparently Alcmaeon of Croton speculated along the same lines, and either he derived the theory from them or they from him; for [Alcmaeon was contemporary with the old age of Pythagoras, and] his doctrines were very similar to theirs. He says that the majority of things in the world of men are in pairs; but the contraries which he mentions are not, as in the case of the Pythagoreans, carefully defined, but are taken at random, *e.g.* white and black, sweet and bitter, good and bad, great and small. Thus Alcmaeon only threw out vague hints with regard to the other instances of contrariety, but the Pythagoreans pronounced how many and what the contraries are. Thus from both these authorities we can gather thus much, that the contraries are first principles of things; and from the former, how many and what the contraries are. How these can be referred to our list of causes is not definitely expressed by them, but they appear to reckon their elements as material; for they say that these are the original constituents of which Being is fashioned and composed.

From this survey we can sufficiently understand the meaning of those ancients who taught that the elements of the natural world are a plurality. Others, however, theorized about the universe as though it were a single entity; but their doctrines are not all alike either in point of soundness or in respect of conformity with the facts of nature. For the purposes of our present inquiry an account of their teaching is quite irrelevant, since they do not, while assuming a unity, at the same time make out that Being is generated from the unity as from matter, as do some physicists, but give a different explanation; for the physicists assume motion also, at any rate when explaining the generation of the universe; but these thinkers hold that it is immovable. Nevertheless thus much is pertinent to our present inquiry. It appears that Parmenides conceived of the Unity as one in definition, but Melissus as materially one. Hence the former says that it is finite, and the latter that it is infinite. But Xenophanes, the first exponent of the Unity (for Parmenides is said to have been his disciple), gave no definite teaching, nor does he seem to have grasped either of these conceptions of unity; but regarding the whole material universe he stated that the Unity is God. This school then, as we have said, may be disregarded for the purposes of our present inquiry; two of them, Xenophanes and Melissus, may be completely ignored, as being somewhat too crude in their views. Parmenides, however, seems to speak with rather more insight. For holding as he does that Not-being, as contrasted with Being, is nothing, he necessarily supposes that Being is one and that there is nothing else (we have discussed this point in greater detail in the *Physics*); but being compelled to accord with phenomena, and assuming that Being is one in definition but many in respect of sensation, he posits in his turn two causes, *i.e.* two first principles, Hot and Cold; or in other words, Fire and Earth. 987 A Of these he ranks Hot under Being and the other under Not-being.

From the account just given, and from a consideration of those thinkers who have already debated this question, we have acquired the following information. From the earliest philosophers we have learned that the first principle is corporeal (since water and fire and the like are bodies); some of them assume one and others more than one corporeal principle, but both parties agree in making these principles material. Others assume in addition to this cause the *source of motion*, which some hold to be one and others two. Thus down to and apart from the Italian philosophers the other thinkers have expressed themselves vaguely on the subject, except that, as we have said, they actually employ two causes, and one of these—the source of motion—some regard as one and others as two. The Pythagoreans, while they likewise spoke of two principles, made this further addition, which is peculiar to them: they believed, not that the Limited and the Unlimited are separate entities, like fire or water or some other such thing, but that the Unlimited itself and the One itself are essence of those things of which they are predicated, and hence that number is the essence of all things. Such is the nature of their pronouncements on this subject. They also began to discuss and define the "what" of things; but their procedure was far too simple. They defined superficially, and supposed that the essence of a thing is that to which the term under consideration first applies—*e.g.* as if it were to be thought that "double" and "2" are the same, because 2 is the first number which is double another. But presumably "to be double a number" is not the same as "to be the number 2." Otherwise, one thing will be many—a consequence which actually followed in their system. This much, then, can be learned from other and earlier schools of thought.

VI. The philosophies described above were succeeded by the system of Plato, which in most respects accorded with them, but contained also certain peculiar features distinct from the philosophy of the Italians. In his youth Plato first became acquainted with Cratylus and the Heraclitean doctrines—that the whole sensible world is always in a state of flux, and that there is no scientific knowledge of it—and in after years he still held these opinions. And when Socrates, disregarding the physical universe and confining his study to moral questions, sought in this sphere for the universal and was the first to concentrate upon definition, Plato followed him and assumed that the problem of definition is concerned not with any sensible thing but with entities of another kind; for the reason that there can be no general definition of sensible things which are always changing. These entities he called "Ideas," and held that all sensible things are named after them and in virtue of their relation to them; for the plurality of things which bear the same name as the Forms exist by participation in them. (With regard to the "participation," it was only the term that he changed; for whereas the Pythagoreans say that things exist by imitation of numbers, Plato says that they exist by participation—merely a change of term. As to what this "participation" or "imitation" may be, they left this an open question.)

Further, he states that besides sensible things and the Forms there exists an intermediate class, the *objects of mathematics*, which differ from sensible things in being eternal and immutable, and from the Forms in that there are many similar objects of mathematics, whereas each Form is itself unique.

Now since the Forms are the causes of everything else, he supposed that their elements are the elements of all things. Accordingly the material principle is the "Great and Small," and the essence [or formal principle] is the One, since the numbers are derived from the "Great and Small" by participation in the One. In treating the One as a substance instead of a predicate of some other entity, his teaching resembles that of the Pythagoreans, and also agrees with it in stating that the numbers are the causes of Being in everything else; but it is peculiar to him to posit a duality instead of the single Unlimited, and to make the Unlimited consist of the "Great and Small." He is also peculiar in regarding the numbers as distinct from sensible things, whereas they hold that things themselves *are* numbers, nor do they posit an intermediate class of mathematical objects. His distinction of the One and the numbers from ordinary things (in which he differed from the Pythagoreans) and his introduction of the Forms were due to his investigation of logic (the earlier thinkers were strangers to Dialectic); his conception of the other principle as a duality to the belief that numbers other than primes can be readily generated from it, as from a matrix. The fact, however, is just the reverse, and the theory is illogical; for whereas the Platonists derive multiplicity from matter although their Form generates only once, it is obvious that only one table can be made from one piece of timber, and yet he who imposes the form upon it, although he is but one, can make many tables. Such too is the relation of male to female: the female is impregnated in one coition, but one male can impregnate many females. And these relations are analogues of the principles referred to.

This, then, is Plato's verdict upon the question which we are investigating. From this account it is clear that he only employed two causes; that of the essence, and the material cause; for the Forms are the cause of the essence in everything else, and the One is the cause of it in the Forms. He also tells us what the material substrate is of which the Forms are predicated in the case of sensible things, and the One in that of the Forms—that it is this duality, the "Great and Small." Further, he assigned to these two elements respectively the causation of good and of evil; a problem which, as we have said, had also been considered by some of the earlier philosophers, e.g. Empedocles and Anaxagoras.

VII. We have given only a concise and summary account of those thinkers who have expressed views about the causes and reality, and of their doctrines. Nevertheless we have learned thus much from them: that not one of those who discuss principle or cause has mentioned any other type than those which we have distinguished in the *Physics*. Clearly it is after these types that they are groping, however uncertainly. Some speak of the first principle as material, whether they regard it as one or several, as corporeal or incorporeal: e.g. Plato speaks of the "Great and Small"; the Italians of the Unlimited; Empedocles of Fire, Earth, Water and Air; Anaxagoras of the infinity of homoeomeries. All these have apprehended this type of cause; and all those too who make their first principle air or water or "something denser than fire but rarer than air" (for some have so described the primary element). These, then, apprehended this cause only, but others apprehended the *source of motion*—e.g. all such as make Love and Strife, or Mind, or Desire a first principle. As for the *essence* or *essential nature*, nobody has definitely introduced it; but the inventors of the Forms express it most nearly. For they do not conceive of the Forms as the *matter* of sensible things (and the One as the matter of the Forms), nor as producing the *source of motion* (for they hold that they are rather the cause of immobility and tranquility); but they adduce the Forms as the *essential nature* of all other things, and the One as that of the Forms. The *end* towards which actions, changes and motions tend they do in a way treat as a cause, but not in this sense, i.e. not in the sense in which it is naturally a cause. Those who speak of Mind or Love assume these causes as being something *good;* but nevertheless they do not profess that anything exists or is generated *for the sake* of them, but only that motions originate from them. Similarly also those who hold that Unity or Being is an entity of this kind state that it is the cause of existence, but not that things exist

988 B

or are generated for the sake of it. So it follows that in a sense they both assert and deny that the Good is a cause; for they treat it as such not absolutely, but incidentally. It appears, then, that all these thinkers too (being unable to arrive at any other cause) testify that we have classified the causes rightly, as regards both number and nature. Further, it is clear that all the principles must be sought either along these lines or in some similar way. . . .

Book II

993 A   I. The study of Truth is in one sense difficult, in another easy. This is shown by the fact that whereas no one person can obtain an adequate
993 B grasp of it, we cannot *all* fail in the attempt; each thinker makes some statement about the natural world, and as an individual contributes little or nothing to the inquiry; but a combination of all conjectures results in something considerable. Thus in so far as it seems that Truth is like the proverbial door which no one can miss, in this sense our study will be easy; but the fact that we cannot, although having some grasp of the whole, grasp a particular part, shows its difficulty. However, since difficulty also can be accounted for in two ways, its cause may exist not in the objects of our study but in ourselves; just as it is with bats' eyes in respect of daylight, so it is with our mental intelligence in respect of those which are by nature most obvious.

It is only fair to be grateful not only to those whose views we can share but also to those who have expressed rather superficial opinions. They too have contributed something; by their preliminary work they have formed our mental experience. If there had been no Timotheus, we should not possess much of our music, and if there had been no Phrynis, there would have been no Timotheus. It is just the same in the case of those who have theorized about reality: we have derived certain views from some of them, and they in turn were indebted to others.

Moreover, philosophy is rightly called a knowledge of Truth. The object of theoretic knowledge is truth, while that of practical knowledge is action; for even when they are investigating *how* a thing is so, practical men study not the eternal principle but the relative and immediate application. But we cannot know the truth apart from the cause. Now every thing through which a common quality is communicated to other things is itself of all those things in the highest degree possessed of that quality (*e.g.* fire is hottest, because it is the cause of heat in everything else); hence that also is most true which causes all subsequent things to be true. Therefore in every case the first principles of things must necessarily be true above everything else—since they are not merely *sometimes* true, nor is anything the cause of their existence, but they are the cause of the existence of other things,—and so as each thing is in respect of existence, so it is in respect of truth.

II. Moreover, it is obvious that there is some first principle, and that the causes of things are not infinitely many either in a direct sequence or in kind. For the material generation of one thing from another cannot go on in an infinite progression (*e.g.* flesh from earth, earth from air, air from fire, and so on without a stop); nor can the source of motion (*e.g.* man be moved by air, air by the sun, the sun by Strife, with no limit to the series). In the same way neither can the Final Cause recede to infinity—walking having health for its object, and health happiness, and happiness something else: one thing always being done for the sake of another. And it is just the same with the Formal Cause. For in the case of all intermediate terms of a series which are contained between a first and last term, the prior term is necessarily the cause of those which follow it; because if we had to say which of the three is the cause, we should say "the first." At any rate it is not the last term, because what comes at the end is not the cause of anything. Neither, again, is the intermediate term, which is only the cause of one (and it makes no difference whether there is one intermediate term or several, nor whether they are infinite or limited in number). But of series which are infinite in this way, and in general of the infinite, all the parts are equally intermediate, down to the present moment. Thus if there is no first term, there is no cause at all.

On the other hand there can be no infinite progression downwards (where there is a beginning in the upper direction) such that from fire comes water, and from water earth, and in this way some other kind of thing is always being produced. There are two senses in which one thing "comes from" another—apart from that in which one thing is said to come *after* another, *e.g.* the Olympian "from" the Isthmian games—either as a man comes from a child as it develops, or as air comes from water. Now we say that a man "comes from" a child in the sense that that which *has* become something comes from that which *is* becoming: *i.e.* the perfect from the imperfect. (For just as "becoming" is always intermediate between being and not-being, so is that which is becoming between what is and what is not. The learner is becoming informed, and that is the meaning of the statement that the informed person "comes from" the learner.) On the other hand A comes from B in the sense that water comes from air by the destruction of B. Hence the former class of process is not reversible (*e.g.* a child cannot come from a man, for the result of the process of becoming is not the thing which is becoming, but that which exists after the process is complete. So day comes from early dawn, because it is after dawn; and hence dawn does not come from day). But the other class is reversible. In both cases progression to infinity is impossible; for in the former the intermediate terms must have an end, and in the second the process is reversible, for the destruction of one member of a pair is the generation of the other. At the same time the first cause, being eternal, cannot be destroyed; because, since the process of generation is not infinite in the upper direction, that cause which first, on its destruction, becomes something else, cannot possibly be eternal.

Further, the Final cause of a thing is an *end,* and is such that it does not happen for the sake of something else, but all other things happen for its sake. So if there is to be a last term of this kind, the series will not be infinite; and if there is no such term, there will be no Final cause. Those who introduce infinity do not realize that they are abolishing the nature of the Good (although no one would attempt to do anything if he were not likely to reach some limit); nor would there be any intelligence in the world, because the man who has intelligence always acts for the sake of something, and this is a limit, because the *end* is a limit.

Nor again can the Formal cause be referred back to another fuller definition; for the prior definition is always closer, and the posterior is not; and where the original definition does not apply, neither does the subsequent one. Further, those who hold such a view do away with scientific knowledge, for on this view it is impossible to know anything until one comes to terms which cannot be analysed. Understanding, too, is impossible; for how can one conceive of things which are infinite in this way? It is different in the case of the line, which, although in respect of divisibility it never stops, yet cannot be conceived of unless we make a stop (which is why, in examining an infinite line, one cannot count the sections). Even matter has to be conceived under the form of something which changes, and there can be nothing which is infinite. In any case the concept of infinity is not infinite.

Again, if the kinds of causes were infinite in *number* it would still be impossible to acquire knowledge; for it is only when we have become acquainted with the causes that we assume that we know a thing; and we cannot, in a finite time, go completely through what is additively infinite.

III. The effect of a lecture depends upon the habits of the listener; because we expect the language to which we are accustomed, and anything beyond this seems not to be on the same level, but somewhat strange and unintelligible on account of its unfamiliarity; for it is the familiar that is intelligible. The powerful effect of familiarity is clearly shown by the laws, in which the fanciful and puerile survivals prevail, through force of habit, against our recognition of them. Thus some people will not accept the statements of a speaker unless he gives a mathematical proof; others will not unless he makes use of illustrations; others expect to have a poet adduced as witness. Again, some require exactness in everything, while others are annoyed by it, either because they cannot follow the reasoning or because of its pettiness; for there is something about exactness which seems to some people to be mean, no less in an argument than in a business transaction.

Hence one must have been already trained how to take each kind of argument, because it is absurd to seek simultaneously for knowledge and for the method of obtaining it; and neither is easy to acquire. Mathematical accuracy is not to be demanded in everything, but only in things which do not contain matter. Hence this method is not that of natural science, because presumably all nature is concerned with matter. Hence we should first inquire what nature is; for in this way it will become clear what the objects of natural science are [and whether it belongs to one science or more than one to study the causes and principles of things].

Book IV

I. There is a science which studies Being *qua* Being, and the properties inherent in it in virtue of its own nature. This science is not the same as any of the so-called particular sciences, for none of the others contemplates Being generally *qua* Being; they divide off some portion of it and study the attribute of this portion, as do for example the mathematical sciences. But since it is for the first principles and the most ultimate causes that we are searching, clearly they must belong to something in virtue of its own nature. Hence if these principles were investigated by those also who investigated the elements of existing things, the elements must be elements of Being not incidentally, but *qua* Being. Therefore it is of Being *qua* Being that we too must grasp the first causes.

II. The term "being" is used in various senses, but with reference to one central idea and one definite characteristic, and not as merely a common epithet. Thus as the term "healthy" always relates to health (either as preserving it or as producing it or as indicating it or as receptive of it), and as "medical" relates to the art of medicine (either as possessing it or as naturally adapted for it or as being a function of medicine)—and we shall find other terms used similarly to these—so "being" is used in various senses, but always with reference to one principle. For some things are said to "be" because they are substances; others because they are modifications of substance; others because they are a process towards substance, or destructions or privations or qual-

1003 A

1003 B

ities of substance, or productive or generative of substance or of terms relating to substance, or negations of certain of these terms or of substance. (Hence we even say that not-being *is* not-being.) And so, just as there is one science of all healthy things, so it is true of everything else. For it is not only in the case of terms which express one common notion that the investigation belongs to one science, but also in the case of terms which relate to one particular characteristic; for the latter too, in a sense, express one common notion. Clearly then the study of things which *are, qua* being, also belongs to one science. Now in every case knowledge is principally concerned with that which is primary, *i.e.* that upon which all other things depend, and from which they get their names. If, then, substance is this primary thing, it is of substances that the philosopher must grasp the first principles and causes.

Now of every single class of things, as there is one perception, so there is one science: *e.g.*, grammar, which is one science, studies all articulate sounds. Hence the study of all the species of Being *qua* Being belongs to a science which is generically one, and the study of the several species of Being belongs to the specific parts of that science.

Now if Being and Unity are the same, *i.e.* a single nature, in the sense that they are associated as principle and cause are, and not as being denoted by the same definition (although it makes no difference but rather helps our argument if we understand them in the same sense), since "one man" and "man" and "existent man" and "man" are the same thing, *i.e.* the duplication in the statement "he is a man and an *existent* man" gives no fresh meaning (clearly the concepts of humanity and existence are not dissociated in respect of either coming to be or ceasing to be), and similarly in the case of the term "one," so that obviously the additional term in these phrases has the same significance, and Unity is nothing distinct from Being; and further if the substance of each thing is one in no accidental sense, and similarly is of its very nature something which *is*—then there are just as many species of Being as of Unity. And to study the essence of these species (I mean, *e.g.*, the study of Same and Other and all the other similar concepts—roughly speaking all the "contraries" are reducible to this first principle; but we may consider that they have been sufficiently studied in the "Selection of Contraries") is the province of a science which is generally one.

1004 A

And there are just as many divisions of philosophy as there are kinds of substance; so that there must be among them a First Philosophy and one which follows upon it. For Being and Unity at once entail genera, and so the sciences will correspond to these genera. The term "philosopher" is like the term "mathematician" in its uses; for mathematics too has divisions,—there is a primary and a secondary science, and others successively, in the realm of mathematics.

Now since it is the province of one science to study opposites, and the opposite of unity is plurality, and it is the province of one science to study the negation and privation of Unity, because in both cases we are studying Unity, to which the negation (or privation) refers, stated either in the simple form that Unity is not present, or in the form that it is not present in a particular class; in the latter case Unity is modified by the differentia, apart from the content of the negation (for the negation of Unity is its absence); but in privation there is a substrate of which the privation is predicated.—The opposite of Unity, then, is Plurality; and so the opposites of the above-mentioned concepts—Otherness, Dissimilarity, Inequality and everything else which is derived from these or from Plurality or Unity—fall under the cognizance of the aforesaid science. And one of them is Oppositeness; for this is a form of Difference, and Difference is a form of Otherness. Hence since the term "one" is used in various senses, so too will these terms be used; yet it pertains to one science to take cognizance of them all. For terms fall under different sciences, not if they are used in various senses, but if their definitions are neither identical nor referable to a common notion. And since everything is referred to that which is primary, *e.g.* all things which are called "one" are referred to the primary "One," we must admit that this is also true of Identity and Otherness and the Contraries. Thus we must first distinguish all the senses in which each term is used, and then attribute them to the primary in the case of each predicate, and see how they are related to it; for some will derive their name from possessing and others from producing it, and others for similar reasons.

Thus clearly it pertains to one science to give an account both of these concepts and of substance (this was one of the questions raised in the "Difficulties"), and it is the function of the philosopher to be able 1004 B to study all subjects. If this is not so, who is it who will investigate whether "Socrates" and "Socrates seated" are the same thing; or whether one thing has one contrary, or what the contrary is, or how many meanings it has? and similarly with all other such questions. Thus since these are the essential modifications of Unity *qua* Unity and of Being *qua* Being, and not *qua* numbers or lines or fire, clearly it pertains to that science to discover both the essence and the attributes of these concepts. And those who investigate them err, not in being unphilosophical, but because the substance, of which they have no real knowledge, is prior. For just as number *qua* number has its peculiar modifications, *e.g.* oddness and evenness, commensurability and equality, excess and defect, and these things are inherent in numbers both considered independently and in relation to other numbers; and as similarly other peculiar modifications are inherent in the solid and the immovable and the moving and the weightless and that which has weight;

so Being *qua* Being has certain peculiar modifications, and it is about these that it is the philosopher's function to discover the truth. And here is evidence of this fact. Dialecticians and sophists wear the same appearance as the philosopher, for sophistry is Wisdom in appearance only, and dialecticians discuss all subjects, and Being is a subject common to them all; but clearly they discuss these concepts because they appertain to philosophy. For sophistry and dialectic are concerned with the same class of subjects as philosophy, but philosophy differs from the former in the nature of its capability and from the latter in its outlook on life. Dialectic treats as an exercise what philosophy tries to understand, and sophistry seems to be philosophy, but is not.

Further, the second column of contraries is privative, and everything is reducible to Being and Not-being, and Unity and Plurality; *e.g.* Rest falls under Unity and Motion under Plurality. And nearly everyone agrees that substance and existing things are composed of contraries; at any rate all speak of the first principles as contraries—some as Odd and Even, some as Hot and Cold, some as Limit and Unlimited, some as Love and Strife. And it is apparent that all other things also 1005 A are reducible to Unity and Plurality (we may assume this reduction); and the principles adduced by other thinkers fall entirely under these as genera. It is clear, then, from these considerations also, that it pertains to a single science to study Being *qua* Being; for all things are either contraries or derived from contraries, and the first principles of the contraries are Unity and Plurality. And these belong to one science, whether they have reference to one common notion or not. Probably the truth is that they have not; but nevertheless even if the term "one" is used in various senses, the others will be related to the primary sense (and similarly with the contraries)—even if Being or Unity is not a universal and the same in all cases, or is not separable from particulars (as it presumably is not; the unity is in some cases one of reference and in others one of succession). For this very reason it is not the function of the geometrician to inquire what is Contrariety or Completeness or Being or Unity or Identity or Otherness, but to proceed from the assumption of them.

Clearly, then, it pertains to one science to study Being *qua* Being, and the attributes inherent in it *qua* Being; and the same science investigates, besides the concepts mentioned above, Priority and Posteriority, Genus and Species, Whole and Part, and all other such concepts.

III. We must pronounce whether it pertains to the same science to study both the so-called axioms in mathematics and substance, or to different sciences. It is obvious that the investigation of these axioms too pertains to one science, namely the science of the philosopher; for they apply to all existing things, and not to a particular class separate and distinct from the rest. Moreover all thinkers employ them—because they are axioms of Being *qua* Being, and every genus possesses Being—but employ them only in so far as their purposes require; *i.e.*, so far as the genus extends about which they are carrying out their proofs. Hence since these axioms apply to all things *qua* Being (for this is what is common to them), it is the function of him who studies Being *qua* Being to investigate them as well. For this reason no one who is pursuing a particular inquiry—neither a geometrician nor an arithmetician—attempts to state whether they are true or false; but some of the physicists did so, quite naturally; for they alone professed to investigate nature as a whole, and Being. But inasmuch as there is a more ultimate type of thinker than the natural philosopher (for nature is only a genus of Being), the investigation of these axioms too will belong to the universal thinker who studies the primary reality. Natural philosophy is a kind of Wisdom, but not the primary kind. As for the attempts of some of those who discuss how the truth should be received, they are due to lack of training in logic; for they should understand these things before they approach their task, and not investigate while they are still learning. Clearly then it is the function of the philosopher, *i.e.* the student of the whole of reality in its essential nature, to investigate also the principles of syllogistic reasoning. And it is proper for him who best understands each class of subject to be able to state the most certain principles of that subject; so that he who understands the modes of Being *qua* Being should be able to state the most certain principles of all things. Now this person is the philosopher, and the most certain principle of all is that about which one cannot be mistaken; for such a principle must be both the most familiar (for it is about the unfamiliar that errors are always made), and not based on hypothesis. For the principle which the student of any form of Being must grasp is no hypothesis; and that which a man must know if he knows anything he must bring with him to this task.

Clearly, then, it is a principle of this kind that is the most certain of all principles. Let us next state *what* this principle is. "It is impossible for the same attribute at once to belong and not to belong to the same thing and in the same relation"; and we must add any further qualifications that may be necessary to meet logical objections. This is the most certain of all principles, since it possesses the required definition; for it is impossible for anyone to suppose that the same thing is and is not, as some imagine that Heraclitus says—for what a man says does not necessarily represent what he believes. And if it is impossible for contrary attributes to belong at the same time to the same subject (the usual qualifications must be added to this premiss also), and an opinion which contradicts another is contrary to it, then clearly it is impossible

1005 B

for the same man to suppose at the same time that the same thing is and is not; for the man who made this error would entertain two contrary opinions at the same time. Hence all men who are demonstrating anything refer back to this as an ultimate belief; for it is by nature the starting-point of all the other axioms as well.

IV. There are some, however, as we have said, who both state themselves that the same thing can be and not be, and say that it is possible to hold this view. Many even of the physicists adopt this theory. But we have just assumed that it is impossible at once to be and not to be, and by this means we have proved that this is the most certain of all principles. Some, indeed, demand to have the law proved, but this is because they lack education; for it shows lack of education not to know of what we should require proof, and of what we should not. For it is quite impossible that everything should have a proof; the process would go on to infinity, so that even so there would be no proof. If on the other hand there are some things of which no proof need be sought, they cannot say what principle they think to be more self-evident. Even in the case of this law, however, we can demonstrate the impossibility by refutation, if only our opponent makes some statement. If he makes none, it is absurd to seek for an argument against one who has no arguments of his own about any thing, in so far as he has none; for such a person, in so far as he is such, is really no better than a vegetable. And I say that proof by refutation differs from simple proof in that he who attempts to prove might seem to beg the fundamental question, whereas if the discussion is provoked thus by someone else, refutation and not proof will result. The starting-point for all such discussions is not the claim that he should state that something is or is not so (because this might be supposed to be a begging of the question), but that he should say something significant both to himself and to another (this is essential if any argument is to follow; for otherwise such a person cannot reason either with himself or with another); and if this is granted, demonstration will be possible, for there will be something already defined. But the person responsible is not he who demonstrates but he who acquiesces; for though he disowns reason he acquiesces to reason. Moreover, he who makes such an admission as this has admitted the truth of something apart from demonstration [so that not everything will be "so and that so"].

Thus in the first place it is obvious that this at any rate is true: that the term "to be" or "not to be" has a definite meaning; so that not everything can be "so and not so." Again, if "man" has one meaning, let this be "two-footed animal." By "has one meaning" I mean this: if X means "man," then if anything is a man, its humanity will consist in being X. And it makes no difference even if it be said that "man" has several meanings, provided that they are limited in number; for one 1006 B could assign a different name to each formula. For instance, it might be said that "man" has not one meaning but several, one of which has the formula "two-footed animal," and there might be many other formulae as well, if they were limited in number; for a particular name could be assigned to each formula. If on the other hand it be said that "man" has an infinite number of meanings; obviously there can be no discourse; for not to have one meaning is to have no meaning, and if words have no meaning there is an end of discourse with others, and even, strictly speaking, with oneself; because it is impossible to think of anything if we do not think of one thing; and even if this were possible, one name might be assigned to that of which we think. Now let this name, as we said at the beginning, have a meaning; and let it have *one* meaning. Now it is impossible that "being man" should have the same meaning as "not being man," that is, if "man" is not merely predicable of one subject but has one meaning (for we do not identify "having one meaning" with "being predicable of one subject," since in this case "cultured" and "white" and "man" would have one meaning, and so all things would be one; for they would all have the same meaning). And it will be impossible for the same thing to be and not to be, except by equivocation, as *e.g.* one whom we call "man" others might call "not-man"; but the problem is whether the same thing can at once and not be "man," not in *name,* but in *fact.* If "man" and "not-man" have not different meanings, clearly "not being a man" will mean nothing different from "being a man"; and so "being a man" will be "not being a man"; they will be one. For "to be one" means, as in the case of "garment" and "coat," that the formula is one. And if "being man" and "being not-man" are to be one, they will have the same meaning; but it has been proved above that they have different meanings. If then any thing can be truly said to be "man," it must be "two-footed animal"; for this is what "man" was intended to mean. And if this is necessarily so, it is impossible that at the same time the same thing should *not* be "two-footed animal." For "to be necessarily so" means this: that it is impossible not to be so. Thus it cannot be true to say at the same time that the same thing is and is not man. And the same argument holds also in the case of not being man; because "being man" 1007 A and "being not-man" have different meanings if "being white" and "being man" have different meanings (for the opposition is much stronger in the former case so as to produce different meanings). And if we are told that "white" too means one and the same thing, we shall say again just what we said before, that in that case all things, and not merely the opposites, will be one. But if this is impossible, what we have stated follows; that is, if our opponent answers our question; but if when

asked the simple question he includes in his answer the negations, he is
not answering our question. There is nothing to prevent the same thing
from being "man" and "white" and a multitude of other things; but
nevertheless when asked whether it is true to say that X is man, or not,
one should return an answer that means one thing, and not add that X
is white and large. It is indeed impossible to enumerate all the infinity
of accidents; and so let him enumerate either all or none. Similarly
therefore, even if the same thing is ten thousand times "man" and "not-
man," one should not include in one's answer to the question whether
it is "man" that it is at the same time also "not-man," unless one is
also bound to include in one's answer all the other accidental things that
the subject is or is not. And if one does this, he is not arguing properly.

In general those who talk like this do away with substance and essence, for they are compelled to assert that all things are accidents, and
that there is no such thing as "being essentially man" or "animal."
For if there is to be such a thing as "being essentially man," this will
not be "being not-man" or "not-being man" (and yet these are negations of it); for it was intended to have one meaning, *i. e.* the substance
of something. But to denote a substance means that the essence is that
and nothing else; and if for it "being essentially man" is the same as
either "being essentially not-man" or "essentially not-being man," the
essence will be something else. Thus they are compelled to say that nothing can have such a definition as this, but that all things are accidental;
for this is the distinction between substance and accident: "white" is
an accident of "man," because although he is white, he is not white in
essence. And since the accidental always implies a predication about
some subject, if all statements are accidental, there will be nothing pri-
1007 B mary about which they are made; so the predication must proceed to
infinity. But this is impossible, for not even more than two accidents
can be combined in predication. An accident cannot be an accident of
an accident unless both are accidents of the same thing. I mean, *e.g.*,
that "white" is "cultured" and "cultured" "white" merely because
both are accidents of a man. But it is not in this sense—that both terms
are accidents of something else—that Socrates is cultured. Therefore
since some accidents are predicated in the latter and some in the former
sense, such as are predicated in the way that "white" is of Socrates
cannot be an infinite series in the upper direction; *e.g.* there cannot be
another accident of "white Socrates," for the sum of these predications
does not make a single statement. Nor can "white" have a further accident, such as "cultured"; for the former is no more an accident of
the latter than *vice versa;* and besides we have distinguished that although
some predicates are accidental in this sense, others are accidental in the
sense that "cultured" is to Socrates; and whereas in the former case the

accident is an accident of an accident, it is not so in the latter; and thus not all predications will be of accidents. Therefore even so there will be something which denotes substance. And if this is so, we have proved that contradictory statements cannot be predicated at the same time.

Again, if all contradictory predications of the same subject at the same time are true, clearly all things will be one. For if it is equally possible either to affirm or deny anything of anything, the same thing will be a trireme and a wall and a man; which is what necessarily follows for those who hold the theory of Protagoras. For if anyone thinks that a man is not a trireme, he is clearly not a trireme; and so he also is a trireme if the contradictory statement is true. And the result is the dictum of Anaxagoras, "all things mixed together"; so that nothing truly exists. It seems, then, that they are speaking of the Indeterminate; and while they think that they are speaking of what exists, they are really speaking of what does not; for the Indeterminate is that which exists potentially but not actually. But indeed they must admit the affirmation or negation of any predicate of any subject, for it is absurd that in the case of each term its own negation should be true, and the negation of some other term which is not true of it should not be true. I mean, *e.g.*, that if it is true to say that a man is not a man, it is obviously also true to say that he is or is not a trireme. Then if the affirmation is true, so must the negation be true; but if the affirmation is not true the negation 1008 A will be even truer than the negation of the original term itself. Therefore if the latter negation is true, the negation of "trireme" will also be true; and if this is true, the affirmation will be true too.

And not only does this follow for those who hold this theory, but also that it is not necessary either to affirm or to deny a statement. For if it is true that X is both man and not-man, clearly he will be neither man nor not-man; for to the two statements there correspond two negations, and if the former is taken as a single statement compounded out of two, the latter is also a single statement and opposite to it.

Again, either this applies to all terms, and the same thing is both white and non-white, and existent and non-existent, and similarly with all other assertions and negations; or it does not apply to all, but only to some and not to others. And if it does not apply at all, but only to some and not to others. And if it does not apply to all, the exceptions will be admitted; but if it does apply to all, again either (a) the negation will be true wherever the affirmation is true, and the affirmation will be true wherever the negation is true, or (b) the negation will be true wherever the assertion is true, but the assertion will not always be true where the negation is true. And in the latter case there will be something which definitely is not, and this will be a certain belief; and if that it is not is certain and knowable, the opposite assertion will be still more knowable. But if what is denied can be equally truly asserted, it must be either true or false to state the predicates separately and say, *e.g.*, that a thing is white, and again that it is not-white. And if it is not-true to state them separately, our opponent does not say what he professes to say, and nothing exists; and how can that which does not exist speak or walk? And again all things will be one, as we said before, and the same thing will be "man" and "God" and "trireme" and the negations of these terms. For if it is equally possible to assert or deny anything of anything, one thing will not differ from another; for if anything does differ, it will be true and unique. And similarly even if it is possible to make a true statement while separating the predicates, what we have stated follows. Moreover it follows that all statements would be true and all false; and that our opponent himself admits that what he says is false. Besides, it is obvious that discussion with him is pointless, because he makes no real statement. For he says neither "yes," nor "no," but "yes and no"; and again he denies both of these and says "neither yes nor no"; otherwise there would be already some definite statement.

Again, if when the assertion is true the negation is false, and when the latter is true the affirmation is false, it will be impossible to assert 1008 B and deny with truth the same thing at the same time. But perhaps it will be said that this is the point at issue.

Again, is the man wrong who supposes that a thing is so or not so, and he who supposes both right? If he is right, what is the meaning of saying that "such is the nature of reality"? And if he is not right, but is more right than the holder of the first view, reality will at once have a definite nature, and this will be true, and not at the same time not-true. And if all men are equally right and wrong, an exponent of this view can neither speak nor mean anything, since at the same time he says both "yes" and "no." And if he forms no judgement, but "thinks" and "thinks not" indifferently, what difference will there be between him and the vegetables?

Hence it is quite evident that no one, either of those who profess this theory or of any other school, is really in this position. Otherwise, why does a man walk to Megara and not stay at home, when he thinks he ought to make the journey? Why does he not walk early one morning into a well or ravine, if he comes to it, instead of clearly guarding against doing so, thus showing that he does *not* think that it is equally good and not good to fall in? Obviously then he judges that the one course is better and the other worse. And if this is so, he must judge that one thing is man and another not man, and that one thing is sweet and another not sweet. For when, thinking that it is desirable to drink water and see a man, he goes to look for them, he does not look for and judge all things indifferently; and yet he should, if the same thing were equally man and not-man. But as we have said, there is no one who does not evidently avoid some things and not others. Hence, as it seems, all men form unqualified judgements, if not about all things, at least about what is better or worse. And if they do this by guesswork and without knowledge, they should be all the more eager for truth; just as a sick man should be more eager for health than a healthy man; for indeed the man who guesses, as contrasted with him who knows, is not in a healthy relation to the truth.

Again, however much things may be "so and not so," yet differences of degree are inherent in the nature of things. For we should not say that 2 and 3 are equally even; nor are he who thinks that 4 is 5, and he who thinks it is 1000, equally wrong: hence if they are not equally wrong, the one is clearly less wrong, and so more right. If then that which has more the nature of something is nearer to that something, 1009 A there will be some truth to which the more true is nearer. And even if there is not, still there is now something more certain and true, and we shall be freed from the undiluted doctrine which precludes any mental determination.

V. From the same view proceeds the theory of Protagoras, and both alike must be either true or false. For if all opinions and appearances are true, everything must be at once true and false; for many people form judgements which are opposite to those of others, and imagine that those who do not think the same as themselves are wrong: hence the same thing must both be and not be. And if this is so, all opinions must be true; for those who are wrong and those who are right think contrarily to each other. So if reality is of this nature, everyone will be right.

Clearly then both these theories proceed from the same mental outlook. But the method of approach is not the same for all cases; for some require persuasion and others compulsion. The ignorance of those who have formed this judgement through perplexity is easily remedied, because we are dealing not with the theory but with their mental outlook; but those who hold the theory for its own sake can only be cured by refuting the theory as expressed in their own speech and words.

This view comes to those who are perplexed from their observation of sensible things. (i.) The belief that contradictions and contraries can be true at the same time comes to them from seeing the contraries generated from the same thing. Then if what is not cannot be generated, the thing must have existed before as both contraries equally—just as Anaxagoras says that everything is mixed in everything; and also Democritus, for he too says that Void and Plenum are present equally in any part, and yet the latter *is,* and the former *is not.* To those, then, who base their judgement on these considerations, we shall say that although in one sense their theory is correct, in another they are mistaken.

For "being" has two meanings, so that there is a sense in which something can be generated from "not-being," and a sense in which it cannot; and a sense in which the same thing can at once be and not be; but not in the same respect. For the same thing can "be" contraries at the same time potentially, but not actually. And further, we shall request them to conceive another kind also of substance of existing things, in which there is absolutely no motion or destruction or generation.

1009 B And (ii.) similarly the theory that there is truth in appearances has come to some people from an observation of sensible things. They think that the truth should not be judged by the number or fewness of its upholders; and they say that the same thing seems sweet to some who taste it, and bitter to others; so that if all men were diseased or all insane, except two or three who were healthy or sane, the latter would seem to be diseased or insane, and not the others. And further they say that many of the animals as well get from the same things impressions which are contrary to ours, and that the individual himself does not always think the same in matters of sense-perception. Thus it is uncertain which of these impressions are true or false; for one kind is no more true than another, but equally so. And hence Democritus says that either there is no truth or we cannot discover it.

And in general it is because they suppose that thought is sense-perception, and sense-perception physical alteration, that they say that the impression given through sense-perception is necessarily true; for it is on these grounds that both Empedocles and Democritus and practically all the rest have become obsessed by such opinions as these. For Empedocles says that those who change their bodily condition change their thought:

> For according to that which is present to them doth thought increase in men.

And in another passage he says:

> And as they change into a different nature, so it ever comes to them to think differently.

And Parmenides too declares in the same way:

> For as each at any time hath the temperament of his many-jointed limbs, so thought comes to men. For for each and every man the substance of his limbs is that very thing which thinks; for thought is that which preponderates.

There is also recorded a saying of Anaxagoras to some of his disciples, that things would be for them as they judged them to be. And they say that Homer too clearly held this view, because he made Hector, when he was stunned by the blow, lie with thoughts deranged—thus implying that even those who are "out of their minds" still think, although not the same thoughts. Clearly then, if both are kinds of thought, reality also will be "both so and not so." It is along this path that the consequences are most difficult; for if those who have the clearest vision of such truth as is possible (and these are they who seek and love it most) hold such opinions and make these pronouncements about the truth, surely those who are trying to be philosophers may well despair; for the pursuit of truth will be "chasing birds in the air."

But the reason why these men hold this view is that although they 1010 A studied the truth about reality, they supposed that reality is confined to sensible things, in which the nature of the Indeterminant, *i.e.* of Being in the sense which we have explained, is abundantly present. (Thus their statements, though plausible, are not true; this form of the criticism is more suitable than that which Epicharmus applied to Xenophanes.) And further, observing that all this indeterminate substance is in motion, and that no true predication can be made of that which changes, they supposed that it is impossible to make any true statement about that which is in all ways and entirely changeable. For it was from this supposition that there blossomed forth the most extreme view of those which we have mentioned, that of the professed followers of Heraclitus, and such as Cratylus held, who ended by thinking that one need not say anything, and only moved his finger; and who criticized Heraclitus for saying that one cannot enter the same river twice, for he himself held that it cannot be done even once.

But we shall reply to this theory also that although that which is changeable supplies them, when it changes, with some real ground for supposing that it "is not," yet there is something debatable in this; for that which is shedding any quality retains something of that which is being shed, and something of that which is coming to be must already exist. And in general if a thing is ceasing to be, there will be something there which *is;* and if a thing is coming to be, that from which it comes and by which it is generated must *be;* and this cannot go on to infinity. But let us leave this line of argument and remark that quantitative and qualitative change are not the same. Let it be granted that there is nothing permanent in respect of quantity; but it is by the *form* that we recognize everything. And again those who hold the theory that we are attacking deserve censure in that they have maintained about the whole material universe what they have observed in the case of a mere minority of sensible things. For it is only the realm of sense around us which continues subject to destruction and generation, but this is a practically negligible part of the whole; so that it would have been fairer for them to acquit the former on the ground of the latter than to condemn the latter on account of the former.

Further, we shall obviously say to these thinkers too the same as we said some time ago; for we must prove to them and convince them that there is a kind of nature that is not moved (and yet those who claim that things can at once be and not be are logically compelled to admit rather that all things are at rest than that they are in motion; for there is nothing for them to change into, since everything exists in every-

1010 B thing).

And as concerning reality, that not every appearance is real, we shall say, first, that indeed the perception, at least of the proper object of a sense, is not false, but the impression we get of it is not the same as the perception. And then we may fairly express surprise if our opponents raise the question whether magnitudes and colours are really such as they appear at a distance or close at hand, as they appear to the healthy or to the diseased; and whether heavy things are as they appear to the weak or to the strong; and whether truth is as it appears to the waking or to the sleeping. For clearly they do not really believe the latter alternative—at any rate no one, if in the night he thinks that he is at Athens whereas he is really in Africa, starts off to the Odeum. And again concerning the future (as indeed Plato says) the opinion of the doctor and that of the layman are presumably not equally reliable, *e.g.* as to whether a man will get well or not. And again in the case of the senses themselves, our perception of a foreign object and of an object proper to a given sense, or of a kindred object and of an actual object of that sense itself, is not equally reliable; but in the case of colours sight, and not taste, is authoritative, and in the case of flavour taste, and not sight. But not one of the senses ever asserts at the same time of the same object that it is "so and not so." Nor even at another time does it make a conflicting statement about the quality, but only about that to which the quality belongs. I mean, *e.g.*, that the same wine may seem, as the result of its own change or of that of one's body, at one time sweet and at another not; but sweetness, such as it is when it exists, has never yet changed, and there is no mistake about it, and that which is to be sweet is necessarily of such a nature. Yet all these theories destroy the possibility of anything's existing by necessity, inasmuch as they destroy the existence of its essence; for "the necessary" cannot be in one way and in another; and so if anything exists of necessity, it cannot be "both so and not so."

And in general, if only the sensible exists, without animate things there would be nothing; for there would be no sense-faculty. That there would be neither sensible qualities nor sensations is probably true (for these depend upon an effect produced in the percipient), but that the substrates which cause the sensation should not exist even apart from the sensation is impossible. For sensation is not of itself, but there is something else too besides the sensation, which must be prior to the sensation; because that which moves is by nature prior to that which is moved, and this is no less true if the terms are correlative.   1011 A

VI. But there are some, both of those who really hold these convictions and of those who merely profess these views, who raise a difficulty; they inquire who is to judge of the healthy man, and in general who is to judge rightly in each particular case. But such questions are like wondering whether we are at any given moment asleep or awake; and all problems of this kind amount to the same thing. These people demand a reason for everything. They want a starting-point, and want to grasp it by demonstration; while it is obvious from their actions that they have no conviction. But there case is just what we have stated before; for they require a reason for things which have no reason, since the starting-point of a demonstration is not a matter of demonstration. The first class, then, may be readily convinced of this, because it is not hard to grasp. But those who look only for cogency in argument look for an impossibility, for they claim the right to contradict themselves, and lose no time in doing so. Yet if not everything is relative, but some things are self-existent, not every appearance will be true; for an appearance is an appearance to someone. And so he who says that all appearances are true makes everything relative. Hence those who demand something cogent in argument, and at the same time claim to make out a case, must guard themselves by saying that the appearance is true not in itself, but *for him to whom* it appears, and *at the time when* it appears, and in the *way* and *manner* in which it appears. And if they make out a case without this qualification, as a result they will soon contradict themselves; for it is possible in the case of the same man for a thing to appear honey to the sight, but not to the taste, and for things to appear different to the sight of each of his two eyes, if their sight is unequal. For to those who assert (for the reasons previously stated) that appearances are true, and that all things are therefore equally false and true, because they do not appear the same to all, nor always the same to the same person, but often have contrary appearances at the same time (since if one crosses the fingers touch says that an object is two, while sight says that it is only one), we shall say "but not to the same sense or to the same part of it in the same way and at the same time";   1011 B
so that with this qualification the appearance will be true. But perhaps it is for this reason that those who argue not from a sense of difficulty but for argument's sake are compelled to say that the appearance is not true in itself, but true to the percipient; and, as we have said before, are compelled also to make everything relative and dependent upon opinion and sensation, so that nothing has happened or will happen unless someone has first formed an opinion about it; otherwise clearly all things would not be relative to opinion.

Further, if a thing is one, it is relative to one thing or to something determinate. And if the same thing is both a half and an equal, yet the equal is not relative to the double. If to the thinking subject "man" and the object of thought are the same, "man" will be not the thinking subject but the object of thought; and if each thing is to be regarded as relative to the thinking subject, the thinking subject will be relative to an infinity of specifically different things.

That the most certain of all beliefs is that opposite statements are not both true at the same time, and what follows for those who maintain that they are true, and why these thinkers maintain this, may be regarded as adequately stated. And since the contradiction of a statement cannot be true at the same time of the same thing, it is obvious that contraries cannot apply at the same time to the same thing. For in each pair of contraries one is a privation no less than it is a contrary—a privation of substance. And privation is the negation of a predicate to some defined genus. Therefore if it is impossible at the same time to affirm and deny a thing truly, it is also impossible for contraries to apply to a thing at the same time; either both must apply in a modified sense, or one in a modified sense and the other absolutely.

VII. Nor indeed can there by any intermediate between contrary statements, but of one thing we must either assert or deny one thing, whatever it may be. This will be plain if we first define truth and falsehood. To say that what is is not, or that what is not is, is false; but to say that what is is, and what is not is not, is true; and therefore also he who says that a thing is or is not will say either what is true or what is false. But neither what is nor what is not is said not to be *or* to be. Further, an intermediate between contraries will be intermediate either as grey in between black and white, or as "neither man nor horse" is between man and horse. If in the latter sense, it cannot change (for change is from not-good to good, or from good to not-good); but in fact it is clearly always changing; for change can only be into the opposite and the intermediate. And if it is a true intermediate, in this case too there would be a kind of change into white not from not-white; but in fact this is not seen. Further, the understanding either affirms or denies every object of understanding or thought (as is clear from the definition) whenever it is right or wrong. When, in asserting or denying, it combines the predicates in one way, it is right; when in the other, it is wrong.

Again, unless it is maintained merely for argument's sake, the intermediate must exist beside all contrary terms; so that one will say what is neither true nor false. And it will exist beside what is and what is not; so that there will be a form of change beside generation and destruction.

Again, there will also be an intermediate in all classes in which the negation of a term implies the contrary assertion; e.g., among numbers

1012 A

there will be a number which is neither odd nor not-odd. But this is impossible, as is clear from the definition.

Again, there will be an infinite progression, and existing things will be not only half as many again, but even more. For again it will be possible to deny the intermediate in reference to its assertion and to its negation, and the result will be something; for its essence is something distinct.

Again, when a man is asked whether a thing is white and says "no," he has denied nothing except that it is [white], and its not-being [white] is a negation.

Now this view has occurred to certain people in just the same way as other paradoxes have also occurred; for when they cannot find a way out from eristic arguments, they submit to the argument and admit that the conclusion is true. Some, then, hold the theory for this kind of reason, and others because they require an explanation for everything. In dealing with all such persons the starting-point is from definition; and definition results from the necessity of their meaning something; because the formula, which their term implies, will be a definition. The doctrine of Heraclitus, which says that everything is and is not, seems to make all things true; and that of Anaxagoras seems to imply an intermediate in contradiction, so that all things are false; for when things are mixed, the mixture is neither good nor not-good; and so no statement is true.

VIII. It is obvious from this analysis that the one-sided and sweeping statements which some people make cannot be substantially true—some maintaining that nothing is true (for they say that there is no reason why the same rule should not apply to everything as applies to the commensurability of the diagonal of a square), and some that everything is true. These theories are almost the same as that of Heraclitus. For the theory which says that all things are true and all false also makes each of these statements separately; so that if they are impossible in combination they are also impossible individually. And again obviously 1012 B there are contrary statements which cannot be true at the same time. Nor can they all be false, although from what we have said this might seem more possible. But in opposing all such theories we must demand, as was said in our discussion above, not that something should be or not be, but some significant statement; and so we must argue from a definition, having first grasped what "falsehood" or "truth" means. And if to assert what is true is nothing else than to deny what is false, everything cannot be false; for one part of the contradiction must be true. Further, if everything must be either asserted or denied, both parts cannot be false; for one and only one part of the contradiction is false. Indeed, the consequence follows which is notorious in the case of all such theories, that they destroy themselves; for he who says that everything is true makes the opposite theory true too, and therefore his own untrue (for the opposite theory says that his is not true); and he who says that everything is false makes himself a liar. And if they make exceptions, the one that the opposite theory alone is not true, and the other that his own theory alone is not false, it follows none the less that they postulate an infinite number of true and false statements. For the statement that the true statement is true is also true; and this will go on to infinity.

Nor, as is obvious, are those right who say that all things are at rest; nor those who say that all things are in motion. For if all things are at rest, the same things will always be true and false, whereas "this state of affairs" is obviously subject to change; for the speaker himself once did not exist, and again he will not exist. And if all things are in motion, nothing will be true, so everything will be false; but this has been proved to be impossible. Again, it must be that which *is* that changes, for change is from something into something. And further, neither is it true that all things are at rest or in motion sometimes, but nothing continuously; for there is something which always moves that which is moved, and the "prime mover" is itself unmoved.

Book VI

1025 B   I. It is the principles and causes of the *things which are* that we are seeking; and clearly of the things which are *qua* being. There is a cause of health and physical fitness; and mathematics has principles and elements and causes; and in general every intellectual science or science which involves intellect deals with causes and principles, more or less exactly or simply considered. But all these sciences single out some existent thing or class, and concern themselves with that; not with Being unqualified, nor *qua* Being, nor do they give any account of the essence; but starting from it, some making it clear to perception, and others assuming it as a hypothesis, they demonstrate, more or less cogently, the essential attributes of the class with which they are dealing. Hence obviously there is no demonstration of substance or essence from this method of approach, but some other means of exhibiting it. And similarly they say nothing as to whether the class of objects with which they are concerned exists or not; because the demonstration of its essence and that of its existence belong to the same intellectual process. And since physical science also happens to deal with a genus of Being (for it deals with the sort of substance which contains in itself the principle of motion and rest), obviously it is neither a practical nor a productive science. For in the case of things produced the principle of motion (either mind or art or some kind of potency) is in the producer; and in the case of things done the will is the agent—for the thing done and the thing willed are the same. Thus if every intellectual activity is either practical or productive or speculative, physics will be a speculative science; but speculative about that kind of Being which can be moved, and about formulated substance for the most part only *qua* inseparable from matter. But we must not fail to observe *how* the essence and the formula exist, since without this our inquiry is ineffectual.

Now of things defined, *i.e.* of essences, some apply in the sense that "snub" does, and some in the sense that "concave" does. The difference is that "snub" is a combination of form with matter; because "the snub" is a concave *nose*, whereas concavity is independent of sensible matter. Now if all physical terms are used in the same sense as "snub"— 1026 A *e.g.* nose, eye, face, flesh, bone, and in general animal; leaf, root, bark, and in general vegetable (for not one of these has a definition without motion; the definition invariably includes matter)—it is clear how we should look for and define the essence in physical things, and why it is the province of the physicist to study even some aspects of the soul, so far as it is not independent of matter.

It is obvious, then, from these considerations, that physics is a form of speculative science. And mathematics is also speculative; but it is not clear at present whether its objects are immutable and separable from matter; it is clear, however, that some branches of mathematics study their objects *qua* immutable and *qua* separable from matter. Obviously it is the province of a speculative science to discover whether a thing is eternal and immutable and separable from matter; not, however, of physics (since physics deals with mutable objects) nor of mathematics, but of a science prior to both. For physics deals with things which exist separately but are not immutable; and some branches of mathematics deal with things which are immutable, but presumably not separable, but present in matter; but the primary science treats of things which are both separable and immutable. Now all causes must be eternal, but these especially; since they are the causes of what is visible of things divine. Hence there will be three speculative philosophies: mathematics, physics, and theology—since it is obvious that if the divine is present anywhere, it is present in this kind of entity; and also the most honourable science must deal with the most honourable class of subject.

The speculative sciences, then, are to be preferred to the other sciences, and "theology" to the other speculative sciences. One might indeed raise the question whether the primary philosophy is universal or deals with some one genus or entity; because even the mathematical sciences differ in this respect—geometry and astronomy deal with a particular kind of entity, whereas universal mathematics applies to all kinds alike. Then if there is not some other substance besides those which are naturally composed, physics will be the primary science; but if there is a substance which is immutable, the science which studies this will be prior to physics, and will be primary philosophy, and universal in this sense, that it is primary. And it will be the province of this science to study Being *qua* Being; what it is, and what the attributes are which belong to it *qua* Being.

II. But since the simple term "being" is used in various senses, of which we saw that one was *accidental,* and another *true* (not-being being used in the sense of "false"); and since besides these there are the cat-
1026 B egories, *e.g.* the "what," quality, quantity, place, time, and any other similar meanings; and further besides all these the *potential* and *actual:* since the term "being" has various senses, it must first be said of what "is" accidentally, that there can be no speculation about it. This is shown by the fact that no science, whether practical, productive or speculative, concerns itself with it. The man who produces a house does not produce all the attributes which are accidental to the house in its construction; for they are infinite in number. There is no reason why the house so produced should not be agreeable to some, injurious to others, and beneficial to others, and different perhaps from every other existing thing; but the act of building is productive of none of these results. In the same way the geometrician does not study the accidental attributes of his figures, not whether a triangle is different from a triangle the sum of whose angles is equal to two right angles. And this accords with what we should reasonably expect, because "accident" is only, as it were, a sort of name. Hence in a way Plato was not far wrong in making sophistry deal with what is non-existent; because the sophists discuss the accident more, perhaps, than any other people—whether "cultured" and "grammatical," and "cultured Coriscus" and "Coriscus," are the same or different; and whether everything that is, but has not always been, has come into being, so that if a man who is cultured has become grammatical, he has also, being grammatical, become cultured; and all other such discussions. Indeed it seems that the accidental is something closely akin to the non-existent. This is clear too from such considerations as the following: of things which *are* in other senses there is generation and destruction, but of things which *are* accidentally there is not. Nevertheless we must state further, so far as it is possible, with regard to the accidental, what its nature is and through what cause it exists. At the same time it will doubtless also appear why there is no science of it.

Since, then, there are among existing things some which are invariable and of necessity (not necessity in the sense of compulsion, but that by which we mean that it cannot be otherwise), and some which are not necessarily so, nor always, but usually; this is the principle and this the cause of the accidental. For whatever is neither always nor usually so, we call an accident. *E.g.*, if in the dog-days we have storm and cold, we call it an accident; but not if we have stifling and intense heat, because the latter always or usually comes at this time, but not the former. It is accidental for a man to be white (since this is neither always nor usually so), but it is not accidental for him to be an animal. It is by accident that a builder restores to health, because it is not a builder but 1027 A a doctor who naturally does this; but the builder happened accidentally to be a doctor. A confectioner, aiming at producing enjoyment, may produce something health-giving; but not in virtue of his confectioner's art. Hence, we say, it was accidental; and he produces it in a sense, but not in an unqualified sense. For there are potencies which produce other things, but there is no art or determinate potency of accidents, since the cause of things which exist or come to be by accident is also accidental. Hence, since not everything is or comes to be of necessity and always, but most things happen usually, the accidental must exist. *E.g.*, the white man is neither always nor usually cultured; but since this sometimes happens, it must be regarded as accidental. Otherwise, everything must be regarded as of necessity. Therefore the cause of the accidental is the matter, which admits of variation from the usual.

We must take this as our starting-point: Is everything either "always" or "usually"? This is surely impossible. Then besides these alternatives there is something else: the fortuitous and accidental. But again, are things *usually* so, but nothing *always*, or are there things which are eternal? These questions must be inquired into later; but it is clear that there is no science of the accidental—because all scientific knowledge is of that which is *always* or *usually* so. How else indeed can one learn it or teach it to another? For a fact must be defined by being so always or usually; *e.g.*, honey-water is usually beneficial in case of fever. But science will not be able to state the exception to the rule: when it is not beneficial—*e.g.* at the new moon; because that which happens at the new moon also happens either always or usually; but the accidental is contrary to this. We have now explained the nature and cause of the accidental, and that there is no science of it.

III. It is obvious that there are principles and causes which are generable and destructible apart from the actual processes of generation and destruction; for if this is not true, everything will be of necessity: that is, if there must necessarily be some cause, other than accidental, of that which is generated and destroyed. Will A be, or not? Yes, if B happens; otherwise not. And B will happen if C does. It is clear that in this way, as time is continually subtracted from a limited period, we 1027 B shall come to the present. Accordingly So-and-so will die by disease or violence if he goes out; and this if he gets thirsty; and this if something else happens; and thus we shall come to what is the case now, or to something which has already happened. *E.g.* "if he is thirsty"; this will happen if he is eating pungent food, and this is either the case or not. Thus of necessity he will either die or not die. And similarly if one jumps over to the past, the principle is the same; for this—I mean that which has just happened—is already present in something. Everything, then, which is to be, will be of necessity; *e.g.*, he who is alive must die—for some stage of the process has been reached already; *e.g.*, the contraries are present in the same body—but whether by disease or violence is not yet determined; it depends upon whether so-and-so happens. Clearly, then, the series goes back to some starting-point, which does not go back to something else. This, therefore, will be the starting-point of the fortuitous, and nothing else is the cause of its generation. But to what sort of starting-point and cause this process of tracing back leads, whether to a material or final or moving cause, is a question for careful consideration.

IV. So much, then, for the accidental sense of "being"; we have defined it sufficiently. As for "being" *qua* truth, and "not-being" *qua* falsity, since they depend upon combination and separation, and taken together are concerned with the arrangement of the parts of a contradiction (since the true has affirmation when the subject and predicate are combined, and negation where they are divided; but the false has the contrary arrangement. How it happens that we combine or separate in thought is another question. By "combining or separating in thought" I mean thinking them not as a succession but as a unity); for "falsity" and "truth" are not in *things*—the good, for example, being true, and the bad false—but in *thought;* and with regard to simple concepts and essences there is no truth or falsity even in thought;—what points we must study in connexion with being and not-being in this sense, we must consider later. But since the combination and separation exists in thought and not in things, and this sense of "being" is different from the proper senses (since thought attaches or detaches essence or quality or quantity or some other category), we may dismiss the accidental and real senses of "being." For the cause of the one is indeterminate, and of the other an affection of thought; and both are connected with the remaining genus of "being," and do not indicate any objective reality. Let us therefore dismiss them, and consider the causes and principles of Being itself *qua* Being. [We have made it clear in our distinction of the number of senses in which each term is used that "being" has several senses.]

1028 A

Book VII

I. The term "being" has several senses, which we have classified in our discussion of the number of senses in which terms are used. It denotes first the *"what"* of a thing, *i.e.* the individuality; and then the quality or quantity or any other such category. Now of all these senses which "being" has, the primary sense is clearly the "what," which denotes the *substance* (because when we describe the quality of a particular thing we say that it is "good" or "bad," and not "five feet high" or "a man"; but when we describe *what* it is, we say not that it is "white" or "hot" or "five feet high," but that it is "a man" or "a god"), and all other things are said to "be" because they are either quantities or qualities or affections or some other such thing.

Hence one might raise the question whether the terms "to walk" and "to be well" and "to sit" signify each of these things as "being," or not; and similarly in the case of any other such terms; for not one of them by nature has an independent existence or can be separated from its substance. Rather, if anything it is the *thing* which walks or sits or is well that is existent. The reason why these things are more truly existent is because their subject is something definite; *i.e.* the substance and the individual, which is clearly implied in a designation of this kind, since apart from it we cannot speak of "the good" or "the sitting." Clearly then it is by reason of the substance that each of the things referred to exists. Hence that which *is* primarily, not in a qualified sense but absolutely, will be substance.

Now "primary" has several meanings; but nevertheless substance is primary in all senses, both in definition and in knowledge and in time. For none of the other categories can exist separately, but substance alone; and it is primary also in definition, because in the formula of each thing the formula of substance must be inherent; and we assume that we know each particular thing most truly when we know *what* "man" or "fire" 1028B is—rather than its quality or quantity or position; because we know each of these points too when we know *what* the quantity or quality is. Indeed, the question which was raised long ago, is still and always will be, and which always baffles us—"What is Being?"—is in other words "What is substance?" Some say that it is one; others, more than one; some, finite; others, infinite. And so for us too our chief and primary and practically our only concern is to investigate the nature of "being" in the sense of substance.

II. Substance is thought to be present most obviously in bodies. Hence we call animals and plants and their parts substances, and also natural bodies, such as fire, water, earth, etc., and all things which are parts of these or composed of these, either of parts of them or of their totality; *e.g.* the visible universe and its parts, the stars and moon and sun. We must consider whether (*a*) these are the only substances, or (*b*) these and some others, or (*c*) some of these, or (*d*) some of these and some others, or (*e*) none of these, but certain others. Some hold that the bounds of body—*i.e.* the surface, line, point and unit—are substances, and in a truer sense than body or the solid. Again, some believe that there is nothing of this kind besides sensible things, while others believe in eternal entities more numerous and more real than sensible things. Thus Plato posited the Forms and the objects of mathematics as two kinds of substance, and as a third the substance of sensible bodies; and Speusippus assumed still more kinds of substances, starting with "the One," and positing principles for each kind: one for numbers, another for magnitudes, and then another for the soul. In this way he multiplies the kinds of substance. Some again hold that the Forms and numbers have the same nature, and that other things—lines and planes—are dependent upon them; and so on back to the substance of the visible universe and sensible things. We must consider, then, with regard to these matters, which of the views expressed is right and which wrong; and what things are substances; and whether there are any substances besides the sensible substances, or not; and how sensible substances exist; and whether there is any separable substance (and if so, why and how) or no substance besides the sensible ones. We must first give a rough sketch of what substance is.

III. The term "substance" is used, if not in more, at least in four principal cases; for both the essence and the universal and the genus are held to be the substance of the particular, and fourthly the substrate. The substrate is that of which the rest are predicated, while it is not 1029 A itself predicated of anything else. Hence we must first determine its nature, for the primary substrate is considered to be in the truest sense substance.

Now in one sense we call the *matter* the substrate; in another, the *shape*; and in a third, the combination of the two. By matter I mean, for instance, bronze; by shape, the arrangement of the form; and by the combination of the two, the concrete thing: the statue. Thus if the form is prior to the matter and more truly existent, by the same argument it will also be prior to the combination.

We have now stated in outline the nature of substance—that it is not that which is predicated of a subject, but that of which the other things are predicated. But we must not merely define it so, for it is not enough. Not only is the statement itself obscure, but also it makes matter substance; for if matter is not substance, it is beyond our power to say what else is. For when everything else is removed, clearly nothing but matter remains; because all the other things are affections, products and potencies of bodies, and length, breadth and depth are kinds of quantity, and not substances. For quantity is not a substance; rather the substance is that to which these affections primarily belong. But when we take away length and breadth and depth we can see nothing remaining, unless it be the something bounded by them; so that on this view matter must appear to be the only substance. By matter I mean that which in itself is neither a particular thing nor a quantity nor designated by any of the categories which define Being. For there is something of which each of these is predicated, whose being is different from that of each one of the categories; because all other things are predicated of substance, but this is predicated of matter. Thus the ultimate substrate is in itself neither a particular thing nor a quantity nor anything else. Nor indeed is it the negations of these; for the negations too will only apply to it accidentally.

If we hold this view, it follows that matter is substance. But this is impossible; for it is accepted that separability and individuality belong especially to substance. Hence it would seem that the form and the combination of form and matter are more truly substance than matter is. The substance, then, which consists of both—I mean of matter and form—may be dismissed, since it is posterior and obvious. Matter too is in a sense evident. We must consider the third type, for this is the most perplexing.

Now it is agreed that some sensible things are substances, and so we should begin our inquiry in connexion with these. IV. It is convenient to advance to the more intelligible; for learning is always acquired in this way, by advancing through what is less intelligible by nature to what is more so. And just as in actions it is our task to start from the good of the individual and make absolute good good for the individual, so it is our task to start from what is more intelligible to oneself and make what is by nature intelligible intelligible to oneself. Now that which is intelligible and primary to individuals is often but slightly intelligible, and contains but little reality; but nevertheless, starting from that which is imperfectly intelligible to oneself, we must try to understand the absolutely intelligible; advancing, as we have said, by means of these very things which are intelligible to us.

Since we distinguished at the beginning the number of ways in which substance is defined, and since one of these appeared to be essence, we must investigate this. First, let us make certain linguistic statements about it.

The essence of each thing is that which it is said to be *per se*. "To be you" is not "to be cultured," because you are not of your own nature

1029B

cultured. Your essence, then, is that which you are said to be of your own nature. But not even all of this is the essence; for the essence is not that which is said to be *per se* in the sense that whiteness is said to belong to a surface, because "being a surface" is not "being white." Nor is the essence the combination of both, "being a white surface." Why? Because the word itself is repeated. Hence the formula of the essence of each thing is that which defines the term but does not contain it. Thus if "being a white surface" is the same as "being a smooth surface," "white" and "smooth" are one and the same.

But since in the other categories too there are compounds with substance (because there is a substrate for each category, *e.g.* quality, quantity, time, place and motion), we must inquire whether there is a formula of the essence of each of them; whether these compounds, *e.g.* "white man," also have an essence. Let the compound be denoted by X. What is the essence of X?

"But this is not even a *per se* expression." We reply that there are two ways in which a definition can be not *per se* true of its subject: (*a*) by an addition, and (*b*) by an omission. In one case the definition is not *per se* true because the term which is being defined is combined with something else; as if, *e.g.*, in defining whiteness one were to state the definition of a white man. In the other, because something else (which is not in the definition) is combined with the subject; as if, *e.g.*, X were to denote "white man," and X were defined as "white." "White man"
1030 A is white, but its essence is not "to be white." But is "to be X" an essence at all? Surely not. The essence is an individual type; but when a subject has something distinct from it predicated of it, it is not an individual type. *E.g.*, "white man" is not an individual type; that is, assuming that individuality belongs only to substances. Hence essence belongs to all things the account of which is a definition. We have a definition, not if the name and the account signify the same (for then all accounts would be definitions; because any account can have a name, so that even "the *Iliad*" will be a definition), but if the account is of something primary. Such are all statements which do not involve the predication of thing of another. Hence essence will belong to nothing except species of a genus, but to these only; for in these the predicate is not considered to be related to the subject by participation or affection, nor as an accident. But of everything else as well, if it has a name, there will be a formula of *what it means*—that X belongs to Y; or instead of a simple formula one more exact—but no definition, nor essence.

Or perhaps "definition," like the "what," has more than one sense. For the "what" in one sense means the substance and the individual, and in another each one of the categories: quantity, quality, etc. Just as "is" applies to everything, although not in the same way, but pri-

marily to one thing and secondarily to others; so "what it is" applies
in an unqualified sense to substance, and to other things in a qualified
sense. For we might ask also what quality "is," so that quality also is
a "what it is"; not however without qualification, but just as in the case
of not-being some say by a verbal quibble that not-being "is"—not in
an unqualified sense, but "is" not-being—so too with quality.

Now although we must also consider how we should express ourselves in each particular case, it is still more important to consider what
the facts are. Hence now, since the language which we are using is clear,
similarly essence also will belong primarily and simply to substance, and
secondarily to other things as well; just as the "what it is" is not essence
simply, but the essence of a quality or quantity. For it must be either
by equivocation that we say that these things *are*, or by adding and sub-
tracting qualifications, as we say that the unknowable is known; since
the truth is that we use the terms neither equivocally nor in the same
sense, but just as we use the term "medical" in *relation* to one and the
same thing; but not *of* one and the same thing, nor yet equivocally. The
term "medical" is applied to a body and a function and an instrument,
neither equivocally nor in one sense, but in relation to one thing.

1030 B

However, in whichever way one chooses to speak of these things, it
matters nothing; but this point is clear: that the primary and unqualified
definition, and the essence, belong to substances. It is true that they
belong equally to other things too, but not *primarily*. For if we assume
this, it does not necessarily follow that there is a definition of anything
which means the same as any formula; it must mean the same as a
particular kind of formula, *i.e.* the formula of one thing—one not by
continuity, like the *Iliad*, or things which are arbitrarily combined, but
in one of the proper senses of "one." And "one" has the same variety
of senses as "being." "Being" means sometimes the individual thing,
sometimes the quantity, sometimes the quality. Hence even "white
man" will have a formula and definition; but in a different sense from
the definition of "whiteness" and "substance."

V. The question arises: If one denies that a formula involving an
added determinant is a definition, how can there be a definition of terms
which are not simple but coupled? Because they can only be explained
by adding a determinant. I mean, *e.g.*, there is "nose" and "concavity"
and "snubness," the term compounded of the two, because the one is
present in the other. Neither "concavity" nor "snubness" is an accidental, but a *per se* affection of the nose. Nor are they attributes in the
sense that "white" is of Callias or a man, because Callias is white and
is by accident a man; but in the sense that "male" is an attribute of
animal, and equality of quantity, and all other attributes which we say
belong *per se*. That is, all things which involve the formula or name of

the subject of the affection, and cannot be explained apart from it. Thus "white" can be explained apart from "man," but not "female" apart from "animal." Thus either these terms have no essence or definition, or else they have it in a different sense, as we have said.

But there is also another difficulty about them. If "snub nose" is the same as "concave nose," "snub" will be the same as "concave." But if not, since it is impossible to speak of "snub" apart from the thing of which it is a *per se* affection (because "snub" means a concavity in the nose), either it is impossible to call the nose snub, or it will be a tautology, "concave-nose nose" because "snub nose" will equal "concave-nose nose." Hence it is absurd that such terms as these should have an essence. Otherwise there will be an infinite regression; for in "snub-nose nose" there will be yet another nose.

1031 A

Clearly, then, there is definition of substance alone. If there were definition of the other categories also, it would have to involve an added determinant, as in the case of the qualitative; and of the odd, for this cannot be defined apart from number; nor can "female" apart from "animal." By "involving an added determinant" I mean descriptions which involve a tautology, as in the above examples. Now if this is true, there will be no definition of compound expressions either; e.g., "odd number." We fail to realize this because our terms are not used accurately. If on the other hand there are definitions of these too, either they are defined in a different way, or, as we have said, "definition" and "essence" must be used in more than one sense; thus in one sense there will be no definition of anything, and nothing will have an essence, except substances; and in another those other things will have a definition and essence. It is obvious, then, that the definition is the formula of the essence, and that the essence belongs either *only* to substances, or especially and primarily and simply.

VI. We must inquire whether the essence is the same as the particular thing, or different. This is useful for our inquiry about substance; because a particular thing is considered to be nothing other than its own substance, and the essence is called the substance of the thing. In accidental predications, indeed, the thing itself would seem to be different from its essence; e.g., "white man" is different from "essence of white man." If it were the same, "essence of man" and "essence of white man" would be the same. For "man" and "white man" are the same, they say, and therefore "essence of white man" is the same as "essence of man." But perhaps it is not necessarily true that the essence of accidental combinations is the same as that of the simple terms; because the extremes of the syllogism are not identical with the middle term in the same way. Perhaps it might be thought to follow that the accidental extremes are identical; e.g., "essence of white" and "essence of cultured"; but this is not admitted.

But in *per se* expressions, is the thing necessarily the same as its essence, *e.g.*, if there are substances which have no other substances or entities prior to them, such as some hold the Ideas to be? For if the Ideal Good is to be different from the essence of good, and the Ideal Animal and Being from the essence of animal and being, there will be other substances and entities and Ideas besides the ones which they describe; 1031 B and prior to them, if essence is substance. And if they are separate from each other, there will be no knowledge of the Ideas, and the essences will not exist (by "being separate" I mean if neither the essence of good is present in the Ideal Good, nor "being good" in the essence of good); for it is when we know the essence of it that we have knowledge of a thing. And it is the same with other essences as with the essence of good; so that if the essence of good is not good, neither will the essence of being "be," nor the essence of one be one. Either all essences exist alike, or none of them; and so if not even the essence of being "is," neither will any other essence exist. Again that to which "essentially good" does not apply cannot be good. Hence "the good" must be one with the essence of good, "the beautiful" with the essence of beauty, and so with all terms which are not dependent upon something else, but self-subsistent and primary. For it is enough if this is so, even if they are not Forms; or perhaps rather even if they are. (At the same time it is clear also that if the Ideas are such as some hold, the substrate will not be substance; for the Ideas must be substances, but not involving a substrate, because if they did involve one they would exist in virtue of its participation in them.)

That each individual thing is one and the same with its essence, and not merely accidentally so, is apparent, not only from the foregoing considerations, but because to have knowledge of the individual is to have knowledge of its essence; so that by setting out examples it is evident that both must be identical. But as for the accidental term, *e.g.* "cultured" or "white," since it has two meanings, it is not true to say that the term itself is the same as its essence; for both the accidental term and that of which it is an accident are "white," so that in one sense the essence and the term itself are the same, and in another they are not, because the essence is not the same as "the man" or "the white man," but it is the same as the affection.

The absurdity [of separating a thing from its essence] will be apparent also if one supplies a name for each essence; for then there will be another essence besides the original one, *e.g.* the essence of "horse" will have a further essence. Yet why should not some things be identified with their essence from the outset, if essence is substance? Indeed not 1032 A only are the thing and its essence one, but their formula is the same, as is clear from what we have just stated; for it is not by accident that the essence of "one," and "the one," are one. Moreover, if they are different, there will be an infinite series; for the essence of "one" and "the one" will both exist; so that in that case too the same principle will apply. Clearly, then, in the case of primary and self-subsistent terms, the individual thing and its essence are one and the same.

It is obvious that the sophistical objections to this thesis are met in the same way as the question whether Socrates is the same as the essence of Socrates; for there is no difference either in the grounds for asking the question or in the means of meeting it successfully. We have now explained in what sense the essence is, and in what sense it is not, the same as the individual thing.

VII. Of things which are generated, some are generated naturally, others artificially, and others spontaneously; but everything which is generated is generated by something and from something and becomes something. When I say "becomes something" I mean in any of the categories; it may come to me either a particular thing or of some quantity or quality or in some place.

Natural generation is the generation of things whose generation is by nature. That from which they are generated is what we call matter; that by which, is something which exists naturally; and that which they become is a man or a plant or something else of this kind, which we call substance in the highest degree. All things which are generated naturally or artificially have matter; for it is possible for each one of them both to be and not to be, and this possibility is the matter in each individual thing. And in general both that from which and that in accordance with which they are generated, is nature; for the thing generated, *e.g.* plant or animal, has a nature. And that by which they are generated is the so-called "formal" nature, which has the same form as the thing generated (although it is in something else); for man begets man.

Such is the generation of things which are naturally generated; the other kinds of generation are called productions. All productions proceed from either art or potency or thought. Some of them are also generated spontaneously and by chance in much the same way as things which are naturally generated; for sometimes even in the sphere of nature the same things are generated both from seed and without it. We shall consider cases of this kind later.

1032 B   Things are generated artificially whose form is contained in the soul (by "form" I mean the essence of each thing, and its primary substance); for even contraries have in a sense the same form. For the substance of the privation is the opposite substance; *e.g.*, health is the substance of disease; for disease is the absence of health, and health is the formula and knowledge in the soul. Now the healthy subject is produced as the result of this reasoning; since health is so-and-so, if the subject is to be healthy, it must have such-and-such a quality, *e.g.* homogeneity; and if so, it must have heat. And the physician continues reasoning until he arrives at what he himself finally can do; then the process from this point onwards, *i.e.* the process towards health, is called "production." Therefore it follows in a sense that health comes from health and a house from a house; that which has matter from that which has not (for the art of medicine or of building is the *form* of health or the house). By substance without matter I mean the essence.

In generations and motions part of the process is called cogitation, and part production—that which proceeds from the starting-point and the form is cogitation, and that which proceeds from the conclusion of the cogitation is production. Each of the other intermediate measures is carried out in the same way. I mean, *e.g.*, that if A is to be healthy, his physical condition will have to be made uniform. What, then, does being made uniform entail? So-and-so; and this will be achieved if he is made hot. What does this entail? So-and-so; now this is potentially present, and the thing is now in his power.

The thing which produces, and from which the process of recovering health begins, is the form in the soul, if the process is artificial; if spontaneous, it is whatever is the starting-point of the production for the artificial producer; as in medical treatment the starting-point is, perhaps, the heating of the patient; and this the doctor produces by friction. Heat in the body, then, is either a part of health, or is followed (directly or through several intermediaries) by something similar which is a part of health. This is the ultimate thing, namely that produces, and in this sense is a part of, health—or of the house (in the form of stones) or of other things. Therefore, as we say, generation would be impossible if nothing were already existent. It is clear, then, that some part must necessarily pre-exist; because the matter is a part, since it is matter which pre-exists in the product and becomes something. But then is matter part of the formula? Well, we define bronze circles in both ways; we describe the matter as bronze, and the form as such-and-such a shape; and this shape is the proximate genus in which the circle is placed. The bronze circle, then, has its matter in its formula. Now as for that from which, as matter, things are generated, some things when they are generated are called not "so-and-so," but "made of so-and-so"; *e.g.*, a statue is not called stone, but made of stone. But the man who becomes healthy is not called after that from which he becomes healthy. This is because the generation proceeds from the privation and the substrate, which we call matter (*e.g.*, both "the man" and "the invalid" become healthy), but it is more properly said to proceed from the privation; *e.g.*, a man becomes healthy from being an invalid rather than from being a man. Hence a healthy person is not called an invalid, but a man, and

a healthy man. But where the privation is obscure and has no name—
e.g. in bronze the privation of any given shape, or in bricks and wood
the privation of the shape of a house—the generation is considered to
proceed from these materials, as in the former case from the invalid.
Hence just as in the former case the subject is not called that from which
it is generated, so in this case the statue is not called wood, but is called
by a verbal change not wood, but wooden; not bronze, but made of
bronze; not stone, but made of stone; and the house is called not bricks,
but made of bricks. For if we consider the matter carefully, we should
not even say without qualification that a statue is generated from wood,
or a house from bricks; because that from which a thing is generated
should not persist, but be changed. This, then, is why we speak in this
way.

VIII. Now since that which is generated is generated *by* something
(by which I mean the starting-point of the process of generation), and
from something (by which let us understand not the privation but the
matter; for we have already distinguished the meanings of these), and
becomes something (*i.e.* a sphere or circle or whatever else it may be);
just as the craftsman does not produce the substrate, *i.e.* the bronze, so
neither does he produce the sphere; except accidentally, inasmuch as
the bronze sphere is a sphere, and he makes the former. For to make
an individual thing is to make it out of the substrate in the fullest sense.
I mean that to make the bronze round is not to make the round or the
sphere, but something else; *i.e.* to produce this form in another medium.
For if we make the form, we must make it out of something else; for
this has been assumed. *E.g.*, we make a bronze sphere; we do this in
the sense that from A, *i.e.* bronze, we make B, *i.e.* a sphere. If, then,
we make the spherical form itself, clearly we shall have to make it in
the same way; and the processes of generation will continue to infinity.

It is therefore obvious that the form (or whatever we should call the
shape in the sensible thing) is not generated—generation does not apply
to it—nor is the essence generated; for this is that which is induced in
something else either by art or by nature or by potency. But we do cause
a bronze sphere to be, for we produce it from bronze and a sphere; we
induce the form into this particular matter, and the result is a bronze
sphere. But if the essence of sphere in general is generated, something
must be generated from something; for that which is generated will always have to be divisible, and be partly one thing and partly another;
I mean partly matter and partly form. If then a sphere is the figure
whose circumference is everywhere equi-distant from the centre, part
of this will be the medium in which that which we produce will be contained, and part will be in that medium; and the whole will be the thing
generated, as in the case of the bronze sphere. It is obvious, then, from

1033 B

what we have said, that the thing in the sense of form or essence is not generated, whereas the concrete whole which is called after it is generated; and that in everything that is generated matter is present, and one part is matter and the other form.

Is there then some sphere besides the particular spheres, or some house besides the bricks? Surely no individual thing would ever have been generated if form had existed thus independently. Form means "of such a kind"; it is not a definite individual, but we produce or generate from the individual something "of such a kind"; and when it is generated it is an individual "of such a kind." The whole individual, Callias or Socrates, corresponds to "this bronze sphere," but "man" and "animal" correspond to bronze sphere in general.

Obviously therefore the cause which consists of the Forms (in the sense in which some speak of them, assuming that there are certain entities besides particulars), in respect at least of the generation and destruction, is useless; nor, for this reason at any rate, should they be regarded as self-subsistent substances. Indeed in some cases it is even obvious that that which generates is of the same kind as that which is generated—not however identical with it, nor numerically one with it, but formally one—*e.g.* in natural productions (for man begets man), unless something happens contrary to nature, as when a horse sires a mule. And even these cases are similar; for that which would be common to both horse and ass, the genus immediately above them, has no 1034 A name; but it would probably be both, just as the mule is both.

Thus obviously there is no need to set up a form as a pattern (for we should have looked for Forms in these cases especially, since living things are in a special sense substances); the thing which generates is sufficient to produce, and to be the cause of the form in the matter. The completed whole, such-and-such a form induced in this flesh and these bones, is Callias or Socrates. And it is different from that which generated it, because the matter is different; but identical in form, because the form is indivisible. . . .

XVII. As for what and what sort of thing we mean by substance, 1041 A let us explain this by making, as it were, another fresh start. Perhaps in this way we shall also obtain some light upon that kind of substance which exists in separation from sensible substances. Since, then, substance is a kind of principle and cause, we had better pursue our inquiry from this point.

Now when we ask why a thing is, it is always in the sense "why does A belong to B?" To ask why the cultured man is a cultured man is to ask either, as we have said, why the man is cultured, or something else. Now to ask why a thing is itself in no question; because when we ask the reason of a thing the fact must first be evident; *e.g.*, that the

moon suffers eclipse; and "because it is itself" is the one explanation
and reason which applies to all questions such as "why is man man?"
or "why is the cultured person cultured?" (unless one were to say that
each thing is indivisible from itself, and that this is what "being one"
really means); but this, besides being a general answer, is a summary
one. We may, however, ask why a man is an animal of such-and-such
a kind. It is clear, then, that we are not asking why he who is a man is
a man; therefore we are asking why A, which is predicated of B, belong
to B. (The fact that A does belong to B must be evident, for if this is
not so, the question is pointless.) *E.g.*, "Why does it thunder?" means
"why is a noise produced in the clouds?" for the true form of the question is one thing predicated in this way of another. Or again, "Why are
these things, *e.g.* bricks and stones, a house?" Clearly then we are inquiring for the cause (*i.e.*, to speak abstractly, the essence); which is in
the case of some things, *e.g.* house or bed, the *end*, and in others the
prime mover—for this also is a cause. We look for the latter kind of
cause in the case of generation and destruction, but for the former also
in the case of existence.

1041 B   What we are now looking for is most obscure when one term is not
predicated of another; *e.g.* when we inquire what man is; because the
expression is a simple one not analysed into subject and attributes. We
must make the question articulate before we ask it; otherwise we get
something which shares the nature of a pointless and of a definite question. Now since we must know that the fact actually exists, it is surely
clear that the question is "why is the *matter* so-and-so?" *e.g.* "why are
these materials a house?" Because the essence of house is present in
them. And this matter, or the body containing this particular form, is
man. Thus what we are seeking is the cause (*i.e.* the form) in virtue of
which the matter is a definite thing; and this is the substance of the
thing.

Clearly then in the case of simple entities inquiry and explanation
are impossible; in such cases there is a different mode of inquiry.

Now since that which is composed of something in such a way that
the whole is a unity; not as an aggregate is a unity, but as a syllable
is—the syllable is not the letters, nor is BA the same as B and A; nor
is flesh fire and earth; because after dissolution the compounds, *e.g.* flesh
or the syllable, no longer exist; but the letters exist, and so do fire and
earth. Therefore the syllable is some particular thing; not merely the
letters, vowel and consonant, but something else besides. And flesh is
not merely fire and earth, or hot and cold, but something else besides.
Since then this something else must be either an element or composed
of elements, (*a*) if it is an element, the same argument applies again;
for flesh will be composed of *this* and fire and earth, and again of another

element, so that there will be an infinite regression. And (*b*) if it is composed of elements, clearly it is composed not of one (otherwise it will itself be that element) but of several; so that we shall use the same argument in this case as about the flesh or the syllable. It would seem, however, that this "something else" is something that is not an element, but is the cause that *this* matter is flesh and *that* matter a syllable, and similarly in other cases. And this is the substance of each thing, for it is the primary cause of its existence. And since, although some things are not substances, all substances are constituted in accordance with and by nature, substance would seem to be this "nature," which is not an element but a principle. An element is that which is present as matter in a thing, and into which the thing is divided; *e.g.*, A and B are the elements of the syllable.

Book IX

I. We have now dealt with Being in the primary sense, to which all 1045 B the other categories of being are related; *i.e.* substance. For it is from the concept of substance that all the other modes of being take their meaning; both quantity and quality and all other such terms; for they will all involve the concept of substance, as we stated it in the beginning of our discussion. And since the senses of being are analysable not only into substance or quality or quantity, but also in accordance with potentiality and actuality and function, let us also gain a clear understanding about potentiality and actuality; and first about potentiality in the sense which is most proper to the word, but not most useful for our 1046 A present purpose—for potentiality and actuality extend beyond the sphere of terms which only refer to motion. When we have discussed this sense of potentiality we will, in the course of our definitions of actuality, explain the others also.

We have made it plain elsewhere that "potentiality" and "can" have several senses. All senses which are merely equivocal may be dismissed; for some are used by analogy, as in geometry, and we call things possible or impossible because they "are" or "are not" in some particular way. But the potentialities which conform to the same type are all principles, and derive their meaning from one primary sense of potency, which is the source of change in some other thing, or in the same thing *qua* other.

One kind of potentiality is the power of being affected; the principle in the patient itself which initiates a passive change in it by the action of some other thing, or of itself *qua* other. Another is a positive state of impassivity in respect of deterioration or destruction by something else or by itself *qua* something else; *i.e.* by a transformatory principle—for all these definitions contain the formula of the primary sense of potentiality. Again, all these potentialities are so called either because they merely act or are acted upon in a particular way, or because they do so *well*. Hence in their formulae also the formulae of potentiality in the senses previously described are present in some degree.

Clearly, then, in one sense the potentiality for acting and being acted upon is one (for a thing is "capable" both because it itself possesses the power of being acted upon, and also because something else has the power of being acted upon by it); and in another sense it is not; for it is partly in the patient (for it is because it contains a certain principle, and because even the matter is a kind of principle; that the patient is acted upon; *i.e.*, one thing is acted upon by another; oily stuff is inflammable, and stuff which yields in a certain way is breakable, and similarly in other cases)—and partly in the agent; *e.g.* heat and the art of building; the former in that which produces heat, and the latter in that which builds. Hence in so far as it is a natural unity, nothing is acted upon by itself; because it is one, and not a separate thing. "Incapacity" and "the incapable" is the privation contrary to "capacity" in this sense; so that every "capacity" has a contrary incapacity for producing the same result in respect of the same subject.

Privation has several senses—it is applied (i.) to anything which does not possess a certain attribute; (ii.) to that which would naturally possess it, but does not; either (*a*) in general, or (*b*) when it would naturally possess it; and either (1) in a particular way, *e.g.* entirely, or (2) in any way at all. And in some cases if things which would naturally possess some attribute lack it as the result of constraint, we say that they are "deprived."

II. Since some of these principles are inherent in inanimate things, and others in animate things and in the soul and in the rational part of the soul, it is clear that some of the potencies also will be irrational and some rational. Hence all arts, *i.e.* the productive sciences, are potencies; because they are principles of change in another thing, or in the artist himself *qua* other.

Every rational potency admits equally of contrary results, but irrational potencies admit of one result only. *E.g.*, heat can only produce heat, but medical science can produce disease and health. The reason of this is that science is a rational account, and the same account explains both the thing and its privation, though not in the same way; and in one sense it applies to both, and in another sense rather to the actual fact. Therefore such sciences must treat of contraries—essentially of the one, and non-essentially of the other; for the rational account also applies essentially to the one, but to the other in a kind of accidental

1046 B

way, since it is by negation and removal that it throws light on the contrary. For the contrary is the primary privation, and this is the removal of that to which it is contrary. And since contrary attributes cannot be induced in the same subject, and science is a potency which depends upon the possession of a rational formula, and the soul contains a principle of motion, it follows that whereas "the salutary" can only produce health, and "the calefactory" only heat, and "the frigorific" only cold, the scientific man can produce both contrary results. For the rational account includes both, though not in the same way; and it is in the soul, which contains a principle of motion, and will therefore, by means of the same principle, set both processes in motion, by linking them with the same rational account. Hence things which have a rational potency produce results contrary to those of things whose potency is irrational; for the results of the former are included under one principle, the rational account. It is evident also that whereas the power of merely producing (or suffering) a given effect is implied in the power of producing that effect *well*, the contrary is not always true; for that which produces an effect well must also produce it, but that which merely produces a given effect does not necessarily produce it well.

III. There are some, *e.g.* the Megaric school, who say that a thing only has potency when it functions, and that when it is not functioning it has no potency. *E.g.*, they say that a man who is not building cannot build, but only the man who is building, and at the moment when he is building; and similarly in the other cases. It is not difficult to see the absurd consequences of this theory. Obviously a man will not be a builder unless he is building, because "to be a builder" is "to be capable of building"; and the same will be true of the other arts. If, therefore, it is impossible to possess these arts without learning them at some time and having grasped them, and impossible not to possess them without having lost them at some time (through forgetfulness or some affection or the lapse of time; not, of course, through the destruction of the object of the art, because it exists always), when the artist ceases to practise his art, he will not possess it; and if he immediately starts building again, how will he have re-acquired the art? 1047 A

The same is true of inanimate things. Neither the cold nor the hot nor the sweet nor in general any sensible thing will exist unless we are perceiving it (and so the result will be that they are affirming Protagoras' theory). Indeed, nothing will have the faculty of sensation unless it is perceiving, *i.e.* actually employing the faculty. If, then, that is blind which has not sight, though it would naturally have it, and when it would naturally have it, and while it still exists, the same people will be blind many times a day; and deaf too.

Further, if that which is deprived of its potency is incapable, that which is not happening will be incapable of happening; and he who says that that which is incapable of happening *is* or *will be*, will be in error, for this is what "incapable" meant. Thus these theories do away with both motion and generation; for that which is standing will always stand, and that which is sitting will always sit; because if it is sitting it will not get up, since it is impossible that anything which is incapable of getting up should get up. Since, then, we cannot maintain this, obviously potentiality and actuality are different. But these theories make potentiality and actuality identical; hence it is no small thing that they are trying to abolish.

Thus it is possible that a thing may be capable of being and yet not be, and capable of not being and yet be; and similarly in the other categories that which is capable of walking may not walk, and that which is capable of not walking may walk. A thing is capable of doing something if there is nothing impossible in its having the actuality of that of which it is said to have the potentiality. I mean, *e.g.*, that if a thing is capable of sitting and is not prevented from sitting, there is nothing impossible in its actually sitting; and similarly if it is capable of being moved or moving or standing or making to stand or being or becoming or not being or not becoming.

The term "actuality," with its implication of "complete reality," has been extended from motions, to which it properly belongs, to other things; for it is agreed that actuality is properly motion. Hence people do not invest non-existent things with motion, although they do invest them with certain other predicates. *E.g.*, they say that non-existent things are conceivable and desirable, but not that they are in motion. This is because, although these things do not exist actually, they will exist actually; for some non-existent things exist potentially; yet they do not exist, because they do not exist in complete reality.

1047 B   IV. Now if, as we have said, that is possible which does not involve an impossibility, obviously it cannot be true to say that so-and-so is possible, but will not be; this view entirely loses sight of the instances of impossibility. I mean, suppose that someone—*i.e.* the sort of man who does not take the impossible into account—were to say that it is possible to measure the diagonal of a square, but that it will not be measured, because there is nothing to prevent a thing which is capable of being or coming to be from neither being nor being likely ever to be. But from our premises this necessarily follows; that if we are to assume that which is not, but is possible, to be or to have come to be, nothing impossible must be involved. But in this case something impossible will take place; for the measuring of the diagonal is impossible.

The false is of course not the same as the impossible for although it is false that you are now standing, it is not impossible. At the same time it is also clear that if B must be real if A is, then if it is possible for A to be real, it must also be possible for B to be real; for even if B is not necessarily possible, there is nothing to prevent its being possible. Let A, then, be possible. Then when A was possible, if A was assumed to be real, nothing impossible was involved; but B was necessarily real too. But *ex hypothesi* B was impossible. Let B be impossible. Then if B is impossible, A must also be impossible. But A was by definition possible. Therefore so is B.

If, therefore, A is possible, B will also be possible; that is if their relation was such that if A is real, B must be real. Then if, A and B being thus related, B is not possible on this condition, A and B will not be related as we assumed; and if when A is possible B is necessarily possible, then if A is real B must be real too. For to say that B must be possible if A is possible means that if A is real at the time when and in the way in which it was assumed that it was possible for it to be real, then B must be real at that time and in that way.

V. Since all potencies are either innate, like the senses, or acquired by practice, like flute-playing, or by study, as in the arts, some—such as are acquired by practice or a rational formula—we can only possess when we have first exercised them; in the case of others which are not of this kind and which imply passivity, this is not necessary.

Since anything which is possible is something possible at some time 1048 A and in some way, and with any other qualifications which are necessarily included in the definition; and since some things can set up processes rationally and have rational potencies, while others are irrational and have irrational potencies; and since the former class can only belong to a living thing, whereas the latter can belong both to living and to inanimate things: it follows that as for potencies of the latter kind, when the agent and the patient meet in accordance with the potency in question, the one must act and the other be acted upon; but in the former kind of potency this is not necessary, for whereas each single potency of the latter kind is productive of a single effect, those of the former kind are productive of contrary effects, so that one potency will produce at the same time contrary effects. But this is impossible. Therefore there must be some other deciding factor, by which I mean *desire* or *conscious choice*. For whichever of two things an animal desires decisively it will do, when it is in circumstances appropriate to the potency and meets with that which admits of being acted upon. Therefore everything which is rationally capable, when it desires something of which it has the capability, and in the circumstances in which it has the capability, must do that thing. Now it has the capability when that which admits of being acted upon is present and is in a certain state; otherwise it will not be able to act. (To add the qualification "if anything external prevents it" is no longer necessary; because the agent has the capability in so far as it is a capability of acting; and this is not in all, but in certain circumstances, in which external hindrances will be excluded; for they are precluded by some of the positive qualifications in the definition.) Hence even if it wishes or desires to do two things or contrary things simultaneously, it will not do them, for it has not the capability to do them under these conditions, nor has it the capability of doing things simultaneously, since it will only do the things to which the capability applies and under the appropriate conditions.

VI. Since we have now dealt with the kind of potency which is related to motion, let us now discuss actuality; what it is, and what its qualities are. For as we continue our analysis it will also become clear with regard to the potential that we apply the name not only to that whose nature it is to move or be moved by something else, either without qualification or in some definite way, but also in other senses; and it is on this account that in the course of our inquiry we have discussed these as well.

"Actuality" means the presence of the thing, not in the sense which we mean by "potentially." We say that a thing is present potentially as Hermes is present in the wood, or the half-line in the whole, because it can be separated from it; and as we call even a man who is not studying "a scholar" if he is capable of studying. That which is present in the opposite sense to this is present actually. What we mean can be plainly seen in the particular cases by induction; we need not seek a definition for every term, but must comprehend the analogy; that as that which is actually building is to that which is capable of building, 1048 B so is that which is awake to that which is asleep; and that which is seeing to that which has the eyes shut, but has the power of sight; and that which is differentiated out of matter to the matter; and the finished article to the raw material. Let actuality be defined by one member of this antithesis, and the potential by the other.

But things are not all said to exist actually in the same sense, but only by analogy—as A is in B or to B, so is C in or to D; for the relation is either that of motion to potentiality, or that of substance to some particular matter.

Infinity and void and other concepts of this kind are said to "be" potentially or actually in a different sense from the majority of existing things, *e.g.* that which sees, or walks, or is seen. For in these latter cases the predication may sometimes be truly made without qualification, since "that which is seen" is so called sometimes because it is seen and sometimes because it is capable of being seen; but the Infinite does not exist potentially in the sense that it will ever exist separately in actuality; it is separable only in knowledge. For the fact that the process of division never ceases makes this actuality exist potentially, but not separately.

Since no action which has a limit is an end, but only a means to the end, as, *e.g.*, the process of thinning; and since the parts of the body themselves, when one is thinning them, are in motion in the sense that they are not already that which it is the object of the motion to make them, this process is not an action, or at least not a complete one, since it is not an end; it is the process which includes the end that is an action. *E.g.*, at the same time we see and have seen, understand and have understood, think and have thought; but we cannot at the same time learn and have learnt, or become healthy and be healthy. We are living well and have lived well, we are happy and have been happy, at the same time; otherwise the process would had to cease at some time, like the thinning-process; but it has not ceased at the present moment; we both are living and have lived.

Now of these processes we should call the one type motions, and the other actualizations. Every motion is incomplete—the process of thinning, learning, walking, building—these are motions, and incomplete at that. For it is not the same thing which at the same time is walking and has walked, or is building and has built, or is becoming and has become, or is being moved and has been moved, but two different things: and that which is causing motion is different from that which has caused motion. But the same thing at the same time is seeing and has seen, is thinking and has thought. The latter kind of process, then, is what I mean by actualization, and the former what I mean by motion.

What the actual is, then, and what it is like, may be regarded as demonstrated from these and similar considerations.

VII. We must, however, distinguish when a particular thing exists potentially, and when it does not; for it does not so exist at any and every time. *E.g.*, is earth potentially a man? No, but rather when it has already become semen, and perhaps not even then; just as not *everything* can be healed by medicine, or even by chance, but there is some definite kind of thing which is capable of it, and this is that which is potentially healthy. 1049 A

The definition of that which as a result of thought comes, from existing potentially, to exist actually, is that, when it has been willed, if no external influence hinders it, it comes to pass; and the condition in the case of the patient, *i.e.* in the person who is being healed, is that nothing in him should hinder the process. Similarly a house exists potentially if there is nothing in X, the matter, to prevent it from becoming a house, *i.e.*, if there is nothing which must be added or removed or changed; then X is potentially a house; and similarly in all other cases where the generative principle is contained in the thing itself, one thing is potentially another when, if nothing external hinders, it will of itself become the other. *E.g.*, the semen is not yet potentially a man; for it must further undergo a change in some other medium. But when, by its own generative principle, it has already come to have the necessary attributes, in this state it is now potentially a man, whereas in the former state it has need of another principle; just as earth is not yet potentially a statue, because it must undergo a change before it becomes bronze.

It seems that what we are describing is not a particular thing, but a definite material; *e.g.*, a box is not wood, but wooden material, and wood is not earth, but earthen material; and earth also is an illustration of our point if it is similarly not some other thing, but a definite material—it is always the latter term in this series which is, in the fullest sense, potentially something else. *E.g.*, a box is not earth, nor earthen, but wooden; for it is this that is potentially a box, and this is the matter of the box—that is, wooden material in general is the matter of "box" in general, whereas the matter of a particular box is a particular piece of wood.

If there is some primary stuff, which is not further called the material of some other thing, this is primary matter. *E.g.*, if earth is "made of air," and air is not fire, but "made of fire," then fire is primary matter, not being an individual thing. For the subject or substrate is distinguishable into two kinds by either being or not being an individual thing. Take for example as the subject of the attributes "man," or "body" or "soul," and as an attribute "cultured" or "white." Now the subject, when culture is induced in it, is called not "culture" but "cultured," and the man is called not whiteness but white; nor is he called "ambulation" or "motion," but "walking" or "moving"; just as we said that things are of a definite material. Thus where "subject" has this sense, the ultimate substrate is substance; but where it has not this sense, and the predicate is a form or individuality, the ultimate substrate is matter or material substance. It is quite proper that both matter and attributes should be described by a derivative predicate, since
1049 B they are both indefinite.

Thus it has now been stated when a thing should be said to exist potentially, and when it should not.

VIII. Now since we have distinguished the several senses of priority, it is obvious that actuality is prior to potentiality. By potentiality I mean not that which we have defined as "a principle of change which is in something other than the thing changed, or in that same thing *qua* other," but in general any principle of motion or of rest; for nature also is in the same genus as potentiality, because it is a principle of motion, although not in some other thing, but in the thing itself *qua* itself. To every potentiality of this kind actuality is prior, both in formula and in substance; in time it is sometimes prior and sometimes not.

That actuality is prior in formula is evident; for it is because it can be actualized that the potential, in the primary sense, is potential, I mean, *e.g.*, that the potentially constructive is that which can construct, the potentially seeing that which can see, and the potentially visible that which can be seen. The same principle holds in all other cases too, so that the formula and knowledge of the actual must precede the knowledge of the potential.

In time it is prior in this sense; the actual is prior to the potential with which it is formally identical, but not to that with which it is identical numerically. What I mean is this: that the matter and the seed and the thing which is capable of seeing, which are potentially a man and corn and seeing, but are not yet so actually, are prior in time to the individual man and corn and seeing subject which already exist in actuality. But prior in time to these potential entities are other actual entities from which the former are generated; for the actually existent is always generated from the potentially existent *by* something which is actually existent—*e.g.*, man by man, cultured by cultured—there is always some prime mover; and that which initiates motion exists already in actuality.

We have said in our discussion of substance that everything which is generated is generated from something and by something; and by something formally identical with itself. Hence it seems impossible that a man can be a builder if he has never built, or a harpist if he has never played a harp; because he who learns to play the harp learns by playing it, and similarly in all other cases. This was the origin of the sophists' quibble that a man who does not know a given science will be doing that which is the object of that science, because the learner does not know the science. But since something of that which is being generated is already generated, and something of that which is being moved as a whole is already moved (this is demonstrated in our discussion on Motion), presumably the learner too must possess something of the science. At any rate from this argument it is clear that actuality is prior to potentiality in this sense too, *i.e.* in respect of generation and time. 1050 A

But it is also prior in substantiality; (*a*) because things which are posterior in generation are prior in form and substantiality; *e.g.*, adult is prior to child, and man to semen, because the one already possesses the form, but the other does not; and (*b*) because everything which is generated moves toward a principle, *i.e.* its *end*. For the object of a thing is its principle; and generation has as its object the *end*. And the actuality is the end, and it is for the sake of this that the potentiality is acquired; for animals do not see in order that they may have sight, but have sight in order that they may see. Similarly men possess the art of building in order that they may build, and the power of speculation that they may speculate; they do not speculate in order that they may have the power of speculation—except those who are learning by practice; and they do not really speculate, but only in a limited sense, or about a subject about which they have no desire to speculate.

Further, matter exists potentially, because it may attain to the form; but when it exists actually, it is then *in* the form. The same applies in all other cases, including those where the end is motion. Hence, just as teachers think that they have achieved their end when they have exhibited their pupil performing, so it is with nature. For if this is not so, it will be another case of "Pauson's Hermes"; it will be impossible to say whether the knowledge is *in* the pupil or outside him, as in the case of the Hermes. For the activity is the end, and the actuality is the activity; hence the term "actuality" is derived from "activity," and tends to have the meaning of "complete reality."

Now whereas in some cases the ultimate thing is the use of the faculty, as, *e.g.*, in the case of sight seeing is the ultimate thing, and sight produces nothing else besides this; but in other cases something is produced, *e.g.*, the art of building produces not only the act of building but a house; nevertheless in the one case the use of the faculty is the end, and in the other it is more truly the end than is the potentiality. For the act of building resides in the thing built; *i.e.*, it comes to be and exists simultaneously with the house.

Thus in all cases where the result is something other than the exercise of the faculty, the actuality resides in the thing produced; *e.g.* the act of building in the thing built, the act of weaving in the thing woven, and so on; and in general the motion resides in the thing moved. But where there is no other result besides the actualization, the actualization resides in the subject; *e.g.* seeing in the seer, and speculation in the speculator, and life in the soul (and hence also happiness, since happiness is a particular kind of life). Evidently, therefore, substance or form is actuality. Thus it is obvious by this argument that actuality is prior in substantiality to potentiality; and that in point of time, as we have said, one actuality presupposes another right back to that of the prime mover in each case.

It is also prior in a deeper sense; because that which is eternal is prior in substantiality to that which is perishable, and nothing eternal is potential. The argument is as follows. Every potentiality is at the same time a potentiality for the opposite. For whereas that which is incapable of happening cannot happen to anything, everything which is capable may fail to be actualized. Therefore that which is capable of being may both be and not be. Therefore the same thing is capable both of being and of not being. But that which is capable of not being may possibly not be; and that which may possibly not be is perishable; either absolutely, or in the particular sense in which it is said that it may possibly not be; that is, in respect either of place or of quantity or of quality. "Absolutely" means in respect of substance. Hence nothing which is

absolutely imperishable is absolutely potential (although there is no reason why it should not be potential in some particular respect; *e.g.* of
quality or place); therefore all imperishable things are actual. Nor can
anything which is of necessity be potential; and yet these things are
primary, for if they did not exist, nothing would exist. Nor can motion
be potential, if there is any external motion. Nor, if there is anything
eternally in motion, is it potentially in motion (except in respect of some
starting-point or destination), and there is no reason why the matter of
such a thing should not exist. Hence the sun and stars and the whole
visible heaven are always active, and there is no fear that they will ever
stop—a fear which the writers on physics entertain. Nor do the heavenly
bodies tire in their activity; for motion does not imply for them, as it
does for perishable things, the potentiality for the opposite, which makes
the continuity of the motion distressing; this results when the substance
is matter and potentiality, not actuality.

Imperishable things are resembled in this respect by things which
are always undergoing transformation, such as earth and fire; for latter
too are always active, since they have their motion independently and
in themselves. Other potentialities, according to the distinctions already
made, all admit of the opposite result; for that which is capable of causing motion in a certain way can also cause it not in that way; that is if
it acts rationally. The same irrational potentialities can only produce
opposite results by their presence or absence.

Thus if there are any entities or substances such as the dialecticians
describe the Ideas to be, there must be something which has much more
knowledge than absolute knowledge, and much more mobility than motion; for there will be in a truer sense actualities, whereas knowledge 1051 A
and motion will be their potentialities. Thus it is obvious that actuality
is prior both to potentiality and to every principle of change.

IX. That a good actuality is both better and more estimable than
a good potentiality will be obvious from the following arguments. Everything of which we speak as capable is alike capable of contrary results;
e.g., that which we call capable of being well is alike capable of being
ill, and has both potentialities at once; for the same potentiality admits
of health and disease, or of rest and motion, or of building and of pulling
down, or of being built and of falling down. Thus the capacity for two
contraries can belong to a thing at the same time, but the contraries
cannot belong at the same time; *i.e.*, the actualities, *e.g.* health and disease, cannot belong to a thing at the same time. Therefore one of them
must be the good; but the potentiality may equally well be both or neither. Therefore the actuality is better.

Also in the case of evils the end or actuality must be worse than the
potentiality; for that which is capable is capable alike of both contraries.

Clearly, then, evil does not exist apart from *things;* for evil is by nature posterior to potentiality. Nor is there in things which are original and eternal any evil or error, or anything which has been destroyed—for destruction is an evil.

Geometrical constructions, too, are discovered by an actualization, because it is by dividing that we discover them. If the division were already done, they would be obvious; but as it is the division is only there potentially. Why is the sum of the interior angles of a triangle equal to two right angles? Because the angles about one point [in a straight line] are equal to two right angles. If the line parallel to the side had been already drawn, the answer would have been obvious at sight. Why is the angle in a semicircle always a right angle? If three lines are equal, the two forming the base, and the one set upright from the middle of the base, the answer is obvious to one who knows the former proposition. Thus it is evident that the potential constructions are discovered by being actualized. The reason for this is that the actualization is an act of thinking. Thus potentiality comes from actuality (and therefore it is by constructive action that we acquire knowledge). [But this is true only in the abstract], for the individual actuality is posterior in generation to its potentiality.

X. The terms "being" and "not-being" are used not only with reference to the types of predication, and to the potentiality or actuality, or non-potentiality and non-actuality; of these types, but also (in the strictest sense) to denote truth and falsity. This depends, in the case of the objects, upon their being united or divided; so that he who thinks that what is divided is divided, or that what is united is united, is right; while he whose thought is contrary to the real condition of the objects is in error. Then *when* do what we call truth and falsity exist or not exist? We must consider what we mean by these terms.

It is not because we are right in thinking that you are white that you are white; it is because you are white that we are right in saying so. Now if whereas some things are always united and cannot be divided, and others are always divided and cannot be united, others again admit of both contrary states, then "to be" is to be united, *i.e.* a unity; and "not to be" is to be not united, but a plurality. Therefore as regards the class of things which admit of both contrary states, the same opinion or the same statement comes to be false and true, and it is possible at one time to be right and at another wrong; but as regards things which cannot be otherwise the same opinion is not sometimes true and sometimes false, but the same opinions are always true or always false.

But with regard to incomposite things, what is being or not-being, and truth or falsity? Such a thing is not composite, so as to be when it is united and not to be when it is divided, like the proposition that "the wood is white," or "the diagonal is incommensurable"; nor will truth and falsity apply in the same way to these cases as to the previous ones. In point of fact, just as truth is not the same in these cases, so neither is being. Truth and falsity are as follows: contact and assertion are truth (for assertion is not the same as affirmation), and ignorance is non-contact. I say ignorance, because it is impossible to be deceived with respect to what a thing is, except accidentally; and the same applies to incomposite substances, for it is impossible to be deceived about them. And they all exist actually, not potentially; otherwise they would be generated and destroyed; but as it is, Being itself is not generated (nor destroyed); if it were, it would be generated out of something. With respect, then, to all things which are essences and actual, there is no question of being mistaken, but only of thinking or not thinking them. Inquiry as to *what* they are takes the form of inquiring whether they are of such-and-such a nature or not.

As for being in the sense of truth, and not-being in the sense of falsity, a unity is true if the terms are combined, and if they are not combined it is false. Again, if the unity exists, it exists in a particular 1052 A way, and if it does not exist in that way, it does not exist at all. Truth means to think these objects, and there is no falsity or deception, but only ignorance—not, however, ignorance such as blindness is; for blindness is like a total absence of the power of thinking. And it is obvious that with regard to immovable things also, if one assumes that there are immovable things, there is no deception in respect of time. *E.g.,* if we suppose that the triangle is immutable, we shall not suppose that it sometimes contains two right angles and sometimes does not, for this would imply that it changes; but we may suppose that one thing has a certain property and another has not; *e.g.,* that no even number is a prime, or that some are primes and others are not. But about a single number we cannot be mistaken even in this way, for we can no longer suppose that one instance is of such a nature, and another not, but whether we are right or wrong, the fact is always the same.

Book XII

I. Our inquiry is concerned with substance; for it is the principles 1069 A and causes of substances that we are investigating. Indeed if the universe is to be regarded as a whole, substance is its first part; and if it is to be regarded as a succession, even so substance is first, then quality, then quantity. Moreover, the latter hardly exist at all in the full sense, but are merely qualifications and affections of Being. Otherwise "not-white" and "not-straight" would also exist; at any rate we say that they too "are," *e.g.,* "it is not white." Further, none of the other categories is separately existent. Even the ancients in effect testify to this, for it was of substance that they sought the principles and elements and causes. Present-day thinkers tend to regard universals as substance, because genera are universal, and they hold that these are more truly principles and substances because they approach the question theoretically; but the ancients identified substance with particular things, *e.g.* fire and earth, and not with body in general.

Now there are three kinds of substance. One is *sensible* (and may be either eternal or perishable; the latter, *e.g.* plants and animals, is universally recognized); of this we must apprehend the elements, whether they are one or many. Another is *immutable*, which certain thinkers hold to exist separately; some dividing it into two classes, others combining the Forms and the objects of mathematics into a single class, and others recognizing only the objects of mathematics as of this nature. The first two kinds of substance come within the scope of physics, since they involve motion; the last belongs to some other science, if there is no principle common to all three.

Sensible substance is liable to change. Now if change proceeds from opposites or intermediates—not however from all opposites (for speech is not white), but only from the contrary—then there must be something underlying which changes into the opposite contrary; for the contraries do not change.

II. Further, something persists, whereas the contrary does not persist. Therefore besides the contraries there is some third thing, the *matter*. Now if change is of four kinds, in respect either of substance or of quality or of quantity or of place, and if change of substance is generation or destruction in the simple sense, and change of quantity is increase or decrease, and change of affection is alteration, and change of place is locomotion, then changes must be in each case into the corresponding contrary state. It must be the matter, then, which admits of both contraries, that changes. And since "that which is" is twofold, everything changes from that which is potentially to that which is actually; *e.g.* from potentially white to actually white. The same applies to increase and decrease. Hence not only may there be generation accidentally from that which is not, but also everything is generated from that which is, but is potentially and is not actually. And this is the "one" of Anaxagoras; for his "all things were together," and the "mixture" of Empedocles and Anaximander and the doctrine of Democritus would be better expressed as "all things were together potentially, but not actually." Hence these thinkers must have had some conception of matter. All things which change have matter, but different things have different kinds; and of eternal things such as are not generable but are movable by locomotion have matter; matter, however, which admits not of generation, but of motion from one place to another.

One might raise the question from what sort of "not-being" generation takes place; for not-being has three senses. If a thing exists through a potentiality, nevertheless it is not through a potentiality for any chance thing; different things are derived from different things. Nor is it satisfactory to say that "all things were together," for they differ in their matter, since otherwise why did they become an infinity and not one? For Mind is one; so that if matter is also one, only that could have come to be in actuality whose matter existed potentially. The causes and principles, then, are three; two being the pair of contraries, of which one is the formula or form and the other the privation, and the third being the matter.

III. We must next observe that neither matter nor form (I mean in the proximate sense) is generated. All change is of some subject by some agent into some object. The agent is the immediate mover; the subject 1070 A is the matter; and the object is the form. Thus the process will go on to infinity if not only the bronze comes to be round, but also roundness or bronze comes to be; there must, then, be some stopping-point.

We must next observe that every substance is generated from something which has the same name ("substances" including not only natural but all other products). Things are generated either by art or by nature or by chance or spontaneously. Art is a generative principle in something else; nature is a generative principle in the subject itself (for man begets man); the other causes are privations of these.

There are three kinds of substance: (i.) matter, which exists individually in virtue of being apparent (for everything which is characterized by contact and not by coalescence is matter and substrate; e.g. fire, flesh and head; these are all matter, and the last is the matter of a substance in the strictest sense); (ii.) the "nature" (existing individually)—i.e. a kind of positive state which is the terminus of motion; and (iii.) the particular combination of these, e.g. Socrates or Callias. In some cases the individuality does not exist apart from the composite substance (e.g., the form of a house does not exist separately, except as the art of building; nor are these forms liable to generation and destruction; there is a distinct sense in which 'house' and 'health' and every natural product, considered in the abstract, do or do not exist; if it does so at all, it does so in the case of natural objects. Hence Plato was not far wrong in saying that there are as many Forms as there are kinds of natural objects; that is if there are Forms distinct from the thing in our world.

Moving causes are causes in the sense of pre-existent things, but formal causes coexist with their effects. For it is when the man becomes healthy that health exists, and the shape of the bronze sphere comes into being simultaneously with the bronze sphere. Whether any form remains also afterwards is another question. In some cases there is nothing to prevent this, *e.g.*, the soul may be of this nature (not all of it, but the intelligent part; for presumably all of it cannot be). Clearly then there is no need on these grounds for the Ideas to exist; for man begets man, the individual begetting the particular person. And the same is true of the arts, for the art of medicine is the formula of health.

IV. In one sense the causes and principles are different for different things; but in another, if one speaks generally and analogically, they are the same for all. For the question might be raised whether the principles and elements of substance and of relations are the same or different; and similarly with respect to each of the other categories. But it is absurd that they should be the same for all; for then relations and substance would have the same constituents. What then can their common constituent be? For there is nothing common to and yet distinct from substance and the other predictable categories, yet the element is prior to that of which it is an element. Moreover substance is not an element of relations, nor is any of the latter an element of substance. Further, how can all the categories have the same elements? For no elements can be the same as that which is composed of elements; *e.g.*, neither B nor A can be the same as BA (nor indeed can any of the 'intelligibles,' *e.g.* Unity or Being, be an element; for these apply in every case, even to composite things); hence no element can be either substance or relation. But it must be one or the other. Therefore the categories have not all the same element.

The truth is that, as we say, in one sense all things have the same elements and in another they have not. *E.g.*, the elements of sensible bodies are, let us say, (1) as form, the hot, and in another sense the cold, which is the corresponding privation; as matter, that which directly and of its own nature is potentially hot or cold. And not only these are substances, but so are (2) the compounds of which they are principles, and (3) any unity which is generated from hot and cold, *e.g.* flesh or bone; for the product of hot and cold must be distinct from them. These things, then, have the same elements and principles, although specifically different things have specifically different elements; we cannot, however, say that all things have the same elements in this sense, but only by analogy; *i.e.*, one might say that there are three principles, form, privation, and matter. But each of these is different in respect of each class of things, *e.g.*, in the case of colour they are white, black, surface; or again, there is light, darkness and air, of which day and night are composed. And since not only things which are inherent in an object are its causes, but also certain external things, *e.g.* the mov-

1070 B

ing cause, clearly 'principle' and 'element' are not the same; but both are causes. Principles are divided into these two kinds, and that which moves a thing or brings it to rest is a kind of principle and substance. Thus analogically there are three elements and four causes or principles; but they are different in different cases, and the proximate moving cause is different in different cases. Health, disease, body; and the moving cause is the art of medicine. Form, a particular kind of disorder, bricks; and the moving cause is the art of building. And since in the sphere of natural objects the moving cause of man is man, while in the sphere of objects of thought the moving cause is the form of its contrary, in one sense there are three causes and in another four. For in a sense the art of medicine is health, and the art of building is the form of a house, and man begets man; but besides these there is that which as first of all things moves all things.

V. Now since some things can exist in separation and others cannot, it is the former that are substances. And therefore all things have 1071 A the same causes, because without substance there can be no affections and motions. Next we shall see that these causes are probably soul and body, or mind, appetite and body. Again, there is another sense in which by analogy the principles are the same, *viz.* actuality and potentiality; but these are different for different things, and apply to them in different ways. For in some cases the same thing exists now actually and now potentially; *e.g.* wine or flesh or man (actuality and potentiality also fall under the causes as already described; for the form exists actually if it is separable, and so does the compound of form and matter, and the privation, *e.g.* darkness or disease; and the matter exists potentially, for it is this which has the potentiality of becoming both); but the distinction in virtue of actuality and potentiality applies in a different sense to cases where the matter of cause and effect is not the same, in some of which the form is not the same but different. *E.g.*, the cause of a man is (i) his elements; fire and earth as matter, and the particular form; (ii) some external formal cause, *viz.* his father; and besides these (iii) the sun and the ecliptic, which are neither matter nor form nor privation nor identical in form with him, but cause motion.

Further, we must observe that some causes can be stated universally, but others cannot. The proximate principles of all things are the proximate actual individual and another individual which exists potentially. Therefore the proximate principles are not universal. For it is the particular that is the principle of particulars; 'man' in general is the principle of 'man' in general, but there is no such person as 'man,' whereas Peleus is the principle of Achilles and your father of you, and this particular B of this particular BA; but B in general is the principle of BA regarded absolutely. Again, even if the causes of substance are universal, still, as has been said, different things, *i.e.*, things which are not in the same genus, as colours, sounds, substances and quantity, have different causes and elements, except in an analogical sense; and the causes of things which are in the same species are different, not in species, but because the causes of individuals are different; your matter and form and moving cause being different from mine, although in their universal formula they are the same.

As for the question what are the principles or elements of substances and relations and qualities, whether they are the same or different, it is evident that when the terms "principle" and "element" are used with several meanings they are the same for everything; but when the meanings are distinguished, they are not the same but different, except that in a certain sense they are the same for all. In a certain sense they are the same or analogous, because (*a*) everything has matter, form, privation and a moving cause; (*b*) the causes of substances may be regarded as the causes of all things, since if substances are destroyed everything is destroyed; and further (*c*) that which is first in complete reality is the cause of all things. In another sense, however, proximate causes are different; there are as many proximate causes as there are contraries which are predicated neither as genera nor with a variety of meanings; and further the particular material causes are different.

Thus we have stated what the principles of sensible things are, and how many they are, and in what sense they are the same and in what sense different.

VI. Since we have seen that there are three kinds of substance, two of which are natural and one immutable, we must now discuss the last named and show that there must be some substance which is eternal and immutable. Substances are the primary reality, and if they are all perishable, everything is perishable. But motion cannot be either generated or destroyed, for it always existed; nor can time, because there can be no priority or posteriority if there is no time. Hence as time is continuous, so too is motion; for time is either identical with motion or an affection of it. But there is no continuous motion except that which is spatial, and of spatial motion only that which is circular.

But even if we are to suppose that there is something which is kinetic and productice although it does not actually move or produce, there will not necessarily be motion; for that which has a potentiality may not actualize it. Thus it will not help matters if we posit eternal substances, as do the exponents of the Forms, unless there is in them some principle which can cause change. And even this is not enough, nor is it enough if there is another substance besides the Forms; for unless it actually functions there will not be motion. And it will still not be enough even if it does function, if its essence is potentiality; for there will not be eternal motion, since that which exists potentially may not exist. Therefore there must be a principle of this kind whose essence is actuality. Furthermore these substances must be immaterial; for they must be eternal if anything is. Therefore they are actuality.

There is a difficulty, however; for it seems that everything which actually functions has a potentiality, whereas not everything which has a potentiality actually functions; so that potentiality is prior. But if this is so, there need be no reality; for everything may be capable of existing, but not yet existent. Yet if we accept the statements of the cosmologists who generate everything from Night, or the doctrine of the physicists that "all things were together," we have the same impossibility; for how can there be motion if there is no actual cause? Wood will not move itself—carpentry must act upon it; nor will the menses or the earth move themselves—the seeds must act upon the earth, and the semen on the menses. Hence some, *e.g.* Leucippus and Plato, posit an eternal actuality, for they say that there is always motion; but why there is, and what it is, they do not say; nor, if it moves in this or that particular way, what the cause is. For nothing is moved at haphazard, but in every case there must be some reason present; as in point of fact things are moved in one way by nature, and in another by force or mind or some other agent. And further, what kind of motion is primary? For this is an extremely important point. Again, Plato at least cannot even explain what it is that he sometimes thinks to be the source of motion, *i.e.*, that which moves itself; for according to him the soul is posterior to motion and coeval with the sensible universe. Now to suppose that potentiality is prior to actuality is in one sense right and in another wrong; we have explained the distinction. But that actuality is prior is testified by Anaxagoras (since mind is actuality), and by Empedocles with his theory of Love and Strife, and by those who hold that motion is eternal, *e.g.* Leucippus. 1072 A

Therefore Chaos or Night did not endure for an unlimited time, but the same things have always existed, either passing through a cycle or in accordance with some other principle—that is, if actuality is prior to potentiality. Now if there is a regular cycle, there must be something which remains always active in the same way; but if there is to be generation and destruction, there must be something else which is always active in two different ways. Therefore this must be active in one way independently, and in the other in virtue of something else, *i.e.* either of some third active principle or of the first. It must, then, be in virtue of the first; for this is in turn the cause both of the third and of the second. Therefore the first is preferable, since it was the cause of perpetual regular motion, and something else was the cause of variety and obviously both together make up the cause of perpetual variety. Now this is just what actually characterizes motions; therefore why need we seek any further principles?

VII. Since (*a*) this is a possible explanation, and (*b*) if it is not true, we shall have to regard everything as coming from "Night" and "all things together" and "not-being," these difficulties may be considered to be solved. There is something which is eternally moved with an unceasing motion, and that circular motion. This is evident not merely in theory, but in fact. Therefore the "ultimate heaven" must be eternal. Then there is also something which moves it. And since that which is moved while it moves is intermediate, there is something which moves without being moved; something eternal which is both substance and actuality.

Now it moves in the following manner. The object of desire and the object of thought move without being moved. The primary objects of desire and thought are the same. For it is the apparent good that is the object of appetite, and the real good that is the object of the rational will. Desire is the result of opinion rather than opinion that of desire; it is the act of thinking that is the starting-point. Now thought is moved by the intelligible, and one of the series of contraries is essentially intelligible. In this series substance stands first, and of substance that which is simple and exists actually. (The one and the simple are not the same; for one signifies a measure, whereas "simple" means that the subject itself is in a certain state.) But the Good, and that which is in itself desirable, are also in the same series; and that which is first in a class is always best or analogous to the best.

1072 B

That the final cause may apply to immovable things is shown by the distinction of its meanings. For the final cause is not only "the good *for something*," but also "the good which is *the end of some action*." In the latter sense it applies to immovable things, although in the former it does not; and it causes motion as being an object of love, whereas all other things cause motion because they are themselves in motion. Now if a thing is moved, it can be otherwise than it is. Therefore if the actuality of "the heaven" is primary locomotion, then in so far as "the heaven" is moved, in this respect at least it is possible for it to be otherwise; *i.e.* in respect of place, even if not of substantiality. But since there is something—X—which moves while being itself unmoved, existing actually, X cannot be otherwise in any respect. For the primary kind of change is locomotion, and of locomotion circular locomotion; and this is the motion which X induces. Thus X is necessarily existent; and *qua* necessary it is good, and is in this sense a first principle. For the necessary has all these meanings; that which is by constraint because it is contrary to impulse; and that without which excellence is impossible; and that which cannot be otherwise, but is absolutely necessary.

Such, then, is the first principle upon which depend the sensible universe and the world of nature. And its life is like the best which we temporarily enjoy. It must be in that state always (which for us is impossible), since its actuality is also pleasure. (And for this reason waking, sensation and thinking are most pleasant, and hopes and memories are pleasant because of them.) Now thinking in itself is concerned with that which is in itself best, and thinking in the highest sense with that which is in the highest sense best. And thought thinks itself through participation in the object of thought; for it becomes an object of thought by the act of apprehension and thinking, so that thought and the object of thought are the same, because that which is receptive of the object of thought, *i.e.* essence, is thought. And it actually functions when it possesses this object. Hence it is actuality rather than potentiality that is held to be the divine possession of rational thought, and its active contemplation is that which is most pleasant and best. If, then, the happiness which God always enjoys is as great as that which we enjoy sometimes, it is marvellous; and if it is greater, this is still more marvellous. Nevertheless it is so. Moreover, life belongs to God. For the actuality of thought is life, and God is that actuality; and the essential actuality of God is life most good and eternal. We hold, then, that God is a living being, eternal, most good; and therefore life and a continuous eternal existence belong to God; for that is what God is.

Those who suppose, as do the Pythagoreans and Speusippus, that perfect beauty and goodness do not exist in the beginning (on the ground that whereas the first beginnings of plants and animals are causes, it is in the products of these that beauty and perfection are found) are mistaken in their views. For seed comes from prior creatures which are perfect, and that which is first is not the seed but the perfect creature. *E.g.,* one might say that prior to the seed is the man—not he who is produced from the seed, but another man from whom the seed comes. 1073 A

Thus it is evident from the foregoing account that there is some substance which is eternal and immovable and separate from sensible things; and it has also been shown that this substance can have no magnitude, but is impartible and indivisible (for it causes motion for infinite time, and nothing finite has an infinite potentiality; and therefore since every magnitude is either finite or infinite, it cannot have finite magnitude, and it cannot have infinite magnitude because there is no such thing at all); and moreover that it is impassive and unalterable; for all the other kinds of motion are posterior to spatial motion. Thus it is clear why this substance has these attributes.

VIII. We must not disregard the question whether we should hold that there is one substance of this kind or more than one, and if more than one, how many; we must review the pronouncements of other thinkers and show that with regard to the number of the substances they have said nothing that can be clearly stated. The theory of the Ideas contains no peculiar treatment of the question, for the exponents of the theory call the Ideas numbers, and speak of the numbers now as though they were unlimited and now as though they were limited by the number 10; but as for why there should be just so many numbers, there is no explanation given with demonstrative accuracy. We, however, must discuss the question on the basis of the assumptions and distinctions which we have already made.

The first principle and primary reality is immovable, both essentially and accidentally, but it excites the primary form of motion, which is one and eternal. Now since that which is moved must be moved by something, and the prime mover must be essentially immovable, and eternal motion must be excited by something eternal, and one motion by some one thing; and since we can see that besides the simple spatial motion of the universe (which we hold to be excited by the primary immovable substance) there are other spatial motions—those of the planets—which are eternal (because a body which moves in a circle is eternal and is never at rest—this has been proved in our physical treatises); then each of these spatial motions must also be excited by a substance which is essentially immovable and eternal. For the nature of the heavenly bodies is eternal, being a kind of substance; and that which moves is eternal and prior to the moved; and that which is prior to a substance must be a substance. It is therefore clear that there must be an equal number of substances, in nature eternal, essentially immov-

1073 B able, and without magnitude; for the reason already stated.

Thus it is clear that the movers are substances, and that one of them is first and another second and so on in the same order as the spatial motions of the heavenly bodies. As regards the number of these motions, we have now reached a question which must be investigated by the aid of that branch of mathematical science which is most akin to philosophy, *i.e.* astronomy; for this has as its object a substance which is sensible but eternal, whereas the other mathematical sciences, *e.g.* arithmetic and geometry, do not deal with any substance. That there are more spatial motions than there are bodies which move in space is obvious to those who have even a moderate grasp of the subject, since each of the non-fixed stars has more than one spatial motion. As to how many these spatial motions actually are we shall now, to give some idea of the subject, quote what some of the mathematicians say, in order that there may be some definite number for the mind to grasp; but for the rest we must partly investigate for ourselves and partly learn from other investigators, and if those who apply themselves to these matters come to some conclusion which clashes with what we have just stated, we must appreciate both views, but follow the more accurate.

Eudoxus held that the motion of the sun and moon involves in either case three spheres, of which the outermost is that of the fixed stars, the second revolves in the circle which bisects the zodiac, and the third revolves in a circle which is inclined across the breadth of the zodiac; but the circle in which the moon moves is inclined at a greater angle than that in which the moon moves is inclined at a greater angle than that in which the sun moves. And he held that the motion of the planets involved in each case four spheres, and that of these the first and second are the same as before (for the sphere of the fixed stars is that which carries round all the other spheres, and the sphere next in order, which has its motion in the circle which bisects the zodiac, is common to all the planets); the third sphere of all the planets has its poles in the circle which bisects the zodiac; and the fourth sphere moves in the circle inclined to the equator of the third. In the case of the third sphere, while the other planets have their own peculiar poles, those of Venus and Mercury are the same.

Callippus assumed the same arrangement of the spheres as did Eudoxus (that is, with respect to the order of their intervals), but as regards their number, whereas he assigned to Jupiter and Saturn the same number of spheres as Eudoxus, he considered that two further spheres should be added both for the sun and for the moon, if the phenomena are to be accounted for, and one for each of the other planets.

But if all the spheres in combination are to account for the phenomena, there must be for each of the other planets other spheres, one less in number than those already mentioned, which counteract these and 1074 A restore to the same position the first sphere of the star which in each case is next in order below. In this way only can the combination of forces produce the motion of the planets. Therefore since the forces by which the planets themselves are moved are 8 for Jupiter and Saturn, and 25 for the others, and since of these the only ones which do not need to be counteracted are those by which the lowest planet is moved, the counteracting spheres for the first two planets will be 6, and those of the remaining four will be 16; and the total number of spheres, both those which move the planets and those which counteract these, will be 55. If we do not invest the moon and the sun with the additional motions which we have mentioned, there will be 47 (?) spheres in all.

This, then, may be taken to be the number of the spheres; and thus it is reasonable to suppose that there are as many immovable substances and principles,—the statement of logical necessity may be left to more competent thinkers.

If there can be no spatial motion which is not conducive to the motion of a star, and if moreover every entity and every substance which is impassive and has in itself attained to the highest good should be regarded as an end, then there can be no other entity besides these, and the number of the substances must be as we have said. For if there are other substances, they must move something, since they are the end of spatial motion. But there can be no other spatial motions besides those already mentioned. This is a reasonable inference from a general consideration of spatial motion. For if everything which moves exists for the sake of that which is moved, and every motion for the sake of something which is moved, no motion can exist for the sake of itself or of some other motion, but all motions must exist for the sake of the stars. For if we are to suppose that one motion is for the sake of another, the latter too must be for the sake of something else; and since the series cannot be infinite, the end of every motion must be one of the divine bodies which are moved through the heavens.

It is evident that there is only one heaven. For if there is to be a plurality of heavens (as there is of men), the principle of each must be one in kind but many in number. But all things which are many in number have matter (for one and the same definition applies to many individuals, *e.g.* that of "man"; but Socrates is one), but the primary essence has no matter, because it is complete reality. Therefore the prime mover, which is immovable, is one both in formula and in number; and therefore so also is that which is eternally and continuously in motion. Therefore there is only one heaven.

1074 B A tradition has been handed down by the ancient thinkers of very early times, and bequeathed to posterity in the form of a myth, to the effect that these heavenly bodies are gods, and that the Divine pervades the whole of nature. The rest of their tradition has been added later in a mythological form to influence the vulgar and as a constitutional and utilitarian expedient; they say that these gods are human in shape or are like certain other animals, and make other statements consequent upon and similar to those which we have mentioned. Now if we separate these statements and accept only the first, that they supposed the primary substances to be gods, we must regard it as an inspired saying; and reflect that whereas every art and philosophy has probably been repeatedly developed to the utmost and has perished again, these beliefs of theirs have been preserved as a relic of former knowledge. To this extent only, then, are the views of our forefathers and of the earliest thinkers intelligible to us.

IX. The subject of Mind involves certain difficulties. Mind is held to be of all phenomena the most supernatural; but the question of how we must regard it if it is to be of this nature involves certain difficulties. If Mind thinks nothing, where is its dignity? It is in just the same state as a man who is asleep. If it thinks, but something else determines its thinking, then since that which is its essence is not thinking but potentiality, it cannot be the best reality: because it derives its excellence from the act of thinking. Again, whether its essence is thought or thinking, what does it think? It must think either itself or something else; and if something else, then it must think either the same thing always, or different things at different times. Then does it make any difference, or not, whether it thinks that which is good or thinks at random? Surely it would be absurd for it to think about some subjects. Clearly, then, it thinks that which is most divine and estimable, and does not change; for the change would be for the worse, and anything of this kind would immediately imply some sort of motion. Therefore if Mind is not thinking but a potentiality, (a) it is reasonable to suppose that the continuity of its thinking is laborious; (b) clearly there must be something else which is more excellent than Mind; i.e. the object of thought; for both thought and the act of thinking will belong even to the thinker of the worst thoughts. Therefore if this is to be avoided (as it is, since it is better not to see some things than to see them), thinking cannot be the supreme good. Therefore Mind thinks itself, if it is that which is best; and its thinking is a thinking of thinking.

Yet it seems that knowledge and perception and opinion and understanding are always of something else, and only incidentally of themselves. And further, if to think is not the same as to be thought, in respect of which does goodness belong to thought? for the act of thinking and the object of thought have not the same essence. The answer is that 1075 A in some cases the knowledge is the object. In the productive sciences, if we disregard the matter, the substance, i.e. the essence, is the object; but in the speculative sciences the formula or the act of thinking is the object. Therefore since thought and the object of thought are not different in the case of things which contain no matter, they will be the same, and the act of thinking will be one with the object of thought.

There still remains the question whether the object of thought is composite; for if so, thought would change in passing from one part of the whole to another. The answer is that everything which contains no matter is indivisible. Just as the human mind, or rather the mind of composite beings, is in a certain space of time (for it does not possess the good at this or at that moment, but in the course of a certain whole period it attains to the supreme good, which is other than itself), so is absolute self-thought throughout all eternity.

X. We must also consider in which sense the nature of the universe contains the good or the supreme good; whether as something separate and independent, or as the orderly arrangement of its parts. Probably in both senses, as an army does; for the efficiency of an army consists partly in the order and partly in the general; but chiefly in the latter, because he does not depend upon the order, but the order depends upon him. All things, both fishes and birds and plants, are ordered together in some way, but not in the same way; and the system is not such that there is no relation between one thing and another; there is a definite connexion. Everything is ordered together to one end; but the arrangement is like that in a household, where the free persons have the least liberty to act at random, and have all or most of their actions preordained for them, whereas the slaves and animals have little common responsibility and act for the most part at random; for the nature of each class is a principle such as we have described. I mean, for example, that everything must at least come to dissolution; and similarly there are other respects in which everything contributes to the good of the whole.

We must not fail to observe how many impossibilities and absurdities are involved by other theories, and what views the more enlightened thinkers hold, and what views entail the fewest difficulties. All thinkers maintain that all things come from contraries; but they are wrong both in saying "all things" and in saying that they come from contraries, nor do they explain how things in which the contraries really are present come from the contraries, for the contraries cannot act upon each other. For us, however, this problem is satisfactorily solved by the fact that there is a third factor. Other thinkers make one of the two contraries matter; *e.g.*, this is done by those who make the Unequal matter for the Equal, or the Many matter for the One. But this also is disposed of in the same way! for the one matter of two contraries is contrary to nothing. Further, on their view everything except Unity itself will partake of evil; for "the Bad" is itself one of the elements. The other school does not even regard the Good and the Bad as principles; yet the Good is in the truest sense a principle in all things. The former school is right in holding that the Good is a principle, but they do not explain how it is a principle—whether as an end or as a moving cause or as form.

1075 B

Empedocles' theory is also absurd, for he identifies the Good with Love. This is a principle both as causing motion (since it combines) and as matter (since it is part of the mixture). Now even if it so happens that the same thing is a principle both as matter and as causing motion, still the essence of the two principles is not the same. In which respect, then, is Love a principle? And it is also absurd that Strife should be imperishable; strife is the very essence of evil.

Anaxagoras makes the Good a principle as causing motion; for Mind moves things, but moves them for some end, and therefore there must be some other Good—unless it is as we say; for on our view the art of medicine is in a sense health. It is absurd also not to provide a contrary for the Good, *i.e.* for Mind. But all those who recognize the contraries fail to make use of the contraries, unless we systematize their theories.

And none of them explains why some things are perishable and others imperishable; for they make all existing things come from the same first principles. Again, some make existing things come from not-being, while others, to avoid this necessity, make all things one. Again, no one explains why there must always be generation, and what the cause of generation is.

Moreover, those who posit two principles must admit another superior principle, and so must the exponents of the Forms; for what made or makes particulars participate in the Forms? And on all other views it follows necessarily that there must be something which is contrary to Wisdom or supreme knowledge, but on ours it does not. For there is no contrary to that which is primary, since all contraries involve matter, and that which has matter exists potentially; and the ignorance which is contrary to Wisdom would tend towards the contrary of the object of Wisdom; but that which is primary has no contrary.

Further, if there is to be nothing else besides sensible things, there will be no first principle, no order, no generation, and no celestial motions, but every principle will be based upon another, as in the accounts of all the cosmologists and physicists. And if the Forms or numbers are to exist, they will be causes of nothing; or if not of nothing, at least not of motion.

Further, how can extension, *i.e.* a continuum, be produced from that which is unextended? Number cannot, either as a moving or as a formal cause, produce a continuum. Moreover, no contrary can be essentially productive and kinetic, for then it would be possible for it not to exist; and further, the act of production would in any case be posterior to the potentiality. Therefore the world of reality is not eternal. But there are real objects which are eternal. Therefore one of these premisses must be rejected. We have described how this may be done.

Further, in virtue of what the numbers, or soul and body, or in general the form and the object, are one, no one attempts to explain; nor is it possible to do so except on our theory, that it is the moving cause that makes them one. As for those who maintain that mathematical number is the primary reality, and so go on generating one substance after another and finding different principles for each one, they make the substance of the universe incoherent (for one substance in no way affects another by its existence or non-existence) and give us a great many governing principles. But the world must not be governed badly:

> The rule of many is not good; let one be the ruler.

XX

NICOMACHEAN ETHICS

Book I

Chapter I

1094 A   Every art and every investigation, and likewise every practical pursuit or undertaking, seems to aim at some good: hence it has been well said that the Good is That at which all things aim. (It is true that a certain variety is to be observed among the ends at which the arts and sciences aim: in some cases the activity of practising the art is itself the end, whereas in others the end is some product over and above the mere exercise of the art; and in the arts whose ends are certain things beside the practice of the arts themselves, these products are essentially superior in value to the activities.) But as there are numerous pursuits and arts and sciences, it follows that their ends are correspondingly numerous: for instance, the end of the science of medicine is health, that of the art of shipbuilding a vessel, that of strategy victory, that of domestic economy wealth. Now in cases where several such pursuits are subordinate to some single faculty—as bridle-making and the other trades concerned with horses' harness are subordinate to horsemanship, and this and every other military pursuit to the science of strategy, and similarly other arts to different arts again—in all these cases, I say, the ends of the master arts are things more to be desired than all those of the arts subordinate to them; since the latter ends are only pursued for the sake of the former. (And it makes no difference whether the ends of the pursuits are the activities themselves or some other thing beside these, as in the case of the sciences mentioned.)

Reprinted by permission of the publishers and The Loeb Classical Library from Aristotle, *Nicomachean Ethics*, translated by H. Rackham, Cambridge, Mass.: Harvard University Press, 1946.

Chapter II

If therefore among the ends at which our actions aim there be one which we wish for its own sake, while we wish the others only for the sake of this, and if we do not choose everything for the sake of something else (which would obviously result in a process *ad infinitum*, so that all desire would be futile and vain), it is clear that this one ultimate End must be the Good, and indeed the Supreme Good. Will not then a knowledge of this Supreme Good be also of great practical importance for the conduct of life? Will it not better enable us to attain what is fitting, like archers having a target to aim at? If this be so, we ought to make an attempt to determine at all events in outline what exactly this Supreme Good is, and of which of the theoretical or practical sciences it is the object.

Now it would be agreed that it must be the object of the most authoritative of the sciences—some science which is pre-eminently a master-craft. But such is manifestly the science of Politics; for it is this that ordains which of the sciences are to exist in states, and what branches of knowledge the different classes of the citizens are to learn, and up to what point; and we observe that even the most highly esteemed of the faculties, such as strategy, domestic economy, oratory, are subordinate to the political science. Inasmuch then as the rest of the sciences are employed by this one, and as it moreover lays down laws as to what people shall do and what things they shall refrain from doing, the end of this science must include the ends of all the others. Therefore, the Good of man must be the end of the science of Politics. For even though it be the case that the Good is the same for the individual and for the state, nevertheless, the good of the state is manifestly a greater and more perfect good, both to attain and to preserve. To secure the good of one person only is better than nothing; but to secure the good of a nation or a state is a nobler and more divine achievement.

1094 B

This then being its aim, our investigation is in a sense the study of Politics.

Chapter III

Now our treatment of this science will be adequate, if it achieves that amount of precision which belongs to its subject matter. The same exactness must not be expected in all departments of philosophy alike, any more than in all the products of the arts and crafts. The subjects studied by political science are Moral Nobility and Justice; but these conceptions involve much difference of opinion and uncertainty, so that they are sometimes believed to be mere conventions and to have no real existence in the nature of things. And a similar uncertainty surrounds the conception of the Good, because it frequently occurs that good things have harmful consequences: people have before now been ruined by wealth, and in other cases courage has cost men their lives. We must therefore be content if, in dealing with subjects and starting from premises thus uncertain, we succeed in presenting a broad outline of the truth: when our subjects and our premises are merely generalities, it is enough if we arrive at generally valid conclusions. Accordingly we may ask the student also to accept the various views we put forward in the same spirit; for it is the mark of an educated mind to expect that amount of exactness in each kind which the nature of the particular subject admits. It is equally unreasonable to accept merely probable conclusions from a mathematician and to demand strict demonstration from an orator.

1095 A   Again, each man judges correctly those matters with which he is acquainted; it is of these that he is a competent critic. To criticize a particular subject, therefore, a man must have been trained in that subject: to be a good critic generally, he must have had an all-round education. Hence the young are not fit to be students of Political Science. For they have no experience of life and conduct, and it is these that supply the premises and subject matter of this branch of philosophy. And moreover they are led by their feelings; so that they will study the subject to no purpose or advantage, since the end of this science is not knowledge but action. And it makes no difference whether they are young in years or immature in character: the defect is not a question of time, it is because their life and its various aims are guided by feeling; for to such persons their knowledge is of no use, any more than it is to persons of defective self-restraint. But Moral Science may be of great value to those who guide their desires and actions by principle.

Let so much suffice by way of introduction as to the student of the subject, the spirit in which our conclusions are to be received, and the object that we set before us.

Chapter IV

To resume, inasmuch as all studies and undertakings are directed to the attainment of some good, let us discuss what it is that we pronounce to be the aim of Politics, that is, what is the highest of all the goods that action can achieve. As far as the name goes, we may almost say that the great majority of mankind are agreed about this; for both the multitude and persons of refinement speak of it as Happiness, and conceive 'the good life' or 'doing well' to be the same thing as 'being happy.' But what constitutes happiness is a matter of dispute; and the popular account of it is not the same as that given by the philosophers. Ordinary people identify it with some obvious and visible good, such as pleasure or wealth or honour—some say one thing and some another, indeed very often the same man says different things at different times: when he falls sick he thinks health is happiness, when he is poor, wealth. At other times, feeling conscious of their own ignorance, men admire those who propound something grand and above their heads; and it has been held by some thinkers that beside the many good things we have mentioned, there exists another Good, that is good in itself, and stands to all those goods as the cause of their being good.

Now perhaps it would be a somewhat fruitless task to review all the different opinions that are held. It will suffice to examine those that are most widely prevalent, or that seem to have some argument in their favour.

And we must not overlook the distinction between arguments that start from first principles and those that lead to first principles. It was a good practice of Plato to raise this question, and to enquire whether the right procedure was to start from or to lead up to the first principles, as in a race-course one may run from the judges to the far end of the track or reversely. Now no doubt it is proper to start from the known. But 'the known' has two meanings—'what is known to us,' which is one thing, and 'what is knowable in itself,' which is another. Perhaps then for us at all events it is proper to start from what is known to us. This is why in order to be a competent student of the Right and Just, and in short of the topics of Politics in general, the pupil is bound to have been well trained in his habits. For the starting-point or first principle is the fact that a thing is so; if this be satisfactorily ascertained, there will be no need also to know the reason why it is so. And the man of good moral training knows first principles already, or can easily acquire them. As for the person who neither knows nor can learn, let him hear the words of Hesiod:

> Best is the man who can himself advise;
> He too is good who hearkens to the wise;
> But who, himself being witless, will not heed
> Another's wisdom, is worthless indeed.

Chapter V

But let us continue from the point where we digressed. To judge from men's lives, the more or less reasoned conceptions of the Good or Happiness that seem to prevail among them are the following. On the one hand the generality of men and the most vulgar identify the Good

with pleasure, and accordingly are content with the Life of Enjoyment—
for there are three specially prominent Lives, the one just mentioned,
the Life of Politics, and thirdly, the Life of Contemplation. The generality of mankind then show themselves to be utterly slavish, by pre-
ferring what is only a life for cattle; but they get a hearing for their view
as reasonable because many persons of high position share the feelings
of Sardanapallus.

Men of refinement, on the other hand, and men of action think that
the Good is honour—for this may be said to be the end of the Life of
Politics. But honour after all seems too superficial to be the Good for
which we are seeking; since it appears to depend on those who confer
it more than on him upon whom it is conferred, whereas we instinctively
feel that the Good must be something proper to its possessor and not
easy to be taken away from him. Moreover men's motive in pursuing
honour seems to be to assure themselves of their own merit; at least they
seek to be honoured by men of judgement and by people who know
them, that is, they desire to be honoured on the ground of virtue. It is
clear therefore that in the opinion at all events of men of action, virtue
is a greater good than honour; and one might perhaps accordingly suppose that virtue rather than honour is the end of the Political Life. But
even virtue proves on examination to be too incomplete to be the End;
since it appears possible to possess it while you are asleep, or without
putting it into practice throughout the whole of your life; and also for
1096 A the virtuous man to suffer the greatest misery and misfortune—though
no one would pronounce a man living a life of misery to be happy,
unless for the sake of maintaining a paradox. But we need not pursue
this subject, since it has been sufficiently treated in the ordinary discussions.

The third type of life is the Life of Contemplation, which we shall
consider in the sequel.

The Life of Money-making is a constrained kind of life, and clearly
wealth is not the Good we are in search of, for it is only good as being
useful, a means to something else. On this score indeed one might conceive the ends before mentioned to have a better claim, for they are
approved for their own sakes. But even they do not really seem to be
the Supreme Good; however, many arguments have been laid down in
regard to them, so we may dismiss them.

Chapter VI

But perhaps it is desirable that we should examine the notion of a
Universal Good, and review the difficulties that it involves, although
such an enquiry goes against the grain because of our friendship for the

authors of the Theory of Ideas. Still perhaps it would appear desirable, and indeed it would seem to be obligatory, especially for a philosopher, to sacrifice even one's closest personal ties in defence of the truth. Both are dear to us, yet 'tis our duty to prefer the truth.

The originators of this theory, then, used not to postulate Ideas of groups of things in which they posited an order of priority and posteriority (for which reason they did not construct an Idea of numbers in general). But Good is predicated alike in the Categories of Substance, of Quality, and of Relation; yet the Absolute, or Substance, is prior in nature to the Relative, which seems to be a sort of offshoot or 'accident' of Substance; so that there cannot be a common Idea corresponding to the absolutely good and the relatively good.

Again, the word 'good' is used in as many senses as the word 'is'; for we may predicate good in the Category of Substance, for instance of God or intelligence; in that of Quality—the excellences; in that of Quantity—moderate in amount; in that of Relation—useful; in that of Time—a favourable opportunity; in that of Place—a suitable 'habitat'; and so on. So clearly good cannot be a single and universal general notion; if it were, it would not be predicable to all the Categories, but only in one.

Again, things that come under a single Idea must be objects of a single science; hence there ought to be a single science dealing with all good things. But as a matter of fact there are a number of sciences even for the goods in one Category: for example, opportunity, for opportunity in war comes under the science of strategy, in disease under that of medicine; and the due amount in diet comes under medicine, in bodily exercise under gymnastics.

One might also raise the question what precisely they mean by their expression 'the Ideal so-and-so,' seeing that one and the same definition of man applies both to 'the Ideal man' and to 'man,' for in so far as both are man, there will be no difference between them; and if so, no more will there be any difference between 'the Ideal Good' and 'Good' in so far as both are good. Nor yet will the Ideal Good be any more good because it is eternal, seeing that a white thing that lasts a long time is no whiter than one that lasts only a day.

1096 B

The Pythagoreans seem to give a more probable doctrine on the subject of the Good when they place Unity in their column of goods; and indeed Speusippus appears to have followed them. But this subject must be left for another discussion.

We can descry an objection that may be raised against our arguments on the ground that the theory in question was not intended to apply to every sort of good, and that only things pursued and accepted for their own sake are pronounced good as belonging to a single species, while things productive or preservative of these in any way, or preventive of their opposites, are said to be good as a means to these, and in a different sense. Clearly then the term 'good' would have two meaning, (1) things good in themselves and (2) things good as a means to these; let us then separate things good in themselves from things useful as means, and consider whether the former are called good because they fall under a single Idea. But what sort of things is one to class as good in themselves? Are they not those things which are sought after even without any accessory advantage, such as wisdom, sight, and certain pleasures and honours? for even if we also pursue these things as means to something else, still one would class them among things good in themselves. Or is there nothing else good in itself except the Idea? If so, the species will be of no use. If on the contrary the class of things good in themselves includes these objects, the same notion of good ought to be manifested in all of them, just as the same notion of white is manifested in snow and in white paint. But as a matter of fact the notions of honour and wisdom and pleasure, as being good, are different and distinct. Therefore, good is not a general term corresponding to a single Idea.

But in what sense then are different things called good? For they do not seem to be a case of things that bear the same name merely by chance. Possibly things are called good in virtue of being derived from one good; or because they all contribute to one good. Or perhaps it is rather by way of a proportion: that is, as sight is good in the body, so intelligence is good in the soul, and similarly another thing in something else.

Perhaps however this question must be dismissed for the present, since a detailed investigation of it belongs more properly to another branch of philosophy. And likewise with the Idea of the Good; for even if the goodness predicated of various things in common really is a unity or something existing separately and absolute, it clearly will not be practicable or attainable by man; but the Good which we are now seeking is a good within human reach.

1097 A   But possibly someone may think that to know the Ideal Good may be desirable as an aid to achieving those goods which are practicable and attainable: having the Ideal Good as a pattern we shall more easily know what things are good for us, and knowing them, obtain them. Now it is true that this argument has a certain plausibility; but it does not seem to square with the actual procedure of the sciences. For these all aim at some good, and seek to make up their deficiencies, but they do not trouble about a knowledge of the Ideal Good. Yet if it were so potent an aid, it is improbable that all the professors of the arts and sciences should not know it, nor even seek to discover it. Moreover, it is not easy to see *how* knowing that same Ideal Good will help a weaver or carpenter in the practice of his own craft, or how anybody will be a better physician or general for having contemplated the absolute Idea. In fact it does not appear that the physician studies even health in the abstract; he studies the health of the human being—or rather of some particular human being, for it is individuals that he has to cure.

Let us here conclude our discussion of this subject.

Chapter VII

We may now return to the Good which is the object of our search, and try to find out what exactly it can be. For good appears to be one thing in one pursuit or art and another in another: it is different in medicine from what it is in strategy, and so on with the rest of the arts. What definition of the Good then will hold true in all the arts? Perhaps we may define it as that for the sake of which everything else is done. This applies to something different in each different art—to health in the case of medicine, to victory in that of strategy, to a house in architecture, and to something else in each of the other arts; but in every pursuit or undertaking it describes the end of that pursuit or undertaking, since in all of them it is for the sake of the end that everything else is done. Hence if there be something which is the end of all the things done by human action, this will be the practicable Good—or if there be several such ends, the sum of these will be the Good. Thus by changing its ground the argument has reached the same result as before. We must attempt however to render this still more precise.

Now there do appear to be several ends at which our actions aim; but as we choose some of them—for instance wealth, or flutes, and instruments generally—as a means to something else, it is clear that not all of them are final ends; whereas the Supreme Good seems to be something final. Consequently if there be some one thing which alone is a final end, this thing—or if there be several final ends, the one among them which is the most final—will be the Good which we are seeking. In speaking of degrees of finality, we mean that a thing pursued as an end in itself is more final than one pursued as a means to something else, and that a thing never chosen as a means to anything else is more final than things chosen both as ends in themselves and as means to that thing; and accordingly a thing chosen always as an end and never as a means we call absolutely final. Now happiness above all else appears to 1097 B be absolutely final in this sense, since we always choose it for its own sake and never as a means to something else; whereas honour, pleasure, intelligence, and excellence in its various forms, we choose indeed for their own sakes (since we should be glad to have each of them although no extraneous advantage resulted from it), but we also choose them for the sake of happiness, in the belief that they will be a means to our securing it. But no one chooses happiness for the sake of honour, pleasure, etc., nor as a means to anything whatever other than itself.

The same conclusion also appears to follow from a consideration of the self-sufficiency of happiness—for it is felt that the final good must be a thing sufficient in itself. The term self-sufficient, however, we employ with reference not to oneself alone, living a life of isolation, but also to one's parents and children and wife, and one's friends and fellow citizens in general, since man is by nature a social being. On the other hand a limit has to be assumed in these relationships; for if the list be extended to one's ancestors and descendants and to the friends of one's friends, it will go on *ad infinitum*. But this is a point that must be considered later on; we take a self-sufficient thing to mean a thing which merely standing by itself alone renders life desirable and lacking in nothing, and such a thing we deem happiness to be. Moreover, we think happiness the most desirable of all good things without being itself reckoned as one among the rest; for if it were so reckoned, it is clear that we should consider it more desirable when even the smallest of other good things were combined with it, since this addition would result in a larger total of good, and of two goods the greater is always the more desirable.

Happiness, therefore, being found to be something final and self-sufficient, is the End at which all actions aim.

To say however that the Supreme Good is happiness will probably appear a truism; we still require a more explicit account of what constitutes happiness. Perhaps then we may arrive at this by ascertaining what is man's function. For the goodness or efficiency of a flute-player or sculptor or craftsman of any sort, and in general of anybody who has some function or business to perform, is thought to reside in that function; and similarly it may be held that the good of man resides in the function of man, if he has a function.

Are we then to suppose that, while the carpenter and the shoemaker have definite functions or businesses belonging to them, man as such has none, and is not designed by nature to fulfil any function? Must we not rather assume that, just as the eye, the hand, the foot and each of the various members of the body manifestly has a certain function of its own, so a human being also has a certain function over and above all the functions of his particular members? What then precisely can this function be? The mere act of living appears to be shared even by plants, whereas we are looking for the function peculiar to man; we must therefore set aside the vital activity of nutrition and growth. Next in the scale will come some form of sentient life; but this too appears to be shared by horses, oxen, and animals generally. There remains therefore what

1098 A

may be called the practical life of the rational part of man. (This part has two divisions, one rational as obedient to principle, the other as possessing principle and exercising intelligence). Rational life again has two meanings; let us assume that we are here concerned with the active exercise of the rational faculty, since this seems to be the more proper sense of the term. If then the function of man is the active exercise of the soul's faculties in conformity with rational principle, or at all events not in dissociation from rational principle, and if we acknowledge the function of an individual and of a good individual of the same class (for instance, a harper and a good harper, and so generally with all classes) to be generically the same, the qualification of the latter's superiority in excellence being added to the function in his case (I mean that if the function of a harper is to play the harp, that of a good harper is to play the harp well): if this is so, and if we declare that the function of man is a certain form of life, and define that form of life as the exercise of the soul's faculties and activities in association with rational principle, and say that the function of a good man is to perform these activities well and rightly, and if a function is well performed when it is performed in accordance with its own proper excellence—from these premises it follows that the Good of man is the active exercise of his soul's faculties in conformity with excellence or virtue, or if there be several human excellences or virtues, in conformity with the best and most perfect among them. Moreover this activity must occupy a complete lifetime; for one swallow does not make spring, nor does one fine day; and similarly one day or a brief period of happiness does not make a man supremely blessed and happy.

Let this account then serve to describe the Good in outline—for no doubt the proper procedure is to begin by making a rough sketch, and to fill it in afterwards. If a work has been well laid down in outline, to carry it on and complete it in detail may be supposed to be within the capacity of anybody; and in this working out of details Time seems to be a good inventor or at all events coadjutor. This indeed is how advances in the arts have actually come about, since anyone can fill in the gaps. Also the warning given above must not be forgotten; we must not look for equal exactness in all departments of study, but only such as belongs to the subject matter of each, and in such a degree as is appropriate to the particular line of enquiry. A carpenter and a geometrician both seek after a right angle, but in different ways; the former is content with that approximation to it which satisfies the purpose of his work; the latter, being a student of truth, looks for its essence or essential attributes. We should therefore proceed in the same manner in other subjects also, and not allow side issues to outweigh the main task in hand.

Nor again must we in all matters alike demand an explanation of
1098 B the reason why things are what they are; in some cases it is enough if
the fact that they are so is satisfactorily established. This is the case with
first principles; and the fact is the primary thing—it *is* a first principle.
And principles are studied—some by induction, others by perception,
others by some form of habituation, and also others otherwise; so we
must endeavour to arrive at the principles of each kind in their natural
manner, and must also be careful to define them correctly, since they
are of great importance for the subsequent course of the enquiry. The
beginning is admittedly more than half of the whole, and throws light
at once on many of the questions under investigation.

Chapter VIII

Accordingly we must examine our first principle not only as a logical
conclusion deduced from certain premises but also in the light of the
current opinions on the subject. For if a proposition be true, all the facts
harmonize with it, but if it is false, it is soon found to be discordant
with them.

Now things good have been divided into three classes, external goods
on the one hand, and goods of the soul and of the body on the other;
and of these three kinds of goods, those of the soul we commonly pronounce good in the fullest sense and the highest degree. But it is our
actions and the soul's active exercise of its functions that we posit (as
being Happiness); hence so far as this opinion goes—and it is of long
standing, and generally accepted by students of philosophy—it supports
the correctness of our definition of Happiness.

It also shows it to be right merely in declaring the End to consist in
actions or activities of some sort, for thus the End is included among
goods of the soul, and not among external goods.

Again, our definition accords with the description of the happy man
as one who 'lives well' or 'does well'; for it has virtually identified happiness with a form of good life or doing well.

And moreover all the various characteristics that are looked for in
happiness are found to belong to the Good as we define it. Some people
think happiness is goodness or virtue, others prudence, others a form
of wisdom; others again say it is all of these things, or one of them, in
combination with pleasure, or accompanied by pleasure as an indispensable adjunct; another school include external prosperity as a concomitant factor. Some of these views have been held by many people
and from ancient times, others by a few distinguished men, and neither
class is likely to be altogether mistaken; the probability is that their beliefs are at least partly, or indeed mainly, correct.

Now with those who pronounce happiness to be virtue, or some particular virtue, our definition is in agreement; for 'activity in conformity with virtue' involves virtue. But no doubt it makes a great difference whether we conceive the Supreme Good to depend on possessing virtue or on displaying it—on disposition, or on the manifestation of a disposition in action. For a man may possess the disposition without its 1099 A producing any good result, as for instance when he is asleep, or has ceased to function from some other cause; but virtue in active exercise cannot be inoperative—it will of necessity act, and act well. And just as at the Olympic games the wreaths of victory are not bestowed upon the handsomest and strongest persons present, but on men who enter for the competitions—since it is among these that the winners are found—so it is those who act rightly who carry off the prizes and good things of life.

And further, the life of active virtue is essentially pleasant. For the feeling of pleasure is an experience of the soul, and a thing gives a man pleasure in regard to which he is described as 'fond of' so-and-so: for instance a horse gives pleasure to one fond of horses, a play to one fond of the theatre, and similarly just actions are pleasant to the lover of justice, and acts conforming with virtue generally to the lover of virtue. But whereas the mass of mankind take pleasure in things that conflict with one another, because they are not pleasant of their own nature, things pleasant by nature are pleasant to lovers of what is noble, and so always are actions in conformity with virtue, so that they are pleasant essentially as well as pleasant to lovers of the noble. Therefore their life has no need of pleasure as a sort of ornamental appendage, but contains its pleasure in itself. For there is the further consideration that the man who does not enjoy doing noble actions is not a good man at all: no one would call a man just if he did not like acting justly, nor liberal if he did not like doing liberal things, and similarly with the other virtues. But if so, actions in conformity with virtue must be essentially pleasant.

But they are also of course both good and noble, and each in the highest degree, if the good man judges them rightly; and his judgement is as we have said. It follows therefore that happiness is at once the best, the noblest, and the pleasantest of things: these qualities are not separated as the inscription at Delos makes out—

> Justice is noblest, and health is best,
> But the heart's desire is the pleasantest—

for the best activities possess them all; and it is the best activities, or one activity which is the best of all, in which according to our definition happiness consists.

Nevertheless it is manifest that happiness also requires external goods in addition, as we said; for it is impossible, or at least not easy, to play a noble part unless furnished with the necessary equipment. For many 1099 B noble actions require instruments for their performance, in the shape of friends or wealth or political power; also there are certain external advantages, the lack of which sullies supreme felicity, such as good birth, satisfactory children, and personal beauty: a man of very ugly appearance or low birth, or childless and alone in the world, is not our idea of a happy man, and still less so perhaps is one who has children or friends that are worthless, or who has had good ones but lost them by death. As we said before, happiness does seem to require the addition of external prosperity, and this is why some people identify it with good fortune (though some identify it with virtue). . . .

Book II

Chapter I

(1103 A)   VIRTUE being, as we have seen, of two kinds, intellectual and moral, intellectual virtue is for the most part both produced and increased by instruction, and therefore requires experience and time; whereas moral or ethical virtue is the product of habit (*ethos*), and has indeed derived its name, with a slight variation of form, from that word. And therefore it is clear that none of the moral virtues is engendered in us by nature, for no natural property can be altered by habit. For instance, it is the nature of a stone to move downwards, and it cannot be trained to move upwards, even though you should try to train it to do so by throwing it up into the air ten thousand times; nor can fire be trained to move downwards, nor can anything else that naturally behaves in one way be trained into a habit of behaving in another way. The virtues therefore are engendered in us neither by nature nor yet in violation of nature; nature gives us the capacity to receive them, and this capacity is brought to maturity by habit.

Moreover, the faculties given us by nature are bestowed on us first in a potential form; we exhibit their actual exercise afterwards. This is clearly so with our senses: we did not acquire the faculty of sight or hearing by repeatedly seeing or repeatedly listening, but the other way about—because we had the senses we began to use them, we did not get them by using them. The virtues on the other hand we acquire by first having actually practised them, just as we do the arts. We learn an art or craft by doing the things that we shall have to do when we have learnt it: for instance, men become builders by building houses, harpers 1103 B by playing on the harp. Similarly we become just by doing just acts, temperate by doing temperate acts, brave by doing brave acts. This truth is attested by the experience of states: lawgivers make the citizens good by training them in habits of right action—this is the aim of all legislation, and if it fails to do this it is a failure; this is what distinguishes a good form of constitution from a bad one. Again, the actions from or through which any virtue is produced are the same as those through which it also is destroyed—just as is the case with skill in the arts, for both the good harpers and the bad ones are produced by harping, and similarly with builders and all the other craftsmen: as you will become a good builder from building well, so you will become a bad one from building badly. Were this not so, there would be no need for teachers of the arts, but everybody would be born a good or bad craftsman as the case might be. The same then is true of the virtues. It is by taking part in transactions with our fellow-men that some of us become just and others unjust; by acting in dangerous situations and forming a habit of fear or of confidence we become courageous or cowardly. And the same holds good of our dispositions with regard to the appetites, and anger; some men become temperate and gentle, other profligate and irascible, by actually comporting themselves in one way or the other in relation to those passions. In a word, our moral dispositions are formed as a result of the corresponding activities. Hence it is incumbent on us to control the character of our activities, since on the quality of these depends the quality of our dispositions. It is therefore not of small moment whether we are trained from childhood in one set of habits or another; on the contrary it is of very great, or rather of supreme, importance.

Chapter II

As then our present study, unlike the other branches of philosophy, has a practical aim (for we are not investigating the nature of virtue for the sake of knowing what it is, but in order that we may become good, without which result our investigation would be of no use), we have consequently to carry our enquiry into the region of conduct, and to ask how we are to act rightly; since our actions, as we have said, determine the quality of our dispositions.

Now the formula 'to act in conformity with right principle' is common ground, and may be assumed as the basis of our discussion. (We shall speak about this formula later, and consider both the definition of right principle and its relation to the other virtues.)

But let it be granted to begin with that the whole theory of conduct 1104 A is bound to be an outline only and not an exact system, in accordance with the rule we laid down at the beginning, that philosophical theories must only be required to correspond to their subject matter; and matters of conduct and expediency have nothing fixed or invariable about them, any more than have matters of health. And if this is true of the general theory of ethics, still less is exact precision possible in dealing with particular cases of conduct; for these come under no science or professional tradition, but the agents themselves have to consider what is suited to the circumstances on each occasion, just as is the case with the art of medicine or of navigation. But although the discussion now proceeding is thus necessarily inexact, we must do our best to help it out.

First of all then we have to observe, that moral qualities are so constituted as to be destroyed by excess and by deficiency—as we see is the case with bodily strength and health (for one is forced to explain what is invisible by means of visible illustrations). Strength is destroyed both by excessive and by deficient exercises, and similarly health is destroyed both by too much and by too little food and drink; while they are produced, increased and preserved by suitable quantities. The same therefore is true of Temperance, Courage, and the other virtues. The man who runs away from everything in fear and never endures anything becomes a coward; the man who fears nothing whatsoever but encounters everything becomes rash. Similarly he that indulges in every pleasure and refrains from none turns out a profligate, and he that shuns all pleasure, as boorish persons do, becomes what may be called insensible. Thus Temperance and Courage are destroyed by excess and deficiency, and preserved by the observance of the mean.

But not only are the virtues both generated and fostered on the one hand, and destroyed on the other, from and by the same actions, but they will also find their full exercise in the same actions. This is clearly the case with the other more visible qualities, such as bodily strength: for strength is produced by taking much food and undergoing much exertion, while also it is the strong man who will be able to eat most food and endure most exertion. The same holds good with the virtues. We become temperate by abstaining from pleasures, and at the same time we are best able to abstain from pleasures when we have become 1104 B temperate. And so with Courage: we become brave by training ourselves to despise and endure terrors, and we shall be best able to endure terrors when we have become brave.

Chapter III

An index of our dispositions is afforded by the pleasure or pain that accompanies our actions. A man is temperate if he abstains from bodily pleasures and finds this abstinence itself enjoyable, profligate if he feels it irksome; he is brave if he faces danger with pleasure or at all events without pain, cowardly if he does so with pain.

In fact pleasures and pains are the things with which moral virtue is concerned.

For (1) pleasure causes us to do base actions and pain causes us to abstain from doing noble actions. Hence the importance, as Plato points out, of having been definitely trained from childhood to like and dislike the proper things; this is what good education means.

(2) Again, if the virtues have to do with actions and feelings, and every feeling and every action is attended with pleasure or pain, this too shows that virtue has to do with pleasure and pain.

(3) Another indication is the fact that pain is the medium of punishment; for punishment is a sort of medicine, and it is the nature of medicine to work by means of opposites.

(4) Again, as we said before, every formed disposition of the soul realizes its full nature in relation to and in dealing with that class of objects by which it is its nature to be corrupted or improved. But men are corrupted through pleasures and pains, that is, either by pursuing and avoiding the wrong pleasures and pains, or by pursuing and avoiding them at the wrong time, or in the wrong manner, or in one of the other wrong ways under which errors of conduct can be logically classified. This is why some thinkers define the virtues as states of impassivity or tranquillity, though they make a mistake in using these terms absolutely, without adding 'in the right (or wrong) manner' and 'at the right (or wrong) time' and the other qualifications.

We assume therefore that moral virtue is the quality of acting in the best way in relation to pleasures and pains, but that vice is the opposite.

But the following considerations also will give us further light on the same point.

(5) There are three things that are the motives of choice and three that are the motives of avoidance; namely, the noble, the expedient, and the pleasant, and their opposites, the base, the harmful, and the painful. Now in respect of all these the good man is likely to go right and the bad to go wrong, but especially in respect of pleasure; for pleasure is common to man with the lower animals, and also it is a concomitant of all the objects of choice, since both the noble and the expedient appear to us pleasant. 1105 A

(6) Again, the susceptibility to pleasure has grown up with all of us from the cradle. Hence this feeling is hard to eradicate, being engrained in the fabric of our lives.

(7) Again, pleasure and pain are also the standards by which we all, in a greater or less degree, regulate our actions. On this account therefore pleasure and pain are necessarily our main concern, since to feel pleasure and pain rightly or wrongly has a great effect on conduct.

(8) And again, it is harder to fight against pleasure than against anger (hard as that is, as Heracleitus says); but virtue, like art, is con-

stantly dealing with what is harder, since the harder the task the better is success. For this reason also therefore pleasure and pain are necessarily the main concern both of virtue and of political science, since he who comports himself towards them rightly will be good, and he who does so wrongly, bad.

We may then take it as established that virtue has to do with pleasures and pains, that the actions which produce it are those which increase it, and also, if differently performed, destroy it, and that the actions from which it was produced are also those in which it is exercised.

Chapter IV

A difficulty may however be raised as to what we mean by saying that in order to become just men must do just actions, and in order to become temperate they must do temperate actions. For if they do just and temperate actions, they are just and temperate already, just as, if they spell correctly or play in tune, they are scholars or musicians.

But perhaps this is not the case even with the arts. It is possible to spell a word correctly by chance, or because some one else prompts you; hence you will be a scholar only if you spell correctly in the scholar's way, that is, in virtue of the scholarly knowledge which you yourself possess.

Moreover the case of the arts is not really analogous to that of the virtues. Works of art have their merit in themselves, so that it is enough if they are produced having a certain quality of their own; but acts done in conformity with the virtues are not done justly or temperately if they themselves are of a certain sort, but only if the agent also is in a certain state of mind when he does them: first he must act with knowledge; secondly he must deliberately choose the act, and choose it for its own sake; and thirdly the act must spring from a fixed and permanent disposition of character. For the possession of an art, none of these conditions is included, except the mere qualification of knowledge; but for the possession of the virtues, knowledge is of little or no avail, whereas the other conditions, so far from being of little moment, are all-important, inasmuch as virtue results from the repeated performance of just and temperate actions. Thus although actions are entitled just and temperate when they are such acts as just and temperate men would do, the agent is just and temperate not when he does these acts merely, but when he does them in the way in which just and temperate men do them. It is correct therefore to say that a man becomes just by doing just actions and temperate by doing temperate actions; and no one can

1105 B

have the remotest chance of becoming good without doing them. But the mass of mankind, instead of doing virtuous acts, have recourse to discussing virtue, and fancy that they are pursuing philosophy and that this will make them good men. In so doing they act like invalids who listen carefully to what the doctor says, but entirely neglect to carry out his prescriptions. That sort of philosophy will no more lead to a healthy state of soul than will the mode of treatment produce health of body.

Chapter V

We have next to consider the formal definition of virtue.

A state of the soul is either (1) an emotion, (2) a capacity, or (3) a disposition; virtue therefore must be one of these three things. By the emotions, I mean desire, anger, fear, confidence, envy, joy, friendship, hatred, longing, jealousy, pity; and generally those states of consciousness which are accompanied by pleasure or pain. The capacities are the faculties in virtue of which we can be said to be liable to the emotions, for example, capable of feeling anger or pain or pity. The dispositions are the formed state of character in virtue of which we are well or ill disposed in respect of the emotions; for instance, we have a bad disposition in regard to anger if we are disposed to get angry too violently or not violently enough, a good disposition if we habitually feel a moderate amount of anger; and similarly in respect of the other emotions.

Now the virtues and vices are not emotions because we are not pronounced good or bad according to our emotions, but we are according to our virtues and vices; nor are we either praised or blamed for our emotions—a man is not praised for being frightened or angry, nor is he blamed for being angry merely, but for being angry in a certain way—but we are praised or blamed for our virtues and vices. Again, we are not angry or afraid from choice, but the virtues are certain modes of choice, or at all events involve choice. Moreover, we are said to be 'moved' by the emotions, whereas in respect of the virtues and vices we are not said to be 'moved' but to be 'disposed' in a certain way.

And the same considerations also prove that the virtues and vices are not capacities; since we are not pronounced good or bad, praised or blamed, merely by reason of our capacity for emotion. Again, we possess certain capacities by nature, but we are not born good or bad by nature: of this however we spoke before.

If then the virtues are neither emotions nor capacities, it remains that they are dispositions.

Thus we have stated what virtue is generically.

1106 A

Chapter VI

But it is not enough merely to define virtue generically as a disposition; we must also say what species of disposition it is. It must then be premised that all excellence has a twofold effect on the thing to which it belongs: it not only renders the thing itself good, but it also causes it to perform its function well. For example, the effect of excellence in the eye is that the eye is good *and* functions well; since having good eyes means having good sight. Similarly excellence in a horse makes it a good horse, and also good at galloping, at carrying its rider, and at facing the enemy. If therefore this is true of all things, excellence or virtue in a man will be the disposition which renders him a good man and also which will cause him to perform his function well. We have already indicated what this means; but it will throw more light on the subject if we consider what constitutes the specific nature of virtue.

Now of everything that is continuous and divisible, it is possible to take the larger part, or the smaller part, or an equal part, and these parts may be larger, smaller, and equal either with respect to the thing itself or relatively to us; the equal part being a mean between excess and deficiency. By the mean of the thing I denote a point equally distant from either extreme, which is one and the same for everybody; by the mean relative to us, that amount which is neither too much nor too little, and this is not one and the same for everybody. For example, let 10 be 1106 B many and 2 few; then one takes the mean with respect to the thing if one takes 6; since $6 - 2 = 10 - 6$, and this is the mean according to arithmetical proportion. But we cannot arrive by this method at the mean relative to us. Suppose that 10 lb. of food is a large ration for anybody and 2 lb. a small one: it does not follow that a trainer will prescribe 6 lb., for perhaps even this will be a large ration, or a small one, for the particular athlete who is to receive it; it is a small ration for a Milo, but a large one for a man just beginning to go in for athletics. And similarly with the amount of running or wrestling exercise to be taken. In the same way then an expert in any art avoids excess and deficiency, and seeks and adopts the mean—the mean, that is, not of the thing but relative to us. If therefore the way in which every art or science performs its work well is by looking to the mean and applying that as a standard to its productions (hence the common remark about a perfect work of art, that you could not take from it nor add to it— meaning that excess and deficiency destroy perfection, while adherence to the mean preserves it)—if then, as we say, good craftsmen look to the mean as they work, and if virtue, like nature, is more accurate and better than any form of art, it will follow that virtue has the quality of hitting the mean. I refer to moral virtue, for this is concerned with emotions and actions, in which one can have excess or deficiency or a due mean. For example, one can be frightened or bold, feel desire or anger or pity, and experience pleasure and pain in general, either too much or too little, and in both cases wrongly; whereas to feel these feelings at the right time, on the right occasion, towards the right people, for the right purpose and in the right manner, is to feel the best amount of them, which is the mean amount—and the best amount is of course the mark of virtue. And similarly there can be excess, deficiency, and the due mean in actions. Now feelings and actions are the objects with which virtue is concerned; and in feelings and actions excess and deficiency are errors, while the mean amount is praised, and constitutes success; and to be praised and to be successful are both marks of virtue. Virtue, therefore, is a mean state in the sense that it is able to hit the mean. Again, error is multiform (for evil is a form of the unlimited, as in the old Pythagorean imagery, and good of the limited), whereas success is possible in one way only (which is why it is easy to fail and difficult to succeed—easy to miss the target and difficult to hit it); so this is another reason why excess and deficiency are a mark of vice, and observance of the mean a mark of virtue:

Goodness is simple, badness manifold.

Virtue then is a settled disposition of the mind determining the choice of actions and emotions, consisting essentially in the observance of the mean relative to us, this being determined by principle, that is, as the prudent man would determine it.   1107 A

And it is a mean state between two vices, one of excess and one of defect. Furthermore, it is a mean state in that whereas the vices either fall short of or exceed what is right in feelings and in actions, virtue ascertains and adopts the mean. Hence while in respect of its substance and the definition that states what it really is in essence virtue is the observance of the mean, in point of excellence and rightness it is an extreme.

Not every action or emotion however admits of the observance of a due mean. Indeed the very names of some directly imply evil, for instance malice, shamelessness, envy, and, of actions, adultery, theft, murder. All these and similar actions and feelings are blamed as being bad in themselves; it is not the excess or deficiency of them that we blame. It is impossible therefore ever to go right in regard to them—one must always be wrong; nor does right or wrong in their case depend on the circumstances, for instance, whether one commits adultery with the right woman, at the right time, and in the right manner; the mere commission of any of them is wrong. One might as well suppose there could be a due mean and excess and deficiency in acts of injustice or cowardice or profligacy, which would imply that one could have a medium amount of excess and of deficiency, an excessive amount of excess and a deficient amount of deficiency. But just as there can be no excess or deficiency in temperance and justice, because the mean is in a sense an extreme, so there can be no observance of the mean nor excess nor deficiency in the corresponding vicious acts mentioned above, but however they are committed, they are wrong; since, to put it in general terms, there is no such thing as observing a mean in excess or deficiency, nor as exceeding or falling short in the observance of a mean.

Chapter VII

We must not however rest content with stating this general definition, but must show that it applies to the particular virtues. In practical philosophy, although universal principles have a wider application, those covering a particular part of the field possess a higher degree of truth; because conduct deals with particular facts, and our theories are bound to accord with these.

Let us then take the particular virtues from the diagram.

1107 B   The observance of the mean in fear and confidence is Courage. The man that exceeds in fearlessness is not designated by any special name (and this is the case with many of the virtues and vices); he that exceeds in confidence is Rash; he that exceeds in fear and is deficient in confidence is Cowardly. In respect of pleasures and pains—not all of them, and to a less degree in respect of pains—the observance of the mean is Temperance, the excess Profligacy. Men deficient in the enjoyment of pleasures scarcely occur, and hence this character also has not been assigned a name, but we may call it Insensible. In regard to giving and getting money, the observance of the mean is Liberality; the excess and deficiency are Prodigality and Meanness, but the prodigal man and the mean man exceed and fall short in opposite ways to one another: the prodigal exceeds in giving and is deficient in getting, whereas the mean man exceeds in getting and is deficient in giving. For the present then we describe these qualities in outline and summarily, which is enough for the purpose in hand; but they will be more accurately defined later.

There are also other dispositions in relation to money, namely, the mode of observing the mean called Magnificence (the magnificent man being different from the liberal, as the former deals with large amounts and the latter with small ones), the excess called Tastelessness or Vulgarity, and the defect called Paltriness. These are not the same as Liberality and the vices corresponding to it; but the way in which they differ will be discussed later.

In respect of honour and dishonour, the observance of the mean is

Greatness of Soul, the excess a sort of Vanity, as it may be called, and the deficiency, Smallness of Soul. And just as we said that Liberality is related to Magnificence, differing from it in being concerned with small amounts of money, so there is a certain quality related to Greatness of Soul, which is concerned with great honours, while this quality itself is concerned with small honours; for it is possible to aspire to minor honours in the right way, or more than is right, or less. He who exceeds in these aspirations is called ambitious, he who is deficient, unambitious; but the middle character has no name, and the dispositions of these persons are also unnamed, except that that of the ambitious man is called Ambitiousness. Consequently the extreme characters put in a claim to the middle position, and in fact we ourselves sometimes call the middle person ambitious and sometimes unambitious: we sometimes praise a man for being ambitious, sometimes for being unambitious. 1108 A Why we do so shall be discussed later; for the present let us classify the remaining virtues and vices on the lines which we have laid down.

In respect of anger also we have excess, deficiency, and the observance of the mean. These states are virtually without names, but as we call a person of the middle character gentle, let us name the observance of the mean Gentleness, while of the extremes, he that exceeds may be styled irascible and his vice Irascibility, and he that is deficient, spiritless, and the deficiency Spiritlessness.

There are also three other modes of observing a mean which bear some resemblance to each other, and yet are different; all have to do with intercourse in conversation and action, but they differ in that one is concerned with truthfulness of speech and behaviour, and the other with pleasantness, in its two divisions of pleasantness in social amusement and pleasantness in the general affairs of life. We must then discuss these qualities also, in order the better to discern that in all things the observance of the mean is to be praised, while the extremes are neither right nor praiseworthy, but reprehensible. Most of these qualities also are unnamed, but in these as in the other cases we must attempt to coin names for them ourselves, for the sake of clearness and so that our meaning may be easily followed.

In respect of truth then, the middle character may be called truthful, and the observance of the mean Truthfulness; pretence in the form of exaggeration is Boastfulness, and its possessor a boaster; in the form of understatement, Self-depreciation, and its possessor the self-depreciator.

In respect of pleasantness in social amusement, the middle character is witty and the middle disposition Wittiness; the excess is Buffoonery and its possessor a buffoon; the deficient man may be called boorish, and his disposition Boorishness. In respect of general pleasantness in life, the man who is pleasant in the proper manner is friendly, and the observance of the mean is Friendliness; he that exceeds, if from no interested motive, is obsequious, if for his own advantage, a flatterer; he that is deficient, and unpleasant in all the affairs of life, may be called quarrelsome and surly.

There are also modes of observing a mean in the sphere of and in relation to the emotions. For in these also one man is spoken of as moderate and another as excessive—for example the bashful man whose modesty takes alarm at everything; while he that is deficient in shame, or abashed at nothing whatsoever, is shameless, and the man of middle character modest. For though Modesty is not a virtue, it is praised, and so is the modest man.

1108 B

Again, Righteous Indignation is the observance of a mean between Envy and Malice, and these qualities are concerned with pain and pleasure felt at the fortunes of one's neighbours. The righteously indignant man is pained by undeserved good fortune; the jealous man exceeds him and is pained by all the good fortune of others; while the malicious man so far falls short of being pained that he actually feels pleasure.

These qualities however it will be time to discuss in another place. After them we will treat Justice, distinguishing its two kinds—for it has more than one sense—and showing in what way each is a mode of observing the mean. [And we will deal similarly with the logical virtues.]

Chapter VIII

There are then three dispositions—two vices, one of excess and one of defect, and one virtue which is the observance of the mean; and each of them is in a certain way opposed to both the others. For the extreme states are the opposite both of the middle state and of each other, and the middle state is the opposite of both extremes; since just as the equal is greater in comparison with the less and less in comparison with the greater, so the middle states of character are in excess as compared with the defective states and defective as compared with the excessive states, whether in the case of feelings or of actions. For instance, a brave man appears rash in contrast with a coward and cowardly in contrast with a rash man; similarly a temperate man appears profligate in contrast with a man insensible to pleasure and pain, but insensible in contrast with a profligate; and a liberal man seems prodigal in contrast with a mean man, mean in contrast with one who is prodigal. Hence either extreme character tries to push the middle character towards the other extreme; a coward calls a brave man rash and a rash man calls him a coward, and correspondingly in other cases.

But while all three dispositions are thus opposed to one another, the greatest degree of contrariety exists between the two extremes. For the extremes are farther apart from each other than from the mean, just as great is farther from small and small from great than either from equal. Again some extremes show a certain likeness to the mean—for instance, Rashness resembles Courage, Prodigality Liberality, whereas the extremes display the greatest unlikeness to one another. But it is things farthest apart from each other that logicians define as contraries, so that the farther apart things are the more contrary they are.

And in some cases the defect, in others the excess, is more opposed 1109 A to the mean; for example Cowardice, which is a vice of deficiency, is more opposed to Courage than is Rashness, which is a vice of excess; but Profligacy, or excess of feeling, is more opposed to Temperance than is Insensibility, or lack of feeling. This results from either of two causes. One of these arises from the thing itself; owing to one extreme being nearer to the mean and resembling it more, we count not this but rather the contrary extreme as the opposite of the mean; for example, because Rashness seems to resemble Courage more than Cowardice does, and to be nearer to it, we reckon Cowardice rather than Rashness as the contrary of Courage; for those extremes which are more remote from the mean are thought to be more contrary to it. This then is one cause, arising out of the thing itself. The other cause has its origin in us: those things appear more contrary to the mean to which we are ourselves more inclined by our nature. For example, we are of ourselves more inclined to pleasure, which is why we are prone to Profligacy [more than to Propriety]. We therefore rather call those things the contrary of the mean, into which we are more inclined to lapse; and hence Profligacy, the excess, is more particularly the contrary of Temperance.

Chapter IX

Enough has now been said to show that moral virtue is a mean, and in what sense this is so, namely that it is a mean between two vices, one of excess and the other of defect; and that it is such a mean because it aims at hitting the middle point in feelings and in actions. This is why it is a hard task to be good, for it is hard to find the middle point in anything: for instance, not everybody can find the centre of a circle, but only someone who knows geometry. So also anybody can become angry—that is easy, and so it is to give and spend money; but to be angry with or give money to the right person, and to the right amount, and at the right time, and for the right purpose, and in the right way— this is not within everybody's power and is not easy; so that to do these things properly is rare, praiseworthy, and noble.

Hence the first rule in aiming at the mean is to avoid that extreme which is the more opposed to the mean, as Calypso advises—

Steer the ship clear of yonder spray and surge.

For of the two extremes one is a more serious error than the other. Hence, inasmuch as to hit the mean extremely well is difficult, the second best way to sail, as the saying goes, is to take the least of the evils; and the best way to do this will be the way we enjoin.

The second rule is to notice what are the errors to which we are ourselves most prone (as different men are inclined by nature to different faults)—and we shall discover what these are by observing the pleasure or pain that we experience—; then we must drag ourselves away in the opposite direction, for by steering wide of our besetting error we shall make a middle course. This is the method adopted by carpenters to straighten warped timber.

Thirdly, we must in everything be most of all on our guard against what is pleasant and against pleasure; for when pleasure is on her trial we are not impartial judges. The right course is therefore to feel towards pleasure as the elders of the people felt towards Helen, and to apply their words to her on every occasion; for if we roundly bid her be gone, we shall be less likely to err.

These then, to sum up the matter, are the precautions that will best enable us to hit the mean. But no doubt it is a difficult thing to do, and especially in particular cases: for instance, it is not easy to define in what manner and with what people and on what sort of grounds and how long one ought to be angry; and in fact we sometimes praise men who err on the side of defect in this matter and call them gentle, sometimes those who are quick to anger and style them manly. However, we do not blame one who diverges a little from the right course, whether on the side of the too much or of the too little, but one who diverges more widely, for his error is noticed. Yet to what degree and how seriously a man must err to be blamed is not easy to define on principle. For in fact no object of perception is easy to define; and such questions of degree depend on particular circumstances, and the decision lies with perception.

Thus much then is clear, that it is the middle disposition in each department of conduct that is to be praised, but that one should lean sometimes to the side of excess and sometimes to that of deficiency, since this is the easiest way of hitting the mean and the right course.

XXI

POLITICS

Book I: The Theory of The Household

I. Every state is as we see a sort of partnership, and every partner- 1252 A
ship is formed with a view to some good (since all the actions of all
mankind are done with a view to what they think to be good). It is
therefore evident that, while all partnerships aim at some good, the partnership that is the most supreme of all and includes all the others does
so most of all, and aims at the most supreme of all goods; and this is
the partnership entitled the state, the political association. Those then
who think that the natures of the statesman, the royal ruler, the head
of an estate and the master of a family are the same, are mistaken; they
imagine that the difference between these various forms of authority is
one of greater and smaller numbers, not a difference in kind—that is,
that the ruler over a few people is a master, over more the head of an
estate, over more still a statesman or royal ruler, as if there were no
difference between a large household and a small city; and also as to
the statesman and the royal ruler, they think that one who governs as
sole head is royal, and one who, while the government follows the principles of the science of royalty, takes turns to govern and be governed
is a statesman; but these views are not true. And a proof of what we
assert will appear if we examine the question in accordance with our
regular method of investigation. In every other matter it is necessary to
analyze the composite whole down to its uncompounded elements (for
these are the smallest parts of the whole); so too with the state, by examining the elements of which it is composed we shall better discern in
relation to these different kinds of rulers what is the difference between
them, and whether it is possible to obtain any scientific precision in
regard to the various statements made above.

Reprinted by permission of the publishers and The Loeb Classical Library from Aristotle, *Politics*, translated by H. Rackham, Cambridge, Mass.: Harvard University Press,
1967.

In this subject as in others the best method of investigation is to study things in the process of development from the beginning. The first coupling together of persons then to which necessity gives rise is that between those who are unable to exist without one another, namely the union of female and male for the continuance of the species (and this not of deliberate purpose, but with man as with the other animals and with plants there is a natural instinct to desire to leave behind one another being of the same sort as oneself), and the union of natural ruler and natural subject for the sake of security (for one that can foresee with his mind is naturally ruler and naturally master, and one that can do these things with his body is subject and naturally a slave; so that master and slave have the same interest). Thus the female and the slave are by nature distinct (for nature makes nothing as the cutlers make the Delphic knife, in a niggardly way, but one thing for one purpose; for so each tool will be turned out in the finest perfection, if it serves not many uses but one). Yet among barbarians the female and the slave have the same rank; and the cause of this is that barbarians have no class of natural rulers, but with them the conjugal partnership is a partnership of female slave and male slave. Hence the saying of the poets—

'Tis meet that Greeks should rule barbarians,—

implying that barbarian and slave are the same in nature. From these two partnerships then is first composed the household, and Hesiod was right when he wrote:

First and foremost a house and a wife and an ox for the ploughing—

for the ox serves instead of a servant for the poor. The partnership therefore that comes about in the course of nature for everyday purposes is the 'house,' the persons whom Charondas speaks of as 'meal-tub-fellows' and the Cretan Epimenides as 'manger-fellows.'

On the other hand the primary partnership made up of several households for the satisfaction of not mere daily needs is the village. The village according to the most natural account seems to be a colony from a household, formed of those whom some people speak of as 'fellow-nurslings,' sons and sons' sons. It is owing to this that our cities were at first under royal sway and that foreign races are so still, because they were made up of parts that were under royal rule; for every household is under the royal rule of its eldest member, so that the colonies from the household were so too, because of the kinship of their members. And this is what Homer means:

And each one giveth law
To sons and eke to spouses—

1252 B

for his Cyclopes live in scattered families; and that is the way in which people used to live in early times. Also this explains why all races speak of the gods as ruled by a king, because they themselves too are some of them actually now so ruled and in other cases used to be of old; and as men imagine the gods in human form, so also they suppose their manner of life to be like their own.

The partnership finally composed of several villages is the city-state; it has at last attained the limit of virtually complete self-sufficiency, and thus, while it comes into existence for the sake of life, it exists for the good life. Hence every city-state exists by nature, inasmuch as the first partnerships so exist; for the city-state is the end of the other partnerships, and nature is an end, since that which each thing is when its growth is completed we speak of as being the nature of each thing, for instance of a man, a horse, a household. Again, the object for which a 1253 A thing exists, its end, is its chief good; and self-sufficiency is an end, and a chief good. From these things therefore it is clear that the city-state is a natural growth, and that man is by nature a political animal, and a man that is by nature and not merely by fortune citiless is either low in the scale of humanity or above it (like the 'clanless, lawless, heartless' man reviled by Homer, for he is by nature citiless and also a lover of war) inasmuch as he resembles an isolated piece at draughts. And why man is a political animal in a greater measure than any bee or any gregarious animal is clear. For nature, as we declare, does nothing without purpose; and man alone of the animals possesses speech. The mere voice, it is true, can indicate pain and pleasure, and therefore is possessed by the other animals as well (for their nature has been developed so far as to have sensations of what is painful and pleasant and to signify those sensations to one another), but speech is designed to indicate the advantageous and the harmful, and therefore also the right and the wrong; for it is the special property of man in distinction from the other animals that he alone has perception of good and bad and right and wrong and the other moral qualities, and it is partnership in these things that makes a household and a city-state.

Thus also the city-state is prior in nature to the household and to each of us individually. For the whole must necessarily be prior to the part; since when the whole body is destroyed, foot or hand will not exist except in an equivocal sense, like the sense in which one speaks of a hand sculptured in stone as a hand; because a hand in those circumstances will be a hand spoiled, and all things are defined by their function and capacity, so that when they are no longer such as to perform their function they must not be said to be the same things, but to bear their names in an equivocal sense. It is clear therefore that the state is also prior by nature to the individual; for if each individual when separate is not self-sufficient, he must be related to the whole state as other parts are to their whole, while a man who is incapable of entering into partnership, or who is so self-sufficing that he has no need to do so, is no part of a state, so that he must be either a lower animal or a god.

Therefore the impulse to form a partnership of this kind is present in all men by nature; but the man who first united people in such a partnership was the greatest of benefactors. For as man is the best of the animals when perfected, so he is the worst of all when sundered from law and justice. For unrighteousness is most pernicious when possessed of weapons, and man is born possessing weapons for the use of wisdom and virtue, which it is possible to employ entirely for the opposite ends. Hence when devoid of virtue man is the most unscrupulous and savage of animals, and the worst in regard to sexual indulgence and gluttony. Justice on the other hand is an element of the state; for judicial procedure, which means the decision of what is just, is the regulation of the political partnership.

XXII

PHYSICS

Book II

Chapter I

Some things exist, or come into existence, by nature; and some oth- (192 B)
erwise. Animals and their organs, plants, and the elementary substances—earth, fire, air, water—these and their likes we say exist by
nature. For all these seem distinguishable from those that are not constituted by nature; and the common feature that characterizes them all
seems to be that they have within themselves a principle of movement
(or change) and rest—in some cases local only, in others quantitive, as
in growth and shrinkage, and in others again qualitive, in the way of
modification. But a bedstead or a garment or the like, in the capacity
which is signified by its name and in so far as it is craft-work, has within
itself no such inherent trend towards change, though owing to the fact
of its being composed of earth or stone or some mixture of substances,
it incidentally has within itself the principles of change which inhere
primarily in these materials. For nature is the principle and cause of
motion and rest to those things, and those things only, in which she
inheres primarily, as distinct from incidentally. What I mean by 'as
distinct from incidentally' is like this: If a man were a physician and
prescribed successfully for himself, the patient would cure himself; but
it would not be *qua* patient that he possessed the healing art, though in
this particular case it happened that the physician's personality coin-
cided with that of the patient, which is not always the case. And so it
is with all manufactured or 'made' things: none of them has within itself
the principle of its own making. Generally this principle resides in some

Reprinted by permission of the publishers and The Loeb Classical Library from Aristotle, *Physics*, translated by F. M. Cornford and F. Wicksteed, Cambridge, Mass.: Harvard University Press, 1935.

external agent, as in the case of the house and its builder, and so with all hand-made things. In other cases, such as that of the physician-patient, though the patient does indeed contain in himself the principle of action, yet he does so only incidentally, for it is not *qua* subject acted on that he has in himself the causative principle of the action.

This, then, being what we mean by 'nature,' anything that has in itself such a principle as we have described may be said to 'possess a nature' of its own inherently. And all such things have a substantive existence; for each of them is a substratum or 'subject' presupposed by any other category, and it is only in such substrata that nature ever has her seat.

Further, not only nature itself and all things that 'have a nature,' but also the behaviour of these things in virtue of their inherent characteristics is spoken of as 'natural.' For instance, for fire actually to rise, as distinct from having the tendency to rise, neither *is* nature nor *has* a nature; but it comes about 'by nature' and is 'natural.'

193 A   Such, then, are the definitions of 'nature,' of what exists 'by nature,' and of what is 'natural.' Any attempt to prove that nature, in this sense, is a reality would be childish; for it is patent that many things corresponding to our definitions do actually exist; and to set about proving the obvious from the unobvious betrays confusion of mind as to what is self-evident and what is not. Such confusion, however, is not unknown, though it is like a man born blind arguing about colours, and amounts to reasoning about names without having any corresponding concept in the mind.

Now some hold that the nature and substantive existence of natural products resides in their material on the analogy of the wood of a bedstead or the bronze of a statue. (Antiphon took it as an indication of this that if a man buried a bedstead and the sap in it took force and threw out a shoot it would be tree and not bedstead that came up, since the artificial arrangement of the material by the craftsman is merely an incident that has occurred to it, whereas its essential and natural quality is to be found in that which persists continuously throughout such experiences.) And in like manner, it is thought, if the materials themselves bear to yet other substances the same relation which the manufactured articles bear to them—if, for instance, water is the material of bronze or gold, or earth of bone or timber, and so forth—then it is in the water or earth that we must look for the 'nature' and essential being of the gold and so forth. And this is why some have said that it was earth that constituted the nature of things, some fire, some air, some water, and some several and some all of these elemental substances. For whichever substance or substances each thinker assumed to be primary he regarded as constituting the substantive existence of all things in general, all else being mere modifications, states, and dispositions of them. Any such ultimate substance they regarded as eternal (for they did not admit the transformation of elementary substances into each other), while they held that all else passed into existence and out of it endlessly.

This then is one way of regarding 'nature'—as the ultimately underlying material of all things that have in themselves the principle of movement and change. But from another point of view we may think of the nature of a thing as residing rather in its form, that is to say in the 'kind' of thing it is by definition. For as we give the name of 'art' to a thing which is the product of art and is itself artistic, so we give the name of 'nature' to the products of nature which themselves are 'natural.' And as, in the case of art, we should not allow that what was only potentially a bedstead and had not yet received the form of bed had in it as yet any art-formed element, or could be called 'art,' so in the case of natural products; what is potentially flesh or bone has not yet the 'nature' of flesh until it actually assumes the form indicated by the definition that constitutes it the thing in question, nor is this potential flesh or bone as yet a product of nature. These considerations would lead us to revise our definition of nature as follows: Nature is the distinctive form or quality of such things as have within themselves a principle of motion, such form or characteristic property not being separable from the things themselves, save conceptually. (The *compositum*—a man, for example—which material and form combine to constitute, is not itself a 'nature,' but a thing that comes to be by natural process.) And this view of where to look for the nature of things is preferable to that which finds it in the material; for when we speak of the thing into the nature of which we are inquiring, we mean by its name an actuality not a potentiality merely.

Again men propagate men, but bedsteads do not propagate bedsteads; and that is why they say that the natural factor in a bedstead is not its shape but the wood—to wit, because wood and not bedstead would come up if it germinated. If, then, it is this incapacity of reproduction that makes a thing art and not nature, then the form of natural things will be their nature, as in the parallel case of art; for man is generated by man, whereas a bedstead is not generated from a bedstead.

Again, *na-ture* is etymologically equivalent to *gene-sis* and (in Greek) is actually used as a synonym for it; nature, then, *qua* genesis proclaims itself as the path to nature *qua* goal. Now, it is true that healing is so called, not because it is the path to the healing art, but because it is the path to health, for of necessity healing proceeds from the healing art, not to the healing art itself; but this is not the relation of nature to nature, for that which is born starts as something and advances or grows towards something else. Towards what, then, does it grow? Not towards

193 B

its original state at birth, but towards its final state or goal. It is, then, the form that is nature; but, since 'form' and 'nature' are ambiguous terms, inasmuch as shortage is a kind of form, we shall leave to future investigation whether shortage is, or is not, a sort of contrasted term (opposed to positive form) in absolute generation.

Chapter II

Now that we have determined the different senses in which "nature" may be understood (as signifying either 'material' or 'form'), we have next to consider how the mathematician differs from the physicist or natural philosopher; for natural bodies have surfaces and occupy spaces, have lengths and present points, all which are subjects of mathematical study. And then there is the connected question whether astronomy is a separate science from physics or only a special branch of it; for if the student of Nature is concerned to know what the sun and moon are, it were strange if he could avoid inquiry into their essential properties; especially as we find that writers on Nature have, as a fact, discoursed on the shape of the moon and sun and raised the question whether the earth, or the cosmos, is spherical or otherwise.

Physicists, astronomers, and mathematicians, then, all have to deal with lines, figures and the rest. But the mathematician is not concerned with these concepts *qua* boundaries of natural bodies, nor with their properties as manifested in such bodies. Therefore he abstracts them from physical conditions; for they are capable of being considered in the mind in separation from the motions of the bodies to which they pertain, and such abstraction does not affect the validity of the reasoning or lead to any false conclusions.

Now the exponents of the philosophy of 'Ideas' also make abstractions, but in doing so they fall unawares into error; for they abstract physical entities, which are not really susceptible to the process as math-194 A ematical entities are. And this would become obvious if one should undertake to define, respectively, the mathematical and the 'idea' entities, together with their properties; for the concepts 'odd,' 'even,' 'straight,' 'curved,' will be found to be independent of movement; and so too with 'number,' 'line,' and 'figure.' But of 'flesh' and 'bone' and 'man' this is no longer true, for these are in the same case as a 'turned-up nose,' not in the same case as 'curved.' The point is further illustrated by those sciences which are rather physical than mathematical, though combining both disciplines, such as optics, harmonies, and astronomy; for the relations between them and geometry are, so to speak, reciprocal; since the geometer deals with physical lines, but not *qua* physical, whereas optics deals with mathematical lines, but *qua* physical not *qua* mathematical.

Since 'nature' is used ambiguously, either for the form or for the matter. Nature, as we have seen, can be regarded from two points of view, and therefore our speculations about it may be likened to an inquiry as to what 'snubnosed-ness' is; that is to say, it can neither be isolated from the material subject in which it exists, nor is it constituted by it.

At this point, in fact, we may again raise two questions. Which of the two aspects of Nature is it that claims the attention of the physicist? Or is his subject the *compositum* that combines the two? In that case—if he is concerned with the *compositum*—he must also inquire into its two factors; and then we must ask further whether this inquiry is the same for both factors or different for each.

In reading the ancients one might well suppose that the physicist's only concern was with the material; for Empedocles and Democritus have remarkably little to say about kinds of things and what is the constituent essence of whom. But if art imitates Nature, and if in the arts and crafts it pertains to the same branch of knowledge both to study its own distinctive aspect of things and likewise (up to a point) the material in which the same is manifested (as the physician, for instance, must study health and also bile and phlegm, the state of which constitutes health; and the builder must know what the house is to be like and also that it is built of bricks and timber; and so in all other cases), it seems to follow that physics must take cognisance both of the formal and of the material aspect of Nature.

And further the same inquiry must embrace both the purpose or end and the means to that end. And the 'nature' is the goal for the sake of which the rest exist; for if any systematic and continuous movement is directed to a goal, this goal is an end in the sense of the purpose to which the movement is a means. (A confusion on this point betrayed the poet into the unintentionally comic phrase in reference to a man's death: 'He has reached his end, for the sake of which he was born.' For the 'goal' does not mean any kind of termination, but only the best.) For in the arts, too, it is in view of the end that the materials are either made or suitably prepared, and we make use of all the things that we have at our command as though they existed for our sake; for we too are, in some sort, a goal ourselves. For the expression 'that for the sake of which' a thing exists or is done has two senses (as we have explained in our treatise On Philosophy). Accordingly, the arts which control the material and possess the necessary knowledge are two: the art which uses the product and the art of the master-craftsman who directs the manufacture. Hence the art of the user also may in a sense be called

194 B

the master-art; the difference is that this art is concerned with knowing the form, the other, which is supreme as controlling the manufacture, with knowing the material. Thus, the helmsman knows what are the distinctive characteristics of the helm as such—that is to say, its form— and gives his orders accordingly; while what the other knows is out of what wood and by what manipulations the helm is produced. In the crafts, then, it is we that prepare the material for the sake of the function it is to fulfil, but in natural products Nature herself has provided the material. In both cases, however, the preparation of the material is commanded by the end to which it is directed.

And again, the conception of 'material' is relative, for it is different material that is suited to receive the several forms.

How far then, is the physicist concerned with the form and identifying essence of things and how far with their material? With the form primarily and essentially, as the physician is with health; with the material up to a certain point, as the physician is with sinew and the smith with bronze. For his main concern is with the goal, which is formal; but he deals only with such forms as are conceptually, but not factually, detachable from the material in which they occur. In Nature man generates man; but the process presupposes and takes place in natural material already organized by the solar heat and so forth. But how we are to take the sejunct and what it is, is a question for First Philosophy to determine.

Chapter III

We have next to consider in how many senses 'because' may answer the question 'why.' For we aim at understanding, and since we never reckon that we understand a thing till we can give an account of its 'how and why,' it is clear that we must look into the 'how and why' of things coming into existence and passing out of it, or more generally into the essential constituents of physical change, in order to trace back any object of our study to the principles so ascertained.

Well then, (1) the existence of *material* for the generating process to start from (whether specifically or generically considered) is one of the essential factors we are looking for. Such is the bronze for the statue, or the silver for the phial. (Material *aitia*.) Then, naturally, (2) the thing in question cannot be there unless the material has actually received the *form* or characteristics of the type, conformity to which brings it within the definition of the thing we say it is, whether specifically or generically. Thus the interval between two notes is not an octave unless the notes are in the ratio of 2 to 1; nor do they stand at a musical interval at all unless they conform to one or other of the recognized ratios. (Formal *aitia*.) Then again, (3) there must be something to initiate the process of the change or its cessation when the process is completed, such as the act of a voluntary agent (of the smith, for instance), or the father who begets a child; or more generally the prime, conscious or unconscious, *agent* that produces the effect and starts the material on its way to the product, changing it from what it was to what it is to be. (Efficient *aitia*.) And lastly, (4) there is the *end* or purpose, for the sake of which the process is initiated, as when a man takes exercise for the sake of his health. 'Why does he take exercise?' we ask. And the answer 'Because he thinks it good for his health' satisfies us. (Final *aitia*.) Then there are all the intermediary agents, which are set in motion by the prime agent and make for the goal, as means to the end. Such are the reduction of superfluous flesh and purgation, or drugs and surgical instruments, as means to health. For both actions and tools may be means, or '*media*,' through which the efficient cause reaches the end aimed at.

195 A

This is a rough classification of the causal determinants (*aitiai*) of things; but it often happens that, when we specify them, we find a number of them coalescing as joint factors in the production of a single effect, and that not merely incidentally; for it is *qua* statue that the statue depends for its existence alike on the bronze and on the statuary. The two, however, do not stand on the same footing, for one is required as the material and the other as initiating the change.

Also, it can be said of certain things indifferently that either of them is the cause or the effect of the other. Thus we may say that a man is in fine condition 'because' he has been in training, or that he has been in training 'because' of the good condition he expected as the result. But one is the cause as aim (final *aitia*) and the other as initiating the process (efficient *aitia*).

Again, the same cause is often alleged for precisely opposite effects. For if its presence causes one thing, we lay the opposite to its account if it is absent. Thus, if the pilot's presence would have brought the ship safe to harbour, we say that he caused its wreck by his absence.

But in all cases the essential and causal determinants we have enumerated fall into four main classes. For letters are the causes of syllables, and the material is the cause of manufactured articles, and fire and the like are causes of physical bodies, and the parts are causes of the whole, and the premises are causes of the conclusion, in the sense of that out of which these respectively are made; but of these things some are causes in the sense of the *substratum* (*e.g.* the parts stand in this relation to the whole), others in the sense of the *essence*—the whole or the synthesis or the form. And again, the fertilizing sperm, or the physician, or briefly the voluntary or involuntary *agent* sets going or arrests the transformation or movement. And finally, there is the goal or *end* in view, which animates all the other determinant factors as the best they can attain to; for the attainment of that 'for the sake of which' anything exists or is done is its final and best possible achievement (though of course 'best' in this connexion means no more than 'taken to be the best').

These are the main classes of determinant factors and causes; and, though within these many other distinctions may be drawn, yet they too can be reduced to a manageable number of classes.

Thus, (1) causes belonging to one and the same class may be more or less closely determined by being reduced to subordination to each other. Health may be restored by a 'physician,' or by a 'professional man' (a term which includes physicians). The octave may be described as a case of the ratio 2:1, or less specifically as a 'number'; and generally, an inclusive term may be used instead of a more special one.

And again, (2) an agent may be described not *qua* agent, but as something that characterizes him incidentally; and in this case also the specification may be more or less inclusive. We may say that the statue was made by 'the sculptor,' or that it was made by 'Polycleitus,' in as much as the art resided in the person of Polycleitus and was incidentally associated with all his other irrelevant characteristics. Incidentally, too, the sculptor was a man, or more generally still an animal. And the 'incidental' itself may be more or less remotely related to the essential. Thus the sculptor's being a man of culture or light in complexion is even more incidental and irrelevant to his production of a statue than his being Polycleitus or a man.

(3) Besides all these ways of describing the agent, whether in his agential capacity or by attributes that fall to him incidentally, we may be speaking of his potentialities merely or of the actual exertion of his powers. Thus, we may say that 'the builder' caused the house to be built, meaning the man who knew how to build, but it was only when he was in the act of building that he was really causing the house to be built.

195 B And all this holds just as good for the product as for the producer. The product may be regarded as this particular statue, or as a statue in general, or still more generally as an image; or again the craftsman as working upon this particular piece of bronze, or upon bronze in general, or still more generally upon material. And these distinctions, too, may be crossed by the distinction between 'directly' and 'incidentally.' And again both the incidental and the direct may be united together, if we speak, not of 'Polycleitus,' nor of 'the sculptor,' but of 'Polycleitus the sculptor.'

All these distinctions, however, may be brought under six heads, each of which may be predicated in two different senses. For every determining factor, *qua* determinant, may be designated (1) individually, or (2) as belonging to a class; and (3) incidental coincidences may have a more specific character, or (4) a more general one; and both direct and indirect agency or passion may be indicated (5) separately or (6) in combination. And finally in every case it may be either (*a*) a potentiality that is indicated, or (*b*) an actual energizing. But they differ to this extent, that the actual energizing agent, being an individual, exists as energizing, or ceases to do so, according as that which is experiencing its energy ceases or continues so to experience it (for instance, a particular physician ceases from the actual exercise of his art at the same moment as the particular patient ceases from being actually in the process of restoration to health; and a particular builder ceases from actual building at the same moment as the house ceases from being actually in course of erection); but in the case of potentiality it is not always so, for the potential builder and the house need not perish at the same time.

And in every case we must try to determine the point at which the causality is focused, both here and elsewhere. Thus a man builds *qua* builder, and a builder builds *qua* expert in the building art; so it is in the application of the building art to the material that the building art is focused. And so with all the rest.

Again, the general is related to the general, and the individual to the individual: a statue is produced by a sculptor, but this individual statue by such and such an individual sculptor. And the relation of the potential to the potential and of the actualized to the actualized is analogous.

Let this suffice for the definition of the different classes of determinants and the ways in which they are severally related to the result.

Chapter IV

We often allege fortune, or luck, and accident as causes, saying that something came about 'as fortune or luck would have it' or 'accidentally.' What then is the place of fortune and accident amongst the causes we have reviewed? Is there any distinction between them? And, in a word, what are they?

For some question their existence, declaring that nothing happens casually, but that everything we speak of in that way has really a definite cause. For instance, if a man comes to market and there chances on someone he has been wishing to meet but was not expecting to meet there, the reason of his meeting him was that he wanted to go marketing; and so too in all other cases when we allege chance as the cause, there is always some other cause to be found, and it is never really chance. And indeed it might be urged that, if there really were such a thing as luck, it would present a genuine problem, and the question might be raised, why none of the earlier philosophers should have had anything to say about it when discussing causes in relation to genesis

196 A

and perishing, so as apparently to think that nothing comes about by chance.

Maybe. But is it not equally strange that, however freely men admit that every kind of luck and everything that 'happens accidentally' can really be assigned to some definite cause, still, while accepting this venerable argument for the elimination of chance from their thoughts, they nevertheless invariably distinguish, in fact, between things that do, and the things that do not, depend upon chance or luck? So in any case the philosophers should have given some account of what are called chance happenings. If they gave none, it was not because they identified chance with any one of the causes they recognized—Love or Strife, Mind, or Fire or some other element. But surely, whether they believed or disbelieved in chance, they were bound in reason to take some note of it; especially as, on occasion, they actually had recourse to it, as when Empedocles says that air is sifted out upwards not uniformly but as it happens—for he says of it, in his *Cosmogony,*

Thus did it chance to hit one while, but other whiles not thus—

and he says that the members of animals, for the most part, came out haphazard.

Some indeed attribute our Heaven and all the worlds to chance happenings, saying that the vortex and shifting that disentangled the chaos and established the cosmic order came by chance. This is surely most amazing—for these people actually to say that, whereas neither animals nor plants are, or come to be, by chance, but are all caused by Nature or Mind or what else (for it is not a matter of chance what springs from a given sperm, since an olive comes from such an one, and a man from such another), yet the heaven and the divinest things that our sight reveals come anyhow and have no such causes as animals and plants have. But if this really were so, that very fact ought to give us pause and 196 B convince us that the matter needs investigation. For, in addition to the inherently paradoxical nature of such an assertion, we may note that it is exactly in the movements of the heavenly bodies that we never observe what we call casual or accidental variations, whereas in all that these people tell us is exempt from chance such things are common. Of course it ought to be just the other way.

Some, moreover, hold that fortune is a genuine cause of things, but one that has a something divine and mysterious about it, that makes it inscrutable to the human intelligence.

So we must obviously investigate the whole matter, and must see whether the phrases in question can be classified or distinguished from each other, and how they fall in with the causes and determinants we have defined.

Chapter V

To begin with, then, we note that some things follow upon others uniformly or generally, and it is evidently not such things that we attribute to chance or luck. Necessary or customary successions, therefore, are excluded from our present inquiry. On the other hand irregular and exceptional consequences do occasionally occur, and since it is precisely to this class of actual happenings that we ourselves apply such terms as 'luck' or 'lucky' and of this class that we think when anyone else uses these terms, it follows that what we call luck or chance corresponds to some reality and is not a mere fiction.

Or taking it from another side: some things make for a purpose and some not; and of the 'ends' actually achieved some are those we aimed at, but some are not. In this latter case our actions were as a fact making for the uncontemplated result just as much as if it had been intended; so that an action may actually 'serve a purpose' which does not necessarily or normally follow upon it, and which it was not intended to serve. In this sense any action may be regarded as purpose-serving if it leads to a result that *might have been* voluntarily sought, or to a result which stands in the corresponding relation to the movements of Nature. Now when such results accrue incidentally, we say that they come 'by chance.' 'Incidentally,' I say; for as a thing takes its name, and is what it is, in virtue of certain essential attributes, but incidentally has other attributes, not essential to it as that thing, so too it may be with causes. Thus the essential efficient cause of a house being built is the application of the builder-craft to the task by a builder; but if the man in whom that builder-craft is embodied is a pale-complexioned or cultivated person, then these characteristics are incidentally part and parcel with the direct cause of the building. Thus direct causation is determinate and calculable, but incidental causation indeterminate; for one and the same person or thing may have an indefinite number of incidental qualifications.

As we said, then, what we mean by luck or chance (for at present we are attempting no distinction between different terms within this general purport) is the incidental production of some significant result by a cause that took its place in the causal chain incidentally, and without the result in question being contemplated. I call actions purpose-serving, and speak of them as accomplishing 'ends,' when the result is such as *would have been* recognized as a purpose and *would have* determined the action, had it been anticipated. Thus the man who came to the market-place for some other reason would have come there on purpose to recover his debt if he had known that he would there meet his debtor in the act of receiving the sum subscribed by his friends; and

though he did not come for that reason, yet his coming there incidentally
made for that end, though directed to another. But we must suppose
that he did not habitually go to the place (frequented occasionally by
197 A his debtor), and still less that he was compelled to go there habitually
on some other business; so that in his case the achieved end of recovering his debt was a result not normally involved in his action, but was
yet of the class of things that may be deliberately determined upon and
purposed. In this case he would in fact be said to have come there 'by
luck'; whereas, if that had been the purpose he contemplated, or if he
always went to market, or if he generally recovered a debt when he did,
we should not say that the result came by luck. Clearly then luck itself,
regarded as a cause, is the name we give to causation which incidentally
inheres in deliberately purposeful action taken with respect to some other
end but leading to the event we call fortunate. And the significant results
of such causes we say 'come by luck.' Thus, since choice implies intention, it follows that luck and intention are concerned with the same field
of objects.

The incidentally causative forces are, in the nature of the case, indefinite as to number. This is why luck appears to have something eva-
sive about it and to be inscrutable by man; and why, on the other hand
(since everything really *has* a definite cause) there is a sense in which it
might seem that nothing at all really goes by luck or chance. For all
these opinions have some justification in the facts; inasmuch as there is
a sense in which things do go by luck, when they come to pass incidentally to some other chain of causation, and 'luck' is the name we give
to causes that act incidentally; but in the absolute sense, without this
qualification, luck is not the cause of anything. For instance, the builder,
as such, is the efficient cause of the house being built, but his skill in
flute-playing is incidental, and therefore might equally well attach itself
to any other man, not a builder. In like manner the man's meeting his
debtor was a by-product incidentally determined by the purpose, whatever it was, that brought him to the market-place; and it would have
attached itself in the same incidental way to any other of the countless
reasons that might have brought him there at that moment, such as the
desire to meet a friend, or legal business as prosecutor or defendant. It
is only if he had come on purpose to meet his debtor that his meeting
him would have followed not incidentally but primarily from his purposeful action. And this is why we are justified in saying that luck cannot
be calculated; for we can calculate only from necessary or normal se-
quences, and luck acts outside such. So the indeterminate nature of these
incidental lines of causation makes luck indeterminate.

But when we have said all this, the question still remains in some
cases how far we are to carry back our search for this incidental causation. If a man has his head shaved for some special treatment, and

afterwards goes out for some reason indifferent to his cure, and the air and sun cure him, is the exposure to air and sun (which is the efficient cause of his cure) incident to his going out? Or must we go further back and say that it is incident to his being shaved, without reference to going out, his going out itself being without reference to the cure? The only answer to such questions is that, here as elsewhere, 'incidence' may be more or less proximate or remote.

We speak of 'good luck' when luck brings us something good, and 'bad luck' in the opposite event, or, in serious cases, of 'good fortune' or 'misfortune'; and accordingly if we just miss some important good thing or just escape a bad one, we call that also bad or good fortune, because by anticipation we regard the good or ill as having been actually present, so close did it seem.

Yet again, we may well say that good fortune is unstable; for so is all luck, inasmuch as nothing that is constant or normal can be attributed to luck.

Both luck and chance, then, as we have said, are causes that come into play incidentally and produce effects that possibly, but not necessarily or generally, follow from the purposeful action to which in this case they are incident, though the action might have been taken directly and primarily for their sake.

Chapter VI

In Greek *tyche* and *automaton* differ in this, that *automaton* is the more general term and includes *tyche* as a special class.

197 B

For (1) *tyche* itself, as a cause, and the results that accrue by the action of *tyche*, are only spoken of in connexion with beings capable of enjoying good fortune, or more generally of 'doing well' or 'doing ill,' in the sense either of 'faring' or of 'acting' so. Therefore *tyche* must always be connected with our doings and farings—a truth indicated by the common belief that good fortune (*tyche*) is the same, or much the same, thing as 'happiness'; and to be 'happy' is to have 'done well' in life; so that 'doing well' or 'ill' by *tyche* is impossible to creatures that have no self-direction. That is why neither inanimate things nor brute beasts nor infants can ever accomplish anything by *tyche*, since they exercise no deliberate choice; nor can such be said to have good or bad *tyche*, except by a figure of speech, as when Protarchus speaks of the 'fortunate' stones that have been built into altars and are treated with reverence, while their fellows are trampled under foot. But even such things may be brought, as passive agents, under the action of *tyche*, if a rational agent does something with them which turns out by *tyche* to affect his well-being; but not otherwise.

(2) *Automaton*, on the other hand, may be used to describe the be-

haviour of brute beasts and even of many inanimate things. For instance, we attribute it to *automaton* if a horse escapes a danger by coming accidentally to a place of safety. Or again, if a tripod chances to fall on its feet for a man to sit down upon, this is due to *automaton*, for though a man would put it on its feet *with a view to* its being a seat, the forces of Nature that controlled its fall had no such aim.

It is clear, then, that when *any* causal agency incidentally produces a significant result outside its aim, we attribute it to *automaton;* and in the special cases where such a result springs from deliberate action (though not aimed at it) on the part of a being capable of choice, we may say that it comes by *tyche*.

(The etymology of *automaton* indicates this; for the expression *maten*—'for nothing,' 'to no purpose'—is used in cases where the end or purpose is not realized, but only the means to it. Walking, for instance, is a means to evacuation; if a man takes a walk and this natural effect does not follow, we say that he took his walk 'for nothing' and the walk was 'to no purpose,' meaning by this phrase what fails to accomplish that purpose to which it is naturally a means. 'Naturally a means,' for it would be ridiculous to say one had taken a bath 'to no purpose' because an eclipse of the sun did not follow: an eclipse is not a natural consequence of taking a bath. So then *automaton*, as the form of the word implies, means an occurrence that is *in itself* (*auto*) *to no purpose* (*maten*). A stone falls and hits someone, but it does not fall for the purpose of hitting him; the fall accordingly was 'in-itself-to-no-purpose'—a chance result—because the fall might have been caused by someone who had the purpose of hitting the man.)

It would be most inappropriate of all to speak of *tyche* in cases where Nature herself produces unnatural monstrosities; and accordingly in these cases we may attribute it to an 'accident' (*automaton*) in Nature, but can hardly say that a piece of bad 'luck' (*tyche*) has come to her. But this case is different from that of the horse; for the horse's escape was due to an external cause, but the causes of Nature's miscarriage are internal to her own processes.

198 A   What *automaton* and *tyche* are, and how they differ, has now been stated; and it follows that both are causes of the 'efficient' order, that set processes in motion; for they are always attached to efficient causes either of the natural or volitional order, such attachments being indefinite in number.

And since the results of *automaton* and *tyche* are always such as might have been aimed at by mind or Nature, though in fact they emerged incidentally, and since there can be nothing incidental unless there is something primary for it to be incidental to, it follows that there can be no incidental causation except as incident to direct causation. Chance and fortune, therefore, imply the antecedent activity of mind and Nature as causes; so that, even if the cause of the heavens were ever so casual, yet mind and Nature must have been causes antecedently, not only of many other things we could mention, but of this universe itself.

Chapter VII

It is clear, then, that there are such things as causes, and that they can be classified under the four heads that have been enumerated. For these are the four ways of apprehending the 'how and why' of things: we may refer it either (1) to the essential nature of the thing in question, in the sphere of unchanging objects (as in mathematics, where the conclusions ultimately depend upon the definitions of straight line, or commensurability, or whatever it may be); or (2) to that which first initiated the movement (as in: 'Why did they go to war? Because the others had raided them') or (3) to the result aimed at (as: 'To gain an empire'); or (4) in the case of anything that comes into existence out of something already there, to the material.

Clearly, then, the 'becauses' being such and so classified, it behoves the natural philosopher to understand all four, and to be able to indicate, in answer to the question 'how and why,' the material, the form, the moving force, and the goal or purpose, so far as they come within the range of Nature. But in many cases three of these 'becauses' coincide; for the essential nature of a thing and the purpose for which it is produced are often identical (so that the final cause coincides with the formal), and moreover the efficient cause must bear some resemblance in 'form' to the effect (so that the efficient cause too must, so far, coincide with the formal); for instance, man is begotten by man. And this applies universally to all things that cause motion and are themselves moved. (Where that is not the case, we are no longer in the domain of Physics at all, since we are dealing, not with things that move other things in virtue of their own motion or because they have the principle of motion in themselves, but with something that moves other things, though itself motionless. So that we have three fields of inquiry, concerned respectively with (1) things motionless, (2) things that, though in motion, are imperishable, and (3) things perishable.) Thus to give an account of the how and why of anything is to trace it to its material, to its essential characteristics, and to its provoking cause; for in investigating the genesis of a thing men are chiefly concerned with the nature of what emerges from the process, with the impulse that initiates the process, and with what was already there to undergo the process, at the start; together with all the successive steps that lie between the starting-point and the end.

But the principles which direct physical movement or change are of two orders, one of which is not itself physical, for it is not in motion, nor has it in itself the principle of motion. Such would be anything that should move other things while itself motionless, as being absolutely unchanging and primary, and such the essential characteristic or form in its capacity of constituting the end and aim to be reached, and therefore, since Nature is purposeful, demanding to be recognized by the natural philosopher. In short, under all four aspects, we must give an account of the how and why, so as to show (1) that from this *efficient* cause this result must follow, or if the cause in question does not absolutely involve a certain definite result, we must show that it will lead to it normally. We must also show (2) that, if such and such a thing is to exist, there must be a *material* substrate, related to it as the premisses to the conclusion, and (3) that the result manifests the *essential nature* aimed at by the process, and (4) why it was *better* thus—not absolutely, but relatively to the being of the thing in question.

Chapter VIII

We must now consider why Nature is to be ranked among causes that are final, that is to say purposeful; and further we must consider what is meant by 'necessity' when we are speaking of Nature. For thinkers are for ever referring things to necessity as a cause, and explaining that, since hot and cold and so forth are what they are, this or that exists or comes into being 'of necessity'; for even if one or another of them alleges some other cause, such as 'Sympathy and Antipathy' or 'Mind,' he straight away drops it again, after a mere acknowledgement.

So here the question rises whether we have any reason to regard Nature as making for any goal at all, or as seeking any one thing as preferable to any other. Why not say, it is asked, that Nature acts as Zeus drops the rain, not to make the corn grow, but of necessity (for the rising vapour must needs be condensed into water by the cold, and descend, and incidentally, when this happens, the corn grows) just as, when a man loses his corn on the threshing-floor, it did not rain on purpose to destroy the crop, but the result was merely incidental to the raining? So why should it not be the same with natural organs like the teeth? Why should it not be a coincidence that the front teeth come up with an edge, suited to dividing the food, and the back ones flat and good for grinding it, without there being any design in the matter? And so with all other organs that seem to embody a purpose. In cases where a coincidence brought about such a combination as might have been arranged on purpose, the creatures, it is urged, having been suitably formed by the operation of chance, survived; otherwise they perished, and still perish, as Empedocles says of his 'man-faced oxen.'

Such and suchlike are the arguments which may be urged in raising this problem; but it is impossible that this should really be the way of it. For all these phenomena and all natural things are either constant or normal, and this is contrary to the very meaning of luck or chance. 199 A No one assigns it to chance or to a remarkable coincidence if there is abundant rain in the winter, though he would if there were in the dog-days; and the other way about, if there were parching heat. Accordingly, if the only choice is to assign these occurrences either to coincidence or to purpose, and if in these cases chance coincidence is out of the question, then it must be purpose. But, as our opponents themselves would admit, these occurrences are all natural. There is purpose, then, in what is, and in what happens, in Nature.

Further, in any operation of human art, where there is an end to be achieved, the earlier and successive stages of the operation are performed for the purpose of realizing that end. Now, when a thing is produced by Nature, the earlier stages in every case lead up to the final development in the same way as in the operation of art, and *vice versa*, provided that no impediment balks the process. The operation is directed by a purpose; we may, therefore, infer that the natural process was guided by a purpose to the end that is realized. Thus, if a house were a natural product, the process would pass through the same stages that it in fact passes through when it is produced by art; and if natural products could also be produced by art, they would move along the same line that the natural process actually takes. We may therefore say that the earlier stages are for the purpose of leading to the later. Indeed, as a general proposition, the arts either, on the basis of Nature, carry things further than Nature can, or they imitate Nature. If, then, artificial processes are purposeful, so are natural processes too; for the relation of antecedent to consequent is identical in art and in Nature.

This principle comes out most clearly when we consider the other animals. For their doings are not the outcome of art (design) or of previous research or deliberation; so that some raise the question whether the works of spiders and ants and so on should be attributed to intelligence or to some similar faculty. And then, descending step by step, we find that plants too produce organs subservient to their perfect development—leaves, for instance, to shelter the fruit. Hence, if it is by nature and also for a purpose that the swallow makes her nest and the spider his web, and that plants make leaves for the sake of the fruit and strike down (and not up) with their roots in order to get their nourishment, it is clear that causality of the kind we have described is at work in things that come about or exist in the course of Nature.

Also, since the term 'nature' is applied both to material and to form, and since it is the latter that constitutes the goal, and all else is for the sake of that goal, it follows that the form is the final cause.

Now there are failures even in the arts (for writers make mistakes in writing and physicians administer the wrong dose): so that analogous 199 B failures in Nature may evidently be anticipated as possible. Thus, if in art there are cases in which the correct procedure serves a purpose, and attempts that fail are aimed at a purpose but miss it, we may take it to be the same in Nature, and monstrosities will be like failures of purpose in Nature. So if, in the primal combinations, such 'ox-creatures' as could not reach an equilibrium and goal, should appear, it would be by the miscarriage of some principle, as monstrous births are actually produced now by abortive developments of sperm. Besides, the sperm must precede the formation of the animal, and Empedocles' 'primal all-generative' is no other than such sperm.

In plants, too, though they are less elaborately articulated, there are manifest indications of purpose. Are we to suppose, then, that as there were 'ox-creatures man-faced' so also there were 'vine-growths olive-bearing'? Incongruous as such a thing seems, it ought to follow if we accept the principle in the case of animals. Moreover, it ought still to be a matter of chance what comes up when you sow this seed or that.

In general, the theory does away with the whole order of Nature, and indeed with Nature's self. For natural things are exactly those which do move continuously, in virtue of a principle inherent in themselves, towards a determined goal; and the final development which results from any one such principle is not identical for any two species, nor yet is it any random result; but in each there is always a tendency towards an identical result, if nothing interferes with the process. A desirable result and the means to it may also be produced by chance, as for instance we say it was 'by luck' that the stranger came and ransomed the prisoner before he left, where the ransoming is done as if the man had come for that purpose, though in fact he did not. In this case the desirable result is incidental; for, as we have explained, chance is an incidental cause. But when the desirable result is effected invariably or normally, it is not an incidental or chance occurrence; and in the course of Nature the result always is achieved either invariably or normally, if nothing hinders. It is absurd to suppose that there is no purpose because in Nature we can never detect the moving power in the act of deliberation. Art, in fact, does not deliberate either, and if the shipbuilding art were incorporate in the timber, it would proceed by nature in the same way in which it now proceeds by art. If purpose, then, is inherent in art, so is it in Nature also. The best illustration is the case of a man being his own physician, for Nature is like that—agent and patient at once.

That Nature is a cause, then, and a goal-directed cause, is above dispute.

Chapter IX

The phrase 'must of necessity' may be used of what is uncondition-ally necessary or of what is necessary to this or that.' Of which kind is the necessity that exists in Nature? For people ignore this distinction and talk about things being 'necessarily generated,' much as if they 200 A thought that a wall would come up in the necessary course of things because what is heavy naturally descends and what is light is naturally on the top, so that stones go down and make the foundations, while the lighter brick rises above them, and the timber, lightest of all, roofs them above.

No doubt it is a fact that the building cannot dispense with these materials, and in that sense they 'must be there'; but they do not them-selves 'make' the building in the sense of constructing it, but only in that of constituting its material. What causes the building to be made is the purpose of protecting and preserving certain goods. And so in all other cases where a purpose can be traced. It cannot be accomplished without materials that have the required nature; but it is not they that 'make' the purpose-fulfilling instrument, except materially. For what makes it, in the formative sense, is the purposeful intention of the maker. For instance: 'Why is a saw like this?' 'In order that it may have the essential character of a saw and serve for sawing.' This purpose, how-ever, could not be served if it were not made of iron. So if it is to be a saw, and to do its work, it 'must necessarily' be made of iron. The necessity, then, is conditional, or hypothetical. The purpose, mentally conceived, demands the material as necessary to its accomplishment; but the nature of the material, as already existing, does not 'necessarily' lead to the accomplishment of the purpose.

Note, too, that in a certain respect, there is a kind of inverted par-allelism between mathematics and the things that take place under the control of nature. For a straight line being what it is, if (i) a triangle is straight-sided, then (ii) its angles are equal to two right angles; but it does not follow that if (ii) its angles are equal to two right angles, then (i) the triangle must be straight-sided, though it does follow that if (ii) is not, i.e. its angles are not equal to two right angles, then (i) is not, i.e. the triangle cannot be straight-sided. But in purposeful constructions it is the other way about; for if (ii) the end is to be secured or actually has been secured, then (i) the antecedent conditions must be, or must have been, present; but just as in the case of the triangle the failure of the *consequent* (its angles are equal to two right angles) necessarily in-volves the failure of the *antecedent* (that the triangle be straight-sided), so here the failure of the material *antecedent* (bricks or iron) necessarily carries with it the failure of the proposed *end* (house or saw). But in both cases it is the 'principle' or 'primary factor' that imposes the necessity upon the accessary one; for in the case of the triangle it is the premise that imposes a logical necessity on the conclusion (for the whole construction is logical, and there is no action at all in question), whereas in the other cases, though the purpose (which is the principle that imposes the necessity on the material) has to do with action, yet it is only a logical necessity that it can impose, for it does not actually create or constitute the material. Thus, if there is to be a house, then stones, bricks and so forth, if not already on hand, must be produced (for at any rate they must be there). Or, to put it generally, the purpose-serving materials must be there, if the purpose is to be accomplished; but since they do not themselves fulfil the purpose, except materially, it does not follow that, if they are there, the purpose will be fulfilled. To sum up: the materials will not account for the existence of the house or of the saw, though, if they are simply not there—no stones for the house, no iron for the saw—there will be no house and no saw (just as in the mathematical illustration straight-sidedness does not inhere in biorthogonality, but cannot exist without it).

It is clear, then, that when physicists speak of necessity absolutely, they should limit the term to what is inherent in the material, and should recognize purposeful movement imposed upon the material as a distinct addition to its inherent qualities. And though the physicist has to deal with both material and purpose, he is more deeply concerned with the latter; for purpose directs the moving causes that act upon the material, not the reverse. It is the goal that determines the purpose, and the principle of causation is derived from the definition and rationale of the end, in Nature just as much as in artificial constructions. *E.g.* since this is what a house is, these things must necessarily be ready or be produced; and since this is what health is, such and such things must be provided to secure it. And in like manner, if this is what 'man' is, then there must antecedently be such and such things, and that they again may be there, such and such other things. And the same kind of 'necessity' may be traced on the conceptual side. For if we define 'sawing' as such and such a method of dividing, it follows that it can only be accomplished by teeth of such and such a character, and these teeth can exist only if the saw be made of iron. For a definition, too, contains constituent terms which are, as it were, its materials.

200 B

Book III

206A 9-25

Yet, if we frankly deny that anything at all can be without limit, we commit ourselves to many statements that are obviously false; for we should have to say that time had a beginning and will have an end, and that there are magnitudes that cannot be divided into magnitudes, and that numeration has a limit. So if we conceive the alternative to lie between the existence of some unlimited substance cognizable by the senses and there being nothing unlimited at all, we shall be landed in impossibilities either way; so we must appeal to an umpire, who will obviously have to explain that in one sense the unlimited exists and in another sense not.

Now things are said to exist as potentialities or as actualities; and there is no limit to the addition (or subtraction) of terms in a convergent series; and though we have seen that a magnitude cannot actually be increased beyond limit by multiplication, it may be divided into something smaller yet than any parvitude you choose to mention—for there is no difficulty in refuting the doctrine that there are such things as atomic lines. It results that the unlimited potentiality exists.

But how are we to understand 'potentiality' here? Not in the sense in which we say that the potentiality of the statue exists in the bronze; for that implies that the whole of the bronze may actually become the statue, whereas it is not so with an illimitable potentiality, since it can never become an unlimited actuality. As to this we must not be misled by the ambiguity of the word 'is,' for the only sense in which the unlimited is actualized at all is the sense in which we say that it 'actually is' such and such a day of the month, or that the games 'actually are' on; for in these cases, too, the period of time or the succession of events in question is not (like the statue-potentialities of the bronze) all actualized at once, but is in course of transit as long as it lasts. The Olympic games, *as-a-whole*, are a potentiality only, even when they are in process of actualization.

206B 3-207A 2

There is a certain process of endless addition that can be identified by reciprocity with endless division; for as we see the finite magnitude in process of division *ad infinitum*, so we shall find the process of addition tending towards a definite limit. For if (1) one should take a definite piece away from a limited magnitude and then go on to take away the same *proportion of what is left* (not the same fraction of the original whole), and so on and so on, he will never work through to the end of the original magnitude; whereas, if (2) he increases the proportion of the remainder which he takes away each time, so as to make the actual magnitude taken away always the same, then he will get through to the end; for successive withdrawals of any constant magnitude, however small, will exhaust any limited magnitude whatever. The illimitable, then, exists only the way just described—as an endless potentiality of approximation by reduction of intervals. Illimitability is never actual except in the sense in which we can say 'the day' or 'the games' are actual, wheras as potentiality it is analogous to formless matter; it never exists as a *thing*, as a determined quantum does. In this sense, then, there is also illimitable potentiality of addition, which in a way is the same as whatwe describe as illimitable in respect of division, for in addition it will always be possible to find something beyond the total for the time being (in a convergent series) though the total will never exceed every assigned magnitude in the way that, in the direction of division, the result does pass every assigned magnitude and will always become still smaller. But, in the sense of exceeding *every* finite magnitude as the result of addition, the unlimited cannot exist even potentially, unless we accpe the hypothesis of the physicists who suppose some such actual substance as air or the like to have bodily existence outside the universe and to be unlimited. In that case indeed 'infinity' would incidentally have an actual existence (though not itself substantial). But if (as has been shown) it is impossible that there should exist any such sensible body, as an accomplished actuality, itfollows that there is no potentiality of a sum of additions extending beyond all assignable magnitude. The only potentiality of unlimited additions, then, is the additions thatare the obverse of the subtractions regulated by successive divisions as already explained. And this is why Plato himself distinguishes between two 'infinites,' thinking that he must have an infinite that could exceed all expansion as well as all reduction. But although he postulates such an infinity, he never makes any use of it; for in numbers he does not admit either endless reduction(since the monad is the irreducible minimum), or increase without limit, for the series of numbers stops at the decade.

The fact is that the unlimited is really the exact opposite of its usual description; for it is not that 'beyond which there is nothing,' but 'what is always beyond.'

207A 33–B 21

It follows also from the rationale of infinity that it cannot exceed all magnitude, but depends on the principle of division; for since it is analogous to the 'material' it is contained, whereas it is the 'form' that is the continent.

It is also quite as it should be that in number there should be an inferior limit, whereas it is always possible to transcend any given number, but that in magnitudes, on the other hand, it should always be possible to make the small smaller, but there can be no magnitude of unlimited greatness. The reason is that unity, as unity, is atomic, the human unit, for instance, being one man and not more than one; whereas number is of more units than one, and specifically of 'so many,' so that you cannot go further back than the indivisible (for 'two' and 'three,' that is, two ones and three ones, are both numbers, *qua* more than one, but different numbers, *qua* two or three respectively, and so with the rest). But since you can always make another division of a magnitude into two, however many divisions you have already made to get it, you can always conceive a higher number of divisions than any given number however great; consequently the 'possibility of more' is inexhaustible and incapable of completion, but can be carried on through a greater than any assignable number of steps. This inexhaustible 'number,' however, is not separable from the dichotomy, and its 'illimitability' is not an accomplished *thing* like the magnitude itself that is the subject of the dichotomies, but is the accompaniment of the process of dichotomy, always in the making and never made; just like time, and the numerical register of time. So number cannot be reduced below unity, but can be increased indefinitely; but the reverse is true of magnitude; for a continuous magnitude can be divided beyond any given smallness, but cannot be increased above every assignable greatness. For any magnitude that can exist potentially can exist actually; so since, as we have seen, nothing sense-perceived can be unlimited, a magnitude in excess of every definite magnitude is an impossiblity; it would have to transcend the universe.

207B 28-34

Nor does this account of infinity rob the mathematicians of their study; for all that it denies is the actual existence of anything so great that you can never get to the end of it. And as a matter of fact, mathematicians never ask for or introduce an infinite magnitude; they only claim that the finite line shall be of any length they please; and it is possible to divide any magnitude whatsoever in the same proportion as the greatest magnitude. So that the question under discussion does not affect their demonstrations; whereas actual dimensional existence can only be found in actually existent magnitudes.

Book IV

215B 12-20

But the nonexistent substantiality of vacuity cannot bear any ratio whatever to the substantiality of any material substance, any more than zero can bear a ratio to a number. For if we divide a constant quantity *c* (that which exceeds) into two variable parts, *a* (the excess) and *b* (the exceeded), then, as *a* increases, *b* will decrease and the ratio *a* : *b* will increase; but when the whole of *c* is in section *a* there will be none of *c* for section *b*; and it is absurd to speak of 'none of *c*' as 'a part of *c*.' So the ratio *a* : *b* will cease to exist, because *b* has ceased to exist and only *a* is left, and there is no proportion between something and nothing. (And in the same way there is no such thing as the proportion between a line and a point, because, since a point is no part of a line, taking a point is not taking any of the line.)

219B 1-18

But when we perceive a distinct before and after, then we speak of time; for this is just what time is, the calculable measure or dimension of motion with respect to before-and-afterness.

Time, then, is not movement, but that by which movement can be numerically estimated. To see this, reflect that we estimate any kind of more-and-lessness by number; so, since we estimate all more-or-lessness on some numerical scale and estimate the more-or-lessness of motion by time, time is a scale on which something (to wit movement) can be numerically estimated. But now, since 'number' has two meanings (for we speak of the 'numbers' that are counted in the thing in question, and also of the 'numbers' by which we count them and in which we calculate), we are to note that time is the countable thing that we are counting, not the numbers we count in—which two things are different.

And as motion is a continuous flux, so is time; but at any given moment time is the same everywhere, for the 'now' itself is identical in its essence, but the relations into which it enters differ in different connexions, and it is the 'now' that marks off time as before and after. But this 'now,' which is identical everywhere, itself retains its identity in one sense, but does not in another; for inasmuch as the point in the flux of time which it marks is changing (and so to mark it is its essential function) the 'now' too differs perpetually, but inasmuch as at every moment it is performing its essential function of dividing the past and future it retains its identity.

221A 1-9

It is by reference to the standard unit of time that we determine the relative velocity of two several motions. For we ask what distance either motion has covered during the lapse of the standard unit of time, and pronounce the motion itself fast or slow in proportion as that distance is great or small. But that same standard unit of time measures the duration of a motion. So the way in which a motion exists in time is by both itself and its duration being measured by time. For time measures both the motion and its duration by the same act, and its duration being so measured constitutes it as existing in time. But it is obvious that other things as well as motion exist in time because their existence too is measured by time.

221B 4–22

From all this it is clear that things which exist eternally, as such, are not in time; for they are not embraced by time, nor is their duration measured by time. This is indicated by their not suffering anything under the action of time as though they were within its scope.

And since time is the measure of a motion, it will also incidentally be the measure of rest; for all rest is in time. For a thing being in motion necessitates that it should be moving, but its being in time does not; for time is not identical with motion, but is that in terms of which motion is counted, and even if a thing is at rest, it may be countable by the same count as motion. For not everything that is unmoved is at rest, but that only which by its nature is capable of moving but now lacks its actual motion, as we have already noted. But a thing existing in number means that it 'has' a number and that its existence is measured by that number; and so too in the case of time. And time will measure that which is in motion and that which is at rest, *as such*; for it is their motion and their rest of which it determines the amount. So that the thing in motion is not measured by time in all respects in its capacity of a quantum, but in so far as its motion is defined in quantity; hence that which is neither in motion nor at rest is not in time, since to be 'in time' means to be measured by time, and it is motion and rest of which time is the measure.

Book VIII

263A 4–B 8

This reasoning, further, enables us to meet those who, in the terms of Zeno's argument [see above, pp. 46–48]: ask whether it is true that you must always go half-way to a point before you get there, and there is always a half-way point between the last half-way point that you have reached and the point itself that you are making for, and so you can never get there, because you would have to pass through an infinite number of points. Or, as others put it: If you count the first half of the journey and then the half of what is left and so on, you would have to count an infinite series of numbers before you got to the end of the journey; which is admitted to be impossible. It is true that in our previous studies concerning movement we sloved this puzzle by pointing out that since time, just as much as space, is divisible without limit and with respect to this capacity is illimitable, there is no contradiction in a man passing through an infinite number of points in a time which is 'infinite' in precisely the same sense as the distance to be traversed is. But this solution, though adequate as a reply to the question (which was, whether it is possible in a finite time to go through or to count an infinite number of points), does not really settle the underlying truth or get at realities. For what if a man, dropping the element of distance and the question of the possibility of tranversing an infinite number of distances in a finite time, were to confine his question to the time only; for this contains an illimitable number of divisions? It would then be no solution to say that there is no limit to the divisibility of time itself, but we should have to fall back upon the truth we have just arrived at. For whoever divides the continuous into two halves thereby confers a double function upon the point of division, for he makes it both a beginning and an end. And that is just what the counting man, or the dividing man whose half-sections he counts, is doing; and by the very act of division both the line and the movement cease to be continuous; for the movement is not continuous unless the mobile and the time and the track with which it is concerned are continuous. And though it be true that there is no limit to the potential dichotomy of any continuum, it is not true that it is actually dichotomized to infinity. But to make an actual bisection is to effect a motion that is not continuous but interrupted, as is patent in the case of one who counts the segments; for he must take the bisecting point twice, once as an end and once as a beginning (which we have seen to involve an interruption of continuity)—I mean if he does not count the continuous line as one, but the separated halves as two. Accordingly, if we are asked whether it is possible to go through an unlimited number of points, whether in a period of time or in a length, we must answer that in one sense it is possible but in another not. If the points are actual it is impossible, but if they are potential it is possible.

SELECTIVE BIBLIOGRAPHY

General

Burnet, J. *Greek Philosophy*, Thales to Plato. London, 1950. An excellent survey in brief compass. Developing a theory now generally rejected, Burnet ascribes the content of Plato's middle dialogues to the historical Socrates; but this is a flaw easily corrected for.

Cornford, F. M. *Before and After Socrates*. Cambridge, 1950. A brilliant brief survey, in popular form.

Cornford, F. M. *The Unwritten Philosophy*. Cambridge, 1950. A graceful series of essays on Plato and the Presocratics.

Guthrie, W. K. C. *A History of Greek Philosophy*. 6 vols. Cambridge, 1962–1981. Comprehensive, thorough, and accurate, it sums up the main results of the last fifty years of scholarship on Greek philosophy.

Heath, T. L. *A History of Greek Mathematics*. 2 vols. Oxford: Oxford University Press, 1921. The authoritative history of Greek mathematics. Indispensable for the study of Greek philosophy.

Jaeger, W. *Paideia: The Ideals of Greek Culture*. 3 vols. Transl. Gilbert Highet. Oxford, 1945. A masterful study of Greek concepts of civilization and education.

Robin, L. *Greek Thought*. Transl. M. R. Dobie. London, 1928. A stimulating study by a great French scholar.

Snell, B. *The Discovery of the Mind: The Greek Origins of European Thought*. Transl. T. G. Rosenmeyer. Cambridge, Mass., 1953. A study of the intellectual life of Greece, its literature, art, and religion as well as its philosophy.

Tannery, P. *Pour L'histoire de la science hellène*. 2nd ed. by A. Diès. Paris, 1930: A profoundly influential work.

Presocratics

Text

Diels, H. and Kranz, W. *Die Fragmente der Vorsokratiker*. 8th ed. Berlin, 1956. The Greek texts, with German translation. A monument of scholarship.

Translation and Commentary

Burnet, J. *Early Greek Philosophy*. 4th ed. London, 1930. An enduring work of scholarship, often criticized but perennially fresh. Most complete translations in English.

Kirk, G. S. and Raven, J. E. *The Presocratic Philosophers*. Cambridge, 1957. An admirable survey, which provides the Greek text with translation of the major fragments and testimonia.

General

Bailey, C. *The Greek Atomists and Epicurus*. Oxford, 1928. The standard study, distinguished for its scholarship.

Cherniss, H. *Aristotle's Criticism of Presocratic Philosophy*. Baltimore, 1935. An assessment of Aristotle as a source of evidence for determining the views of the Presocratics.

Cherniss, H. "The Characteristics and Effects of Presocratic Philosophy," *Journal of the History of Ideas*, 12 (1951), 319–45. A masterly short study.

Furley, D. J. and Allen, R. E. *Studies in Presocratic Philosophy*. London, 1970, 1975.

Guthrie, W. K. C. *The Greeks and Their Gods*. London, 1950. An excellent study of Greek religion.

———. "Aristotle as a Historian of Philosophy," *Journal of Hellenic Studies*, 1957 (1), 35–41. A brief estimate, considerably more favorable than Cherniss's.

Kahn, C. H. *Anaximander and the Origins of Greek Cosmology*. New York, 1960. Contains a survey of sources and documentary evidence, and an outline of Anaximander's cosmology.

Kirk, G. S. *Heraclitus, the Cosmic Fragments*. Cambridge, 1954. A fresh interpretation, extremely influential.

Moorelatos, A. D. P. *The Presocratics*. New York, 1974.

Raven, J. E. *Pythagoreans and Eleatics*. Cambridge, 1948. A valuable survey.

Plato

Text

Platonis Opera. Oxford Classical Texts. Oxford, 1900–1907. Recognovit J. Burnet.

Jowett, B. *The Dialogues of Plato*. 4th ed., revised by D. J. Allan and H. E. Dale. Oxford, 1953.

Loeb Classical Library translations by Bury, Fowler, Lamb and Shorey. Published with text. Cambridge, Mass.

General

Allen, R. E. *Studies in Plato's Metaphysics*. London, 1965.

Allen, R. E. *Plato's Euthyphro*. London, 1970.

Allen, R. E. *Socrates and Legal Obligation*. Minneapolis, 1980.

Allen, R. E. *Plato's Parmenides*. Minneapolis, 1983.

Cherniss, H. *Aristotle's Criticism of Plato and the Academy*. New York, 1944. An estimate of the worth of Aristotle's criticisms for interpreting Plato.

Cornford, F. M. *Plato's Cosmology*. New York, 1952. Translation and running commentary on the *Timaeus*. Indispensable.

Cornford, F. M. *Plato and Parmenides*. New York, 1951. Translation and running commentary on the *Parmenides*, with discussion of Pythagoreanism and a translation and commentary on Parmenides' *Way of Truth*. Indispensable.

Cornford, F. M. *Plato's Theory of Knowledge*. New York, 1951. Translation and running commentary on the *Theaetetus* and *Sophist*. Indispensable.

Cornford, F. M. *The Republic of Plato*. Oxford, 1950. Translation with brief analysis.

Festugière, A. J. *Contemplation et vie contemplative selon Platon*. Paris, 1936. A study of Plato's concept of *theoria*, and its philosophical, moral, and religious implications.

Field, G. C. *The Philosophy of Plato*. Oxford, 1949. An excellent brief survey.

Gould, John. *Plato's Ethics*. Cambridge, 1955. A study, primarily, of the early dialogues and the *Laws* and the contrast between them.

Hardie, W. F. R. *A Study in Plato*. Oxford, 1936. A philosophical account of Plato's epistemology and metaphysics.

Nettleship, R. L. *Lectures on the Republic of Plato*. London, 1951. First published in 1897, and strongly influenced by 19th century English rationalism, this book remains perennially fresh.

Robinson, R. *Plato's Earlier Dialectic*. 2nd ed. Oxford, 1953. The standard study.

Ross, W. D. *Plato's Theory of Ideas*. Oxford, 1951. Traces the theory from the early dialogues to the Laws and argues for a development from "immanence" to "transcendence" of the Forms.

Shorey, P. *What Plato Said*. Chicago, 1933. A resume and analysis of the entire Platonic corpus.

Taylor, A. E. *Plato: The Man and his Work*. New York, 1950. A resume and analysis of the entire Platonic corpus.

Aristotle

Text

Aristotelis Opera. Berlin, 1831–1870. The Prussian Academy edition.

Translations

Loeb Classical Library translations by Cornford, Peck, Tredennick and others. Published with text. Cambridge, Mass.

Oxford Translation, ed. by J. A. Smith and W. D. Ross, Oxford, 1908–1931.

General

Ackrill, J. L. *Aristotle's Categories and De Interpretatione*. Oxford, 1963. Translation with notes, amounting to a commentary.

Allan, D. J. *The Philosophy of Aristotle*. Oxford, 1952. An excellent brief survey.

Barker, E. *The Politics of Aristotle*. Oxford, 1948. Translation, with notes.

Bywater, I. *Aristotle on the Art of Poetry*. Oxford, 1909. Text, translation, and commentary.

Hicks, R. D. *Aristotle's De Anima*. Cambridge, 1907. Text, translation, and commentary.

Jaeger, W. *Aristotle: Fundamentals of the History of His Development*. 2nd ed. Transl. Richard Robinson. Oxford, 1948. First published in German in 1923, this has become a widely influential, and seminal, study of the development of Aristotle's thought.

Lukasiewicz, J. *Aristotle's Syllogistic*. 2nd ed. Oxford, 1957. A study of Aristotle's syllogistic in the light of modern formal logic.

Owens, J. *The Doctrine of Being in the Aristotelian Metaphysics*. 2nd ed. Toronto, 1963. A nearly indispensable aid to the study of the *Metaphysics*.

Ross, W. D. *Aristotle*. London, 1949. A survey and analysis of nearly the whole of Aristotle's work.

Ross, W. D. *Aristotle's Metaphysics*. Oxford, 1924. Text, with introduction and commentary.

Ross, W. D. *Aristotle's Physics*. Oxford, 1936. Text, with introduction and commentary.

Ross, W. D. *Aristotle's Prior and Posterior Analytics*. Oxford, 1949. Text, with introduction and commentary.

Solmsen, F. *Aristotle's System of the Physical World*. Ithaca, 1960. Relates Aristotle's natural philosophy to that of his predecessors.

Stewart, J. A. *Notes on the Nicomachean Ethics of Aristotle*. Oxford, 1892. A guide to the *Ethics*.

INDEX